INTERWAR

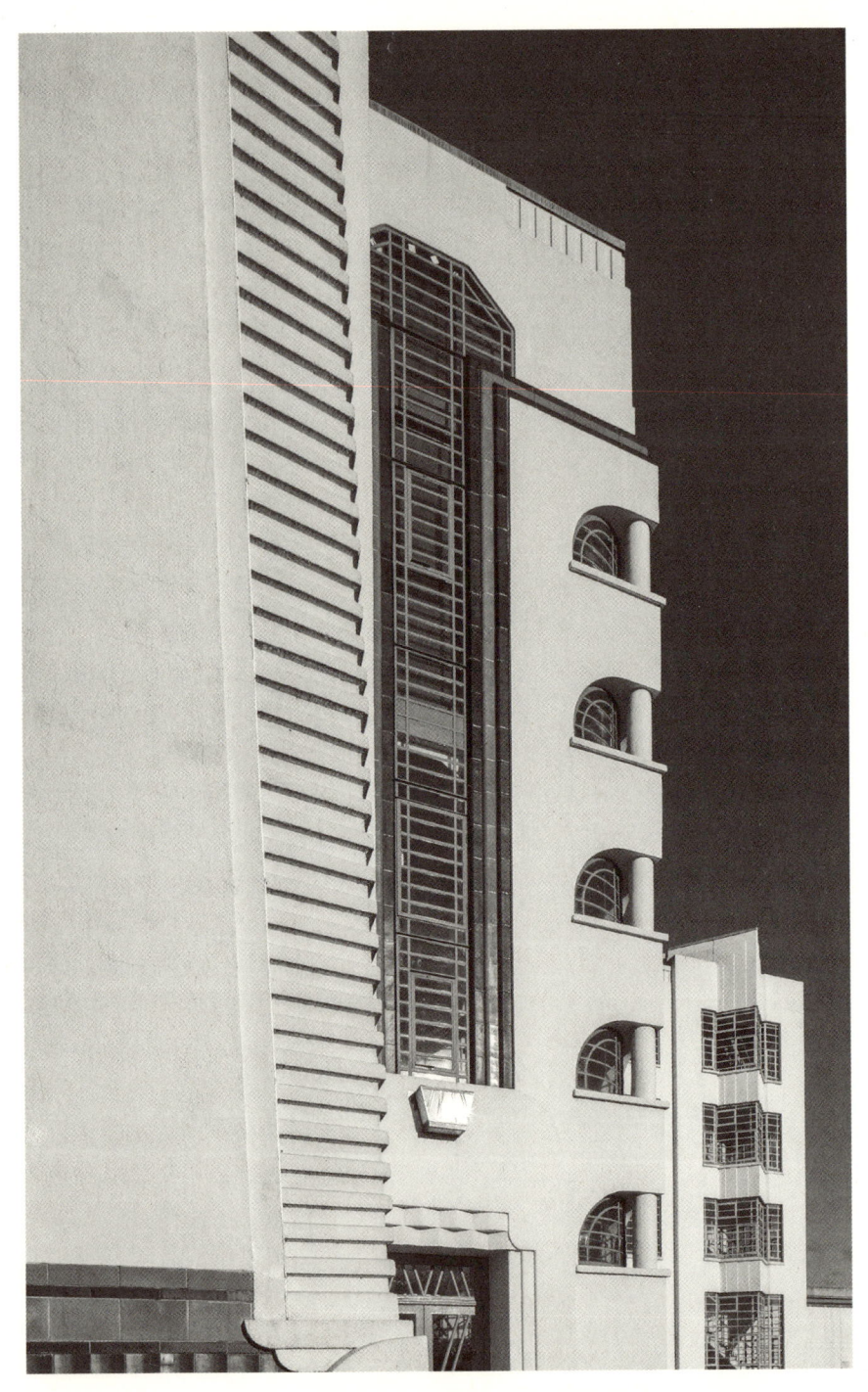

Hoover Factory, Perivale, Greater London (Wallis, Gilbert & Partners, 1932, extended 1935)

INTERWAR

BRITISH ARCHITECTURE 1919–39

──◆──

GAVIN STAMP

With a foreword by Rosemary Hill

Supported by

Profile Books C20 Twentieth Century Society

First published in Great Britain in 2024 by
Profile Books Ltd
29 Cloth Fair
London
EC1A 7JQ

www.profilebooks.com

Copyright © The Estate of Gavin Stamp, 2024
Foreword copyright © Rosemary Hill, 2024
Photography copyright © John East, 2024

All photographs in this book are the work of the photographer John East (john.east@hotmail.com), unless otherwise stated on p. 512, which constitutes an extension of this copyright page.

1 3 5 7 9 10 8 6 4 2

Text design by Carr Design Studio

Printed and bound in Slovenia by
DZS-Grafik d.o.o.

The moral right of the authors has been asserted.

All rights reserved. Without limiting the rights under copyright reserved above, no part of this publication may be reproduced, stored or introduced into a retrieval system, or transmitted, in any form or by any means (electronic, mechanical, photocopying, recording or otherwise), without the prior written permission of both the copyright owner and the publisher of this book.

A CIP catalogue record for this book is available from the British Library.

ISBN 978 1 80081 739 5
eISBN 978 1 80081 741 8

MIX
Paper | Supporting responsible forestry
FSC® C106600

CONTENTS

Foreword		1
Introduction		11
One	Armistice	39
Two	The Grand Manner	79
Three	Swedish Grace	129
Four	Brave New World	177
Five	Tutankhamun	233
Six	Merrie England	271
Seven	New Georgians	339
Eight	Modern Gothic	399
Nine	The Shape of Things to Come	445
Acknowledgements and Picture Credits		521
Notes		523
Bibliography		537
Index		555

Royal Artillery War Memorial, Hyde Park Corner, London (Lionel Pearson; sculptor Charles Sargeant Jagger, 1925)

FOREWORD

When my husband Gavin Stamp died in 2017 at the age of sixty-nine, he left the manuscript that became this book, a study of British architecture between the world wars, unfinished. It was a subject that had interested and preoccupied him since his schooldays. He returned to it on and off for decades; in a sense, the book would never have been finished because Gavin never stopped looking, learning and reconsidering.

Gavin was the most important and influential architectural historian and critic of his generation. Journalist, campaigner, scholar and activist, he continued to develop his ideas and change his mind when the evidence required it, into the last days of his life. He was immensely versatile. As *Private Eye*'s 'Piloti' he was the fearless scourge of vandals, individual or municipal, who tried to spoil good buildings – or even merely average buildings if they added to the quality of life for those who used them. He was among the first architectural conservationists to make the ecological argument, pointing out that buildings are embodied energy and demanding an

Battersea Power Station, London, before reconstruction (Giles Gilbert Scott, 1933)

environmental audit of the case for any demolition. As a scholar, his biography of George Gilbert Scott, junior, *An Architect of Promise*, rescued the most complicated figure of the great Scott dynasty, fated to be known as 'Middle Scott', from the heavy shadows of his famous father Sir Gilbert (designer of the Albert Memorial) and his yet more famous son Sir Giles (Battersea Power Station). Gavin wrote academic articles and organised exhibitions, most notably, with Colin Amery and others, the Lutyens exhibition at the Hayward Gallery in 1980–81, a landmark reassessment of Lutyens's reputation; for some years he taught at the Glasgow School of Architecture, where his lectures were memorably unorthodox; but for most of his life he was a working freelance journalist producing copy on time, to length (more or less), and often illustrated with his own photographs. This allowed him to explore ideas and places, to fill gaps in his knowledge and to revisit buildings over time. As Ian Hislop, his editor at *Private Eye*, once observed, Gavin's success as Piloti lay in his ability to assess readers' comments about a proposed development because he almost invariably knew the town, the street and, often, the building itself.

The architectural writer must conjure up the subject for the reader in words – and here, too, Gavin's range served him well. He could read the subtleties of a building as a musician reads a score. Of Lutyens's Midland Bank in the City of London he says:

> The ground floor is comparatively conventional, although tricks are played with the Doric order of pilasters disappearing into the rustication. Above, the wall dissolves, with banks of windows contained within giant buttresses, or pilasters, of unprecedented form. Not only do these recede, to give the vertical surfaces a pronounced batter, but each course of rustication diminishes in width by one-eighth of an inch as the building rises. Optical subtlety could surely be carried no further.

But technical details are not always relevant. He is equally likely to describe a building as 'wobbly', 'vulgar', 'friendly' or, quite brilliantly, as 'dominatingly unassertive'.

Gavin loved the architecture of Britain. In his later teens, irritated by his contemporaries' enthusiasm for Continental holidays, he made his own Grand Tour of the great industrial cities of the north. Manchester, Leeds, Liverpool and Glasgow remained for him among the most romantic and interesting of places, and he was impatient of his fellow southerners' tendency to know Tuscany better than Lancashire. Yet he also travelled widely himself. His was the generation that could trek with reasonable safety across Afghanistan – and he did, though not in hippy style. He wore a linen jacket and carried a canvas suitcase marked with his initials, being careful always to see that it was strapped on top of the bus before he boarded himself. He travelled too in India, a country for which he developed an enduring fascination, later making pioneering studies of the architecture of the Raj, and in Central and Eastern Europe before the fall of the Berlin Wall. As chairman of the Twentieth Century Society he led foreign trips to cities including Havana and Ljubljana which were always exciting and sometimes hair-raising due to their speed and intensity, as well as Gavin's disregard for physical comfort and local bylaws. He had 20/20 eyesight until middle age and a phenomenal visual memory that allowed him to reach easily for connections and comparisons between, for example, the Nebraska State Capitol and Swansea Town Hall.

The period between the wars interested him for many reasons. He was an historian before he was an architectural historian, and he knew that at any given moment the most inaccessible period is that which is just within living memory. Too much material is still in private hands, too many axes are still being ground; the recent past is always on the move. At the same time it offers unique opportunities. Biography and oral history are two of the implements in the historian's toolkit, and Gavin made ample use of them. He knew many of the architects and critics he writes about here, including John Betjeman, through whom he inherited the *Private Eye* 'Nooks and Corners' column; Ernö Goldfinger, who became a friend; and John Summerson, with whom he enjoyed a long correspondence and who once publicly described Battersea Power Station, which Gavin was campaigning to save, as 'Gavin Stamp's billiard table'. He recorded extensive interviews for the British Sound Archive with Osbert Lancaster and Berthold Lubetkin, and although he just missed one of his heroes, Arthur Shoosmith, he developed a friendship with his widow, Marjorie, which informed his essay on Shoosmith for the *Dictionary of National Biography* and enabled them, together, to ensure that an unjustly forgotten figure was reassessed. Shoosmith's genius and its neglect are explicable in historical terms, and Gavin wanted to explain that (and much more) in order to see the period as a whole. This was something that he believed those historians who confined themselves to architecture had failed to do.

In architectural terms, the decades between 1919 and 1939 have generally been seen to mark a break between the traditional architecture of the Victorians and Edwardians and the start of the rise of Modernism. Too often the period has merely been scanned for evidence of what was to come, when as Nikolaus Pevsner put it: 'our functionalists of the twenties and thirties', carried on the current of the zeitgeist, were led inexorably into 'the ocean of the International style of the 1930s'. This ignored the many continuities between pre- and post-war architecture and it undervalued or ignored the work of those such as Lutyens who were not part of this teleological rise to an inevitable Modernist Truth. It is one thing to argue that the work of the interwar Modernists was the best, aesthetically or even morally, the most interesting or the most cosmopolitan; it is another and simply untrue to suggest that it loomed large in Britain in the period between the world wars. Gavin's counter argument is implicit in the arrangement of his book, which reflects the historical reality. It begins with war memorials, the first and most widespread architectural expressions of the period, and ends with Modernism, a late, rarefied and largely unpopular phenomenon.

The past is always complicated. To understand it means seeing it as nearly as possible in the round – and this is especially true of the history of architecture. A poem can be the work of one person. To build requires collaboration, social momentum, money. Architecture happens to everyone, in their homes, streets, schools and their places of work and leisure. As A. W. N. Pugin demonstrated in his 1841 illustrations of 'Contrasted Towns', comparing the spires and turrets of the Middle Ages with the factory chimneys of the nineteenth century, a skyline will tell you a lot about a society. Since Gavin started work on this book, more light and shade have been added to the picture. Both his own writings and those of others have helped to establish a broader and more nuanced understanding of what Modernism was – and was not – in the Britain of the 1920s and 1930s. Yet nobody has written about the period as he does here, following the overlapping themes and cross-currents of an age of remarkable contrasts in architecture, as in society, but one also of continuities with the Late Victorian and Edwardian years. This was a period when 'British' architecture was built in many places outside Britain, by an Empire that had yet fully to comprehend the signs of its imminent collapse, and when much that was built in Britain was the work of Americans, Russians, Australians and, after 1933, of European fugitives from Nazism. Of course, nobody thought of it at the time as an historic period and certainly not, until it was almost over, one of 'interwar' architecture. For a history to show how events unfolded with the advantage of hindsight while avoiding the condescension of posterity requires imagination as well as scholarship, and Gavin uses both to try and enter into the mood of Britain in 1919. Out of a population of 43 million, 880,000 men had been killed. The number physically wrecked or suffering from 'shell shock' is unknowable. There was no family, town or village that had not known losses, and so his first chapter deals with war memorials, the first works of a nation coming to terms with an unprecedented catastrophe, and its attempts to give expression to the inexpressible, from simple parish crosses to the vast cemeteries of Flanders, culminating in Lutyens's tragic masterpiece, the Memorial to the Missing of the Somme. Here, in monumental forms closer to pure sculpture than most architecture comes, is where the story of the interwar years begins.

If life was cheap in the Great War, death was expensive. Wages and employment fell through the 1920s. There could be few major building programmes, and the post-war years saw a concomitant flowering of architectural journalism. Projects that could not be built could be drawn and described. Visions for the brave new world were argued out in print – not only by specialist critics but by writers of many kinds, including Sacheverell Sitwell, Evelyn Waugh, Aldous Huxley and Robert Byron. A journalist himself, Gavin gives full weight to the arguments that ran through the pages of *Country Life* and especially the *Architectural Review*, the 'Archie Rev' as it was known to its friends. Here Pevsner and Betjeman represented two sides of the Modernism argument. Betjeman characterised his rival as the 'Herr Doktor Professor', complaining that Pevsner saw him as a lightweight enthusiast for Victoriana, a 'waxed-fruit' merchant. Pevsner, to Betjeman's irritation, seems not to have noticed this very British kind of teasing and failed to rise to a quarrel. There was also something of a satire boom. Evelyn Waugh was scathing

Woodland Way, Petts Wood, Greater London (Basil Scruby and Leonard Culliford, c. 1930)

about Modernism in both his journalism and his novels. The extreme Corbusian view represented by Professor Silenus in *Decline and Fall* is so madly doctrinaire that he resents his client's insistence on having a staircase. ('Up and down, in and out, round and round! Why can't they sit still and work?') Meanwhile, at the Archie Rev, the most brilliant architectural satirist who ever lived was in his prime. Osbert Lancaster's gift for language was as great as his ability to find and gently exaggerate the characteristics of any building. The styles he named – 'Stockbroker's Tudor', 'Bypass Variegated', 'Pseudish' and the rest – skewered sections of contemporary society and attached them to the bricks and mortar, concrete, glass, or mock-oak beams that best expressed their tastes and prejudices.

Gavin, especially in his guise as Piloti, shared Lancaster's fondness for satire. He occasionally resorted to it in his sallies against the vision of interwar Britain as a seedbed for Modernism, pointing out for example that Modernist buildings (he was thinking of Lubetkin's London Zoo Penguin Pool and Oliver Hill's hotel at Morecambe) are found mostly in 'fringe conditions, by the seaside or in zoos', or in such 'peculiar locations' as Hampstead and Highgate in London. Apart from its historical inaccuracy, Gavin disliked the characterisation of the interwar period as an early chapter in the rise of Modernism for its snobbery. As he argued elsewhere in an article defending suburbia, 'Neo-Tudor', the semi-detached houses, thatched pubs and 'Elizabethan' shopping parades that represented the greater part of the output of the period were also what most people wanted. The Modernists' desire to distance themselves from popular taste was fully reciprocated; Lubetkin's 1930s block of flats, Highpoint One, intended as a manifesto for high-rise living, prompted local residents to form the Highgate Preservation Society to ensure that nothing like it happened again. Ironically it is the less socially advantaged who have ended up living in the social housing that was the post-war legacy of Corbusian doctrine, and the consequences have often been unhappy.

The question of patronage is always central to the history of architecture. After 1919 the traditional patrons – the landed aristocracy and the Church – no longer dominated. Public bodies, notably London Underground, the War Graves Commission and individual local authorities, largely determined the post-war built environment. The great housing shortage allowed speculative builders to flourish, and Gavin, whose own early childhood was spent in a bungalow on the Orpington bypass, was interested in them too. On either side of this broad middle were the extremes. On the one hand the die-hard Modernists with their 'flat roof Bolshevism', and on the other fringe there was the remarkable lone figure of Blunden Shadbolt, an architect who specialised in 'New "Old" Houses', laying roof tiles on wobbly chicken wire to create an effect of weathered age. His masterpiece, 'Smugglers' Way' in the New Forest, was a 'wildly irregular gabled composition of timber and brick, roofed with both tile and thatch'. Gavin found Shadbolt funny, but he didn't sneer at him, seeing in him one of the many ways in which architecture reflected the contrasts of the times. The Jazz Age, with its fancy factories, was also the age of the Cenotaph, just as the flappers and the Charleston coincided with the Jarrow March and the General Strike.

The architectural profession had its own internal contradictions in this period. The architects practising in 1919 spanned three generations. Some were Victorians carrying on, others were just beginning their careers. How many architects of genius were lost in the trenches we will never know. It was, predominantly, still a man's world, one in which men were known by surnames and initials, wore tweed and horn-rimmed glasses, and there was a distinct whiff of pipe smoke in the office air. Women in 1919 had not yet won the vote and they would not be admitted to degrees at Cambridge until 1948 (the year of Gavin's birth). In this context architecture appears among the more open-minded of the professions. Ethel Charles became the first female member of the Royal Institute of British Architects (RIBA) in 1898 and her sister followed two years later. Practising female architects, however, remained rare. Elisabeth Scott, whose Shakespeare Memorial Theatre of 1927 Gavin campaigned to preserve from destructive alterations, was an exception but, as he wrote in a letter to the *London Review of Books* five months before he died, she was accused in her lifetime of plagiarism: 'In the very masculine profession of architecture, few could then accept that a mere young woman could have possibly been responsible for a sophisticated modern design chosen by independent British and American assessors out of 72 entries.'

Thus, the built environment is shaped by social norms, by politics and by our sense of the past. From the standpoint of the 1920s and 1930s, Georgian architecture still did not appear 'properly old'. Although it was admired by architects, including the Modernists, it was being swept away on a vast scale. 'The great contribution of England is Georgian,' Ernö Goldfinger remarked. 'But hardly had I time to look at it [than] they were pulling it down.' The Georgian Group was founded in 1937 to try and turn the tide. Even Christopher Wren was not safe. In 1919, 'as if to celebrate the peace', as Gavin writes, the Bishop of London proposed the closure of nineteen City of London churches by Wren, Hawksmoor and others, to free up valuable sites for redevelopment and fund new churches in the suburbs. This, at

'Drayneflete 1925'
(Osbert Lancaster,
1949)

least, was stopped, but many battles lay ahead, and from the late 1960s onwards Gavin was usually somewhere in the advance guard. Some things he never forgot or forgave. The fact that Giles Scott's Memorial Court at Clare College, Cambridge, 'unique in British architecture', had been 'gratuitously spoiled' was among them. Overall, however, his tone in this last book is irenic. Surprisingly so, perhaps, for someone whose career involved so many campaigns and controversies. But this was a subject he had had time to come to terms with, to consider, and to arrive if not at a final then at a deeply considered judgement.

Between the manuscript that Gavin left on his computer and the book you now hold in your hands or read on screen, a great deal of work has been needed. I have done as much as I could, but *Interwar* would have been much diminished without the support of the Twentieth Century Society. A decision was made at an early stage by its Director, Catherine Croft, to support the book's illustration. This, and the generosity of the photographer John East, have made it what it is. John not only put his own archive at the disposal of the project, he also undertook original photography, travelling around the country from Petts Wood to the East Neuk of Fife, braving all weathers and obstructions, human and otherwise, in a spirit that Gavin would have appreciated. My debt to him and to the Twentieth Century Society is immense.

Rosemary Hill
December 2023

INTRODUCTION

Seventy years after it was completed, the tallest building in the city of Cambridge is still that strange, stocky, brooding tower which stands over the river to the west of the old colleges. Built of pinky-grey brick, its vertical lines are terminated by a colonnade below a truncated pyramidal roof. Uncollegiate and not particularly Gothic in character, with its walls curving subtly inwards towards the summit, it is reminiscent of monuments of the Ancient World while also looking rather like an early twentieth-century American skyscraper. But it is not a commercial structure. It is rather a tower of learning, for it rises above the Cambridge University Library (Plate 2). This building was designed by a major architect who flourished in the two decades framed by two world wars, became President of the Royal Institute of British Architects and is best known for the last great Gothic Revival cathedral in Britain, two prominent electricity generating stations in London, a bridge across the Thames, and for the design of the once-ubiquitous red telephone kiosk. He was Sir Giles Gilbert Scott (1880–1960), the third generation of a great British architectural dynasty.

In its modernity, its stylistic eclecticism and in its monumentality, the 'UL', as it is familiarly known, may serve as emblematic of British architecture between the wars, for it is very difficult to characterise in architectural terms. In his *Buildings of England* volume on Cambridgeshire (1954), Nikolaus Pevsner could write that 'one is never sure whether the building was meant to be functional or for display, modern or traditional'.[1] The 1920s and 1930s were responsible for a large number of important public buildings which continue to serve their functions as intended and which define the physical and social landscape of Britain, yet it was a time with no one identifiable style, or general agreement about what modern architecture might be. In fact, it was a period as complex, diverse and contradictory as the mid-Victorian decades. In his Inaugural Address at the RIBA in 1933, Scott talked of the urgent need for reconciliation in another Battle of the Styles:

> I hold no brief either for the extreme diehard Traditionalist or the extreme Modernist and it seems to me idle to compare styles and say that one is better than another; the old fight of my grandfather's time between Gothic and Classic and the present fight between Traditionalism and Modernism seem to me issues not worth spilling ink over, but what we do need is a common agreement to use only one style and one style only.[2]

This exasperating pluralism can be seen in interwar Cambridge. The axial approach to the library is framed by elegant neo-Georgian buildings designed by the same architect; in the marketplace a new Guildhall in a stripped, modernised Classical manner in grey-brown brick faces a curved residential block in stone with a strong horizontal modernistic emphasis. Not far away, the laboratory built for Sir Ernest Rutherford is a severe flat-roofed structure of simple volumes lit by large metal-framed windows and only ornamented by a crocodile carved into its yellow brickwork by Eric Gill; elsewhere in Cambridge there were experimental houses with flat roofs, white walls and metal windows, built by young architects for progressive dons. Like other, more typical suburban houses in Cambridge, however, the new block added to Queens' College in the 1930s is in a modern adaptation of the Tudor, looking, as Nikolaus Pevsner put it with mild amusement, 'exactly like a friendly block of flats at, say, Pinner'.[3] In a similar style but rather better was the suave, traditional residential block by Sir Edwin Lutyens added to Magdalene College. Peterhouse, in contrast, built a modernistic residential block in concrete and brick while the nearby Fitzwilliam Museum was extended in a grand American Beaux-Arts Classical manner. Indeed, the impression given by the architectural production of a mere two decades is as chaotic as that given by the architectural ambitions of the first few decades of Victoria's reign in the same city, with the Roman grandeur of the Fitzwilliam Museum and the subtle neo-Classicism of Cockerell's old University Library co-existing with the earnest efforts of the Gothic Revival, while certain colleges chose Alfred Waterhouse's interpretation of Early French Renaissance before the pretty eclecticism of the 'Queen Anne' style of Newnham tried to suggest a resolution to this conflict.

This stylistic diversity worried contemporaries, in both the nineteenth century and the twentieth. 'When the history of the present phase of architectural development is written,' the architect Howard Robertson and the architectural photographer F. R. Yerbury predicted in 1931,

> it may be that the achievement of the years in which we are living will be summed up as mediocre. Emphasis will perhaps be laid on the lack of uniform tendencies, on the amount of individual experiment which has had no sequence, on the divergence between schools of thought which permits a twentieth-century house of the pseudo-thatched and elm-boarded pattern to rise cheek by jowl with a square flat-roofed box which is a pale essay in geometry. Sometimes, even, there may be astonishment on the part of historians to find that these two extremes in the expression of domestic ideals are the work of the same architect.[4]

Faced with this diversity, historians of architecture have tended to concentrate on the particular, while historians of the bigger picture have given way to conventional prejudice.

A comparison between the two eras is again here instructive. In his survey of *English Social History*, published in 1942, the historian G. M. Trevelyan could write how 'the decay of taste between the period of the Regency and the period of the Prince Consort was astonishing. The most refined and educated classes were as bad as any: the monstrosities of architecture erected by order of the Dons of Oxford and Cambridge Colleges in the days of William Butterfield and Alfred Waterhouse gives daily pain to posterity.'[5] Such a blinkered dismissal of some of the most serious buildings of their time was curiously echoed two decades later when A. J. P. Taylor generalised about the more recent architectural achievement in England:

> Architecture continued to follow a decaying Imperial style. Nash's Regent Street was destroyed. A nondescript blatancy took its place. Giles Gilbert Scott outdid the worst achievements of the Victorians in the New Bodleian building at Oxford. All that redeemed the period are some Underground stations by Charles Holden and the *Daily Express* building in Fleet Street.[6]

If architectural historians can be notoriously narrow in outlook, political and social historians can be out of their depth when dealing with aesthetic matters. Trevelyan's remarks were already dated in their time and were soon supplanted by a number of serious studies of Victorian architecture. Taylor's were almost as old-fashioned, but while the foundation of the Thirties Society in 1979 reflected a growing desire to understand and defend British interwar architecture, no major studies have attempted to put the buildings he dismissed into a broad cultural context. There are monographs on individual architects of the period, some traditional, like Edwin Lutyens; more on adherents of the Modern Movement, including Berthold Lubetkin, Ernö Goldfinger and Wells Coates, while exhibition catalogues and other monographs have assessed more problematic and varied figures such as Oliver Hill, Robert Atkinson and H. S. Goodhart-Rendel. There have also been surveys of particular building types, factories, Underground railway stations and cinemas, but the only studies of a more general nature are devoted to what was a significant but nonetheless minority aspect of the period: the Modern Movement. Taylor's opinion would seem to echo the conclusion asserted by the architect and critic J. M. Richards in his influential Pelican paperback on modern architecture published at the very end of the period, in 1940, that:

> Presumably all thinking people now agree that it is absurd to put up houses that look like miniature castles, petrol stations that look like medieval barns, and department stores that look like the palaces of Renaissance bishops – quite apart from being extremely inefficient. No arguments are needed against dressing up our buildings in fancy costumes borrowed from the past. A more profitable occupation is to give our undivided attention to the new architecture of the mid twentieth century which is at last evolving.[7]

Except that many people still thought it absurd to put up houses that looked like factories.

Modernism was always invested with such particular moral virtue and presented itself with such polemic that the problem remains of putting it into that wider picture. As the architectural historian John Summerson put it in 1959:

> It seems natural writing about the past thirty years of English architecture, to write as if the only things worth bothering about were the local initiation, progress and achievements of the 'modern movement'. Historically, this is evidently lop-sided; but also, historically, it would be extremely difficult to write about the architecture of the period as if it could all be evaluated in

much the same way. It cannot be. In architecture, as in poetry and sculpture, there has been a wide and deep gulf between the moderns and those who are vaguely and rather misleadingly described as traditionalists.[8]

In consequence, it was the moderns who were taken seriously first – at least officially. On the advice of Nikolaus Pevsner, the first buildings of the period 1914–39 to be listed in 1970 by the Ministry of Housing and Local Government were almost all by famous English pioneers of Modernism: Lubetkin's Penguin Pool; the Lawn Road flats in Hampstead by Wells Coates; Maxwell Fry's Sun House, also in Hampstead; the Peter Jones store in Sloane Square; and so on, together with the celebrated works of the refugees from Nazi Germany who did so much to encourage the New Architecture in Britain: Eric Mendelsohn, Walter Gropius and Marcel Breuer. Only in 1981, following the sudden, scandalous demolition of the Art Deco Firestone Factory on the Great West Road in Brentford in anticipation of listing, was a more representative selection given statutory protection. Even so, more than half a century on from Summerson's remarks, the attempt to present the whole picture still needs to be made – hence this book. And from the present vantage point, perhaps it can be seen that the gulf was not quite so wide, and that there were continuities and shared characteristics between architects who designed in so many different, contemporary styles.

Despite its international scope, the perception has emerged that the best British architecture of the interwar years was 'Deco',* but this is as misleading a picture as that given by concentrating on the advent and development of the Modern Movement. The name 'Deco' came from the Exposition des Arts Décoratifs held in Paris in 1925, but the style was more influenced by modern American design. When

---

* [This was in the aftermath of an exhibition in 2003 at the Victoria and Albert Museum, which described Deco as 'the most glamorous and popular style of the twentieth century'. RH.]

Peter Jones Department Store, Sloane Square, London (William Crabtree, 1936)

applied to buildings in Britain, the result was best characterised as *moderne*, but the ingredients which give that sense of period style were much more diverse in origin and included the pre-war Jugendstil or Art Nouveau, German and Dutch Expressionist brick architecture and a taste for the exotic as well as the Sublime. The publicity given to the discovery of the tomb of Tutankhamun in 1922 only encouraged an existing interest in the monumental character of ancient buildings in Egypt and elsewhere, as well as in new decorative styles.

Quite how confusing the period was may be gathered from the retrospective published by the Architecture Club in 1947. According to its 'Preface' by Lionel Brett (later fourth Viscount Esher), *Recent English Architecture 1920–40* offered 'a representative selection of English architecture produced between the wars in preparation for the time when fine building can again be undertaken and its progressive evolution be resumed'.[9] The selection certainly indicated the redundancy of any analysis of style by building types; the civic buildings illustrated were Renaissance Classical (Trowbridge) or monumental stripped Classical (Dagenham), Swedish modern (Norwich) and Dutch modern (Hornsey), while even churches were modernistic or Early Christian in addition to the predictable Gothic. Modernism was well represented by an airport (Ramsgate) and a village college (Impington), as well as by several already much celebrated houses.

The building chosen for the book's dustjacket, however, was the monumental brick ziggurat with Art Deco detailing which Herbert Rowse designed to conceal a ventilation shaft above the Mersey Tunnel in Birkenhead, which was clearly inspired by modern American structures, although it also has hints of German Expressionist architecture. Private houses were in almost every style, including that sort of Spanish Colonial which the great architectural critic, satirist and cartoonist Osbert Lancaster dubbed 'Pseudish'. Not represented was the most popular style, that of the new speculative housing developments, which were, in scale alone, a significant aspect of the output of the construction industry in Britain. But, then as now, there was a snobbish prejudice against such a popular taste. Nevertheless, the text of *Recent English Architecture* insisted that the illustrations had been chosen 'for the contribution the originals make to our heritage of building, whether they are modern or traditional in style. It is misleading to discriminate between buildings by mere labels, which are largely a matter of fashion.'

Another useful guide to the architectural aspirations and prejudices of the period was published by *The Architects' Journal* just a few months before another war brought things to a close. *Scoreboard* was the survey of votes for 'six recent British buildings ... considered of the greatest merit' cast by 'well-known people' chosen by the journal's readers. The results are not so much a guide to popular taste as to educated fashionable opinion in London in 1939. The most popular architects were the avant-garde firm Tecton, led by the glamorous Russian *émigré* Berthold Lubetkin, followed by Messrs Adams, Holden & Pearson: that is, Charles Holden, the architect of, amongst other things, Arnos Grove Station on the Piccadilly Line, as well as the headquarters of London University. More revealing, however, are the individual buildings cited.

Top of the poll came the Peter Jones department store in Sloane Square in London. This was another choice that indicated the increasing acceptance of the Modern Movement in Britain; its curving glass and vitrolite curtained-walled exterior was derived from the Schocken Stores in Germany by Eric Mendelsohn, which its architect, the young William Crabtree, had studied. Second, however, came a building designed, on the outside at least, by Sir Giles Gilbert Scott. His Cambridge library may not have been cited, but his Battersea Power Station was much admired as a conspicuous and successful modern industrial building. It was chosen by, amongst others, the scientist J. D. Bernal, Kenneth Clark, director of the National Gallery, the actor Charles Laughton and the writer Rebecca West. Third came another conspicuous modern structure in London: the headquarters of the London Passenger Transport Board above St James's Park Station, designed by Charles Holden. Its supporters included the scientist Julian Huxley, the art critic of *The Times*, Charles Marriott, the Byzantinist David Talbot Rice and, perhaps not surprisingly, Frank Pick, the board's chief executive.

If any conclusion can be drawn from these choices, it is that modernity in the 1930s took several forms. It could be the New Architecture of steel and glass derived from Continental Europe, but it could also be that American-influenced treatment of monumental brickwork which John Betjeman dismissed as 'jazz modern' and today is loosely described as 'Deco'. Or it could be the monumental Classicism abstracted to planes of white Portland stone which was enriched in the case of Holden's building by avant-garde sculpture by Henry Moore, Jacob Epstein and Eric Gill. The survey reflects the tastes of the 1930s, a polarised and anxious decade which saw the increasing acceptance of the arguments in favour of the Modern Movement while Modernism itself was becoming more romantic, more English.

A similar survey undertaken in 1929 would have selected rather more traditional modern buildings; the 1920s was initially a more conservative decade, dominated, in England, by the cult of Sir

Christopher Wren, though it was still characterised by a diversity of approach. There was also the potent influence of Geoffrey Scott's book, *The Architecture of Humanism*, first published in 1914 but revised in 1924, which vaunted style at the expense of nineteenth-century notions of structural integrity. The consequence was a widespread belief that modern British architecture should be a development of the simplified national Classical tradition: that is, the Georgian. Anglophile foreign architects admired the repetitive, elegant severity of Georgian terraces in London and saw them as truly modern. This did not prevent several knighted traditionalists from assisting unbridled private interests in destroying much of the best of Georgian London between the wars, eventually provoking the foundation of the Georgian Group of the Society for the Protection of Ancient Buildings in 1937. This aspect of the period is powerfully conveyed by the uncritical optimism of the egregious Harold P. Clunn, who described those who would preserve John Rennie's Waterloo Bridge as 'short-sighted fanatics'.[10] That modern Georgian aspired to be the national style is suggested by the curiosity of 'The King's House' presented to King George V as a Silver Jubilee gift in 1935 by the Royal Warrant Holders;[11] the winning design by Beresford Marshall was in modernistic neo-Georgian, in brick, with a soberly streamlined Deco interior.*

Well might the critic or historian be bemused by British interwar architecture, especially as the same architect could produce buildings almost simultaneously in different styles. In the 1860s, George Gilbert Scott had been committed to Gothic. His grandson Giles Scott, however, might seem to have been unconstrained in choice. He naturally used the Gothic manner in which he had been trained for his great cathedral in Liverpool, but other churches by him were designed in an abstracted round-arched Early Christian or Romanesque manner, while a refined neo-Georgian was employed

---

* The King chose the design from three which emerged from a limited competition among architects nominated by Sir Giles Scott.

for domestic commissions and 'jazz modern' for his industrial jobs. Although he was happy to employ reinforced-concrete construction to achieve flat roofs, and sometimes used metal windows with a pronounced horizontal emphasis, Scott never designed a building which might be categorised as 'Modern', albeit his new Waterloo Bridge was a model of austere functional elegance. Younger architects could produce flat-roofed, reinforced-concrete houses which were published in several polemical books (including Raymond McGrath's *Twentieth Century Houses* and F. R. S. Yorke's *The Modern House in England*) while also being prepared to design in traditional styles when asked. Marshall Sisson or Hugh Hughes might be cited, but the best example is that supremely versatile architect, Oliver Hill.

Born in 1887, Hill was an exact contemporary of Le Corbusier (1887–1965). He designed a number of much-illustrated Modern houses, like Holthanger at Wentworth in Surrey, and a number of simple, geometrical houses with flat roofs and standard metal windows on the Frinton Estate in Essex. He was responsible for the stylish, streamlined Midland Hotel at Morecambe, the first modern-style hotel in Britain, and the Prospect Inn on the Isle of Thanet, the first modern pub or roadhouse, and was chosen as the architect for the British Pavilion at the 1937 Paris Exposition. On the other hand, Hill also designed London town houses in a neo-Georgian or neo-Regency manner in which the influence of his principal architectural hero, Edwin Lutyens, is clearly evident. He was also responsible for one of the finest houses of the interwar years, designed in a rugged, Arts and Crafts manner, at Cour, on the Kintyre peninsular (Plate 23), while his own home was a restored tile-hung farmhouse in Surrey, reflecting the widespread English taste for the Tudor. Hill was also a talented interior designer, making clever use of mirror and repetitive vertical fluting in a manner best described as Art Deco. After the Second World War, Hill's practice declined; he moved to the Cotswolds and wrote much for the magazine *Country Life* – in whose pages he had first seen the entrancing work of Lutyens.

Hill ought to have been included in *Representative British Architects of Today*, a compilation of articles published by Charles Reilly (1874–1948) in 1931. Reilly, the former Head of the Liverpool School of Architecture, later switched his enthusiasm for American Beaux-Arts Classicism for whatever was modern and fashionable. In 1931, however, he had yet to be converted to the Modern Movement, and the dozen architects selected mostly worked in more traditional styles. In a curious way Reilly's book is representative of the period by being so very unrepresentative. None of the younger architects already producing notably modern buildings were included, while the conspicuous absence of two of Reilly's productive contemporaries, E. Vincent Harris (who triumphed in so many competitions for civic buildings) and Charles Holden (then producing his admired work for London Underground), can only be explained by professional jealousy. The youngest architects included were both older than Hill, being both born in 1883. One was Robert Atkinson, a pioneer in cinema architecture responsible for The Regent at Brighton, with its American-influenced, atmospheric interiors. The other was Clough Williams-Ellis, a glamorous and fashionable figure who would become best known for his recycling of rescued architectural fragments to create a picturesque Mediterranean village on the Welsh coast at Portmeirion (Plate 9).

Both Atkinson and Williams-Ellis, like Reilly himself, had begun their architectural careers before the Great War, as had the other architects he eulogised. Indeed, what is most revealing about Reilly's book is how old and how established they were. Half of them were (or would soon be) knighted. Several were over seventy, and the oldest had been born at the end of the Crimean War. This was the combative Sir Reginald Blomfield (1856–1942), who still had it in him to infuriate younger generations and would soon do so by attempting to commence the rebuilding of Nash's Carlton House Terrace, and by publishing, in 1934, an intemperate attack on Modernism with the consciously xenophobic title *Modernismus*. 'For myself I am prejudiced enough to detest cosmopolitanism,' he announced, despite the fact that his own Classical work had been conspicuously French in inspiration.[12] Others in the book had also made their names by producing Classical or 'Edwardian Baroque' buildings before the war: H. V. Lanchester, whose partnership was then working on the Parkinson Building at Leeds University and a whopping palace in India for the Maharajah of Jodhpur; Arthur J. Davis, who was still building giant Renaissance *palazzi* for banks in the City of London; and Curtis Green, whose unhappy collaboration with the engineer Owen Williams had resulted in the uncharacteristic and controversial Dorchester Hotel. There was also Stanley Adshead, who, in partnership with Stanley Ramsey, had once produced exquisite housing in a clever neo-Regency style.

Some were church architects, best known for Gothic work: Sir Giles Scott, of course, and Sir Walter Tapper. There was also the old Arts and Crafts architect, E. Guy Dawber. And there was Sir Herbert Baker, another knighted architect who managed to combine an Arts and Crafts sensitivity with an Imperial Classicism which he had practised in South Africa and India, as well as in London. That year, 1931, was indeed the year the new capital of British India, New Delhi, was officially inaugurated, and in which Baker's contribution to it was excoriated by Robert Byron in the pages of both the *Architectural Review* and *Country Life* while that of his uncomfortable collaborator, Sir Edwin Lutyens, was lauded. Along with Scott, Lutyens was the only representative of these distinguished Late Victorian and Edwardian architects who fully deserved inclusion in Reilly's book. Unlike several of them, he was still building, having just started on his huge, sublime Roman Catholic cathedral in Liverpool, and, unlike most of them, he was producing work which was still admired by a younger generation.

The differences among, and the conflicts between, these different generations may be one useful way of charting the complexities of interwar architecture. As Reilly's book suggests, the older generation still dominated: almost completely in the 1920s and still, to a considerable extent, in the 1930s. Too old to have fought in the First World War, they carried on regardless and, for a time, unchallenged.

'No age, not even the Victorian, is so remote from today as the Edwardian,' began an editorial in the *Architectural Review* in 1934,[13] going on to concede that 'the most prominent architects today' belonged to that era, and that, 'even when they themselves are dead, the offices which they started are still busy turning out the same sort of thing as they turned out in 1905'.* No wonder their grandchildren's generation often felt exasperated. 'We were born in the war,' yelled the young editors of *Focus*, the new student magazine emanating from the Architectural Association: 'We were born into a civilization whose leaders, whose ideals, whose culture had failed. They are still in power today. But we, the generation who follow, cannot accept their domination. They lead us always deeper into reaction that we are convinced can only end in disaster.'[14]

Polarised by the increasingly extreme politics of the 1930s, this was the voice of a generation ideologically committed to the Modern Movement which would attempt to fulfil its ideals after the Second World War. 'Today we have got our Modern Architecture and very soon it will be absolutely inescapable,' John Summerson could announce in 1941. 'It has the loyalty of the young; it is established, with different degrees of firmness, in every school of architecture in the country. Soon it will not be Modern Architecture any longer. It will just be Architecture.'[15]

It would, however, be a mistake to see the confused interwar years merely as a period of transition. There was, for a start, a generation in between the older Traditionalists and younger Modernists; this generation, which had fought in the war, included a number of thoughtful, broad-minded architects who reacted intelligently to the possibilities offered by Modernism and were open to new ideas from Europe, but who were not prepared to forget the past and to discard the many strengths of the continuing traditions of British architecture. They included such figures as Harry Goodhart-Rendel,

---

* Architectural development seems to go in spurts, followed by lulls, so much the same could have been written in, say, 1980 – or indeed today.

Howard Robertson, Thomas S. Tait, Frederick Etchells (who first translated the polemics of Le Corbusier into English), Herbert Rowse and Arthur Shoosmith – as well as Oliver Hill. These architects were responsible for a rich and allusive modernism, one that could be monumental, decorative and colourful, in contrast to the doctrinaire aesthetic of planar reinforced concrete derived from Le Corbusier and the Bauhaus.

However, for all the differences in outlook between the different generations of architects, they had much in common. Not least was an acceptance of the revolutionary impact new technologies were making on architecture and daily life – modernity in its widest sense. The more conservative architects may have believed in pitched roofs and traditional building materials, but they were happy to enjoy the benefits of electric light, the telephone and the motor car. What is also evident is how a machine aesthetic influenced architecture, for so many 'streamlined' buildings imitated the shape of aeroplanes, biplanes and monoplanes, and the superstructures of ocean liners. Then there were the new forms of construction, whose benefits were not to be denied (reinforced concrete and the steel frame), and new materials: plywoods and plastics, ruboleum for floors, aluminium and welded steel tubing for furniture, and vitrolite and new forms of glass for the walls. The sheer size and weight of the lavish book on *Glass in Architecture and Decoration* by Raymond McGrath and A. C. Frost, published by the Architectural Press in 1937 says much about the enthusiasms of the time.

It is, perhaps, difficult to appreciate the revolutionary impact of technical innovations experienced by architects born in the 1880s. Such men grew up in a world in which, beyond the network of steam railways, the fastest speed was that of a horse. By the beginning of the new century, the first vehicles powered by the internal combustion engine were appearing on the roads, the telephone was becoming widespread, and the first cinematograph films were being shown. Within another twenty years, horse-drawn transport was almost extinct in Britain and the wireless had annihilated time and distance. The development of

Royal Institute of British Architects, Portland Place, London (G. Grey Wornum, 1934)

these inventions was encouraged by a war which saw industrialised slaughter on an unprecedented scale. The Wright brothers had first staggered into the air in North Carolina in 1903; six years later Louis Blériot flew across the English Channel in an aeroplane, and by 1918 the Germans were able to attack London with four-engined Gotha bombers operating from Belgium. Meanwhile, on the ground, strange rhomboidal 'tanks' with continuous caterpillar tracks had proved able to defeat barbed wire and trenches. And there was poison gas. By the 1920s, the turn-of-the-century science fiction fantasies of H. G. Wells had been realised, and there was much more to come.

All this was exhilarating, and architects were not immune from the excitements generated by this momentous technical and social change. Many in Britain after the war wished to turn the clock back as if nothing had happened. But with the Kaiser defeated and the League of Nations founded, perhaps these technical and scientific advances would now be used to make the world a better place. Soon there would be the 'Good New Days' – the title of a book of 1935 by Marjorie and C. H. B. Quennell, when problems that had defeated earlier generations could be solved by science, by reason, by order, by cleanliness, by democracy. Unfortunately, modern technology might also be used to create the *Brave New World* that Aldous Huxley imagined in 1932. What the interwar years were not, either in architecture or other areas of life, was calm or serene. Rather, there seems to have been a general acceptance of continuous upheaval and, for many, a sense of impending doom.

The first published history of the 1930s, which appeared in 1940, began ominously: 'Each moment seems more urgent than all preceding ones; each generation of men are convinced that their difficulties and achievements are unparalleled. One of the few constants in life, for the individual and for the community, is a sense of crisis.'[16] The crises had been many: the General Strike of 1926, the Wall Street Crash of 1929, the economic depression and hunger marches that followed, political instability, the Abdication of Edward VIII in 1937, the rise of Mosley's Blackshirts and of street violence, the Spanish Civil War, Appeasement, the Munich Agreement of 1938, and then the widespread, increasing fear of another war, to be accompanied by devastating aerial bombardment. The old political establishment had been discredited by the Great War, even though the interwar decades continued to be dominated by old men. Ideal solutions were increasingly sought in political extremes whose models were to be found abroad: in Soviet Russia and in Fascist Italy by the mid-1920s and in Nazi Germany after 1933. In that year, the young John Betjeman wrote of the necessity of 'a return to Christendom':

> Whether that Christendom will be a Union of Soviet Republics, a League of Socialistic Nations or an Ecclesiastical Union, it is not for me to say. I only know, like everyone else, that we are changing in a rapid and terrifying manner to some new form of civilization which will demand new architectural expression. Perhaps we are rushing towards annihilation.[17]

Despite, or because of, all these crises, there was a prevailing sense that the Modern Age was profoundly and qualitatively different from all former times, and particularly from the recent but distant Victorian Age. Countless books contrasted spacious, hygienic, modern housing in garden cities with back-to-back slum terraces in smoky industrial towns; tastefully furnished austere rooms, flooded with light, with rich dark interiors stuffed with threatening 'clutter'; sensible, modern body-revealing bathing costumes with crinoline dresses, frock-coats and stove-pipe hats; bright, clean milk bars with rowdy, degenerate Victorian gin palaces; flat-roofed modern houses with extreme examples of suburban Gothic Revival villas; and so on. New inventions – radio, the cinema, air travel – were going to make the world a better, happier place; scientific and social progress was inevitable. If the gas-lit Victorians moved in constant pea-soup fog, smoke and rain, there was now going to be perpetual sunshine.

Not that the picture was simple, for the legacy of the Victorians and Edwardians was everywhere and inescapable. Skirt lengths may have risen dramatically by the mid-1920s, but when the Prime Minister, Neville Chamberlain, returned from Munich and alighted at Heston Aerodrome in 1938 clutching that scrap of paper, he was wearing a stiff wing-collar. In the numerous memoirs written by that cohesive, artistic Bright Young Thing generation born soon after the turn of the century – John Betjeman, Osbert Lancaster, Cecil Beaton, Evelyn Waugh and the rest – parents are presented as remote and incomprehensible, almost a different species. Even the more elderly saw the Victorians as absurd. Giles Scott had a low opinion of the work of his famous grandfather, the architect of the Albert Memorial, but he had been born in 1880 and the roots of his own architecture lay firmly in the nineteenth century. Yet very few took the earnest efforts of the mid-Victorians seriously, especially in the 1920s. In 1949, describing how he came to write his pioneering study of the Gothic Revival, Kenneth Clark found 'the state of feeling towards nineteenth-century architecture which prevailed in 1927' hard to believe:

> In Oxford it was universally believed that Ruskin had built Keble, and that it was the ugliest building in the world. Undergraduates and young dons used to break off on their afternoon walks in order to have a good laugh at the quadrangle . . . One eminent historian . . . went so far as to call me a liar at a public meeting because I denied Ruskin's part in these buildings.[18]

Curiously, in vehemently rejecting what was perceived as the nineteenth-century practice of dressing up buildings in historical styles, architects of the 1920s and 1930s were sharing the Victorian obsession with style. Like them, they followed a quest for the elusive new style for the age, even if the advocates of the Modern Movement insisted that it was not a style but 'the honest product of science and art . . . relating methods of building as closely as possible to real needs'.[19] Not all architects agreed that a house was just a machine for living in, but a respect for simplicity and a desire to avoid excessive ornament, an affection for well-lit interiors and muted colours, for order and rational planning, in contrast to so-called Victorian 'ostentation' and 'clutter', was shared by conservative Traditionalists and by Modernists. 'Revivalism' was the ultimate horror; instead, a new style was surely about to evolve. Some believed that modern architecture would come from developing the English Georgian tradition in its well-proportioned simplicity; others looked to America for a lead, while others saw the way in Holland, or Sweden, or Finland. Many had discovered the possibilities of the future at the Paris Exposition of 1925, others at Gothenburg in 1923 or Stockholm in 1930, and a few were convinced that the New Architecture had already been born in Cologne, Stuttgart and Dessau.

This also indicates a new and remarkable openness to foreign influences by British architects. Edwardian Britain had indeed looked to France and to America, but this was in connection with a growing interest in academic Classicism and the methods of the École des Beaux-Arts. Domestic architecture had remained national and insular in character, while being admired abroad. After the war, however, despite the initial attempts to reassert English values and traditions, there was a distinct loss of confidence among many architects that encouraged them to look abroad and, in particular, to two countries with vigorous national architectural traditions: Holland and Sweden. British architects had always looked to the Continent, of course, but they had always focused on old buildings – no Victorian was much interested in contemporary developments in Italy, France or Germany. What was new was that architects were learning from modern buildings abroad, whether from personal visits and organised student tours or from the articles and publications usually illustrated with photographs by F. R. Yerbury. The number of foreign architects working in Britain was also new. First came the colonials (Uren, Connell, Ward, McGrath, Coates), who were soon followed by the seductive and exotic Europeans (Goldfinger and Lubetkin) in promoting radical new ideas. The great Peter Behrens of Berlin had already been invited to design the first real modern house in Britain, at Northampton in 1924. Then came the distinguished refugees from Nazism after 1933, although here the RIBA bowed to public anxiety and prejudice by insisting that each form a partnership with an established British architect: hence Gropius & Fry, Yorke & Breuer, Mendelsohn & Chermayeff.

The established architectural profession was in general agreement that it was absurd for Modern Man to live in a neo-Tudor house. Well-designed traditional houses in the Arts and Crafts tradition were acceptable, but not suburban houses with fake beams, leaded-light windows and tile-hung gables. This reflected a snobbish and self-interested disapproval of the work of the speculative builder, but also a widespread concern that the vast new housing developments encouraged after the Great War by electrified railways, bus services and the growing ownership of motor cars were wastefully planned and gobbling up large tracts of countryside. By the end of the 1930s, one in four houses was new and three-quarters of these had been built by private enterprise. These new suburbs succeeded in defining what was increasingly regarded as typical and desirable: developments of curving streets of neo-Tudor houses, with the occasional Pseudish example and, even rarer, a Modernistic one, detached or semi-detached, set behind parallel rows of front gardens, occasionally interspersed with a shopping parade, often half-timbered as well, with a large, Modernistic cinema, church and, perhaps, smart new Underground or Southern Electric station.

Unfortunately, in the absence of much effective planning legislation, suburban and industrial development tended to line arterial roads, giving rise to the ugly phenomenon of 'ribbon development' through rural countryside. Such consequences of uncontrolled development increasingly concerned architects and planners, and especially those impressed by the anti-urban bias of the Arts and Crafts and the ordered neatness encouraged by the Garden City movement. Numerous urban and rural plans were produced. Campaigning publications like Clough Williams-Ellis's *England and the Octopus* (1928), with its photographs of outrageous advertisement hoardings and sprawls of bungalows, and the collection of essays entitled *Britain and the Beast* (1938) were informed responses to these problems, while Thomas Sharp's *Town and Countryside* (1932) deplored the blurring of the distinction between urban and rural districts.

The result was an almost universally shared belief in the desirability of planning, which mirrored the contemporary political tendencies towards collectivism and state control. Individualism was blamed for the chaotic and grimy legacy of the Industrial Revolution and unbridled private enterprise for ribbon development. Professorial chairs in town planning had been established before the war, and almost all architects agreed on the virtues of orderly, controlled urban development. These concerns were reflected in the consistently high standards of design encouraged by Frank Pick within the London Passenger Transport Board, whether in buildings, buses, lettering or advertisements, and by the appropriate, urbane buildings, usually sober neo-Georgian, erected by the Ministry of Works for the General Post Office. The former were much admired by the advocates of the New Architecture; the latter rather less so. And planning began to have legal backing: the Town and Country Planning Act of 1932 allowed a local authority to prohibit any building 'likely seriously to injure the amenity of a locality', the irony being that these powers were used chiefly against progressive modern designs.[20]

A British architect did not necessarily have to sympathise with the urban renewal policies, with new public buildings encouraged in Mussolini's Italy, with the economic planning attempted in Soviet Russia, or the public works programmes promoted in Hitler's Germany, to believe in the necessity of planning. The important thing was that the architect should be in charge. In the catalogue of the ambitious exhibition held by the RIBA to mark its centenary, 'International Architecture: 1924–34', Giles Scott, as President, contributed a foreword which stressed that it should:

demonstrate the architect as a PLANNER, and as one of the most important servants of the community, with an invaluable contribution to make towards an improvement in the art of living . . . 'Planning' is the key-word to a form of development peculiar to our own time. We cannot continue to tolerate the poverty, ill-health, waste and ugliness of disorder. The whole world is out of joint through lack of planning.[21]

Planning could not have prevented the outbreak of war in 1914, but there was a determination that such a catastrophe must never happen again. The Great War created the vast gulf between generations; it was responsible for that loss of confidence which lies behind the eclectic confusion in British architecture in the 1920s and 1930s, and in the consequent determination to make a better, safer world; and it lies behind the technological and social optimism that generated the Modern Movement. As with so much else, the movement's origins can be traced before 1914, but it was the post-war climate that allowed such often misguided optimism to flourish. The mood was well caught by the young Australian designer Raymond McGrath, in his enthusiastic 1934 survey of *Twentieth Century Houses*:

> The work of Gropius at Cologne was a certain sign of the great changes coming, but the outburst of war in the same year made these changes seem farther off than ever and in comparison with the military scale of events quite unimportant. It is not possible to say what probable great architects there were among those millions of dead, but on those who did come through undamaged the effect of that time of destruction seems to have been a burning desire for sunlight and clean air and clean thought. The machines did their work at last and Metal took control.[22]

Great Britain may have emerged victorious in 1918, but at a terrible cost. The total British Empire loss was over a million men dead. The proportion of the population killed and wounded in England may not have been as high as in France and Germany, but the social and psychological damage was immense. The older generation, those too old to fight, may have fully supported the war effort and revelled in the final victory, but many members of younger generations became disillusioned by the incompetence and callousness displayed by those in command. Although the effect of the war on society was nothing like as traumatic as it was in Germany, traditional ways of doing things were discredited – and in architecture the consequences of this took some time to emerge.

During the decade after the Armistice, British architecture was often conservative and uninspired, reflecting a society which was damaged and exhausted by four years of war. The dominant impulse at first was to go back to the way things were before 1914, a tendency exacerbated by the cult of Christopher Wren, which reached its height between 1923, the bicentenary of his death, and the tercentenary of his birth in 1932. The prevalent mood was caught by the *Country Life* writer Lawrence Weaver, when he insisted that 'A new method of design is incredible, simply because it is not feasible. We had our misfortunes a few years ago in that pursuit, but even before the war the "New Art" which pleased Germany and Austria so vastly was "dead and damned" in Great Britain.'[23] But this prejudiced and insular view ignored the interest of the more experimental architecture of the Edwardian years, and the fact that even Weaver's hero, Lutyens, had once been influenced by the 'New Art'.

Change was inevitable, and in 1927 the publication of Frederick Etchells's translation of Le Corbusier's *Vers une Architecture* as *Towards a New Architecture* opened up exciting possibilities to a younger generation of architects. The permanent buildings erected for the British Empire Exhibition at Wembley in 1924 were solid, monumental essays in abstracted neo-Classicism, albeit all of reinforced concrete, but by 1927 the international competition for rebuilding the Shakespeare Memorial Theatre at Stratford-upon-Avon resulted in a design neither Classical nor Gothic but strongly influenced by the modern Expressionist brick architecture

Shakespeare Memorial Theatre, Stratford-upon-Avon, Warwickshire (Elisabeth Scott, 1932)

of Holland (Plate 13). Even more remarkably, the architect was a woman, Elisabeth Scott, a cousin of Sir Giles, whose victory signalled, if not the end, then at least the opening up, of a profession exclusively dominated by men.

A special issue of the *Architectural Review* was devoted to the Stratford theatre in 1932. That same year, another one was entirely concerned with the new headquarters of the British Broadcasting Corporation, but not so much with its confused stone-clad exterior as with the unprecedented interior studios designed in a streamlined, modern manner using plywoods and bakelites. British architecture was changing. Another landmark was the competition for the De La Warr Pavilion at Bexhill-on-Sea being won with a modern design by Mendelsohn & Chermayeff, despite local opposition to employing 'alien' architects and that of the British Union of Fascists. It is important, however, to remember that whole issues of the *Architectural Review* were also devoted to more traditional modern buildings, like Norwich City Hall, while the January 1931 issue was a eulogy of Lutyens's achievement at New Delhi – designed before the war.

Nor should it be forgotten that some of the most impressive works of British architects between the wars were to be found in those far-flung parts of the world still coloured red in British atlases. A few miles west of New Delhi stand the massive, pinky-red walls of what by turns resembles both a stepped ziggurat and a buttressed Gothic cathedral (Plate 1). Anciently monumental, but with details reminiscent of German Expressionism or Dutch Modernism, this extraordinary brick construction is in fact a church. Designed in 1928, St Martin's Garrison Church was liked by the military as they thought it could be defended in times of trouble, and came to be known as 'the Cubist church', as Penelope Chetwode, daughter of the Indian Army's Commander-in-Chief, recalled.* At once

---

* [Penelope Chetwode (1910–1986) was the wife of John Betjeman. She and Gavin Stamp became friends in the later years of her life. RH.]

modern and traditional, practical and symbolic, it was also typical of its time in combining the severe industrial character of the factory with echoes of the monumentality of antiquity, both of which were much admired at the time; as Robert Byron argued, the two aesthetics were not necessarily so different.[24] 'Had this church been the work of a French or German architect,' wrote another contemporary admirer, 'Europe would be flabbergasted by the magnificently simple and direct design. But since it is the work of an Englishman, it will probably never be heard of abroad.'[25] That English architect was A. G. Shoosmith, and following his return home, he never built again.[26]

This Introduction ends with his church because it exemplifies many of the contradictory tendencies in architecture in the first three decades of the twentieth century. It also manifests the creative influence of Edwin Lutyens, who, despite his age, was indisputably the greatest living architect in Britain, enjoying the respect of his peers and of the younger generation, in the years between the two world wars. Designed in 1928, Shoosmith's Cubist church is not a building normally mentioned in discussions of British Architecture between the wars — not because it was built far away in India but because it has not been regarded as typical. For a majority of recent historians and critics, what has seemed most important has been the British expression of the Modern Movement in architecture, comparatively limited in both quantity and range though it may have been. The following chapters will attempt to suggest otherwise.

CHAPTER ONE

ARMISTICE

———◆———

EIGHT MONTHS AFTER the signing of the Armistice that ended the fighting on the Western Front, peace celebrations were held in London. On 19 July 1919, British and French troops marched past an unusual temporary structure erected in the middle of Whitehall: a tall pylon of timber and plaster, bearing wreaths, flanked by flags and carrying a symbolic draped coffin. At the end of the day, the watching crowds gathered round it and piled up flowers and wreaths around its base. The designer of this structure, the fashionable country house architect Edwin Lutyens (1869–1944), had not been invited to the unveiling ceremony. Nevertheless, he had created an object that so perfectly expressed the inarticulate grief of a nation in mourning that the government was unable to resist the popular demand that it be re-created in stone. The permanent Cenotaph, the national memorial to the British Empire dead of the Great War of 1914–1918, was unveiled on Armistice Day in 1920.[1] 'Not a catafalque but a Cenotaph,' was Lutyens's response to the Prime Minister Lloyd George's request in 1919 that he emulate the catafalque being erected for the peace celebrations in Paris; he recalled being told that a cenotaph, an

The Cenotaph, Whitehall, London (Edwin Lutyens, 1920)

empty tomb, is a memorial to someone buried elsewhere.* Almost all of those who had died were buried elsewhere, half of them with no known grave. Many cenotaphs were needed.

The Great War cast a long shadow over the twentieth century. Millions died. France lost 1 in 28 of her population, Germany 1 in 35, Austria 1 in 50, Great Britain 1 in 66. Of those British men aged between twenty and twenty-four in 1914, 30 per cent died; 1 in 8 of the 6 million who fought were killed, and 1.5 million were disabled. No wonder, as a modern historian has concluded, 'interwar Britain was probably more obsessed with death than any other period of modern history'.[2] The total loss for the British Empire was well over a million. Such figures transcend ordinary comprehension; in one contemporary Armistice Day broadcast, the enormity of the loss was illustrated by stating that if all the Britons killed in the Great War were to march four abreast from Scotland to London, by the time the leaders reached Whitehall the tail of the column would still be at Durham.

Inevitably, some of the dead were architects. During the war years, the pages of the *Journal of the Royal Institute of British Architects* and the *Architectural Association Journal* were filled with photographs of young architects in uniform who had died. How many, had they lived, might have emerged as great talents after 1918 is impossible to say. Even some stars of the pre-war years, including Edwin Rickards and Cecil Brewer, died from ill-health as a result of their war work. It was the task of those who survived to put into tangible, symbolic form the sense of loss felt by colleagues and friends, wives, parents, siblings and children, and to do so in a dignified manner. Never before and never again would there be such a demand for war memorials, and the visible consequences of the 1914–1918 conflict comprise a significant proportion of British architectural output in

---

* Christopher Hussey describes this as 'one of his flashes of simultaneous intuition, memory, and visual perception', recalling a conversation with Gertrude Jekyll in her Surrey garden about a large rustic podium which she called the Cenotaph of Sigismunda (Hussey (1950), p. 392).

the two decades that followed. By such memorials, wrote Gerald Wellesley in 1925,

> the arts of architecture and sculpture in the present age are going to be judged by posterity for artists have been called in to help the nation to give material expression to a national impulse in a way which is quite without precedent. It is melancholy to think that any village community should have rated the sacrifice of ardent young lives so low that it was held that their adequate commemoration was achieved by a cross of Cornish design and granite sold in various sizes by large department stores.[3]

On the whole, the architectural profession rose to this unprecedented challenge with conspicuous success, but they were well trained to do so. From about 1890, British architects had become increasingly interested in, first, the native Renaissance architecture of Inigo Jones and Christopher Wren, and then in the whole European Classical tradition. By 1914, the ebullience of 'Edwardian Baroque' architecture had been succeeded by a taste for a more monumental and disciplined Classicism. One product of this was the publication in that year of A. E. Richardson's magnificent book *Monumental Classic Architecture in Great Britain and Ireland*. It was Richardson, with R. Randal Phillips, who, during the early years of the war, traced in a series of articles in the *Architectural Review* the history of war memorials, from Greek and Roman monuments, through the precedents provided by Napoleonic France, to the more recent examples furnished by Imperial Germany, which they felt obliged to condemn. These authors concluded that London was not yet worthy of comparison with Paris in this matter, and that:

> at the close of the War the nation will demand the erection of a national memorial to the memory of her fallen sons. There must be no niggardly dealing in connection with it. Isolated statues and mediocre tablets will not suffice to reward the terrific nature of

the struggle and its all-important effect on the destiny of the race. We are too close to the scene at present to estimate its character, but when the time comes for the consideration of a national monument the thing must be undertaken in a spirit of greatness.[4]

There was, however, no immediate precedent in Britain for the type and scale of memorial required. Before 1914, there were few war memorials, as distinct from regimental memorials, monuments to particular military heroes, or the memorials paid for by the families of officers. After Waterloo, the bloodiest conflict in British history before 1914, while the bodies of officers were taken home for burial, those of private soldiers were left in unmarked mass graves. By the end of the nineteenth century, attitudes were changing, and the feeling grew that all the dead deserved commemoration. Even so, while the Boer War (1899–1903) gave rise to individual memorials with lists of casualties in many churches, there is no national memorial to that conflict in Britain.

In the Great War, parliamentary governments, as well as autocracies, committed their populations to the struggle with a ruthlessness inconceivable in earlier centuries. The British Expeditionary Force of 1914 consisted of professional soldiers, but those who went over the top at the Somme in 1916 were largely volunteers, while by 1918 Douglas Haig was commanding a huge army of conscripted soldiers. The patriotic character of the war and the unprecedented scale of casualties sustained by ordinary citizens demanded that every individual sacrifice be commemorated. This could not be achieved before the conflict was over, but while the casualties were still mounting, much thought was given to the nature and design of future war memorials while, at a local level, small shrines listing the names of the dead were often constructed inside or outside parish churches. Advisory committees were established and books published on the subject to provide good models for emulation. A proposal to erect a war shrine in Hyde Park designed by Lutyens was rendered redundant when, at long last, the guns fell silent on 11 November 1918.

The real debate now began. There had already been a scheme to create a national war museum with a Hall of Honour in Hyde Park and proposals for other large, civic memorials.* Now numerous schemes were published to replan swathes of Central London with civic buildings, triumphal avenues and great monuments. In particular, grandiose notions of a national war memorial fused with the long-running saga of the proposal to replace the Charing Cross or Hungerford Bridge across the Thames and move the railway terminus to the South Bank. The Dean of St Paul's proposed 'blowing up' the railway bridge and its replacement as 'our National War Memorial', and by 1916 Aston Webb, Reginald Blomfield and the politician John Burns had proposed a new Charing Cross road bridge as a memorial with triumphal arches at either end.[5] Encouraged by the London Society, other architects came up with similar proposals.† One, in 1919, was for a Tower of Victory to be built on the site of Charing Cross Station, 235 feet tall, with statues representing Liberty, Retribution, Peace and Victory.[6]

Others, however, argued that public money was better spent on useful things for the living rather than piles of stone for the dead. Lloyd George's government tried to assuage the frustrations of demobilised servicemen by proposing a massive state campaign to replace slums by 'homes fit for heroes', but this was not realised on any large scale. In 1919 the architect W. R. Lethaby complained that, 'The people asked for houses and we have given them stones.'[7] With his Arts and Crafts background, Lethaby preferred utilitarian memorials, and

---

* Lutyens made designs for the Hall of Honour in 1917 (see Crellin, (2002), p. 106).

† On 17 November 1916 Herbert Baker wrote to *The Times* about 'A Great Imperial Memorial', asserting that 'The greatest war memorial that we can conceive would be the acquisition by the nation of some splendid and worthy site which would be devoted to the memory of those who have fallen', perhaps on the South Bank of the Thames in connection with a rebuilt Charing Cross Bridge. The 'Bridge of Victory' idea was revived as a double-decker road and rail bridge in 1926: William Walcot made a design with a colossal arched entrance.

he insisted that 'a hall or something useful' was 'probably the best form a memorial could take, for the living are starved for lack of the means of civilization'.[8] Others agreed. Edwin Hodnett, architect to the parish of Ilford, advocated a memorial hospital, arguing that it was 'our bounden duty to replace the lives that had been lost, and every child saved in this hospital would be a valuable asset to the town and the nation'.[9]

In the event, a Celtic cross with a bronze soldier presenting arms, by the sculptor Newbury Trent, was erected in Ilford in 1922, but such arguments were aired in most communities. The writer G. K. Chesterton later recalled the 'great battle of the Beaconsfield War Memorial' and the opposition provoked by the proposal to erect a free-standing cross in the centre of the Buckinghamshire town. The alternative scheme was for a club building, intended for ex-servicemen:

> I pointed out that a parish-pump might seem to some more rational than a Cross, but it was not so half like a War Memorial. A club, or hospital ward, or anything having its own practical purpose, policy and future, would not really be a War Memorial at all; it would not be in practice a memory of the War. If people thought it wrong to have a memory of the War, let them say so. If they did not approve of wasting money on a War Memorial, let us scrap the War Memorial and save the money.[10]

The club proposal turned out to be too expensive and the Rector of Beaconsfield and individual subscribers went ahead with the Cross. As Chesterton appreciated, with a utilitarian memorial, the commemorative purpose of the building is usually soon forgotten, while the memorial itself could become redundant. In Cambridge, for example, part of the county's war memorial was the proposal to build a new nurses' home attached to Addenbrooke's Hospital, but this was subsequently abandoned.[11] A rare example of an enlightened and lasting cultural gesture in this context was the gift in 1922 by

War Memorial, Beaconsfield, Buckinghamshire (J. O. Cheadle, 1921)

Reginald Tatton to Chorley Corporation of Astley Hall, a fine Elizabethan mansion which had been used as a convalescent home and thereafter became the town's war memorial.

In most cases, parish or town councils decided on a purpose-built, symbolic war memorial, if only to give the many bereaved families a focus for mourning. As the war correspondent Philip Gibbs argued, war memorials 'should be not only reminders of the great death that killed the flower of our race but warnings of what war means in slaughter and ruin, in broken hearts and agony'.[12] The arguments in favour of a permanent memorial are well documented in the case of Spalding in Lincolnshire, where the widow of the former MP, Francis McLaren, killed while serving in the Royal Flying Corps, proposed a memorial cloister in the grounds of Ayscoughfee Hall.[13] As Barbara McLaren was the niece of the famous garden designer Gertrude Jekyll, she had employed Jekyll's early collaborator Lutyens before the war and naturally proposed him as the architect for the memorial.* Others in the town proposed utilitarian memorials, including a chiming clock on the Corn Exchange and the conversion of Ayscoughfee Hall into a YMCA hostel. All these were debated at a stormy public meeting, after which it was decided to put the alternatives to a vote. This, however, was restricted to those on the electoral roll, thus excluding not only women but many surviving combatants. In the event, a modified scheme by Lutyens secured the most votes and his triple-arched pavilion at the end of a reflecting pool was unveiled in 1922 – most of the cost having been borne by Mrs McLaren, her father-in-law and the Jekyll family.

It was, of course, possible for a community to remember its dead with both a dedicated memorial and a practical building. At Tewin in Hertfordshire, for instance, a local resident, Sir Otto Beit, who had lost two sons in the war, gave the village a memorial hall in memory of villagers who had served and died. Revitalising village life by providing a hall or club was a topical concern. Tewin's is a particularly fine and appropriate example, built of red brick in the manner of early Lutyens, with tall chimneys and sweeping roof planes embracing two projecting gabled wings. It was opened in 1922; the architect was not Lutyens but Herbert Baker,[14] who was

---

* Lutyens designed an unusual and poignant oak headboard over the grave of Francis McLaren in Busbridge churchyard in Surrey, which was later accompanied by the monumental tomb he created for Sir Herbert and Lady Jekyll.

also responsible for the village's own war memorial, a free-standing churchyard cross placed next to the medieval parish church.

Looking back, twenty years later, from the beginning of another war, Robert Graves and Alan Hodge recalled how:

> in every village in England the problem of the local war memorial was raging – where should it be placed? What form should it take – statue, obelisk, or cross? Could the names of all the dead be inscribed on it? Or would it not be more sensible to use the money collected for a recreation ground and engrave the names on an inexpensive plaque in the church?[15]

So very many and various memorials were raised that generalisation is difficult. Many are of no artistic merit, although to state that is to miss the point. It was a profitable time to be a sculptor, for so many memorials consisted of a pedestal supporting a bronze figure of a Tommy, usually presenting arms or saluting the dead. One curious example is the young soldier striding back from the front, helmet in hand, who is encountered by visitors arriving at Cambridge railway station. It is the work of a Canadian doctor-cum-sculptor, Tait McKenzie, whose idealised portraits of young men were so popular that his work became the subject of the second book written by the *Country Life* architectural writer Christopher Hussey, published in 1929.[16]

In April 1919, the Cambridgeshire war memorial committee came up with three proposals, intended separately to serve the living, to honour the dead, and to celebrate victory. For the living there was to be the extension to Cambridge's hospital, while the 6,000 county dead were to be commemorated in a chapel in Ely Cathedral, where they were to be listed – as equals and not by regiment, rank or class. It was the celebration of victory, however, which created controversy. In the event the initiative was seized by the Master of Christ's College, Sir Arthur Shipley, who chose both the sculptor (McKenzie) and the sculptor's model (an undergraduate he had met

Cambridgeshire War Memorial, Cambridge (sculptor Robert Tait McKenzie, 1922)

at a party in his college). As the historian Ken Inglis has concluded, the committee 'made a sound judgement of popular taste when they chose *The Homecoming*. It is certain that the initiative for their choice came, at a time when widespread consultation had yielded no solution to the problem of how to represent Victory, from a don with a penchant for young men.'[17] This memorial is, however, somewhat unusual in having a celebratory rather than a mournful iconography; what is impressive about so many war memorials – particularly those erected by the Imperial War Graves Commission – is that they are not triumphalist in character.*

If not a bronze soldier, most free-standing village memorials were of two types: the Celtic cross or the crucifix.[18] This last type had been unusual in Britain because of its Catholic associations, but many soldiers had seen wayside crosses in Belgium and France and so the form began to have appropriate connotations, not least the notion of sacrifice. In Chipping Campden in Gloucestershire, the memorial took this form and was designed by F. L. Griggs, an architectural draughtsman, artist and Roman Catholic convert, provoking an opposing proposal to build a nursing station instead. Griggs's design was supported by the local admirers of C. R. Ashbee's Guild of Handicrafts, and Lethaby wrote that 'this was one of the most appropriate and beautiful memorials he had ever seen'.[19] As Chesterton understood, the utilitarian counter-proposal was usually a smoke-screen for religious prejudice and a dislike of Catholic symbolism. At Beaconsfield, the public meeting about the cross project had barely begun before 'there had entered into it the following subjects of debate':

---

* There are, of course, exceptions, such as the curious but repellent war memorial known as the Waggoners' Memorial at Sledmere, Yorkshire, on which naïve friezes by Carlo Magnoni adhered to an iconography that might have been suggested by British wartime propaganda; it was commissioned by Sir Mark Sykes, who spent much of the war with the French diplomat Picot, carving up the former Turkish Empire in the Middle East, so creating intractable problems for the future.

(1) The Position of Woman in the Modern World; (2) Prohibition and the Drink Question; (3) The Excellence or Exaggeration of the Cult of Athletics; (4) The Problem of Unemployment, Especially in Relation to Ex-Service Men; (5) The Question of Support for Hospitals and the General Claims of Surgery and Medicine; (6) The Justice of the War; (7) Above all, or rather under all, for it was in many ways masked or symbolically suggested, the great war of religion which has never ceased to divide mankind.[20]

There was no reason, of course, why a war memorial should conform to a religious model, and in larger towns and cities the war memorials were usually secular in character, Classical and monumental, and sometimes forming part of an exercise in urban improvement. This was the case at Southport, where a new civic space was created and framed by open colonnaded shrines and with an obelisk in the centre. Birmingham's Hall of Memory, a detached, domed, octagonal structure, was intended to be part of a proposed new civic centre. In Aberdeen, a war memorial hall formed part of a prominent extension to the city's Art Gallery designed by Marshall Mackenzie & Son. In Stockport the detached war memorial hall, another grand Classical building, later became the town's art gallery. In London, the grand entrance to Waterloo Station, planned as part of the rebuilding supervised by J. R. Scott, was made into a 'Victory Arch' commemorating the dead of the London and South Western Railway.

In his 1925 survey of new war memorials, Gerald Wellesley divided 'purely architectural memorials' into five categories: the Cenotaph; the Pylon; the Obelisk; the Column; and the *Tempietto*.[21] Some of the cenotaphs were designed by Lutyens himself, such as those at Southampton and Rochdale, where a carved, draped effigy was raised high above a monumental pedestal flanked by painted stone flags hanging eternally still. As for the pylon, one of the best examples is that by Sir John Burnet in front of Glasgow City Chambers, dedicated in 1924 on one side of George Square. In this powerful, abstracted form, flanked by more examples of the lions by

Ernest Gillick he had used to guard his King Edward VII galleries at the British Museum, the Beaux-Arts-trained Classicist combined the pylon with the elements of a cenotaph, as well as subtly incorporating the outline of a cross and a bronze sword.

In such memorials, designed by architects who had discovered the language of a monumental Classicism before the war, any sculpture was firmly subservient to the architectural conception. As Sir Reginald Blomfield, one of the principal architects to the Imperial War Graves Commission, later recalled, 'Many of us had seen terrible examples [of war memorials] in France,* and were haunted by the fear of winged angels in various sentimental attitudes.'[22] For his Royal Air Force Memorial on the Thames Embankment, Blomfield placed a carved and gilded eagle by the sculptor William Reid Dick above a pylon. Occasionally, the sculpture on war memorials would be work of high artistic merit, intelligently integrated with the form. In Liverpool, the war memorial in front of St George's Hall (designed by Lionel Budden) carries long hieratic friezes by Herbert Tyson Smith. On one side, mourners are shown as modern figures; elderly men in high collars and fashionable women in cloche hats give contemporary poignancy to an ancient representational form. Across the Mersey in the Wirral, the obelisk war memorial at Hoylake carries bronze figures by Charles Sargeant Jagger: a symbolic female, 'Humanity', together with a tough soldier, 'Wipers'. Also by Jagger is the powerfully convincing soldier on Thomas S. Tait's Great Western Railway war memorial at platform one of Paddington Station.

Jagger (1885–1934) was the greatest British sculptor of his generation, and the only one with whom Lutyens seems to have been happy to work.[23] His masterpiece is the Artillery Memorial at Hyde Park Corner in London, a collaboration with the architect Lionel Pearson. Between them, they succeeded in carrying off the dubious

---

* Blomfield was probably referring to memorials of the Franco-Prussian War rather than to new ones; according to Geoff Dyer, 30,000 memorials were raised in France between 1920 and 1925 at a rate of fifty a day (Dyer (2009), p. 64).

experiment of making military ordnance into sculpture, for Pearson's massive, rectilinear base carries a full-size howitzer carved in stone.* On the long flanks of the monument are relief friezes carved by Jagger that illustrate the nature of the artilleryman's work, while on each side are bronze figures of soldiers. There is no idealisation here; just truthful, brilliantly modelled realism about the brutal nature of conflict. This great work of art makes a telling contrast with the symbolism of the nearby Machine Gun Corps Memorial, which consists of a naked youth in bronze standing on a pedestal bearing the Biblical text, 'Saul has slain his thousands, but David his tens of thousands.' Jagger had been in the trenches and knew what war was like. His fourth bronze figure was of a dead artilleryman, lying anonymously under a tarpaulin at the back of a monument. This feature met with opposition, but Jagger believed that a memorial should tell the public about the horror and terror of war, and he paid for this part of the work himself.

As a fusion of architecture and sculpture, Jagger's Artillery Memorial is the only monument in Britain worthy to be compared with one of the very finest memorials, the Anzac Memorial in Sydney, a Classical-cum-Deco temple by C. Bruce Dellit within which Rayner Hoff depicted a dead youth held aloft by a trio of stylised grieving women. Like Jagger, Hoff had been in the trenches, and knew.[24] Their work was in marked contrast to all those figures of St George or St Michael in medieval armour used to suggest the romantic chivalric ideal of the war that were common in the immediate post-war years.

For the poet Robert Graves, 'there were two distinct Britains' by the end of 1918: 'the Fighting Forces, meaning literally the soldiers and sailors who had fought, as opposed to garrison and line-of-communication troops, and the Rest, including the Government'.[25]

---

* Lutyens, with the sculptor Derwent Wood, had earlier produced a design, with a feeble representation of a gun, for the Royal Artillery War Commemoration Fund, which wanted 'a realistic thing' (Skelton and Gliddon (2008), pp. 150–51).

And these two Britains had different ways of seeing the conflict. As Jay Winter has pointed out, commemoration was a political act, and often 'the glorification of sacrifice was expressed in a deliberately archaic language, the cadences of knights and valour, of quests and spiritualised combat'. In consequence, 'These two motifs – war as *both* noble and uplifting and tragic *and* unendurably sad – are present in virtually all post-war memorials; they differ in the balance struck between them.'[26] Very occasionally, realism and the chivalric ideal could be combined. At Paisley, the memorial designed by Robert Lorimer is a tall pylon supporting a powerful compact sculptured group by Alice Meredith Williams consisting of a medieval knight on horseback flanked by modern soldiers with rifles and steel helmets.

The chivalric view of the mincing machines of the Somme and Passchendaele tended to be favoured by the public schools, which had enthusiastically provided so many of the officers among the casualties. The responses of these institutions varied in both scale and artistic quality; most were illustrated in a telling survey of the results published in 1927 and compiled by C. F. Kernot, who wrote: 'There are some who desire to forget the War . . . This book would be a stimulant against post-war apathy, a humble contribution to the history of our epoch, and a grateful and sincere tribute to the memory of those who, at the Call, answered, "We are ready."'[27] Many schools provided memorial panels or screens with lists of names, together with a figure of St George, to go in the school chapel; Clifton and Radley erected memorial gateways, while a few schools commissioned new memorial buildings. Oakham built a chapel, Gothic, by Streatfeild & Atwell; Bishop's Stortford, Marlborough, Uppingham, Harrow and Haileybury built halls, by Clough Williams-Ellis, W. G. Newton, his father Sir Ernest Newton, and, for the last two, Sir Herbert Baker, respectively; all are fine conceptions in traditional styles.

Two schools erected memorial buildings which may now seem to be among the best and most representative works of their time. At Winchester College, to commemorate 500 boys killed, out of the 2,330 who served, Herbert Baker added a memorial cloister to the school's medieval buildings that demonstrated his roots in the Arts and Crafts movement. Using traditional materials – timber, stone and flint – he subtly fused two stylistic languages, for while the enclosing colonnades are of Tuscan columns, the cloister was covered by crafted and pegged timber and roofed in slate. The rustic was combined with the monumental. On the internal walls of knapped flint, decorated with inlaid inscriptions, the names of the 500 old boys who never returned from the war are carved. Baker's rather English and literary approach to architecture, and his sentimental delight in symbols and symbolism, here seem justified; he later wrote that, when considering memorials,

> my own thoughts always turned to the beauty associated with the churchyard and cloister, a sacred *place*, a *temenos*. It was also my belief that war and other memorials lose much of their spiritual value and appeal if they are not placed in sites already hallowed by past associations or where associations can grow in the course of years.[28]

Winchester College War Memorial Cloisters, Winchester (Herbert Baker, 1924)

He was pleased that, after visiting Winchester, Rudyard Kipling wrote to him that 'the thing itself is as near perfection to my mind as human work can be', describing it as 'incomparably the best of all the War Memorials'.[29]

The other is the memorial chapel erected by Charterhouse School at Godalming and designed by the architect of Liverpool Cathedral, Giles Gilbert Scott. Inspired by the thirteenth-century cathedral at Albi in southern France, the new chapel stands aloof and detached from the Victorian Gothic school buildings by P. C. Hardwick. Built of a subtle combination of rubble-stone and ashlar, a series of tall, thin 'transepts', each containing a single lancet window, rises from an unbroken plinth and articulates the long side elevations. When first entering the chapel, these windows cannot be seen and so the light which illuminates the cenotaph above the altar seems mysterious. The chapel commemorates the 686 old boys killed, out of 3,000 who served. There was no new parish church built as a war memorial in Britain that bears comparison with Auguste Perret's experimental reinforced-concrete church of Notre-Dame

Memorial Chapel, Charterhouse School, Godalming, Surrey (Giles Gilbert Scott, 1927)

du Raincy, or Dominikus Böhm's Expressionist Gothic memorial church at Neu-Ulm. Scott's chapel at Charterhouse, however, succeeded in honouring the dead with a brilliant modern essay that reconciled the Gothic Revival tradition with the emotional power of monumental Classicism. As Ian Nairn put it, 'There is a good deal of the overpowering semi-mystical spiritual effect of Liverpool [Cathedral].'[30]

Scott was also responsible for the best of the war memorial buildings erected in the old English universities. The Memorial Court of Clare College was built in 1922–24 on the opposite side of the River Cam from the old seventeenth-century court of the college and in a very different style from the Charterhouse chapel. Elegant, reticent ranges in a suave Georgian manner, built of silver-grey bricks, are penetrated by a large open arch, filled by an aedicule in the fashionable *néo-Grec* manner. Either side of this central, memorial arch, walls which bear bronze tablets with the names of dead undergraduates frame an axial vista which, a few years later, would be terminated by Scott's own University Library. It was a

Memorial Court, Clare College, Cambridge (Giles Gilbert Scott, 1924)

grand conception, unique in British architecture, which has since been gratuitously spoiled.*

The public school memorials suggest what a national war memorial in London might have looked like had the headmasters, bishops and generals had their way. Perhaps it might have been more like the Scottish National War Memorial raised on the top of Castle Rock in Edinburgh (Plate 3). This ambitious project, the final masterpiece of Sir Robert Lorimer, is a melancholy shrine marking the dreadful consequences of his nation's tradition of military ardour – Scottish casualties in proportion to the population were much higher than English. With its Hall of Honour, filled with flags and regimental badges, with the names of battles carved in stone and with images of warriors in bronze and stained glass, it seemed to accept the military agenda in its symbolism. In an early guide, Ian Hay (the pseudonym of Major John H. Beith) insisted that 'there is no suggestion anywhere of exultation over a beaten foe'.[31] Even so, 'Scotland alone among the nations has erected a war memorial commemorating in detail the service of every unit of her Arms',[32] and the figure of St Michael, dressed in a suit of armour, carved by Alice Meredith Williams, confirms the idealised romanticism of the whole conception.

Both the site and the design of the Scottish National War Memorial were the product of long and sometimes acrimonious debate. Initially inspired by the national war memorial and museum proposal for London, Lorimer's first scheme was criticised for its effect on the Edinburgh skyline, as well as for being 'too exclusively a glorification of militarism'.[33] The final scheme by Lorimer and his partner John F. Matthew was carried out in 1923–27, converting an existing barrack block on top of the castle into a non-denominational chapel, inspired by such historic buildings as the castle, the Church of

---

* Although alternative sites were available, in 1984 the college chose to block this vista with a new music room and library designed by Philip Dowson of Arup Associates in a gauche manner echoing Scott, ignoring the opposition of, amongst others, the Thirties Society (now the Twentieth Century Society).

Scottish National War Memorial, Edinburgh, Scotland (Robert Lorimer, 1927)

the Holy Rude at Stirling, and by Falkland Palace. Medieval national precedents were combined with the Classical, and the architect's attention to detail and the balance of intricate sculpture against broad masses of rubble walling is as impressive as it is appropriate in its setting. The result is a powerful, purposeful realisation of the high ideals of the Arts and Crafts movement – an essentially English development that had taken root in Edinburgh, where it continued to flourish. 'Here the picked craftsmen and craftswomen in the east of Scotland have been united under the direction of one of the ablest designers of our time,' commented the journal *Architecture*, 'and we should hear less about the feebleness and decadence of modern art now that this notable Hall of Regiments and Shrine have been thrown open to the public.'[34]

After the Edinburgh memorial was opened in 1927, more than one writer compared its richness of expression with the reticent austerity of the Cenotaph in London and suggested that each reflected the national character. General Sir Ian Hamilton admitted that:

> The London Cenotaph is an original conception, God be praised – not a pillar; not a Cleopatra's needle; not a Monolith – it is I suppose an obelisk but of a shape conceived by an artist who is no imitator. Rearing itself quite suddenly as it does from the midst of those rectangular nests of bureaucrats in Whitehall, it strikes an attitude and makes a contrast which just escapes the fantastic and impels the most thoughtless to bare their heads before it.[35]

For Christopher Hussey,

> The difference in character between the English and Scottish peoples has never been more clearly shown than by their respective War Memorials. It is the difference between inarticulate sentiment, and romanticism flowing out of realism under the stress of emotion. . . . The emotion that makes an Englishman bow his head in silence impels the normally silent Scot to lift up his voice* . . . The Scottish National War Memorial is, and will continue to be, a profoundly moving memorial of a great national effort because it is so intensely human.[36]

All of which may be true, but the comparison has little significance; while Lorimer's project evolved slowly over a decade, Lutyens's began as a temporary structure, and he seems to have conceived the Cenotaph in a matter of hours and produced the working drawings in a day. Despite all the grand visions of memorial halls, victory bridges, triumphal arches and replanned streets, London's national war memorial was, in the event, a single small monument that was the product of an almost accidental circumstance.

Assertions about national character are further undermined by consideration of the war memorials in other parts of the United

---

* Echoing Weaver (1927) on the cover of his publication: 'while England has made an ethereal monument of her inarticulateness, Scotland has seized the occasion to mobilize all the resources of her national art into a visible monument with form and colour.'

Welsh National War Memorial, Cardiff, Wales (Ninian Comper; sculptor Alfred Bertram Pegram, 1928)

Kingdom. The Welsh Memorial in Cardiff is an open circular Corinthian colonnade enclosing a naked male figure of Victory,* above three servicemen in uniform. Its style was an appropriate response to its site in the centre of Cathays Park, the city's formally planned Edwardian civic quarter, but otherwise it is a disappointingly feeble composition untypical of its designer, the church architect Ninian Comper, who was Scottish rather than Welsh.[37] For the Irish National War Memorial in Phoenix Park in Dublin, the Englishman Lutyens designed a memorial garden with pergolas and fountains combined with his own abstracted version of a standing cross, an earlier proposal to erect a memorial in Merrion Square having been rejected by the government of the Irish Free State.

---

* The model for the sculptor, A. Bertram Pegram, was Able Seaman Fred Barker, who had been personally chosen by the architect as an ideal of male beauty after reviewing the entire crews of two battleships at the Union Jack Club in the Waterloo Road, London.

Great War Memorial, Dublin, Éire (Edwin Lutyens, 1939)

Lutyens, who had more influence over the appearance of official British war memorials than any other architect, first came to the attention of a wider public with the Cenotaph. He had made proposals for memorials in Hyde Park and was already advising the Imperial War Graves Commission when he was recommended by Sir Alfred Mond, First Commissioner of Works to the Prime Minister, David Lloyd George, who needed to find 'some prominent artist' to design the temporary, non-denominational 'catafalque' for the peace celebrations in 1919.[38] The legend is that Lutyens produced a sketch of his proposal for Sir Frank Baines, chief architect to the Office of Works, in ten minutes, but he had been thinking about it for some time and had explored the idea of a pylon supporting a funeral effigy in his design for Southampton's memorial.* The recumbent effigy was replaced by a symbolic coffin or sarcophagus; when the

---

* More than one 'original' sketch survives; one was done for Baines, another for Lady Sackville (see M. Lutyens (1991), p. 190).

temporary structure unexpectedly became 'the people's shrine' for tens of thousands grieving for men buried abroad or simply lost,[39] the government allowed the Cenotaph to be replicated permanently in stone.[40]

Lutyens knew better than to resort to sentimental symbolism with the Cenotaph, whether the Christian Cross, emblems of Empire, or military badges. Words and symbols were not required, although there are in fact three words carved on it: 'The Glorious Dead' – though it was not necessarily glorious to be machine-gunned or bayoneted or blown to pieces or drowned in mud or burned alive or choked to death by poison gas. The Cenotaph is not simple; it is a highly sophisticated essay in geometry and form. The bulk diminishes as it rises, governed by Lutyens's own personal system of massing, while the verticals and horizontals are not straight lines at all but curves, governed by a system of optical correction to give visual dynamism and what Hussey called its 'magic quality'.[41] Furthermore, all the verticals are curved and sloped so that they would converge at an imaginary point some nine hundred feet in the air.* In its abstraction, the Cenotaph might seem 'modern', but its power comes through its being rooted in a tradition which still had, and still has, resonance: the Classical, Renaissance tradition. According to Paul Fussell and others, it is a mistake to think that the Great War marked a *caesura* between traditional forms of expression and Modernism. As Jay Winter has argued, 'the war gave a new lease of life to a number of traditional languages expressed both conventionally and in unusual and modern forms'.[42]

The Cenotaph is remarkable for the absence of any visible emblems or symbols on it representing triumph, or heroism, or victory; there are only carved wreaths and ribbons, and three flags along each flank. It speaks only of death, of loss. The absence of religious

---

* The 'frightful calculations' for the *entasis*, based on mathematical studies of the Parthenon, are said to have filled a manuscript book of thirty-three pages (Hussey (1950), p. 392).

symbols is surprising in a nation with an established Church. The bishops, indeed, were unhappy about it; the burial of the Unknown Warrior in Westminster Abbey on the day the permanent Cenotaph was unveiled was the Church of England's riposte to this official secularism.[43] But the Great War was a conflict in which men of all religions, and none, had been slaughtered. Lutyens knew this and argued that not only in Whitehall but in all the war cemeteries and memorials there should be forms which had meaning 'irrespective of creed or caste'. The matter was debated in Parliament, and the massed ranks of bishops, cardinals and ministers and other supporters of the symbolic cross were defeated. As Lutyens remarked afterwards, it was important 'to make folk realise the inherent cruelty of the *forced* cross'.[44] That, however, did not deter the *Catholic Herald* from later dismissing the Cenotaph as 'nothing more or less than a pagan memorial . . . a disgrace in a so called Christian land'.[45]

Similar ideas informed the work of the Imperial War Graves Commission (IWGC), eventually charged with the task of building cemeteries to contain some 580,000 identified and 180,000 unidentified bodies, and also erecting memorials to commemorate the 518,000 'missing'. This task, although largely undertaken overseas, represents a most significant aspect of 1920s British architecture. It was, in fact, one of the largest schemes of public works ever undertaken. The Commission's literary adviser, Rudyard Kipling, called it the 'biggest single bit of work since any of the Pharaohs, and they only worked in their own country'.[46] As its founder, the educational reformer and administrator Fabian Ware, recorded in 1937:

> in France and Belgium alone there are 970 architecturally constructed cemeteries surrounded by 50 miles of walling in brick or stone, with nearly 1,000 Crosses of Sacrifice and 560 Stones of Remembrance, and many chapels, record buildings and shelters; there are some 600,000 headstones resting on nearly 250 miles of concrete beam foundations. There are also eighteen larger memorials to those who have no known grave.[47]

Before the IWGC could begin its task, two controversial matters had first to be settled. The first was the proposed equality of treatment of all the graves. Since 1916, it had not been permitted to exhume bodies for reburial in Britain; now the Commission wanted no distinction to be made between ranks, between officers and men. This also again touched on the controversial question of the Cross, for it also wanted a uniform headstone, secular in shape, on which a regimental or religious symbol might be carved. As Lutyens observed, although the cross was a traditional form in Britain, 'All that is done of structure should be of endurance for all time and for equality of honour, for besides Christians of all denominations, there will be Jews, Musselmens, Hindus, and men of other creeds; their glorious names and their mortal bodies all equally deserving enduring record and seemly sepulture.'[48] In the event, a compromise was reached, for while each cemetery would contain a monolithic, secular Great War Stone designed by Lutyens, bearing the inscription chosen by Kipling from *The Book of Ecclesiasticus*, 'Their Name Liveth for Evermore', it would also have a Cross of Sacrifice designed by Blomfield. This rather conventional form, with a bronze sword affixed to the cross, was a recognition that England was culturally a Christian country, and it appeased the many who could not comprehend that the funerary tradition was pagan in origin.

The Imperial War Graves Commission was established in 1917. Fabian Ware, having discovered that the military authorities were not concerned with locating and recording the graves of casualties, lobbied for the establishment of a Graves Registration Commission.[49] Ware was assisted by Sir Frederick Kenyon, Director of the British Museum, who advised on the choice of architects for the IWGC. In July 1917 Ware sent Lutyens and Herbert Baker to the battle zone to understand the problems and to make recommendations. It was on this occasion that Lutyens wrote the often-quoted letter to his wife that reveals so much about him and his vision of the sublime:

What humanity can endure, suffer, is beyond belief.

The battlefields – the obliteration of human endeavour and achievement and the human achievement of destruction is bettered by the poppies and wild flowers that are as friendly to an unexploded shell as they are to the leg of a garden seat in Surrey.

It is all a sense of wonderment, how can such things be.

. . . Ribbons of little crosses each touching each across a cemetery, set in a wilderness of annuals and where one sort of flower is grown the effect is charming, easy and oh so pathetic. One thinks for the moment no other monument is needed. Evanescent but for the moment is almost perfect and how misleading to surmise in this emotion and how some love to sermonise. But the only monument can be one in which the endeavour is sincere to make such a monument permanent – a solid ball of bronze![50]

That sense of monumental permanence was to be given by the Great War Stone that Lutyens proposed for every cemetery, modelled like the Cenotaph with careful curving *entasis*. It was a concept which he advocated with great passion, against those who wanted something like a conventional churchyard cross. 'I most earnestly advise,' he wrote in his Memorandum to the Commission of August 1917,

> that there shall be one kind of main monument throughout, whether in Europe, Asia or Africa, and that it shall take the form of one great fair stone of fine proportions, twelve feet in length, lying raised upon three steps, of which the first and third shall be twice the width of the second; and that each . . . should stand, though in three Continents, as equal monuments of devotion, suggesting the thought of memorial Chapels in one vast cathedral whose vault is the sky.[51]

But he also felt that it was 'important to secure the qualities of repose and dignity. There is no need for the cemeteries to be gloomy or even sad looking places. Good use should be made of the best and most beautiful flowering plants and shrubs.' Lutyens consulted Gertrude Jekyll, and the care taken over planting greatly contributed to the success of the cemeteries. Baker agreed, later recalling: 'My own ideas on the subject were that the homely sense of the English churchyard should strike the key-note of the designs of the cemeteries; and I think that melody does in some degree run through the composition of most of them.'[52]

In 1918, Lutyens, Baker and Reginald Blomfield were officially appointed the Commission's Principal Architects for France and Belgium;* they were joined by Charles Holden in 1920.[53] Although all agreed on essentials, the differing approaches of each architect can be seen in the shelter or lodge buildings incorporated into each cemetery. Blomfield's were the more conventionally Classical, Baker's are characterised by a legible symbolism, while those by Lutyens and Holden were the most abstract and severe. Holden's cemetery at Passchendaele, for instance, has an austere, military character which is intriguingly similar to that of the contemporary South London Underground stations he designed for the Northern Line extension to Morden. The first three experimental cemeteries – at Le Tréport, Forceville and Louvencourt – were completed in 1920 and won the approval of the public for the principles on which the Commission was operating; ostensibly by Blomfield, the latter two were probably the work of Holden acting as his assistant.

One of the best-known of the war cemeteries is at Étaples on the French coast outside Le Touquet. Designed by Lutyens, it has two arched cenotaphs bearing still, unpainted stone flags placed either side of the Great War Stone on a raised platform overlooking some 11,000 graves. But Étaples was a hospital cemetery at a base camp, and it is a mistake to imagine that most British war cemeteries were this large. Many are very small, and what is daunting is the sheer

---

* Presumably on the assumption that the end of the war was in sight, these appointments were made on 5 March 1918, just a few weeks before Ludendorff's offensive smashed through the British lines and seriously threatened defeat.

number of them: over 900 in Belgium and France, stretching from the English Channel to beyond the valley of the Somme.* The Principal Architects could not possibly have undertaken all the necessary design work themselves, and so they were joined by a team of younger Assistant Architects, recruited from the armed forces, who seem to have been responsible for the design of cemeteries with under 250 burials. J. R. Truelove, for one, designed the Chinese Labour Corps Cemetery at Noyelles-sur-Mer; Lutyens wrote on the Commission's standard report sheet that 'I know nothing of Chinese art. I can but express my admiration. Capt. Truelove should go to London and visit the British Museum and the wholesale Chinese warehouses in London.'[54] G. H. Goldsmith was the most active of these Assistant Architects. Baker later described his pupil Gordon Leith, who would later do distinguished work in his native South Africa, as 'the ablest of the devoted band'.[55] Another of them, Wilfred Von Berg, later recalled that Blomfield 'took a meagre and superficial interest in my work and rarely had much to contribute. Lutyens, on the other hand, showed a lively concern coupled with a delicious sense of humour . . . Holden, serious and painstaking, was a senior architect for whom I had the greatest respect.'[56]

The work of the Commission was not confined to the Western Front. Robert Lorimer was appointed Principal Architect for Italy and Macedonia; his rugged designs for cemeteries in remote sites in the Alps and northern Greece reflect his feeling for vernacular forms and for simple building materials. Another Scot, Sir John Burnet, was Principal Architect for Palestine and Gallipoli. His war cemetery at Jerusalem is particularly fine, with an entrance gateway in his best Glaswegian-Classical manner and a fine domed chapel perhaps inspired by the blocky shapes of the mausoleum of Theodoric the Ostrogoth at Ravenna.[57] In what is now Iraq, the several war

---

* Most are illustrated in Hurst's *The Silent Cities* (1929), a work published with the 'sympathetic approval of the Commission', and featuring a preface by Fabian Ware.

cemeteries were the responsibility of the Principal Architect for Mesopotamia, Edward Warren.* The Great War had truly been a world war, and its architectural consequences were global.

Even with the completion of almost all the war cemeteries by the mid-1920s, the task of the Imperial War Graves Commission was far from over, as almost half the casualties remained uncommemorated: the missing. The policy of permanently memorialising every individual who died on active service eventually allowed architects to rise to the challenge of designing pure monumental war memorials. The first of these Memorials to the Missing to be commenced was the Menin Gate in Ypres, in whose defence so many British soldiers died. Blomfield first produced his scheme for a memorial gateway in the smashed ramparts of the ancient Flemish city in 1919. Work began in 1923, after earlier proposals for the British government to acquire the whole of the ruins of Ypres as a memorial had been resisted by its long-suffering, displaced citizens.[58] Some 57,000 names are cut into the walls of a long vaulted tunnel or else on the higher external galleries facing the ramparts. At either end, Blomfield designed a Roman Doric gateway, in brick and stone, inspired by seventeenth-century triumphal gateways. At the city end, a sarcophagus rests on the central attic parapet, and at the other end, facing east, a massive lion modelled by William Reid Dick – 'not fierce and truculent, but patient and enduring, looking outward as a symbol of the latent strength and heroism of our race'.[59]

As Blomfield was the most conservative and conventional of the architects working for the Commission, as well as the oldest, it is easy to see him as part of a comfortable establishment that instigated and tolerated the slaughter of young men. Siegfried Sassoon, one of the war poets whose reaction to the war has coloured our view of it, described the Menin Gate as 'a pile of peace-complacent stone'. Having experienced the reality of the salient, he wrote 'On Passing

---

* In 1997, Warren's Memorial to the Missing in Basra War Cemetery was moved by the Iraqi authorities to a new site some twenty miles outside the city.

the New Menin Gate' soon after it was inaugurated in 1927 and his conclusion was excoriating:

> Was ever an immolation so belied
> As these intolerably nameless names?
> Well might the Dead who struggled in the slime
> Rise and deride this sepulchre of crime.[60]

But this interpretation perhaps needs to be set against the reaction of the Austrian writer and pacifist Stefan Zweig, whose 1928 article on the Menin Gate Blomfield was pleased to quote:

> It is a memorial . . . offered not to victory but to the dead – the victims – without any distinction, to the fallen Australians, English, Hindus and Mohammedans who are immortalised to the same degree, and in the same characters, in the same stone, by virtue of the same death. Here there is no image of the King, no mention of victories, no genuflection to generals of genius, no prattle about Archdukes and Princes: only the laconic, noble inscriptions – *Pro Rege Pro Patria*.
>
> In its really Roman simplicity this monument to the six and fifty thousand is more impressive than any triumphal arch or monument to victory that I have ever seen.[61]

As for Blomfield, the Menin Gate was one of three works he wanted to be remembered by,* and 'perhaps the only building I have ever designed in which I do not want anything altered'.[62]

In the event, the Menin Gate was nowhere near large enough to contain all the names of those who disappeared in what Sassoon called the 'sullen swamp' of Passchendaele; another memorial, designed by Baker, was created at Tyne Cot Cemetery nearby, where

---

* The others were the rebuilding of Lambeth Bridge and the Quadrant of Regent Street.

Menin Gate, Ypres, Belgium (Reginald Blomfield, 1927)

a vast, curving wall contains another 35,000 names. In 1922, Kenyon had proposed that the rest of the principal architects should each design a Memorial to the Missing and that the design for others should be chosen by competition. Most of these were to be in France, but difficulties were sometimes encountered in acquiring the necessary land for these memorials; the Anglo-French Mixed Committee reported in 1926 that the French 'had become disquieted by the number and scale of the Memorials which the Commission proposed to erect'.[63] In consequence, the Commission decided to reduce the number of memorials. One casualty of this decision was the tall ethereal arch that Lutyens had designed for Arras as a Memorial to the Missing of the Royal Flying Corps and the Royal Air Force. Instead, he built a long colonnaded wall at the Faubourg d'Amiens Cemetery to contain panels covered in names which broke back to enclose a pylon bearing the names of the missing airmen.

Other memorials were given to younger architects chosen by competition. Truelove, who would go on to design municipal buildings in Stoke Newington, designed those at Le Touret and Vis-en-Artois; H. Chalton Bradshaw, a star product of the Liverpool

School of Architecture who became the first secretary of the Royal Fine Art Commission, designed those at Ploegsteert in Belgium and at Louverval, Cambrai. The latter monument, completed in 1930, is semi-circular in plan with an internal colonnade and sculptured panels by Jagger. The memorial at Pozières British Cemetery by W. H. Cowlishaw is a fine but surprising Classical design from an architect best known for the wild and eccentric Arts and Crafts Cloisters at Letchworth Garden City. But in the 1920s the Classical language was generally accepted as the most appropriate for memorials.

Then there were the missing who disappeared elsewhere. Those who died at sea are commemorated by identical naval memorials – at Chatham, Portsmouth and Plymouth – consisting of tall pylons supporting a nautical globe. These were designed by Lorimer, who was also responsible for the memorial at Lake Doiran in Macedonia. Merchant Navy sailors are named on the Mercantile Marine Memorial at Tower Hill in London, an open Classical temple designed by Lutyens. This rather conventional design superseded a more original proposal for a memorial on the Victoria Embankment, which, to the dismay of Lutyens and Ware, was rejected by the newly established Royal Fine Art Commission in 1926.[64] At Gallipoli, Burnet designed a tall pylon at Cape Helles to bear the names of 20,000 victims of military bravado and stupidity. Burnet was also responsible for the Memorial to Missing Indians, which, with its superb crouching tigers by Jagger, once stood next to the Suez Canal at Port Tewfik. Other Indians are commemorated on the All India Arch that Lutyens designed to terminate the long vista from Viceroy's House in New Delhi, while those Indians who died at the Western Front are listed on the poignant circular memorial at Neuve-Chapelle, designed by Herbert Baker in an Indian style with respect and thoughtful sympathy.

The missing of New Zealand are commemorated in memorials at several cemeteries in France and Belgium; that at Buttes, Polygon Wood, was designed by Holden, in his austere square-piered London Underground manner. The other Dominion governments decided to erect their own memorials, much to Fabian Ware's distress. As he was responsible for the Union Buildings at Pretoria and much else in South Africa, Herbert Baker was the inevitable choice as architect for the South African Memorial at Delville Wood on the Somme. Typical of its designer, this arched pavilion flanked by curving walls is full of symbolism and enhanced by sculpture. The Canadian government turned to a native for its memorial on Vimy Ridge; the result was a unique departure from the standard treatment favoured by the War Graves Commission. Designed by a sculptor, Walter S. Allward, it is Expressionist rather than Classical, and consists of two subtly asymmetrical pylons which dissolve into sculptured figures as they rise.[65]

As for the Australians, their memorial at Villers-Bretonneux Cemetery near Amiens, where the fury of the final German offensive of March 1918 was eventually checked, has a murky history. This cemetery is heralded by two exquisite lodges with interpenetrating orders and pyramid roofs designed by Lutyens in the manner of eighteenth-century garden pavilions, but the memorial with an observation tower that rose at the top of the concave slope was

Australian National Memorial, Villers-Bretonneux Military Cemetery, Somme, France (Edwin Lutyens, 1938)

originally to have been built to the design of the Australian architect William Lucas, who won a competition held in 1926 and had proposed a tall tower with giant columns of polished trachyte. This expensive proposal was, it later emerged, disliked by the chairman of the Australian assessors, Major General Sir Talbot Hobbs, and, after the project was suspended in 1930 for economic reasons, Lutyens was approached instead.[66]* His solution was unusual in having a partly external staircase to reach the aedicular observation platform at the top of a tall, severe tower flanked by wings on which the architect added stone flags and Classical forms suspended in voids.

With the inauguration of the Australian Memorial in 1938, twenty years after the end of the war, the awful task of commemorating the British Empire dead was at last completed. What is remarkable about it is that, for once, the British government selected architects of great talent, and in at least one case of genius, to execute the official memorials. The architectural traditions and attitudes which had prevailed before the cataclysm of 1914–1918 proved to be neither discredited nor exhausted. The Classical language still had something to say, and the official war memorials had meaning by being designed in the Classical or Renaissance style and so rooted in the European tradition.

One memorial in particular, which was not only the largest to be erected but also a remarkably original interpretation of traditional forms, still seems to be growing in symbolic significance. On the site of what had been Thiepval *château* north-west of Albert, the focus of the British offensive on the Somme in July 1916 and the scene of bitter fighting, stands an extraordinary complex structure of red brick and stone. From some angles it looks like a tower, from others more like a ziggurat, but when viewed on axis it is seen to be a great arch. It is the Memorial to the Missing of the Somme, by Lutyens. Marginally

---

* The unfortunate and justifiably aggrieved Lucas wrote repeatedly to Sir Giles Gilbert Scott when he was President of the RIBA (1933–35) about the way he had been treated; Scott had judged the original competition in 1925.

Memorial to the Missing of the Somme, Thiepval, France (Edwin Lutyens, 1932)

smaller than the Arc de Triomphe in Paris, there is no triumph about this particular arch, dedicated 'Aux Armées Française et Britannique [*sic*]'. It was built in 1928–32, once the initial objections of the French had been overcome and the number of proposed British memorials reduced in 1926.[67] At Thiepval, Lutyens adapted his design for an abandoned memorial at Saint-Quentin based on the theme of an interpenetrating hierarchy of arches, a theme which he developed in the interior of his later, unexecuted design for the Metropolitan Cathedral in Liverpool.*

Arched tunnels penetrate the masonry mass on two planes, with the keystone of the smallest of them being the level of the springing of the next arch, and so on, building up to the largest, which is enclosed within a sort of tower. As the structure rises, its mass is diminished by a series of set-backs, alternately on both planes. The vast, intimidating structure is humanised by details at ground level, by huge wreaths within the voids and by unexpected features like the voussoirs of the vaults using the Buddhist-railing motif Lutyens had deployed on the dome of Viceroy's House in India (Plate 4). But there was a terrible purpose behind this subtle geometry; the series of arches creates sixteen piers on the internal walls, enough space to carve the names of the 73,357 men whose bodies were never found after Douglas Haig unleashed his offensive on 1 July 1916, at the end of which day alone 20,000 British were dead: the defining moment of the British experience of the Great War.

The arrangement of arched tunnels is explicable in terms of the Classical language of architecture. This is not, however, true of the exterior of the memorial, for the outside surfaces are unadorned until more wreaths and the carved stone imperial crowns are reached at a high level on the tower. Nothing projects; there are only set-backs as the structure rises, enhanced by the curve and batter of *entasis*, leaving some surfaces to remain standing as piers. The lines of cornices that appear within the tunnels are continued only as flat stone bands above the brickwork. What matters are the set-backs, which are managed alternately according to Lutyens's

---

* [Andrew Hopkins (2022) has suggested that the nineteenth-century 'Arch of the Four Winds' in Rome may have supplied another inspiration for the Thiepval monument. While there is no single source for what Hopkins calls Lutyens's 'astonishing extrapolation' from many examples, the fact that the Arch *dei Quattro Venti* served as a memorial to those who fell at the gates of Rome in 1849 may have been in his mind. RH.]

personal sensibility: first on one elevation, then on the lateral elevation higher up as the mass rises and diminishes, culminating in a rectilinear tower which is reminiscent of, if anything, the top of an American Deco skyscraper.

Lutyens's memorialist, A. S. G. Butler, described the whole thing as 'a solid geometrical composition of arches and their supports, more advanced than anything Lutyens had previously done towards complete abstraction'.[68] It certainly has no connection with anything in the Classical canon, but it does have roots in the past. The pyramidal composition echoes the shape of the pyramids of Egypt and other monuments of the Ancient World. Nor is this coincidence: the architecture of the West in the first third of the twentieth century was conspicuous for an interest in the abstraction and monumentality of early civilisations; there will be more to say of this in a later chapter, but no architect handled such forms with as much architectural logic and intellectual control as Lutyens did at Thiepval. In being at once Classical and abstract, traditional and exotic, the Memorial to the Missing of the Somme was truly modern in its time.

By the time the Memorial to the Missing of the Somme was finally dedicated, in 1932, the architectural as well as the social climate in Britain was beginning to change. There came a reaction against the national emphasis on commemorating the Glorious Dead. What happened was succinctly stated by the novelist Ian Hay in the conclusion to his 1931 book on the Scottish National War Memorial:

> We are at present far too close to that world tragedy, the Great War, to be able to judge it in any true perspective. It is too soon to decide whether we were right or wrong to take up arms at all . . . History must settle that for us, for we are quite incapable of settling it for ourselves. All we can do at present is to react (and reacting we undoubtedly are) to a series of nation-wide emotions, most of them conflicting and all of them extreme. We have been reacting for sixteen years, and the end is not yet in sight, so tremendous was the backwash of that awful conflict.[69]

Lutyens's masterpiece received virtually no critical notice.

In the previous five years many memoirs had revealed to the public the true horror of the war to end all wars. Ian Hay again:

> War has become a monstrous, unspeakable thing, and all the nations of Christendom are to-day combined in earnest, eager debate to drive it forever from among men. So far, so good. . . . Plainly, then, our reactions and emotions upon the subject of recent history are at present too fluid to have any lasting value. We must leave it to Time to crystallize them.[70]

But the awful facts of recent history were crystallised in masonry, above all at Thiepval – and this by an architect who had begun his career in the last decades of Victoria's reign. Modernism may have been on the rise by 1932, but no Modernist had command of a visual language sufficiently resonant to express what the slaughter of the Battle of the Somme meant.

Six decades on, when time had done some of its work, Geoff Dyer wrote of this memorial, in *The Missing of the Somme*, that 'so much of the meaning of our century is concentrated here', and of how 'the Thiepval Memorial to the Missing casts a shadow into the future, a shadow which extends beyond the dead of the Holocaust, to the Gulag, to the "disappeared" of South America and of Tiananmen'.[71] It also happens to be the greatest British work of architecture of the interwar years, arguably of the whole century: an intellectually distinguished creation by an architect of rare genius that represents its time powerfully, and painfully. And it is of considerable significance that such a creation – like so much of the finest architectural production of the interwar decades – was raised, not in Britain itself, but on the other side of the English Channel.

CHAPTER TWO

THE GRAND MANNER

N EW DELHI, the new capital of British India, was inaugurated in 1931. The city had been two decades in the making, and immense difficulties had been overcome; there had been controversy over the site and style of the buildings, construction work had ceased during the Great War, and, inevitably, there had been problems over money. Not only had there been much British opposition to this grand architectural enterprise, but it had been pursued against a background of growing Indian national feeling, and changes had to be made to accommodate the architectural consequences of the Montagu–Chelmsford political reforms of 1919. These first attempts to introduce self-governing institutions reformed the Imperial Legislative Council, which was now to consist of two chambers: a Central Legislative Assembly and a Council of State.

Comparatively little attention had been paid to the building of New Delhi once it commenced, and it was curiously underplayed at the British Empire Exhibition at Wembley in 1924.[1] Now Britain woke up to the fact that something extraordinary had been achieved by British architects 5,000 miles away from home. To do it justice,

Cascading Fountain, New Delhi, India (Edwin Lutyens, c. 1925)

Country Life commissioned a series of articles on the city, and on its centrepiece and masterpiece, the Viceroy's House, while the *Architectural Review* dedicated a whole issue to New Delhi. Both were the work of the young writer and traveller, Robert Byron (1905–1941) who, in passionate, analytical prose, eulogised this 'seventh Delhi':

> four-square upon an eminence – dome, tower, dome, tower, dome, red, pink, cream, and white, washed gold and flashing in the morning sun. The traveller looses a breath, and with it his apprehensions and preconceptions. Here is something not merely worthy, but whose like has never been. With a shiver of impatience he shakes off contemporary standards, and makes ready to evoke those of Greece, the Renascence, and the Moguls.[2]

New Delhi, Byron argued, 'has revived the permanent verity of humanism', and this was the achievement of its principal designer and the architect of the Viceroy's House, Sir Edwin Lutyens (Plate 4).

For the work of Lutyens's collaborator, Sir Herbert Baker, he had rather less respect.³ Baker's reputation never really recovered from Byron's description of the pierced screens and other details on the Secretariat buildings and the separate, circular Council House as like washing on a line: 'not only pants, but petticoats, camisoles, nightdresses, and even tea gowns'.⁴

Byron praised Lutyens for fusing Oriental elements with the Classical language to create something monumental but also modern because of what he identified as a 'dynamic quality' and the use of a 'faintly pyramidal principle' in its design. 'Our age,' he argued,

> despite its physical enslavement by the machine and the mass, has discovered that joy in the sensuous beauty of the world perpetuated by the works of the Italian Renascence. The Viceroy's House at New Delhi is the first real justification of a new architecture which has already produced much that is worthy, but, till now, nothing of the greatest.⁵

Secretariat, New Delhi, India (Herbert Baker, 1927)

Viceroy's House (Rashtrapati Bhavan), New Delhi, India (Edwin Lutyens, 1929)

Cathedral Church of the Redemption, New Delhi, India (Henry Medd, 1935)

India Gate (All-India War Memorial), New Delhi, India (Edwin Lutyens, 1931)

Although he was not ideologically committed to the New Architecture being imported from Continental Europe, Byron represented the younger generation. Yet the New Delhi he so much admired was conceived before the Great War and, in its axial monumentality, represented the supreme realisation of the architectural and town-planning ideals of Edward VII's reign.

What New Delhi also represented was that continuity of architectural development of the civic ideal of the Grand Manner, the Classical tradition. The principal architects of the city had both

National Museum of Wales, Cardiff, Wales (Smith & Brewer, 1922)

been born in the 1860s, and as Charles Reilly's *Representative British Architects of the Present Day* made clear, in 1931 the field was still dominated by the generation too old to fight who had made their names before 1914. In 1918, a monumental Classicism was the inevitable choice not only for the official war memorials but for public buildings. As the architectural weekly, *The Builder*, put it in 1907, Classical architecture was 'not the style of England, or France, or Germany, but the style of this planet'.[6]

Several conspicuous examples, indeed, remained unfinished because of the war – and not just in faraway India. There was the National Museum of Wales in Cardiff, designed by Smith & Brewer. A grand, domed Classical building adding to the monumental civic formality of Cathays Park, it had been begun in 1910 and was opened in 1922. There was also County Hall, the headquarters of the London County Council, in the centre of the capital by the Thames. Designed by Ralph Knott in 1908 and, with its exuberant rustication and Mannerist sculpture, perfectly representing the ideal of Edwardian England, it was also opened, though still incomplete, in 1922. It was soon followed by an even larger exercise in urban renewal in the Grand Manner: the rebuilding of Regent Street by the Crown

Commissioners. The new street was originally laid out by John Nash, and when the ninety-nine-year leases fell in, its rebuilding seemed inevitable. Already before the war the ill-mannered intrusion of the Piccadilly Hotel had spoiled the arrangement of Nash's Quadrant at the south end. Many shared Ford Madox Ford's dismay at the loss of the Quadrant and the 'broad and gracious sweep' of 'the most beautiful street in the Empire'.[7]

Following the death of its architect, Richard Norman Shaw, in 1912, the rebuilding of the rest of the street was left to three of his knighted disciples, Aston Webb, Ernest Newton and Reginald Blomfield. In the event it was Blomfield who took control. Like Nash, he kept the Quadrant for himself, while other blocks were designed by other architects. What was consistent were Classical façades of Portland stone half as high again as the original Regency buildings.

'The present generation,' complained A. Trystan Edwards as old Regent Street began to disappear, 'may now be paying the penalty for not having successfully assailed the authority of Ruskin, who has moulded the architectural opinions of almost the whole class of "educated" Englishmen now arrived at middle age.'[8] To the Edwardians, brought up in the shadow of the Gothic Revival to believe that Regency painted stucco was despicable, this overweening

County Hall, Lambeth, London (Ralph Knott, 1922)

The Quadrant, Regent Street, London (Reginald Blomfield, 1928)

replacement was an obvious improvement, and Blomfield was praised for simplifying Shaw's pompous elevation in the Quadrant and for meeting the objection of the shopkeepers to plate-glass windows being constrained within rusticated arches. Writing in the *Architectural Review* after Regent Street was formally re-opened in 1927, Stanley Adshead wrote how Blomfield:

> has not hesitated to design his building in a way that is reminiscent of tradition, and there has been no foolish attempt either to develop a new style or to avoid all reference to the well-worn details of the past. Instead, he has ransacked French Renaissance, has given us a new idea of it, has rejuvenated it, adapted it, and so handled it that the style of these new buildings is not an old style, but a new style of his own.[9]

There were critics, however, inevitably much younger than Sir Reginald. Charles Marriott, art critic of *The Times* newspaper, pointed out that the new fronts of Portland stone were no more 'honest' than Nash's plaster as they were 'an elaborate mask' over steel-framed construction. Furthermore, 'To put it brutally, in Nash's day the shops existed for the public; the modern view, tacitly accepted by the public, is that the public exists for the shops – as shop-fodder. . . . No, the only new idea which the new Regent Street expresses is that of our abject subservience to our commercial system.'[10] 'Greed designs our modern streets, turning them into gulfs for traffic, shadowed by dead walls,' complained John Gloag, who thought that Nash's Regent Street had been 'changed into the dreariest disaster that had ever befallen London'.[11] And when Blomfield made a neo-Ruskinian assertion that a deliberate search for originality is futile, Howard Robertson responded, 'Is not an original thought in a mechanical age like ours more valuable, even if it is imperfect, than the same old repetition? What is the meaning in the façades of great department stores, of friezes or sacrificial ox-skulls and garlands? Why are there emblems of immortality carved over the doors of motor showrooms?'[12]

The old Regent Street of painted stucco had its defenders. Although it was not until 1935 that John Summerson published his landmark study of John Nash, Regency architecture was already regarded as modern because of its simplicity and elegance, and had been revived before 1914 by such architects as Adshead, with his partner Ramsey, and Robert Atkinson. The principal defender of old Regent Street was the architect, town planner and prolific author A. Trystan Edwards, who, in his 1924 book on *Good and Bad Manners in Architecture*, argued in favour of a humanely proportioned civic architecture that observed a hierarchy of scale and function in good neighbourliness. In the central section of his influential book, he insisted that painted stucco was more cheerful and practical than stone in smoky cities and that 'Regent Street was the most beautiful street in the world. In its quite perfect scale and rare delicacy of Classic detail, in its expression of a spirit most urbane yet intimate and hospitable it had surpassing merit. . . . Regent Street lent distinction to the very idea of commerce.'[13] Its replacement was 'an act of vandalism', Edwards went on, condemning the 'false dogmas' that required 'the shopkeepers to ape a municipal splendour most unbecoming to their station'.[14] 'Often,' he wrote, 'I lie awake at night and imagine that I can hear an odious grating sound, and that I can see a still more odious sight of ugly little teeth, crooked, self-righteous little teeth – the Ruskinian rats are gnawing, nibbling and picking away at masterpiece after masterpiece of our national civic art.'[15]

Edwards spoke for the post-war generation rather than for the Edwardians, but he remained a Classicist. Undaunted, Blomfield applied his Regent Street design elsewhere. In 1925 he was appointed by the Corporation of Leeds to design uniform façades to an important new commercial street, The Headrow, being laid out by the city surveyor. Again he imposed the grand manner, this time in red brick as well as stone, with giant colonnades, arched openings between blocks and a consistent Classical treatment. As even his biographer would later admit, 'the design lacks wit, imagination, sparkle and originality'.[16] A similar solution was adopted by the architects Scarlett & Ashworth in their competition-winning design for the treatment of Ferensway, in Hull. As the *Architect and Building News* complained in 1930, 'The influence of Regent Street is noticeable in almost all designs sent in. It seems possible that Regent Street may set a fashion in new streets in provincial towns, which while all very well for the town concerned, does not provide any new thought on what is, after all, a changing problem.'[17]

The continuing appeal of the Grand Manner was encouraged by the publication in 1924 of a new edition of Geoffrey Scott's *The Architecture of Humanism*. It strongly influenced Robert Byron, who quoted it at length when writing of Lutyens reviving the 'permanent verity of humanism' in New Delhi.[18] In a new epilogue for the second edition, Scott asserted that his arguments 'seem to have met with a fairly wide assent – at any rate among the younger generation of architects'.[19] His eloquently argued demolitions of the several fallacies which determined the architecture of the nineteenth century – the 'Romantic', the 'Mechanical', the 'Ethical' and the 'Biological Fallacy' – greatly appealed to those reacting against the previous generation but who yet held to the Classical tradition. *The Architecture of Humanism* was reprinted in 1929 and again in 1935. Ostensibly a study of Italian Renaissance architecture, its empathetic argument that the beauty of Renaissance forms, and conceptions of space, resonated with the experience of the human body intrigued a generation increasingly interested in psychology.

Scott's book was profoundly liberating to those who understood its implications. He did not give comfort to those who believed that architecture was a matter of following the rules laid down by Vitruvius and Palladio and taught in the new architectural schools modelled on American interpretations of the École des Beaux-Arts in Paris. 'An academic tradition, allied, as it was in the Renaissance, to a living sense of art, is fruitful; but the academic theory is at all times barren.'[20] He instead allowed for originality of expression:

> Architecture that is spacious, massive and coherent, and whose rhythm corresponds to our delight, has flourished most, and most appropriately, at two periods, antiquity and the period of which antiquity became the base – two periods when thought itself was humanistic. . . . Humanism has two enemies – chaos and inhuman order. . . . But in the thought of the Renaissance humanism was pitted, not against chaos, but against the inhuman rigour of a dead scholastic scheme, whose fault was not lack of logic, but excess of logic with a lack of relevance to man. Thus the emphasis of Renaissance humanism, in all its forms, was less on order than on liberty.[21]

The implication of Scott's arguments was that the verities of humanist architecture were perennial and therefore still relevant. 'For if the scope of classical design could be perpetually enlarged until the eighteenth century,' he argued, 'it is not probable that its history is closed. But first we must discard a century of misplaced logic.'[22]

No wonder that younger reviewers, like the architect and journalist Christian Barman, were enthusiastic:

> We now know that the author was not only looking backward, but forward also. . . . He is not extolling the merits of the architecture of humanism merely to awaken our interest in something that has been done by others. Instead, he finds in this architecture the seeds of future growth. It is a bold and generous creed which holds that the great classical tradition is yet capable of revivification, that its history is not yet closed, its power not yet extinguished.[23]

The Classical tradition in Britain was further strengthened by the continuing national cult of Sir Christopher Wren. 'Who were the two greatest English architects?' asked Trystan Edwards. 'Were they not Wren and Nash?'[24] It is, perhaps, typical of the snobbery of England that this amateur architect should be so revered, especially as he only came to design a great national monument in the capital through an accident of history, but his status as a non-professional and, above all, as an English gentleman largely account for this. The year 1923 saw the foundation of the Wren Society and the beginning of its ambitious publication programme, but justice, as well as architectural history, were also served by the publications of pioneering studies on the native Classical architects Hawksmoor, Vanbrugh and Chambers in 1924.*

In the Edwardian years, Wren's work, at Hampton Court above all, was a direct inspiration to architects like Blomfield – and Lutyens, who seems to have coined the term 'Wrennaissance'. Now,

---

* Seven illustrated books, all published in 1924 by Ernest Benn in the 'Masters of Architecture' series edited by Stanley C. Ramsey, comprised studies of *Inigo Jones* by Ramsey himself; *Nicholas Hawksmoor* by H. S. Goodhart-Rendel; *Sir John Vanbrugh* by Christian Barman; *Sir William Chambers* by A. Trystan Edwards; the Austrian Baroque architect *Fischer von Erlach* by H. V. Lanchester; the Victorian church architect *John Francis Bentley* (whose Westminster Cathedral was still much admired) by W. W. Scott Moncrieff; and the contemporary American firm of *McKim, Mead & White* by C. H. Reilly – an altogether intriguing selection.

in 1923, the architect of St Paul's Cathedral was celebrated in an orgy of patriotic architectural fervour. This was further encouraged by the controversy over the Bishop of London's proposal of 1919 to demolish a number of Wren's City churches and by public concern over the structural condition* of his cathedral.[25] 'The greatness of Wren can be proved to be at least four times that of common human greatness,' Paul Waterhouse, President of the RIBA, could assert in his speech at the anniversary Wren Banquet.[26] In the introduction to a collection of essays published by the Institute, the President of the Royal Academy, Sir Aston Webb, described Wren in terms that were almost universally accepted: 'the greatest of our English architects'.[27]

Not everyone agreed, for there was now a living competitor. 'Poor old Christopher Wren could never have done this!' sobbed Edward Hudson, the aged founder and editor of *Country Life*, when he saw Viceroy's House in 1931.[28] But it needed that sharpest of English architectural critics, Harry Goodhart-Rendel, to put Wren in a proper perspective:

> Sir Christopher Wren stands on a height from which no buts can cast him down; his sustained reputation, together with the obviousness of his defects, show of how little account those defects appear in the eyes of his countrymen. His buildings have that inestimable quality of lovableness which, with our present knowledge of aesthetics, we can recognise but not define.

As for his celebrated church of St Stephen Walbrook,

> It is no doubt clever to support the complex roof of a domical double-aisled cross-church on columns standing about in an oblong room... but great architecture does not consist in inventing

---

* The problems detected in the condition of the piers supporting the dome were beyond the Surveyor to St Paul's, Sir Mervyn Macartney, and a Commission of experts appointed in 1921 produced a report in 1924; in the event, the unstable core of the piers was grouted.

insoluble problems and then very nearly solving them. The love of a puzzle for its own sake, so characteristic of the 'conceited' Renaissance, was Wren's great weakness, and that which will always prevent his masterpieces being completely acceptable by those who love simplicity and directness.[29]

But Rendel's most deflating assault on English sentimentality about Wren came two decades later when he pointed out that 'if he was a *great* architect, as practically all Englishmen and practically no foreigners believe, he was so in virtue of his one outstanding capability, the sculptor's capability of making beautiful shapes'.[30]

That was written in 1944 in an obituary of Sir Edwin Lutyens, whose own tribute to his hero was delivered in the tercentenary of his birth, 1932. It is interesting as much for what it reveals about Lutyens's own response to the increasingly uncongenial modern conditions he found himself in as for his interpretation of Wren's virtues. It was, he believed,

> to the larger issues of the Wren tradition that architects almost involuntarily turn; not so much to the grandeur of St Paul's or the unique silhouette of the steeples of the City churches as to the lessons afforded by the scale and dignity of Wren's brick buildings. We read a good deal of the 'when' and little enough of the 'how'. Wren understood brickwork as no other architect before or since his day has done. . . . It is not difficult to visualize how Wren would have met and solved the problems of our time. He would have accepted the girder, the stanchion, the concrete beam, and all the mysteries of reinforcement. He would have banned surface cement, as will be the universal procedure, say, 50 years hence. He would have banned all ersatz materials as being ungodly. He would have made models to try out his effects of mass on the greater scale demanded by increased spans and taller buildings. He would have framed new building laws and he would have placed grace before the machinations of functionalism. The

difference of outlook between these progressive days and the times in which Wren lived and worked is to be regretted.[31]

Lutyens paid tribute to his hero in many of his houses and public buildings, but above all in a masterpiece begun in 1933 which now has a peculiar status, a building which, as his son later wrote, 'stands quite outside time and period, and which can be judged therefore, as a totally isolated work of art, without social or cultural connotations, and which has been saved from prejudiced denigration by the singular purity – by the abstraction – of its non-completion'.[32]

In 1929, Lutyens was asked to design a cathedral for the Roman Catholics of Liverpool on Brownlow Hill which would challenge the huge Gothic Revival Anglican cathedral by Giles Gilbert Scott then steadily rising at the other end of Hope Street. He produced a domed, Classical design twice the size of St Paul's and which was second only in scale to St Peter's in Rome. Wren was the initial inspiration, and Lutyens designed a composition of spires and towers around a great dome. But he also solved problems

Model, Edwin Lutyens's Metropolitan Cathedral, Liverpool (J. B. Thorpe, 1934)

which had defeated Wren, namely the logical combination of an aisled cruciform plan with a central space. Lutyens's exterior would also have been very different from that of St Paul's: not a screen of superimposed orders but massive walls of granite, brick and stone composed like structural cliffs and pierced by arches. And inside, the spaces were to be contained by a carefully proportioned hierarchy of arches, a development of the system used at Thiepval. A great model of the design for Liverpool Metropolitan Cathedral, inspired by Wren's model for St Paul's, was made by John B. Thorp and exhibited at the Royal Academy in 1934, but all that was built before the Second World War halted the project was a part of the crypt. Finally opened in 1958 and now lurking beneath Frederick Gibberd's mediocre reinterpretation of Brasilia Cathedral (known locally as 'Paddy's Wigwam'), this powerful vaulted space hints at what might have been the greatest British building of its time. As John Summerson later concluded,

> The question whether a building can assume a place of authority in the world of architecture without actually being built is a curious one; but the answer is not in doubt. . . . Lutyens's cathedral . . . will survive as an architectural creation of the highest order, perhaps as the latest and supreme attempt to embrace Rome, Byzantium, the Romanesque and the Renaissance in one triumphal and triumphant synthesis.[33]

In contributing to one of the bicentenary volumes on the modern influence of Wren, Stanley C. Ramsey wrote that:

One of the worst tributes that we could offer to the memory of Wren would be to celebrate his bicentenary with the inauguration of another Wren revival. If he is still to influence our modern work, let it be his breadth of design, his dignity of purpose, his wide and spacious views, his joyful creativeness, that shall inspire us. . . . Many of Wren's problems are our problems. If we are no longer called upon to build great palaces for kings and queens, we have to provide great hotels and places of entertainment for the 'sovereign people'.[34]

Certainly, there were fewer references to Wren in civic architecture after the war than before. Twin towers inspired by the steeple of St Vedast Foster Lane flank the Corinthian portico of Vincent Harris's Civic Hall at Leeds, opened in 1933, and these act as a foil to the great Baroque domed tower which surmounts Cuthbert Broderick's mid-Victorian Town Hall opposite. Another, colossal, version of this most Italian Baroque of City church steeples rises above the new Royal Hospital School at Holbrook in Suffolk, a long, monumental composition in brick and stone inspired by Wren's parent Royal Hospital at Chelsea. Designed by the Birmingham architects Buckland & Haywood, it is the most confidently 'Wrennaissance' of interwar public buildings.

The taste of the 1920s was, however, less for the decorative, sculptural exuberance of the Baroque than for a more monumental simplicity in the handling of the Classical language. This was the manner promoted before the war by the Liverpool School of Architecture under Reilly, where students were encouraged to draw, measure and emulate the neo-Classical buildings in the city by James Elmes and C. R. Cockerell. The contrast between the two approaches to civic design can be seen on a dramatically large scale in Belfast. In the city centre is the imposing City Hall of 1899–1906, inspired by the designs for Whitehall Palace and topped by a Greenwich-like dome. Designed by Sir Alfred Brumwell Thomas, the building is purposeful, vulgar and yet friendly. Very different is the Northern Ireland Parliament, which terminates a long axial vista in the large park at Stormont outside the city. A consequence of the partition of Ireland in 1920, the building is most reminiscent of a state capitol in the American Midwest. A giant Greek Ionic portico on a plinth with a blank attic above is flanked by repetitive rectilinear neo-Palladian wings, giving the whole composition that pyramidal outline characteristic of the time.

Stormont Parliament Building, Belfast, Northern Ireland (Arnold Thornely, 1932)

This complex of government buildings was designed by Ralph Knott and Arnold Thornely. Apart from the Speaker's House, the projected buildings by Knott were cancelled for economic reasons and the principal building was the work of the Liverpool architect Arnold Thornely, of Briggs, Wolstenholme & Thornely, designers of the more Baroque, pre-war Mersey Docks and Harbour Board building on Pierhead. Austere, grammatical, magnificent and cold, Thornely's parliament building might seem to justify Geoffrey Scott's warning against 'The Academic Tradition'.[35] Perhaps the grandest public project of its time, the Stormont building was opened, to little fanfare, in 1932.*

The Council House (now the Guildhall) in Nottingham of 1925–29 by the local architect Cecil Howitt is a similar essay in

---

* C. E. B. Brett compares Stormont favourably with the High Court building in Belfast, 'an interesting study in the Recessional-Imperial style of British architecture' designed by J. G. West of the Office of Works and completed in 1933, adding that 'both are much more satisfactory internally than externally' (C. Brett (1973), p. 50).

Guildhall (formerly the Council House), Nottingham (T. Cecil Howitt, 1929)

the academic Classic manner, but its horizontality is relieved by a Wrennian dome raised on a tower so as to be visible above the wide portico when seen from the marketplace. The new Guildhall was integrated into the city by having shops along its flanks and public arcades through its interior; unfortunately the Council exiled the stalls and the famous annual Goose Fair to the edge of Nottingham, leaving the marketplace as a civic space whose aridity complements Howitt's Portland stone Classicism, a mistake avoided when Norwich City Hall was built above the city's marketplace in the following decade. 'Not much can be said in defence of this kind of neo-Baroque display at a date when the Stockholm Town Hall was complete and a style congenial to the C20 established,' thought Nikolaus Pevsner, who heartily disapproved of this sort of civic pile. 'Wren has much to answer for . . .'[36] Howitt went on to win the competition for Newport Civic Centre in 1936. A Classical solution was again demanded, and even the Modernist architects Connell, Ward & Lucas submitted a vaguely Classical scheme, thus provoking the wrath of their committed colleagues in the Modern Architectural

Research group. The result, completed only in 1964, is etiolated and feeble: 'ghostly classicism'.[37]

Nottingham Guildhall is one of many new town halls built in Britain between the wars, most of them in the monumental Classical style considered appropriate since the late nineteenth century. Reilly, who had earlier encouraged the Grand Manner, was now one of those who regretted it, complaining in an article on 'The Town Hall Problem' in 1935 that there was no evidence that architects were aware of newer ideas at home or abroad.[38] But pomp and circumstance was what aspiring towns wished for. Civic ambition prolonged the Grand Manner – to the end of the 1930s, and beyond. The Wiltshire County Offices at Trowbridge, opened in 1940, were designed by Philip Hepworth in a manner influenced by Lutyens, while the great curving sweep of the Council House at Bristol, designed by Vincent Harris, was not completed until well after the Second World War, when this type of civic architecture was being called into question.* 'One may regret the missed opportunity for a proud modern public building at Bristol,' wrote Pevsner in 1958. 'But the Council House has undeniably more character than similarly traditional buildings in other English cities.'[39]

At their best, the civic buildings of the interwar decades in Classical styles are dignified and appropriate in character, imparting a sense of civic pride. One good example is Chesterfield Town Hall, built 1937–38. With its hexastyle portico standing on an arcaded basement and with a central attic above, and with its long wings with regular fenestration, the general exterior design is similar to Stormont, but the detail is more lively and the facing of red brick as well as stone. The architects were Bradshaw, Gass & Hope of Bolton, whose Victorian Classical town hall they enhanced by placing a crescent of stone-faced municipal buildings axially behind. Completed in 1938,

---

* Harris's last civic building, Kensington Library, of 1955–60, along with Sir Albert Richardson's Bracken House and other traditional buildings, was the object of a hostile demonstration by the 'Anti-Uglies', a group of Modernist architectural students focused at the Royal College of Art.

Chesterfield Town Hall, Chesterfield, Derbyshire (Bradshaw, Gass & Hope, 1938)

Pevsner considered that this marked 'the end of a period. But there is, surprisingly enough, no tiredness.'[40] This most competent provincial firm was also responsible for civic buildings in Wimbledon.

Civic grandeur could be combined with an air of modernity by abstracting the Classical language. Swansea Guildhall is the finest work by the leading Welsh architect of the period, Percy Thomas. He already had experience of designing municipal buildings, having won three separate competitions for combined law courts, police and fire stations, at Bristol, Newcastle and Accrington. At Swansea, he won the competition for an ambitious civic complex in 1930. As built, however, economy demanded the elimination of the Greek Ionic portico, and this, combined with the absence of a crowning cornice, gives the buildings a monumental austerity, typical of the time. As Reilly noted,

> here a definite attempt has been made to get away from porticoes, colonnades, pediments and all the paraphernalia of the property room. The masses of the building have been allowed to tell as

Guildhall, Swansea, Wales (Percy Thomas, 1934)

masses... This building externally, and in spite of the unnecessary tower, is the nearest yet that we have got to a modern town hall in this country.[41]

He praised the architect, who 'aims at simple masses in his plans, and gives to these masses a very simple expression. It is sometimes as if he were trying to make a Classical approach to Modernism, if that were possible.'[42] The plan remained formal, however, with four balancing blocks placed around a courtyard and a tall, thin clock tower on the principal axis. Partly owing to the fall in prices after work started, which enabled Thomas to make improvements, the interior is remarkably grand, with coffered barrel vaults and columnar screens.[43] The council chamber provides 'a heady environment for councillors, like the interior of a temple',[44] and civic pride was further indulged by the acquisition of a cycle of mural paintings by Frank Brangwyn which were installed in the Assembly Hall, having originally been commissioned for the House of Lords.

Most civic buildings of the period were the result of competitions that were administered under the auspices of the RIBA. This allowed designs to be selected on the basis of the merits of planning and organisation rather than style, although in the 1920s the style desired was usually formal and Classical. The doyen of civic architects was E. Vincent Harris. His architectural career, wrote Reilly, 'may be said to have been a series of raids all over England, and mostly carried out single-handed. No one of his age, and no one now living ... has tackled so many competitions and at the same

Detail, Guildhall, Swansea, Wales (Percy Thomas, 1934)

time has been placed in so many.'[45] An austere, diligent character, with no life outside architecture, Harris had won the competition for Glamorgan County Hall in Cardiff in 1908 and that for the Board of Trade in Whitehall just before the First World War, a huge block of government offices which were eventually completed, for a different department of state and to a different design, well after the Second World War.* Harris was responsible for several of the most important interwar civic buildings in the north of England. First came Sheffield Memorial Halls, won in competition in 1920. With its grand Corinthian portico, this shows the influence of St George's Hall in Liverpool, especially the apsidal rear of the building, where an internal hall occupies only the lower part of a giant, curving order of square columns. 'What one admires about so much of Mr Harris's work, and Sheffield City Hall in particular,' wrote John Summerson in 1934, 'is the supremely tactful interpretation of classical material. . . . How few architects would have resisted the temptation to "mark the centre" of the Sheffield portico, to introduce a raised blocking course or to pin a heraldic brooch in the frieze!'[46]

In 1925, Harris won two connected competitions for the centre of Manchester: for an extension to the Town Hall and for a new Central Library. The library is circular, of white Portland stone, with a continuous colonnade at an upper level and a projecting entrance portico. This building does not, however, appear to stand in isolation, for it is framed by the two projecting wings of the adjacent extension to the town hall. This is a brilliant solution to the problem of harmonising with what was then the neighbouring building's unfashionable High Victorian Gothic; Harris continued

---

* This 'monument of tiredness', by then for the Ministry of Defence, was completed in 1959; Pevsner considered that the design was 'strongly undecided and should have been abandoned by the government. There is hardly any Western country that would still have been ready at that time to let itself be represented by giant colonnades. The Edwardian-Imperial optimism of the colossal orders was vanishing even from the City, and Mr Harris clearly at that time no longer possessed it fully either' (Pevsner (1973), p. 538).

Manchester Central Library, Manchester (E. Vincent Harris, 1934)

the scale and vertical rhythm of Alfred Waterhouse's masterpiece, as well as using a similar buff sandstone and giving it a high-pitched roof, while avoiding the use of the pointed arch and any literal borrowings from the Gothic. Harris's building is large, but it does not attempt to compete with the old town hall – while the formality of the library enhances a new urban space containing a war memorial by Lutyens. Harris again demonstrated a peculiar sensitivity to site and context in Leeds, where the new Civic Halls gives formality to a newly cleared space and yet does not attempt to outdo the vigorous Corinthian of the 1850s town hall. But Reilly was typically unimpressed, complaining that its 'façade is a pretty toy which would look well in old Staffordshire stoneware: the twin towers and the great portico are entirely unnecessary, yet erected while Leeds is nobly trying to rebuild a third of the town to afford more decent living conditions for a section of its great working-class population, largely out of work'.[47] Although Harris became

Municipal Offices (West Block), Southampton Civic Centre (E. Berry Webber, 1933)

best known for his Classical civic buildings, he was versatile in both scale and style. His design for the perfumiers Atkinsons in Old Bond Street of 1926 is in a suave Tudor Gothic style, and he also used a simplified Tudor for some of the buildings at Exeter University, where he prepared a master plan in 1931.

Vincent Harris's assistant, E. Berry Webber, also became a successful competition winner, beginning with an abortive scheme for a new Manchester Art Gallery. In 1928 he won the competition for Southampton Civic Centre, which attempted to create a new urban focus to the north of the old city. Like the Swansea Guildhall,* the repetitive wings faced in Portland stone are relieved by porticoes and by discrete blocks penetrated by a large arched entrance – a feature strongly reminiscent of Bertram Goodhue's Nebraska State Capitol. The plan is axial, with four separate institutions arranged around its four sides, but the impression given is that of an asymmetrical

---

* C. H. Reilly, in his profile of Percy Thomas, wrote of the Swansea competition that it was 'on a fine open site allowing a great number of possible solutions. I remember Berry Webber saying he was not going in for it for that reason' (Thomas (1963), p. 62).

arrangement of different buildings. 'It was here,' wrote Reilly in his profile of Webber published in 1930,

> that he showed, I think, that he has in him the makings of a first-class architect as well as of a first-class planner, for out of the heterogeneous group of buildings . . . he has not only produced a symmetrical scheme, with the balanced geometrical pattern on the paper which seems necessary today to win a competition, but he so designed his group of buildings, great and small, that from all points on the common on which they are situated they will, I think, compose into an imaginative whole.[48]

On the principal axis is a very tall tower with a pyramidal roof, although this, like all the Classical elements in Webber's design, is etiolated to the verge of feebleness. It is, however, a distinctive local landmark and the whole civic centre has been described as 'a symbol of Southampton's heyday as a port, prospering while much of the rest of the country was in the darkness of slump'.[49] J. B. Priestley, on the other hand, visiting Southampton at the beginning of his *English Journey* in 1933, formed a different impression:

> The town was making money. . . . Nevertheless, Southampton has not been able, just as their very owners have not been able, to live up to those great ships it harbours. They are the soul of the place. Their coming and going light it up. The citizens are knowledgeable about and proud of these visiting giants, but they have not succeeded yet in building a town or planning a life worthy of such majestic company. What a Southampton that would be![50]

Perhaps he would have changed his view had he returned to see the Civic Centre completed five years later, but probably not.

Charles Cowles-Voysey was another successful builder of town halls. A very different sort of architect from his father, C. F. A. Voysey (who lived through the interwar decades as the crotchety conscience of Arts and Crafts individualism in opposition to the fashionable belief in planning), Cowles-Voysey used the Classical language that his father despised with some flair. The White Rock Pavilion at Hastings is in the 'Spanish Mission style of America' but for his town halls he tended to adopt a big-boned, severe Georgian manner. At Worthing Town Hall (1931–33), formality was increased by a tetrastyle Ionic portico and a Wrennian lantern. The building was detailed by the young John Brandon-Jones, who later rejoined Cowles-Voysey and continued the firm after the Second World War. He worked on the Cambridge Guildhall of 1938–39, a severe, large-scale design in white brick above a rusticated stone base. Regularly spaced windows, proportionally scaled in the Georgian manner, articulate a symmetrical façade, with no portico, which faces the curved, streamlined modernity of Easton & Robertson's St Michael's Court of 1934. Such a simplified, monumental design, relying on proportion and fine detailing, was the typical response of a classically minded architect to a changing architectural climate. Another response was to give a design an air of modernity derived from the elegant, diluted Classicism of Sweden; this is evident with Cowles-Voysey's town hall at Watford of 1940 with its relief panels carved into the dominant brickwork.* Goodhart-Rendel later articulated the growing feeling that the 'Corinthian agony' in town halls was incongruous when he pointed out that the 'chief civic building of a town or suburb should, no doubt, be something better than workmanlike, but gorgeousness is out of place in a Rates Office, grandeur ridiculous in the department of a Borough Surveyor'.[51]

Commercial buildings conceived in the Grand Manner were under attack rather earlier. 'Since they have a purpose which is at least respectable,' argued that sharp and broad-minded critic Charles Marriott in 1924,

---

* This building was included as plate 4 in the Architecture Club's collection *Recent English Architecture 1920–1940* (1947), as 'a good instance of the modern use of brick, the traditional English building material which is as effectively applicable to-day as ever it was'.

most of our public buildings escape the worst consequences of the monumental aim in commercial buildings; but the difference between them is very much like that between public and private speaking; between solemn platitudes and speaking to the point. To rule out the Latin elements in our architecture would be as absurd as to rule out the Latin elements in our language, but it is a fact which anyone may observe that when a person feels strongly and is sure of his ground he tends to avoid Latinisms; and the saying 'I put it to him in plain Anglo-Saxon' has an architectural application.[52]

He might have been thinking of the blocks raised in London's new boulevard, The Kingsway, soon after 1918, like Africa House by Trehearne & Norman, with stone façades overloaded with colonnades and sculpture, hung on a steel frame. All were inferior to the classical building in the Aldwych, which closed the southern end of Kingsway: a block enclosing a giant exedra filled by two giant columns supporting a cornice bearing the inscription 'To the Friendship of the English Speaking Peoples'. This is Bush House, built by the Irving T. Bush's Bush Terminal Company of New York on a site occupied by the American YMCA during the war.* Its architects were also American: Helme & Corbett of New York. It was completed in 1935, but without the skyscraper-tower intended to rise above the Strand elevation. Marriott considered that it was 'in the Bush Terminal building, closing the vista, that the architectural character of Kingsway takes a definitely modern turn as pointing the way to the right solution of the problem of how to reconcile the simple fulfilment of contemporary requirements with formal dignity and respect for the neighbouring works of the past'.[53]

One other commercial building in Kingsway attempted a more straightforward expression: Kodak House, designed before the war

---

* Dominion House, with a Germanic Gothic tower, was proposed for the site by Lord Strathcona in 1913, designed by the Arts and Crafts architect A. Randall Wells (illustrated in Stamp (1982b), p. 132).

Africa House, Kingsway, London (Trehearne & Norman, 1922)

by John James Burnet after he had come from Glasgow to build the King Edward VII Galleries for the British Museum. Here the vertical stone-clad steel stanchions read as a giant order of pilasters as the intervening floors are recessed and faced in metal. It was an American solution to the problem of expressing a multi-storey structure in Classical terms and it would be used on countless commercial buildings which followed. For Marriott in 1924, it had already 'become historical as the first attempt in commercial architecture in England to design in terms of utility and to express fitness for purpose without added ornament . . . Its defect is inadequate consideration for the look of the street; reminding one rather of a self-respecting person who forgets his positive duty in the

Interior, Bush House, Aldwych, London (Helme & Corbett, 1925)

pageant of life.'[54] Burnet certainly did not forget pageantry when he came to complete Selfridges, the huge department store which had been begun before the war to the designs, American again, of Daniel H. Burnham, of Chicago, and Francis Swales, of Canada. The Burnet firm had to continue the elaborate giant colonnade marching along Oxford Street, regardless of the problem that beset architects of the time – that of combining the large plate-glass windows demanded by shopkeepers with heavy masonry façades above. Marriott felt towards Selfridges 'the same indulgence as towards an energetic and amusing commercial traveller. The least wavering of confidence and the spell would be broken. Nothing, of course, can get over the architectural anomaly of a monumental building poised on the edge of plate glass.'[55] The Burnet firm's most enjoyable contributions to the building were the entrance doors and canopy, with an extraordinary clock overhead created by the sculptor Gilbert Bayes. A proposal by Gordon Selfridge to build a skyscraper on top of his palace, designed by Philip Tilden, mercifully remained unexecuted.

No wonder that Marriott, in his survey of *Modern English Architecture*, confessed that:

With the best will in the world it is impossible to be very enthusiastic about modern commercial architecture in England, at any rate so far as shops are concerned, but the reason is only partly architectural. . . . Paradoxical as it may sound, the commonest defect in shops is not that they are too commercial, but that they are not commercial enough. Most of the shops in our larger cities give the impression of being too big for their boots; not so much in mere size as architecturally; of bolstering up what they really perform with the architectural associations of what they claim. In a word, they are pretentious.[56]

As far as he and many others were concerned, the best shop in London was Heal & Son Ltd on Tottenham Court Road, designed by Dunbar Smith and Cecil Brewer. Here a simple, dignified, Classical façade was achieved by trabeation, with a giant order of pilasters containing a lower, interpenetrating order to make a rectilinear pattern which connected logically and structurally with the open, colonnaded ground floor. A further, intervening floor was integrated by being

Heal & Son, Tottenham Court Road, London (A. Dunbar Smith and Cecil Brewer, 1917), with extension (Edward Maufe, 1937)

faced with decorative panels by the ubiquitous architectural sculptor Joseph Armitage.

This solution was soon adopted by other Classical architects, particularly in office blocks and on sites where the shopkeepers were less importunate. In a series of commercial buildings in London, A. E. Richardson, with his partner C. Lovett Gill, used his knowledge of the neo-Classicism of Soane and Schinkel to create austere but elegant façades which expressed both the utilitarian nature of the building and the existence of the internal steel frame behind. This tendency culminated in St Margaret's House on Wells Street, off Oxford Street. The façade here, above the ground floor, consisted of a flat plane of brickwork organised into broad pilaster strips supporting an implied entablature. Behind, in the rear elevation faced in glazed white brick, the Classical system was abandoned altogether and arched windows on a slope revealed the position of the staircase. St Margaret's House won the RIBA's Street Architecture award in 1931. The Grand Manner had evolved into the rational manner.

Nevertheless, full blooded Classicism carried on for certain commercial buildings – and for big banks in particular – until the Second World War and beyond. 'In the troubled times in which we live,' explained Osbert Lancaster in 1938 about the style he termed 'Bankers Georgian', 'it is perhaps not unnatural that many a longing glance should be cast at those periods of the past of which we like to persuade ourselves a profound tranquillity was the keynote. Nor is it surprising that no class of the community should have been so deeply affected by this form of nostalgia as the bankers.'[57] Money seemed more secure behind Doric columns, but there was also the architectural tradition of the City of London which had largely remained aloof from both the Gothic Revival and the eclecticism of the later nineteenth century. Victorian architects like John Gibson and Edward l'Anson, and Edwardians like John Belcher, had built banks and insurance offices in the Grand Manner. The innovation of the early twentieth century was the steel frame, which assisted an increase in height to the eighty-foot cornice line limit imposed by building regulations, but image remained the most important architectural consideration. In reviewing Sir Edwin Cooper's splendid new National Provincial Bank in the heart of the City for the *Architectural Review* in 1932, A. E. Richardson observed that, 'In the course of the last quarter of a century the tradition of bank building took a definite line in favour of Classicality. A distinctive treatment for bank exteriors, the result of experience, has been gradually developed.'[58]

Cooper's bank sits on a chamfered acute street corner next to the Mansion House and faces the Royal Exchange. On the three external elevations, a giant Corinthian order unites three floors above an arcaded basement and mezzanine, and a massive, recessed attic continues above. Refined detail is enriched with sculpture by C. L. J. Doman and Ernest Gillick, all in Portland stone. Richardson praised Cooper's plan, both for 'the devisement of the building, from the foundations, into horizontal and vertical compartments, and the apportioning of exact cubical volume to each internal division' and for 'the regard paid to structural integrity':

> The general effect of the building is that of magnificence. There is none of the severity which is akin to baldness; contrariwise there is evidence of a desire to interest and to capture the richness of life. Only a classicist could have attempted a classicism modified and appropriate to a banking house. Here is a composition which is pictorial, yet academic, severe yet subtly rich, respectful to tradition yet consistently inventive in arrangement.[59]

Another thoughtful architect and critic, Harry Goodhart-Rendel, was, however, unimpressed, particularly by the sculpture:

> Nobody is going to bother about what any of these tiresome pomposities signify, nor will anybody but the least sophisticated be favourably impressed by the large amount of money that must have

been wasted upon them. If the purpose of external walls in a city building were to display figure sculpture and to keep out the light, those of the National Provincial Bank would be hard to better.[60]

Cooper was the doyen of City architects, and he also designed an impressive number of hospital and university buildings. Vincent Harris thought he would 'be remembered for his sincerity of purpose

The former National Provincial Bank, Poultry, City of London (Edwin Cooper, 1932)

and exclusiveness of character which made him the able administrator he was'.[61] Cooper had made his name before the war by winning the competitions for the Port of London Authority building by Tower Hill and for Marylebone Town Hall, the first with a gigantic and grandiose design which might seem to be London's answer to the Vittorio Emanuele Monument in Rome, and which brought Cooper a knighthood on its completion in 1923, and the second with a suavely monumental building opened in 1914. His most impressive and most useful post-war design was for the Star and Garter Home at Richmond, a huge Wrennaissance palace for incurable casualties of the war whose grand terrace commands a magnificent view of the Thames; this was a work for which he took no fee. His taste for the monumental, combined with his skill as a planner, was well demonstrated in his Baggage Hall at Tilbury, a utilitarian structure of brick and reinforced concrete of 1925–30 where he managed 'to rise to the poetry of architecture' and evoke a Roman grandeur, and which once welcomed many visitors arriving by sea from the Continent.[62]

Cooper's best work in the City of London was the new premises for Lloyd's of London, the insurers, which, the architect Albert Richardson considered, 'both internally and externally attains the distinction of being superior to style or fashion'.[63] The site was awkward, for not only was it an acute angle between Lime Street and Leadenhall Street, but its apex was owned by the Royal Mail Steam Packet Company. Cooper contrived to contain both institutions within a restrained Classical façade, with Royal Mail House having its entrance on the corner and that for Lloyd's in Leadenhall Street distinguished by an exedra beneath a pediment. From here, a long vaulted corridor led to a series of noble spaces and the underwriting room; all was of Roman grandeur combined with refined detail. When King George V opened the new Lloyd's in 1928 he is said to have observed that the builders of the ancient basilica which had once stood on the site might recognise 'a lineal descendant worthy of the race'. Above the marble walls and columns, relief sculpture by C. L. J. Doman enlivened the pendentives below the glazed dome and there

Lloyd's of London, Leadenhall Street, City of London (Edwin Cooper, 1928)

were ceiling paintings by William Walcot and Frank Brangwyn. Other, panelled rooms were praised for their 'restrained sumptuousness' by Christopher Hussey, who thought them 'as good as anything done in the City since the time of Grinling Gibbons'. But magnificence and quality are seldom any defence against fashion allied with technical change, and Cooper's masterpiece was swept away in 1979 in favour of the 'high-tech' structure by Richard Rogers, save for the Leadenhall Street exedra left as an archaeological fragment. Its loss encouraged the foundation of the Thirties Society, now the Twentieth Century Society, to defend the best buildings of the interwar decades.

The former Westminster Bank, Threadneedle Street, City of London (Arthur J. Davis, 1931)

There were other architects capable of creating commercial palaces of refinement and distinction. One was Arthur J. Davis, who was unusual in England in having trained at the École des Beaux-Arts in Paris. Mewès & Davis had been responsible for some of the most *chic* of Classical buildings in Edwardian London, beginning with the Ritz Hotel in Piccadilly. Now, in the 1920s, following the death of his French partner, Charles Mewès, Davis's commercial work became less French in character. His finest commercial building was the Westminster Bank in Threadneedle Street, with its long, convex façade inspired by Peruzzi's Palazzo Massimo in Rome. It was typical of the fastidiousness of Davis that a portion of this tall façade was erected full-size in plaster to see if the mouldings would tell. Another skilled Classicist was William Curtis Green, who designed the London Life Building on King William Street, completed in 1937. Here he borrowed the pairs of giant Corinthian columns used by Wren on the west front of St Paul's, and made them the centrepiece of a long, flat façade which is subtly modulated by small recessions in smooth planes of Portland stone.

Curtis Green (1875–1960) was an accomplished draughtsman who emerged from the Arts and Crafts movement, but by the beginning of the new century he was playing Mannerist and Baroque games. He is seen at his best in Piccadilly, where he designed a grand Classical showroom for the Wolseley Motor Company. More pairs of Corinthian columns unite three storeys above a noble basement consisting of three arches filled with elaborate wrought-iron screens – a conception which owed much to bank buildings in America and the Boston Public Library. That this sophisticated essay in the Grand Manner reflected the taste of the time was shown by its being awarded the RIBA's Street Architecture Medal in 1922. It did not, however, remain a motor-car showroom for long; in 1926 Green was brought back by Barclays Bank to insert black and gold lacquered Japanese counters, screens and furniture between the shiny Venetian red-painted columns in the ground-floor interior to create the most enjoyable banking hall in London. What is also impressive is how the building relates to its pre-war Classical neighbours: the Ritz Hotel to the west and, immediately to the east, J. J. Joass's busy essay in Mannerism for the Royal Insurance Company. Charles Marriott thought it was 'difficult to point to any other three neighbouring buildings in London which show the same harmony in variety'.[64]

Wolseley House also makes an interesting relationship with the Westminster Bank building on the opposite side of Piccadilly, completed in 1927 – a relationship which exemplifies the sophisticated understanding of the Classical language by certain practitioners in that decade. Each floor of the bank is treated differently in a Mannerist conception that culminates in an open colonnaded loggia beneath a pitched, pantiled roof. Goodhart-Rendel considered this 'elegant and appropriate branch house . . . to represent the best among the many buildings of the kind that have arisen [between the wars] in the streets of all our large towns'.[65] Trystan Edwards thought the relationship between these two distinguished designs worthy of one of several entertainingly revealing conversations between buildings that he published in journals. In 'High Words in Piccadilly, or *What*

Wolseley House, Piccadilly, London (W. Curtis Green, 1921)

Barclay's Bank *said to* The Westminster Bank', the former begins by complaining that 'You have put on royal robes . . . and then you disgrace both yourself and your order by appearing at the same time in a straw hat. Don't you see, you ridiculous parvenu, that your rustic headgear is entirely out of keeping with the splendour of your lower garments?' But the Westminster Bank replies:

> Are you not perhaps affecting an architectural mode more becoming to a public building than to a commercial one? Those gigantic columns, for instance: are they not a trifle pretentious – forgive my speaking so frankly – do they not symbolize the arrogance of wealth? And just consider for a moment the effect upon the street as a whole if *all* the commercial buildings were so adorned; the result would be a columnar epidemic by which our spirits would be quelled by a universal ponderosity.[66]

Edwards made his attitude clear when he made the Westminster Bank conclude: 'don't you see that if the Classic style is to be a real live thing, it must adapt itself to a variety of circumstances?' But in the end all was well as the two banks became the best of friends when they discovered that they were 'in fact related to each other by the closest possible ties' – that is, they were both designed by William Curtis Green.

Some Classical commercial buildings of the period deserve mention for size rather than for aesthetic merit. One example is the three huge blocks built along Millbank across the axis of Lambeth Bridge: the first for Imperial Chemical Industries, and the next two, called Thames House, for Anglo-Properties. Designed by Sir Frank Baines, Chief Architect to the Office of Works, what was on completion the largest office building in Europe was only distinguished by the quality of the sculptural enrichment by Charles Jagger and for exemplifying the effect of the London Building Act of 1894, for above the principal cornice, eighty feet above the pavement, further set-back storeys are contained by a subsidiary colonnaded wall. As Goodhart-Rendel noted, steel-framed construction allowed architects 'to produce the surprising appearance of a small building standing on the roof of a big one'.[67] As far as Robert Byron was concerned, this 'row of enormous white doll's houses . . . are not architecture; they have no design, neither static nor mobile'.[68] Seen from across the river, the effect of pantiled roofs rising above the upper, smaller building is impressive, but the repetitive bulk of this development can be seen as an awful warning of how London would have looked had the capital been rebuilt as those several knighted Classicists hoped.

Another awful warning was the vast and overweening stone-clad structure the steel frame allowed Herbert Baker to raise above the Bank of England in the 1920s. The partial destruction of its celebrated neo-Classical interiors provoked controversy and further encouraged the contemporary revival of interest in the spare, idiosyncratic architecture of Sir John Soane. What now seems intolerable is not that Baker enlarged the Bank of England but that he attempted to improve what survived of the original building.[69] Not only was Sir Robert Taylor's Court Room rebuilt at a higher level, but its plasterwork details were altered. Again to quote Goodhart-Rendel,

> If the new upper storeys of the Bank of England (1925) had been built in red brick they could hardly have appeared more discordant with Soane's classical work below than they are made already by their incongruous and ignorant design. To the outrage done to what of Soane's masterpiece has been allowed to remain it would be pleasanter to make no reference, but the undertaking, in virtue of its size, requires this minimum record.[70]

It was fortunate that Lutyens did not get the Bank of England commission for which he fervently lobbied; the job might well have damaged his reputation just as it helped ruin Baker's. His daughter later recalled that he 'could eat no dinner after hearing the news'.[71] As might be expected, Lutyens applied his architectural imagination and intelligence to the problem of the modern commercial building with conspicuous aesthetic success. In 1920, he was asked to design a large block of offices for the Anglo-Iranian Oil Company on an irregular site between Moorgate and Finsbury Circus. The consequence was Britannic House, a huge palace whose stone façades ripple and dissolve as the architect played games with arched and square headed windows. The design also defied canons of truthful expression, for the great arched windows between the richly modelled upper Corinthian order on the concave front facing Finsbury Circus light not great reception rooms but two tiers of offices. Lutyens's productions, thought Goodhart-Rendel, 'are, perhaps, less truly architecture than they are scene-painting; or, rather, scene construction, he having had a sculptor's skill in the management of masses "in the round"'.[72] Charles Reilly, in reviewing the building, felt obliged to defend such entertaining deceitfulness high above more severe walling below,

> because the pedants at once ask the justification for these arches and columns. The justification they will accept is that the Board Room, the Chairman's Room and the rooms of the other great officials are on this floor. To me it is sufficient that such windows suggest a few fine apartments among the ordinary offices whether such apartments are on this floor or not. We know no great business is run without heads, and therefore we rightly expect some external expression of the hierarchy within. . . . Indeed by ennobling the externals of city life, by giving this life individuality and character instead of making it more machine-like or ant-like than it really is, he has done a great thing, and at a time when, from the set of the current in the opposite direction, such a thing was all the more needed.[73]

Reilly even claimed that 'One could imagine no better future for English architecture than that it should produce a whole series of such buildings for our office blocks, which of necessity will go on growing bigger'.[74] Indeed, Lutyens even proposed raising a tower, a miniature Classical skyscraper, above the pantiled roof of Britannic House, but this was rejected by the London County Council and the fire brigade.[75]

Lutyens's best commercial buildings were undertaken for the Midland Bank, owing to his friendship with Reginald McKenna, the former politician who became its chairman in 1919. The first commission came in 1921 when the bank acquired the site of the old vestry hall next to St James's, Piccadilly. As a compliment to his hero Wren, Lutyens then designed a cube of brick and stone on whose external elevations he played on the theme of Hampton Court. The result was both an exercise in geometry and an indulgence in whimsy that makes Wren's church seem staid and unimaginative. Goodhart-Rendel caught that latter quality when he wrote of it: '"They label me Midland Bank," it seems to say, "but it's really only little me." Nobody can deny that in its way it is a dear.'[76] Internal details were designed in co-operation with the Midland Bank's own architect, T. B. Whinney of Whinney, Son & Austen Hall. Indeed, on all his banks, Lutyens was working with experienced commercial architects who administered the projects.

The success of the Piccadilly bank led to the commission to design the headquarters of the Midland Bank on a large but awkward site in the heart of the City next to the Bank of England. Working with Gotch & Saunders, Lutyens designed a complex building of extraordinary subtlety, which his memorialist, A. S. G. Butler, considered his 'most learned work'.[77] The most impressive aspect is the longer façade on Poultry, richly modelled in three dimensions. In this, Lutyens further developed his personal Classical language. Only the ground floor is comparatively conventional, although tricks are played with the Doric order of pilasters disappearing into the rustication. Above, the wall dissolves, with banks of windows contained within giant buttresses of unprecedented form. Not only do these recede, but each course of rustication diminishes very slightly in width as the building rises. Optical subtlety could surely be carried no further: 'He would admit of no approximation in the drawings, on the plea that plenty of inaccuracies would creep in without beginning in the office. "About! I don't know what you mean by 'about'," he would say.'[78] And then, above the cornice line, the building is set back to conform with the building regulations, but not as a simple, recessed storey. Instead, the skyline is enlivened with domed rooftop pavilions. 'This necessity suggested a picture to his mind, a very romantic picture most sensitively conceived. So he built the picture in solid stone, and built it with real rooms and real staircases and real lifts and real lavatories all packed away somehow inside it.'[79]

The former Midland Bank, Poultry, City of London (Edwin Lutyens, 1924)

Contemporaries were well aware of how truly original this Midland Bank headquarters was. 'No one, I think,' wrote Reilly in 1928,

> has so successfully till this building solved the . . . difficult problem of a large block *not* a skyscraper . . . Here Sir Edwin had frankly given up the crowning feature of the Italian palace – its great cornice. The Americans did that years ago with their tall buildings, but it was an obvious thing to do on a thirty-storey structure. It was not an obvious thing to do on a six-storey one in an old country like ours. Yet one sees at once that it is right for the narrow City street.[80]

The following year, the young E. Maxwell Fry, Reilly's former pupil, who had not yet reinvented himself as a Modernist, compared the building favourably with the new Lloyd's Bank headquarters in Cornhill. While recognising that both buildings conformed to the 'Gran Cañon' character of City streets, he considered that:

> primarily it seems to me to be a matter of artistic virility that makes Sir Edwin Lutyens's Midland Bank the greater of the two; this and the fact that Mr Tait's cornices and colonnades are a retrogression, where in the Midland Bank the lack of a cornice is a logical concession. In the Midland Bank Sir Edwin seems to have advanced the art of palace building to a farther and more definite stage. . . . The whole effect is one of the exultant piling up of fine masonry. It is alive and expansive, and looks as though it were built stone upon stone, upward from the ground.[81]

In fact, of course, all those precisely cut pieces of masonry were fixed to structural steelwork.

It may seem strange that Lutyens applied a much more original interpretation of the Classical language to his commercial commissions than to his domestic ones. Country houses, however, did not present new problems requiring new solutions. Furthermore, as the accelerating attrition of older country seats began in the 1920s, after a war in which so many sons and heirs were killed, there was little demand for large new country houses. Most new houses in the country were smaller in scale and tended to be in the Tudor or Georgian styles. Nevertheless, a few houses were built in the Grand Manner, and Lutyens designed two of them. The first was Gledstone Hall on the Yorkshire Moors, designed in collaboration with Richard Jacques in 1923. Formal and symmetrical around an Ionic portico, it seems to express the conservatism and uncertainty of a nation damaged and exhausted by war; there is nothing here of the sparkle that Lutyens exhibited in his banks or even in his war memorials.

More interesting and imaginative was Middleton Park, despite it being the only house Lutyens ever built for a member of the old landed aristocracy. The client was the young Earl of Jersey, who also owned Robert Adam's Osterley, and who demolished his Oxfordshire seat in 1934 and then approached Lutyens's wayward architect son Robert. In the event, father and son worked together. The inspiration

Gledstone Hall, West Marton, Yorkshire (Edwin Lutyens, 1927)

for Middleton Park may have been Kinross House in Scotland, Frenchified with shutters. The house is less pretentious and more inventive than Gledstone; there is no portico, and Lutyens carefully played with wall planes, eliding them with the proud rustication on both the main house and the smart entrance lodges (Plate 5). As well as producing an ingenious plan, the architects had to cope with modern challenges; as Christopher Hussey noted when writing about the house in 1946: 'Technically it is interesting as demonstrating how the luxurious requirements of the time, a dozen bathrooms, with accommodation for numerous visiting valets and maids, could be met within the framework of the aesthetic science without a water-pipe or a window conflicting with the symmetrical unity.'[82] The glory of the house, presumably the work of Lutyens *fils* rather than *père*, was Lady Jersey's own bathroom. The current countess was the American actress Virginia Cherrill, formerly married to Cary Grant, and her sumptuous vaulted bathroom lined with white marble and pink onyx was, wrote Hussey, 'a notable instance of the between-wars cult of the tub'.[83]

Lutyens was responsible for one other house, which is curiously representative of its time and yet a fantasy, never to be lived in. Constructed in the year of the Wren bicentenary, it paid formal homage to the architect of Hampton Court and attracted much popular interest, especially when exhibited at the British Empire Exhibition at Wembley in 1924. It still attracts thousands of visitors and is, perhaps, the best-known example of British domestic architecture of the interwar decades even though it remains uninhabited and cannot be entered. It is, of course, a model: the Queen's Dolls' House, today on show in Windsor Castle. First proposed in 1921 as a gift from a grateful nation to Queen Mary for the example she had set during the war and after, the project was designed and controlled by Lutyens but was a collaborative effort, enthusiastically donated to by artists and manufacturers alike.

An astonishing amount was written about the Dolls' House in an embarrassing orgy of whimsy, sycophancy, deference and

Exterior (*above*) and interior (*below*), The Queen's Dolls' House, Windsor Castle (Edwin Lutyens, 1924)

infantilism that can be interpreted as the profoundly conservative response of a disoriented nation to the frightening challenges of the post-war years. Furthermore, as Timothy Rohan has pointed out, the prominence given to the Queen's Dolls' House at the Wembley Exhibition was in contrast to the lack of attention given to New Delhi, the great imperial project with which this chapter began but which, in the 1920s, was threatened both by budgetary constraints and by uncertainty about the future of the British Raj:

> In the Dolls' House, Lutyens found a welcome escape from the mournfulness of the current architectural scene, the frustrations of the Viceroy's House and a chance to build the domestic ideal again in the form of a 'fantasy' palace for the Queen over which he could exert absolute control. The miniature house and its contents became signifiers for the ideal objects that had become too expensive to produce in full scale. . . . Simply put, the Dolls' House is a proxy, substitute or surrogate for the Classical Viceroy's House that was never built in New Delhi.[84]

The Dolls' House displays none of the brilliant invention, the wit or the modernity achieved in New Delhi; it is an ideal 'Wrennaissance' design which, as John Summerson observed in 1937, was 'one of the few really dull things Lutyens has done'.[85] And by that date, the Grand Manner was slowly but inexorably fading, despite much wishful thinking then, and in the face of challenges posed by architectural ideas from abroad.

CHAPTER THREE

SWEDISH GRACE

I N 1931, THE Royal Institute of British Architects announced an open competition for a new headquarters building to be erected in Portland Place, London, to celebrate its forthcoming centenary. The following year, the 284 schemes submitted were put on public display in the new Thames House on Millbank. 'The first impression it must make on all critical minds,' wrote H. S. Goodhart-Rendel of the exhibition, 'is one of hesitation and gaucherie, combined with nervous self-assertion. British architecture is plainly suffering from an inferiority complex.' And that inferiority complex was demonstrated by an indebtedness to ideas and precedents from outside Britain: 'There are in the exhibition several designs for an Institute of Swedish Architects, a clever design for an Institute of Genoese Architects, some interesting designs for warehouses and a large sprinkling of designs for American luxury hotels.'[1] In the event, it was a debt to those Swedish architects that was most evident in the building designed by the competition winner, George Grey Wornum, which was opened in 1934.

British architecture has never, perhaps, before or since been so open to ideas from abroad as it was between the two world wars.

The certainties that underpinned the self-confidence of Edwardian architecture had been undermined by the first of those wars, and while the older generation of architects clung to the old way of doing things, a younger generation felt that it had to look overseas to find new inspiration. British architecture after 1918 suddenly seemed tired and conservative, while new architecture abroad, especially in the countries which had managed to avoid the conflict, now promised better. In 1931, Charles Reilly recalled, in his account of *Representative British Architects of the Present Day*, how, before the war, 'no foreign architectural world was known as it is beginning to be known now. If this little book has any successors, foreign names will have to appear, for the national boundaries of architecture are once more receding, as happened at the Renaissance and indeed in all the really vital periods.'[2] If the advanced ideas imported and demonstrated by Gropius and Mendelsohn, Breuer and Freud, Lubetkin and Goldfinger, were, to a remarkable degree, enthusiastically accepted in Britain by the end of the 1930s, the ground had been prepared by a widespread willingness to learn from a whole range of European architecture already shown by architects in the 1920s.

British architecture of the 1920s and 1930s cannot be catalogued or comprehended without reference to contemporary work in Europe. Some contemporaries feared that, in consequence, it was in danger of losing any distinctive character of its own. Significantly, after surveying the various national pavilions at the 1925 Paris Exposition, the architectural journalist and editor H. de Cronin Hastings concluded that, 'Perhaps the British pavilion, alone among those of foreign nations, fails to reveal its nationality.'[3] One of the designers of that pavilion was the American-born, Paris-trained architect Howard Morley Robertson, who insisted in his book, *Architecture Explained*, that there 'is little doubt but that at the present moment we must look to Europe and America, more especially to Northern and Central Europe, for an architecture more typical of our own modern epoch. In Germany, Holland, Sweden, Finland, Switzerland, and France the traditional classic styles are fighting for their very existence'.[4]

Both in his role as director, and later principal, of the Architectural Association and in his prolific writings, Robertson was instrumental in widening the horizons of British architecture. In the pages of the *Architect and Building News* and other journals, Robertson, usually in collaboration with the Architectural Association (AA) secretary and photographer, F. R. Yerbury, introduced architects to the work of their foreign colleagues. Between 1922 and the early 1930s, Robertson and Yerbury published some two hundred articles.[5] 'Yerbury travels all over the globe,' recorded the Anglophile Dane S. E. Rasmussen, after his first visit to London in 1927. 'Robertson writes well and with facility: after spending just a few days in a country of whose language he understands not a word, he writes a whole string of articles on its architecture. So the lack of direction among London's architects is all the more puzzling.'[6] Thanks to Yerbury, British architects unable to travel to see the buildings for themselves could become familiar with the work of foreign architects, for he published a series of influential books largely illustrated with his own photographs. As one AA student remarked, 'It would be impossible to over-emphasise the importance of Yerbury in the development of fashions in the school.'[7]

'The northern countries of Europe, sealed to us for many years by the war, present to architects a veritable field for discovery.'[8] So Robertson's professional partner, John Murray Easton, the other half of Easton & Robertson, designers of the British Pavilion, began a eulogy in the *Architectural Review* in 1924 of what would become one of the most influential exemplars, Stockholm Town Hall. The countries which now particularly interested architects were, above all, Holland and Sweden. They were also, as it happened, Protestant constitutional monarchies, and hence more sympathetic to British visitors and countries in which a native tradition of building in brick had been invigorated by the Arts and Crafts movement. Indeed, the more intelligent visitors appreciated that what they were now admiring was the imaginative development of English ideas which had produced a modern civic vernacular, rich in symbolism and craftsmanship, on a scale and of a quality never realised back home owing to the Edwardian triumph of Classicism. This was cause for optimism as well as self-congratulation, for that beneficial influence could surely now operate in reverse; as Howard Robertson wrote in 1926, anticipating some of the arguments of Pevsner's *Pioneers of the Modern Movement*:

> The so-called new movement, the cult of pure design combined with a desire for a return to the craft spirit, was fostered in this country by such men as William Morris, but the greater development of this influence has, curiously enough, taken place in foreign countries. Architects of our own time – men like Norman Shaw, Charles Voysey, C. R. Mackintosh, Edgar Wood – have had an immense influence abroad, but in England their seed is largely still below soil ... Later on, when things definite have crystallised therefrom, we shall find a fully developed movement transported back to England and worked upon as the basis of what may ultimately grow into a national expression of modern art in architecture.[9]

Naturally, in conservative Britain, some people feared that this international outlook would lead to even greater confusion and to ignorance of what was valuable in English traditions and practices. Robertson was even once accused by the chairman of the RIBA's Board of Architectural Education, Maurice Webb, 'of pernicious and corrupting influence on the general body of students through publicising modern trends, and in that way doing a disservice to the architectural profession'.[10] Others argued that the apparent originality of modern Dutch or German architecture which seemed so appealing was in fact mere eccentricity. Faced with student drawings at the AA in 1922, which were strongly influenced by Holland, Goodhart-Rendel opined that:

> It does not matter whether a style be new or old, still less does it matter what style it be, so that it be suitable to its use, and that

its user can work in it with ease. . . . No poet, however, could write with ease in Esperanto, and it may be doubted whether any architect works or can work with ease in the arbitrarily invented modern style of Germany and Austria. . . . No man, single-handed, can invent much. Originality and individuality will out, and if an architect possesses these qualities, a severe academic training will provide him with the best means of making use of them.[11]

'We live in hope that fine building will in time produce new academic values, arising from devisement, fitness, close observation of conditions, reasonable use of new materials, etc.,' A. E. Richardson ranted at a conference of teachers at the RIBA in 1928.

It is unwise to discuss loose opinions. Fashion is the greatest bugbear, so called Modern Design is another label for fashion. Let us get rid of the term Modern. Sweep modernism into the limbo of other cant phrases. Fashion or modernism is a 'will o' the wisp' that sheds its fitful light in turn on the Germans, the Dutch, the Swedes, the new old styles and Kamschatkan speculations. Divergence of opinion forsooth! Confusion of photographs. What a policy of despair is shown when the architects of a great nation, at least some of them, imitate the whims of architects of countries dissimilar to their own. The salvation of England must begin in England.[12]

A few months later, in calmer mood, Richardson admitted that, 'As in the past, Englishmen will welcome styles from abroad, but they will not submit entirely to didactic rulings.'[13]

Serious interest in Dutch architecture seems to have begun in 1922 with an exhibition of Dutch housing at the Architectural Association. British architects seem to have recognised an affinity with Dutch architecture, particularly in the use of brick and in the creative development of a vernacular tradition. Many, however, found the wilful Expressionism of the Amsterdam School and of the work of de Klerk and Kramer too eccentric and too reminiscent of the 'New Art' that England had firmly rejected twenty years before. After an AA visit to Holland in 1923, Robert Atkinson, the principal, 'thought the newer work, so far as brickwork and technique were concerned, was astonishingly good', but that 'the qualities of sane architecture and logical architecture ought to be the fundamental basis of design, and that the eccentricities of individualism ought to be put in afterwards if money were available for them'.[14] Even Robertson, his successor, was cautious, fearing that 'there is a danger that the sheer brilliance of the results of individual genius may be dangerously captivating, and that Tradition, the pilot, may be dropped too early on the voyage into future experiments'.[15]

By the late 1920s, following the death of Michel de Klerk, the Expressionism of the Amsterdam School had waned and British architects became more interested in the sober, abstracted brick vernacular of, for instance, A. J. Kropholler. Yerbury, in his 1928 European survey, concluded: 'Perhaps Holland alone is the only country of which it can be said that it has a very pronounced modern national architecture, and this has sprung up and flourished since the War to a remarkable degree.'[16] The father of this modern Dutch architecture was H. P. Berlage (1856–1934), but it is unlikely that many realised that the roots of the direct expression and the emphasis on the integrity of wall planes in the Dutch modernist's Exchange in Amsterdam lay in Ruskin and the work of Alfred Waterhouse. Berlage knew England well, and was responsible for a remarkable building in London: Holland House in Bury Street in the City of London, built during the first years of the war. With its steel structure expressed by a tight vertical rhythm of uprights clad in greenish faience, its stylised ship's prow in black granite on an acute corner and its decorative entrance hall in the Amsterdam School manner, this building was very different from the conventional, Classical buildings all around and could

Holland House, Bury Street, City of London (H. P. Berlage, 1916)

have provided English architects with a vital model for a modern commercial architecture, had they known of it.*

The Dutch architect whose work was most closely studied by British architects was, however, Willem Marinus Dudok (1884–1974), the municipal architect at Hilversum since 1915; it can be

---

* Thomas S. Tait probably did know it, as discussed later in this chapter. The building was only published properly in 1960 by Brian Housden, 'A Note on Holland House', in Dannatt (1960), p. 30.

argued that Dudok had more influence on British architecture between the wars than any other architect. Hilversum is a low-density garden city, some miles from Amsterdam, which in the 1920s was becoming the realisation of the ideal suggested by Letchworth and what Welwyn Garden City aspired to be. Dudok's own work had definite English roots, but the elements in it which British architects perceived as modern were largely derived from the buildings of Frank Lloyd Wright in America. Semi-circular entrances and mannered high-level oriels appear on a number of the schools designed by Dudok which act as landmarks in the small-scale urban topography of Hilversum. Later schools exhibited horizontal bands of fenestration, and staircases within glazed semi-circular projecting bays; these were motifs much imitated in British school buildings. Not all of Dudok's schools were conspicuously modern, however; the Fabritius infant school on the edge of the city combined a strong horizontality with massive thatched roofs. John Brandon-Jones later recalled how, when he was a student at the Architectural Association,

> Tommy Tait introduced the Dudok Style and we had Dudok over to give a lecture. There was a certain amount of barracking when he showed a slide of a school with a thatched roof; he answered back, 'I like it, the children like it, so why shouldn't I do it?'* After that there was an outburst of pseudo-Dudok designs, but the main influence was still Scandinavian. If you did not want to do Swedish classic you could get away with Dudok.[17]

It was Yerbury who persuaded his old friend to visit London and lecture at the AA in 1934, having earlier described Dudok's work as

---

* 'Many of these buildings have flat roofs,' Dudok said in his lecture, 'producing a natural context with the surrounding low houses. I like this pure space-enclosure, without having made a dogma of it. I have often applied the excellent tile roof, nay, I have even built a school with a thatched roof, because I thought that a rural building harmonised well with the modest villas surrounding it' (*Architectural Association Journal*, Vol. L (June 1934), p. 7).

'simple and graceful, at times almost severe, but exhibiting always a pleasant sense of phantasy which finds expression especially in the many schools which he has built'.[18] In a reassessment of Dudok's importance written in 1954 from a standpoint of ideological commitment to the Modern Movement, Robert Furneaux Jordan argued that, 'To English architects who wished to be modern and didn't quite know how, Dudok – applying the superficialities of modernism to traditional brick structures – was a boon.'[19] This might seem to be confirmed by Giles Gilbert Scott's observation after Dudok's lecture that, 'If the traditionalists would study the work he has accomplished I think he would do more to convert them to modernism than any other modern architect of whom I know. . . . Mr Dudok has proved that it is possible to be a real modernist and yet preserve the qualities of traditional architecture.'[20]

Dudok was certainly an invigorating influence in Britain. It can surely now be argued that to have learned from Hilversum resulted in a richer and more harmonious public architecture which has lasted and weathered well. Of the many British buildings directly inspired by Dudok's work, the Royal Masonic Hospital at Ravenscourt Park,

Royal Masonic Hospital, Ravenscourt Park, London (Burnet, Tait & Lorne, 1933)

'Healing' and 'Charity', Royal Masonic Hospital, London (sculptor Gilbert Bayes, 1933)

by Burnet, Tait & Lorne, is a particularly distinguished example. Here, the Dutch style is given a more formal and monumental symmetry, while the wings end on open, curved balconies. The design, which won the RIBA's medal in 1933, reflects the changes made to the Burnet firm by Tait in 1930 to prepare for the new architectural methods he could see coming. The result was, as David Walker has written, that it became 'the premier British practice of the decade', while 'Tait never wavered from the path of modernity again'.[21] The extent to which Dutch modernity influenced this change was also shown by the firm's Curzon Cinema in Mayfair, again strongly influenced by Dudok.

Dudok's masterpiece was the Town Hall at Hilversum, completed in 1931. Although the style of the yellow brick building was derived from Frank Lloyd Wright, the Dutchman created a complex public building of remarkable sophistication and originality. This type of composition was not imitated by any British architect, although elements of Hilversum appeared in Clifford Strange's Wembley Town Hall of 1940. What was imitated was the form of Dudok's

Hilversum Town Hall, Hilversum, North Holland, Netherlands (W. M. Dudok, 1931)

campanile, a subtly asymmetrical rectilinear clock tower which owed something to the De Stijl Movement. A similar tower articulates the asymmetrical composition of the Town Hall at Hornsey designed by the New Zealand architect Reginald Uren and completed in 1935, although the canopied niche above the entrance below was derived from Stockholm Town Hall. The treatment of the brick ranges either side is more formal and Georgian in inspiration, with no hint of Dudok's overlapping asymmetries; a clever design which integrates well into the street pattern of this North London suburb.

Hornsey Town Hall, Crouch End, London (Reginald H. Uren, 1935)

A similar Dudokian clock tower completes the Town Hall at Greenwich designed by Culpin & Son and completed in 1939, a building which has other motifs of Continental derivation, and which, along with Hornsey Town Hall, was included in the Architecture Club's selection of *Recent English Architecture 1920–1940*. No wonder Dudok was awarded the Royal Gold Medal by the RIBA in 1935. By that date, however, the brick tradition had been superseded in Holland by the New Architecture of concrete and glass.

The former Greenwich Town Hall, Greenwich, Greater London (Clifford Culpin, 1939)

Swedish influence is more conspicuous than Dutch in the new municipal buildings raised between the wars. Architectural developments there, whether in a National Romantic manner, or Classical, or Functionalist, were closely followed in the pages of the *Architectural Review* and elsewhere. 'Sweden has experienced a phenomenal revival in architecture which has almost raised it to a level higher than in any other country,' wrote Yerbury in 1928.[22] The indefatigable and resourceful photographer did not have to compile a volume on Swedish buildings, since that had been done, with Yerbury's assistance, by Hakon Ahlberg in 1925. Entitled *Swedish Architecture of the Twentieth Century*, this fat, blue-bound volume of plates was soon on the bookshelf of every ambitious British architect. Yerbury contributed a preface: 'Modern Sweden is producing an architecture which belongs to its own times,' he wrote. 'It is fresh and progressive, but it exhibits neither a striving for sensation nor a contempt for the past.'[23] As with modern Dutch architecture, what impressed British architects about Sweden was the humanity and national character of new buildings in which traditional styles had been given a modern expression, carried out with artistry and skill. Reviewing an exhibition of Swedish architecture in 1924, Howard Robertson wrote:

> There must be in Sweden, as here, much bad architecture. But in making the inevitable comparison, we must in honesty ask ourselves if we can produce, in buildings of all categories outside of domestic architecture, work so calculated to be beloved of the human beings for the enrichment of whose lives these buildings are created. Is it not true that we can do this, but that we are not doing it at present?[24]

The first Swedish building to attract attention was the hugely influential Stockholm Town Hall, conceived in the early years of the century and finally completed in 1923. It was the masterpiece of Ragnar Östberg, who was awarded the RIBA Gold Medal in 1926.* It is not surprising that the town hall was so admired by English architects; it is arguably the finest Arts and Crafts building in the world, a realisation of the dreams of William Morris. Manning Robertson, the architect and author, considered it 'an art creation that ranked with the greatest that the world had ever seen' and one that was comparable with the achievement of Michelangelo, Shakespeare and Beethoven.[25] A truly civic monument, built of brick and with a tall landmark tower rising from its waterside site, it is subtly irregular in plan, both vernacular and Classical in style, and full of historical references in its details and in the work of the artists and sculptors who worked closely with the architect. Decorative themes in the great public rooms – such as the geometrical pattern of timber framing painted canvas in the Council Chamber – appear on the walls of council chambers in countless British municipal buildings and in the

---

* It is surely significant that Östberg's book on *The Stockholm Town Hall* (1929) was published, in Sweden, in an English edition.

Stockholm Town Hall,
Stockholm, Sweden
(Ragnar Östberg, 1923)

interiors of the RIBA Headquarters. John Gloag considered it to be 'perhaps the last European example of collective craftsmanship serving architecture'.[26]

It was, however, the Gothenburg Exhibition in 1923 that first drew British architects across the North Sea. Visitors were impressed by the exhibition buildings and by the quality of Swedish crafts and manufactures. Lawrence Weaver, searching for ideas in his role as director general of United Kingdom Exhibits for the forthcoming British Empire Exhibition at Wembley, reported that, 'In England we have our Design and Industry Association and our British Institute of Industrial Art, and now the Royal Society of Art to take a hand in the task of getting beauty into common things. Sweden is ahead of us in that.' And as for the Gothenburg architects Arvid Bjerke and

Sigfrid Ericson, 'They gave to the temporary parts of the Exhibition just that quality of fantasy, that touch of exaggerated gaiety which is not only permissible but righteous.'[27] Clough Williams-Ellis accompanied Weaver on his mission and later recalled how:

> We had both attended other national and international exhibitions, and had usually been poorly enough rewarded for our pains, but here at Gothenburg one seemed to feel the living breath of a new and vigorous world, where beauty was a natural fact of life and not a rare and exotic thing to be glass-cased and ticketed and made self-conscious by a rather silly fuss. There seemed no solemnity about art in Sweden; it was taken for granted as an essential part of the national civilization, of civic and commercial life.[28]

The fanciful, light Baroque style and attenuated Classicism conspicuous in the exhibition were certainly noticed by visitors, and eventually became an element in what is now categorised as 'Art Deco'. One structure in Gothenburg in particular inspired the sincerest form of flattery, resulting in one of the best and most admired British buildings of the 1920s. The Congress Hall by Bjerke was notable for its structure of transverse elliptical arches supporting a series of clerestory windows which stepped inwards as the building rose, rather as in a modern factory. This conception was adopted for the hall of the Royal Horticultural Society in London, won in competition by Easton & Robertson and built in 1926–28, except that the laminated timber construction of the original was translated into reinforced concrete. 'We felt,' recalled Robertson, 'that the Gothenburg Hall, although constructed in wood, was in conception an admirable answer to our problem, with its tiered clerestory and lighting springing from arched ribs, a principle not new (tiered lighting appears in the Scala Regia at the Vatican), but one not at that time fully exploited in any recent building of large scale.'[29] In front, the administrative building was in a sort of modern neo-Georgian, with modernistic fluting on the recessed brick parapet which replaced the conventional cornice.

Royal Horticultural Society hall, Vincent Square, London (Easton & Robertson, 1928)

Stockholm, however, was the most influential Swedish city. In addition to the Town Hall there were the examples of an Expressionist brick vernacular by Wahlman, Westman and Lallerstedt. The architect most admired in Britain in the 1920s was probably Ivar Tengbom (1878–1968), who became, in 1938, the second Swede to be awarded the Royal Gold Medal. Tengbom's tall, etiolated Högalid Church, of 1923, was derived from seventeenth-century Swedish Baroque and carried out in austere planes of brickwork. Inside, the brick was limewashed and the woodwork limed: this, combined with the use of muted, pale colours and subtle gilding, inspired the characteristic look of the interiors of more progressive British churches between the wars. As Peter Anson wrote in his study of *Fashions in Church Furnishings*, 'ecclesiastical good taste often mirrors contemporary domestic furnishings and dress', and by 1930,

> an 'all white' craze began. Furniture was bleached, pickled or scraped. The sugary magentas and pinks, and the strident yellows and orange of the nineteen-twenties were superseded by white walls, white rugs and white covers for chairs and sofas. Gilt was transformed into silver wherever possible. Where an alternative to

white was required only pale almond greens, greys and soft buffs were permitted. All these found their way into churches as well as houses.[30]

It was, however, Tengbom's Classical work that was largely responsible for that cool, decorative elegance which British admirers called 'Swedish Grace'. His 'Match House' of 1926–28, commissioned as the headquarters of the Swedish Match Company, presented an austere, stuccoed façade to the street while in the colonnaded circular courtyard beyond, sculpture by Carl Milles provided a note of restrained sensuality. Similar qualities were evident in his masterpiece, the Stockholm Concert Hall, a building of blue-painted brickwork with more sculpture by Milles in front of a giant, attenuated portico of a metamorphosed Corinthian order placed close against the façade. Inside was a feast of restrained neo-Classical decorative richness, all carried out with wit and superb craftsmanship.

A simplified neo-Classicism, looking back to the early nineteenth century, became the language of modernity in much of Scandinavia, as it was in Germany before 1914. Its other central exponent in Sweden was Gunnar Asplund, whose principal monument in Stockholm was the new City Library, opened in 1928. Here, the tall stuccoed drum lighting the principal reading room

Swedish Match Company, Stockholm, Sweden (Ivar Tengbom, 1928)

rose above plain, rectilinear façades enlivened only with pseudo-Egyptian hieroglyphics. However, along with his collaborator Sigurd Lerewentz, Asplund changed direction and adopted the planar Functionalist style of the German and French modernists. This he interpreted with a certain nautical gaiety in the temporary buildings he designed for the Stockholm Exhibition of 1930. As Robertson concluded presciently, 'one feels that modernism is on the point of receiving a recognition which is more significant than might be the case in a country less cultured in its standards and less rich in traditions of craftsmanship.'[31] Asplund would surely have been the third Swede to be awarded the Royal Gold Medal in the twentieth century had he not died prematurely in 1940.

Interest in the decorative arts of Sweden remained constant throughout the 1930s, and in March 1931 an issue of the *Architectural Review* was devoted to the Swedish Exhibition held at the Dorland House in Lower Regent Street. 'Swedish Grace' as an image of fashionable modernity was the aspiration of many designers of public buildings in Britain in the 1930s. Among these, two in particular stand among the best and most representative examples of British architecture of their time. The first is the City Hall at Norwich. Robert Atkinson had been appointed in 1928 to advise on the development of the central marketplace in the historic East Anglian city. In the event, however, the winner of the 1931 competition for a new town hall was a design by C. H. James and S. Rowland Pierce. Over 140 entries were submitted, and it was remarked that 'Every damn Swedish architect has gone in'.[32] After local opposition and financial problems had been overcome, it was built in 1937–38. The symmetrical bulk of the building, brick above a stone basement, is treated in a monumental Georgian manner, but enlivened by strong hints of Sweden: the canopied openings on the wings; the stylised guardian bronze lions by Alfred Hardiman flanking the central bronze entrance doors by James Woodford; and, above all, the central portico, inspired by Tengbom's Concert Hall combined with the asymmetrical accent of a campanile which pays

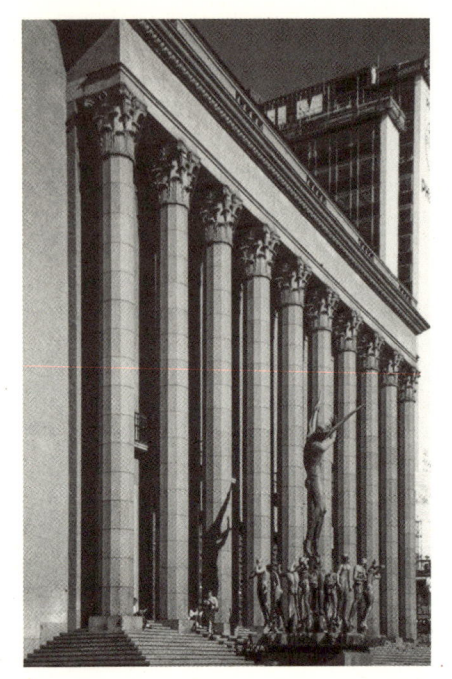

Façade and interior detail, Konserthus, Stockholm, Sweden (Ivar Tengbom, 1926)

intelligent homage to Stockholm Town Hall. Nikolaus Pevsner was surely right to conclude two decades later that, 'In spite of its frankly admitted dependence on Sweden, the Norwich City Hall is likely to go down in history as the foremost English public building of between the wars.'[33]

'Lion Passant', Norwich City Hall, Norwich (sculptor Alfred Hardiman, 1938)

Norwich City Hall, Norwich (C. H. James and S. Rowland Pierce, 1938)

The second example is the design for a Swedish Institute of Architects by Grey Wornum, which had won the competition for the RIBA Headquarters in 1932. As built, without the recessed attic storeys, in 1932–34, the sober and carefully proportioned Portland stone elevations, enlivened with relief figures by Edward Bainbridge Copnall, have the character of the Classicism of Stockholm, while the giant window containing the entrance with bronze doors and flanking sculptural columns is a clear derivation from Asplund's Stockholm Library. The architect Philip Tilden thought it had the character of 'a gentleman dressed in clothes that were not bought in England'.[34] Inside, the modern Swedish character continues, with the

Stockholm City Library, Stockholm, Sweden (E. G. Asplund, 1928)

low relief sculptures on the deep reveals in the Florence Hall, as in the Gallery of the Stockholm Town Hall; the acid etched glass doors, window panels and glass balustrades by Jan Juta, and the rectilinear decorative panelling throughout.[35]

Grey Wornum himself, a dapper figure with a blank monocle who had lost an eye and been badly injured on the Somme, had long been interested in decorative effects and had designed restaurant and domestic interiors in an imaginative neo-Baroque manner. But the distinguished assessors for the RIBA building – Robert Atkinson, Charles Holden, Giles Gilbert Scott, H. V. Lanchester and Percy S. Worthington – did not select Wornum's design because it was modishly Swedish and decorative, but because it was brilliantly planned. Corridors were avoided and most rooms open off the grand staircase hall, which rises through the building, enlivened by four giant fluted black marble columns – with neither bases nor capitals. Grey Wornum eschewed literal traditionalism while not abandoning the humane touch given by decorative art in fine materials.

The result was a most distinguished building that transcended fashion while being truly representative of its time and of the confused aspirations of the contemporary architectural profession. In a guidebook to contemporary architecture published by London Transport in 1938, Hugh Casson described it as 'the most beautifully finished building in London. Although criticised as finicky and glittering, it is unsurpassed in its feeling of internal spaciousness, and few contemporary buildings have been so fully conceived in all three dimensions.'[36]

British architects also took an interest in the other Scandinavian countries; the *Architectural Review* carried an article on the architecture of Finland in 1924, and in 1927 Yerbury published his book of photographs of modern Danish architecture. P. V. Jensen-Klint's brick

Interior, Royal Institute of British Architects, Portland Place, London (engraved glass by Jan Juta and Raymond McGrath; bronze doors by James Woodford, 1934)

Police Headquarters, Copenhagen, Denmark (Hack Kampmann, 1924)

neo-Gothic Grundtvig's Church attracted considerable attention, but the general character of Danish building was coolly Classical. Of particular interest was the large Copenhagen Police Headquarters by Hack Kampmann.

With its vast central circular colonnaded court open to the sky, and its carefully finished interiors in a modernised neo-Classical style, it fulfilled the monumental ideals of English Classicists while avoiding over-elaboration and pomposity. As Yerbury noted, 'the Danish architects of the present day, with few exceptions, have definitely placed their whole architectural faith in the revived Classic'.[37] Nikolaus Pevsner wondered whether the huge, austere Ministry of Pensions building at Acton of 1922, so admired in its day, reflected a Danish influence: 'Its block shape, its roof and its sober decoration all occur almost identical in such Danish blocks of flats as the ones designed by Kay Fisker. And yet one wonders whether an acquaintance with Denmark should be assumed. There is no other indication anywhere to confirm such a hypothesis.'[38]

It would not have been surprising if the new architecture of Britain's defeated and demonised enemy, Germany, was ignored in Britain, but as early as 1922 the *Architectural Review* published an article on the work of Bruno Taut, 'A Visionary in Practice', by the German-American journalist Hermann George Scheffauer. This was soon followed by articles by the same author on Erich Mendelsohn, Hans Poelzig and Walter Gropius.[39] W. G. Newton, the journal's editor, was, however, wary of their influence, and in an editorial in 1927 commented that, 'In Germany, though not so extravagantly as in Russia, there is a tendency, at least on paper, where much of the architecture remains, to be embarrassed by anything which recalls the past; an obsession which proves fatal to poise, balance, and gaiety.'[40] The past in Germany, of course, was more problematic than in victorious Britain, and the fundamental

The former Ministry of Pensions, Acton, London (HM Office of Works, 1922)

conservatism of British architects in the 1920s was shown by such repeated assertions that modernity must be allied with tradition. 'Modern German architecture is unconcerned with leisure or graciousness,' John Gloag maintained in 1931, with typical national prejudice. 'It shouts: "Make something!" "Buy something!" "Go somewhere!" "Eat here!" "Sleep here!" These peremptory orders are the boisterous cries of a child that is still learning how to speak.'[41]

The most sincere tribute to the merits of German modernism was paid by the Northampton engineer Wenman Bassett-Lowke, when in 1924 he commissioned Peter Behrens to design a new suburban house. There will be more to say about this singular case later, but the modern German architecture which most interested British architects in the 1920s was the Expressionism of architects who worked in brick. Fritz Höger's Chilehaus in Hamburg, with its vertical rhythm, irregular plan determined by street lines, and occasional Gothic details, was much illustrated and discussed. 'It is conceived so boldly and frankly,' thought Robertson in 1929, 'that many honest Englishmen consider it to be a wicked building. It has been held up for opprobrium at public lectures. It is almost indecently unashamed. The Chilehaus is in fact both a marvel and an enigma. It attracts and repels at the same time.'[42] The expression of the internal structure by continuous

Chilehaus, Hamburg, Germany (Fritz Höger, 1924)

St Saviour's Church, Eltham, Greater London (N. F. Cachemaille-Day, 1933)

brick projections enclosing tiers of windows was a lesson soon absorbed in England, and it contributed to the vertical fluting in brickwork characteristic of so much modernistic architecture. Church architects also turned their attention to Germany, and to the experimental Protestant churches designed by Otto Bartning and to Expressionist examples such as Höger's in Berlin or the Roman Catholic works of Dominikus Böhm. N. F. Cachemaille-Day, the most consistently innovative of English ecclesiastical designers, may have been influenced by Germany when he translated the massiveness of Albi Cathedral into reinforced concrete and brick at St Saviour's, Eltham (Plate 7). St Alban's Church in North Harrow, by A. W. Kenyon has a rectilinear campanile, pierced at a high level by openings, which is closely derived from Böhm's centrally planned

St Alban's Church, North Harrow, Middlesex (Arthur W. Kenyon, 1936)

church in Cologne, while the conventionally planned interior is articulated by transverse elliptical arches, and the same influences are in play at F. X. Velarde's St Gabriel's, Blackburn.

Although British architects were clearly intrigued by developments in Germany, they felt obliged to associate them with the qualities attributed to their late enemy: the inhumanity of Prussianism. This emerges in the criticism of Adelaide House, the commercial block designed by Sir John Burnet & Partners which rose by the Thames in the early 1920s to destroy the symmetry of the approach to London Bridge: 'That the Fishmongers' Hall is sadly overwhelmed by it is unfortunate . . . But there can be no doubt that two Adelaide Houses, one on each side of London Bridge, would form a most impressive City Gate.'[43] The early proposals had been monumentally Classical in character, but Thomas Tait had transformed these into a towering, vertical composition rising to a bold Egyptian cornice. The steel structure beneath the skin of Portland stone and granite was expressed by an excessively tight rhythm of piers framed by corner pylons, tighter than in fact they needed to be as 'those containing stanchions were supplemented by others not containing stanchions and performing no function except the undesirable one of blocking out useful light'.[44]

The origins of this treatment were probably Dutch, but contemporaries saw Adelaide House as German. Trystan Edwards imagined it claiming to be 'by Uncle Sam out of Germania . . . a cross between an American skyscraper and a German warehouse . . . Inhuman, you say? Well, inhumanity in architecture is rather novel, and I don't mind telling you that I'm out for novelty.'[45] Adelaide House was compared with Lutyens's Britannic House, which was completed the same year, 1925: the former seeming to suggest the future; the latter the end of a tradition. Instead of a palace portico, Tait had designed an entrance with squat, black Doric columns seemingly crushed by the weight of masonry above. 'Massiveness is no defect in architecture, but should it oppress?' asked Vernon Blake in reviewing Adelaide House. 'Can we not leave aside ponderous

Germanic things and learn more of joy from the Latin peoples?' Nevertheless, he recognised that 'Sir John Burnet & Partners have made history; they have given English commercial architecture a definite modern expression.'[46] Nikolaus Pevsner, who, as a German immigrant, was the best judge, thought that, 'There is more of an American accent in Adelaide House, if any foreign accent there is, than a German.'[47]

By the end of the decade, the architecture of the Weimar Republic was being regarded more kindly and, for many, modern Germany seemed a refreshingly vibrant and progressive nation compared with conservative, class-conscious Britain. 'On German traditional architecture there is little to say,' wrote W. P. N. Edwards in 1931. 'Germany has, more than any other Continental country with the possible exception of France, been gripped by the new ideas, and the chief interest of German architecture is, therefore, in the new rather than in the traditional.'[48] One aspect of modern German architecture which had a significant influence on Britain was cinema design. P. Morton Shand's book *Modern Theatres and Cinemas*, published in 1930, was dominated by German examples.

> If the illustrations in this volume are predominantly German, the reason is that the general level of German cinemas is the highest in the world; and that German architects have thought out the cinema as a new and untraditional type of building instead of tinkering with adaptations of the traditional form of the theatre, or aping the barbarous and suffocating magnificence of London, New York and Chicago 'Palaces'.[49]

Shand, in his enthusiasm for the modern, was able to regard Germany without prejudice and with considerable understanding.

> In considering the present trend of cinema design, the fact that Modernist architecture has been adopted in Germany with far greater enthusiasm and on a far wider scale than here or

in America must not be overlooked. . . . Many of the pioneers of Modernism and concrete construction were Germans: men who had been striving to rescue sincerity of structure and the beauty of plain surface and simple proportion from the welter of excrescent ornamentation which was sapping the vitality of architecture. They got their chance when the old *régime* was overthrown, and used it to the full. . . . One of the most striking things about these cinemas is how few of them have seriously begun to 'date' compared to contemporary British and American picture houses.

Furthermore, 'German cinemas cost much less cubic foot for cubic foot than do English ones.'[50] In consequence, they were influential. The clean horizontal lines and curves of Erich Mendelsohn's UFA Universum Kino in Berlin were admired and imitated in the 1930s; more particularly, its prow-like fin above the entrance, together with the fin-tower on the Roxy-Palast in Berlin by Martin Punitzer, led the cinema designer Julian Leathart to design a similar feature on Dreamland at Margate in 1934, and this became the hallmark of Odeon cinemas. Indeed, the style adopted by Oscar Deutsch, founder of the Odeon circuit, to some extent represented the triumph of Morton Shand's advocacy of German modernism. To quote the historian of British cinema architecture, Richard Gray:

> The arrival of the mature Odeon style represents a sea-change in the thinking of what a cinema could be. Architecturally, there was a basic reversal of emphasis from interior to exterior. Gone were the elaborate interiors, be they classical or in some oriental fancy dress, and in their stead were clean-lined interiors with a minimum of decoration. . . . At last a 'cinema style' had arrived, in a fusion of a suitable entertainment architecture with popular heroic modernism – the latter a concept which appealed to the film industry's thinking about itself at the time.[51]

New Victoria Theatre, Wilton Road, London (E. Wamsley Lewis and W. E. Trent, 1930)

The interiors of Berlin's large and spectacular cinemas were certainly influential. When E. Wamsley Lewis won a travelling scholarship to study theatre design in 1927, he visited Germany as well as the United States; the stalactite lighting pendants in Hans Poelzig's Capitol were used in the exotic interior of his innovative New Victoria cinema, completed in 1930, a building which Morton Shand thought 'very German-looking' (Plate 18).[52]

Other elements in this 'mermaid's palace' derived from Oskar Kaufmann's cinemas in Berlin. Not everyone was impressed. Sidney Bernstein was sure that 'People don't want this sort of thing; they want architecture with marble columns, gilt and mirrors. This won't pay.'[53] But it did. Even so, although the New Victoria came in under budget, Lewis never designed another cinema.

In 1930, the designer Oliver P. Bernard – just then working on his illuminated glass and chrome new entrance to the Strand Palace Hotel – visited Berlin and found that 'today it is probably the most extensively organised place of entertainment in the world; it is certainly the most interesting capital of architectural development in Europe.' What particularly interested him were social conditions, and he concluded that:

> Country houses for gentlemen, and more palatial premises for bankers, are still an architectural obsession in little Britain, where hundreds of thousands of families lack adequate space, light, and air to live in. Those who explore the domestic development of Berlin, Stuttgart, Dusseldorf, and even Vienna, may discover that the cities of defeated Empires have triumphed by their examples of progress in living. Art, design, and craft, and their professional distinctions, are worthless until every man, woman and child is allotted an adequate minimum of living accommodation.[54]

The housing schemes in Germany such as those designed by Bruno Taut in Berlin and Frankfurt certainly attracted the attention of architects and planners, but the principal source of ideas for new public housing was Vienna, where, by 1933, some 60,000 dwellings had been erected by the post-war Social Democrat government. Most of these were in large urban blocks of apartments, of which the most visited was the Karl-Marx-Hof. This was a model adopted in Leeds to deal with that city's notorious housing problems. In the pamphlet *Decent Housing for All*, published in 1933 by the clergyman and social reformer Charles Jenkinson, it was recorded how impressed the West Yorkshire Society of Architects was by its visit to the Austrian capital and seeing new blocks of public housing in which every flat had window-boxes. Leeds attempted to emulate this in the Quarry Hill flats, which rose like an urban fortress at the east end of Blomfield's new Headrow after 1934. The elliptical entrance arches which penetrated the long eight-storey blocks were a direct reference to the Karl-Marx-Hof, although the remorselessly horizontal banding which organised the fenestration reflected the admiration of the architect and housing-director, R. A. H. Livett, for Mendelsohn's department stores. Similar ideas influenced the

Quarry Hill Flats, Leeds (R. A. H. Livett, 1938)

St Andrew's Gardens, Liverpool (Lancelot Keay, 1935)

St Andrew's Gardens, Liverpool
(Lancelot Keay, 1935)

appearance of the later housing schemes designed for Liverpool by Lancelot Keay.

Architectural historians like to identify particular details in buildings, but influences were usually diverse and synthetic. What is clear is that Northern European modern architecture had a profound and stimulating impact on Britain. It can be documented, in particular, in the celebrated stations designed in the 1930s by Charles Holden for the London Passenger Transport Board. Holden had already designed his abstracted monumental stone-faced stations on the Northern Line to Morden for Frank Pick, general manager of the LPTB, but a marked change in approach and style had occurred by the time he came to design the stations on the extension to the Piccadilly Line – in part the result of a tour of Holland, Germany, Denmark and Sweden in the summer of 1930. Holden travelled with Pick and W. P. N. Edwards (secretary to Lord Ashfield, chairman of the LPTB), and their impressions were recorded by Edwards in a document entitled *A Note on Contemporary Architecture in Northern Europe*. In this, the two prevalent manners of expressing building frames – the emphasis on verticality and the horizontal line – were examined: 'The new emphasis on the horizontal element is . . . the result, partly of the new steel and concrete construction and the flat roof which usually goes with it, and partly the new ideas of functionalism.' And 'functionalism', Edwards concluded, 'does not take anything on faith and, in revolting against the indiscriminate use of the details of the past, it has contributed towards a simplification of design which, if it has been carried too far in some directions, is at least a sure foundation for the development of a new architecture'.[55]

The simple, utilitarian expression of structure in such buildings as Bussum Station near Hilversum can be seen in the clean, spare booking halls consisting of a reinforced-concrete frame with a brick facing and metal framed windows. In the most illustrated and admired of them all, at Arnos Grove, with its circular hall, can be seen an echo of the great drum of Asplund's Stockholm City Library. Like Asplund, Holden sought modernity through abstracting the simple volumes of neo-Classicism, and at Arnos Grove and other stations a simplified concrete cornice completes the symmetrical elegance of the form (Plate 6). Writing in 1940, J. M. Richards claimed that the LPTB had established as high a standard of design as was once set by the taste of an aristocracy. 'Not only are its Underground Stations,' he wrote (being 'often placed in instructive contrast in the middle of the worst bogus Tudor housing estates'), 'the most satisfactory series of modern buildings in England, but all the details of their equipment – signs, lettering, staircases, and litter-baskets, and the lay-out and typography of time-tables – are well thought out and in a consistent modern taste.'[56] And that taste owed much to Northern Europe and Scandinavia.

Perhaps the supreme example of the positive influence of Northern European modern brick architecture in the 1920s is the Shakespeare Memorial Theatre at Stratford-upon-Avon. For Anthony Bertram, it was 'a remarkable triumph. There was a danger there, not so much of vulgarity as of some absurd bogus Tudor arty-crafty affair that would have tried hard not to look like a big modern theatre.'[57] Furthermore, this important and much-admired structure was historically significant, not least for being the first public building in Britain to be designed by a woman. The old theatre, a Gothic Revival building dating from the 1870s, had been largely destroyed by fire in 1926; in the open international competition for a new building held in 1928, the design by the twenty-nine-year old Elisabeth Scott – a relation of the great Scott dynasty – was chosen by the assessors out of seventy-two entries

(Plate 13). Scott was working for Maurice Chesterton at the time of the competition;* although Chesterton disclaimed 'any personal share whatever in the successful design', prejudice ensured that rumours abounded to the effect that it was not really her own work.[58]

The new Shakespeare Memorial Theatre was faced in red brick rather than stone. Scott redesigned the interior after being sent on a tour of modern theatres in Germany by William Bridges-Adams, the theatre's director, and a German influence may be detected in the vertical brick ribbing and the figure sculpture by Eric Kennington carved into the brickwork. But no single influence can be detected; Scott was successful in gently adapting Northern European modern brick architecture to English conditions. Contemporaries were impressed by the decorative stylishness of the foyers and the staircase and the unprecedented modernity of the whole conception. It was not, however, quite what Stratford had expected; Maxwell Fry described how, at the opening ceremony in 1932,

> The vast crowd moved through the streets, gay with paper flowers, maypoles and English Morris-dancing and a vision sustained it . . . Trailing such clouds of national glory moved the crowd, making for the new theatre by the river. And as it came into sight the vision paled and faltered, for there against a background which photography has firmly implanted in the English mind as for ever to be associated with Elizabethan England stood a great building that was foreign. . . . No doubt timber-framing was expected, and the new brick was very red.[59]

---

* Scott had been assisted in preparing the competition drawings by two fellow students at the Architectural Association, Alison Sleigh and J. C. Shepherd, and the partnership of Scott, Chesterton & Shepherd was formed in 1929 to carry out the commission. Sir Geoffrey Jellicoe, who had been in partnership with Shepherd, recorded in the *Architects' Journal* (12 July 1972, p. 68), that 'in the partnership, Scott provided the initiative, Chesterton the administration and Shepherd the flair'.

Shakespeare Memorial Theatre, Stratford-on-Avon, Warwickshire (Elisabeth Scott, 1932)

As for Sir Edward Elgar, he refused to go inside as he found it 'so unspeakably ugly and wrong'.[60] Nevertheless, a whole issue of the *Architectural Review* was devoted to the new theatre. But ideas of modernity rapidly changed in the 1930s, and Nikolaus Pevsner later wrote that:

> The building strikes us now as being very dated, in its blocky brick shape and its playing with bricks as a chief decorative element – the one inspired by Holland, the other by North Germany.... Modern minded members of the Design and Industries Association from Birmingham showed it proudly to Gropius one day in 1934 or 1935, and it was embarrassing to see his embarrassment.[61]

But there is no reason today why Elisabeth Scott's masterpiece should be compared with the Bauhaus, and as Pevsner had the grace to admit, 'Taken in its English context of 1930, however, it can surely be appreciated, and it has aged well – better than *beton brut* will.'[62]

The influence of Southern Europe on British architecture would seem to have been rather less than that of the Nordic and Teutonic North. This is perhaps surprising as Italy was the traditional destination for British architects, and throughout the interwar decades prize-winning architectural students spent time in Rome. In fulfilment of the Classical ideals of Edwardian educational reformers, the Faculty of Architecture of the British School at Rome was established in 1913.[63] The first winner of the Rome Prize, in 1913, was the Liverpool student Harold Chalton Bradshaw. Bradshaw later simplified and completed the School's building in the Valle Giulia which had been begun by Lutyens, having started life as the British Pavilion at the Rome International Exhibition of 1911.[64] However, the students who were sent to Rome either as winners of the Rome Prize or of the RIBA's Henry Jarvis Prize seem to have been influenced neither by Ancient Roman structures nor by modern Italian architecture. A remarkable number later achieved fame not as Classicists but as Modernists: Amyas Connell, Basil Ward, George Checkley, William Holford, Marshall Sisson.[65] In 1933 Lutyens visited the school to interview a rebellious prize-winner, R. Pearce Hubbard: 'Very good looking, conceited through his own virility, gone off on the German Corbusier tack, bored with having to go through a course of measuring ancient buildings, to no useful purpose, as they have all been measured 100 times before.'[66]

Few British architects or writers seem to have been interested in modern Italian architecture, although something of the Mannerist whimsical spirit of the 'Novecento' style of Giovanni Muzio might be detected in the playfully Baroque decorative interiors of the 1920s designed by Oliver Hill or by Philip Hepworth and his sometime partner Grey Wornum. In their book on *Architecture Here and Now*, published in 1934, Clough Williams-Ellis and John Summerson insisted that the

> great tradition of grandiose building is so ingrained in Italian architects that it still rules almost everything they do. Modern

architecture, as it is understood in Germany or Holland, is hardly adaptable to pompous and grandiloquent ideas, so the Italians have not had much to do with it. They have made a Modernism of their own, which is just as theatrical as their old architecture, but much more adaptable to new materials.[67]

This 'Italian Modernism' was to be seen in Mussolini's favourite architect and town-planner, Marcello Piacentini (1881–1960). Even so, Italian Rationalist architecture would seem to have had similarly little influence on Britain, although the proud, integrated sans-serif capitals of the lettering carved on the Institute of Hygiene and Tropical Medicine in London of 1926–28 by P. Morley Horder and Verner O. Rees might suggest a Fascist influence. Nor did the Italian proponents of the International Style, tolerated by Mussolini until 1938, attract as much attention as their German and French associates; J. M. Richards noted in 1940 that 'Italian architects until recently produced some admirable modern buildings which, overshadowed by the rather showy modernity of her official buildings, have never been given the credit as serious contributions to the mass of modern European architecture which is their due'.[68]

One British architect who seems to have followed developments in Italy was Jack Coia, who was himself Italian in origin. Coia, who inherited the Glasgow firm of Gillespie, Kidd & Coia, had been born in Wolverhampton to itinerant Italian parents, and he designed several striking Roman Catholic churches which betray knowledge of modern churches in Italy. St Anne's, Dennistoun, is in a Romanesque manner with unusual brick detailing over the round-arched windows. The best is St Columbkille's, Rutherglen, in which the Early Christian style is given an Art Deco flavour.

The textured brickwork on the church of St Peter in Chains at Ardrossan, with its Swedish-looking tower, would seem to show the influence of Dudok and Ostberg rather than Piacentini, but this may have been the work of Coia's sometime partner, T. Warnett Kennedy (Plate 8).

Left: St Columba's Catholic Church, Glasgow, Scotland (Gillespie, Kidd & Coia, 1941)
Right: St Peter in Chains, Ardrossan, Scotland (Gillespie, Kidd & Coia, 1938)

For most British architects, the interest of Italy was historical rather than modern. Perhaps the most imaginative tribute to its perennial appeal was Portmeirion, the personal fantasy village built by Clough Williams-Ellis in a secluded cove of the Welsh coast (Plate 9). The inspiration for this was Picturesque: the ideal of an Italian hill town, with a variety of colourful buildings clustered around a baroque steeple. He had been introduced to Portofino by the sculptor Eric Kennington, and in the guidebook Christopher Hussey wrote of 'the dream citadel that had shot up out of wood and water like a fragment of Amalfi or Sorrento'.[69] At Portmeirion, begun in 1925, Williams-Ellis artfully combined architectural fragments rescued from demolished buildings with colour-washed new structures designed in a playful Baroque manner, an aesthetic which was as much modern Swedish as old Italian. Clough Williams-Ellis was an indifferent architect, but he was a good writer and a powerful campaigner against the contemporary tendencies that were spoiling the landscape of Britain. Portmeirion may be in essence stage

Ossulston Estate, Somers Town, London (G. Topham Forrest, 1931)

scenery, but it was intended as an object lesson in how buildings could enhance a landscape. It showed that, for all the talk of progress and modernity, neither the Picturesque tradition nor the romantic, nostalgic impulse in British architecture could easily be eradicated.

Last but not least, there was France, Britain's ally during the late war but, by the later 1920s, regarded once more with ambivalence. Those Edwardians who had been instrumental in establishing architectural schools in Britain to teach Classical values naturally still regarded the École des Beaux-Arts with respect. Modern French architecture, however, did not at first seem particularly inspiring; Howard Robertson later recalled that, compared with Holland, Sweden and Germany, 'France exerted very little influence except in matters of detail.'[70] A few years later, Williams-Ellis and Summerson warned that, 'although we must not deceive ourselves into thinking that England is doing particularly well, it is worth remembering that not every building abroad is a model of sense and excellence. In France and Belgium, for instance, the general level of design is far from good, and well below that of either Sweden or Germany.[71] The most admired new French buildings were the churches of the first great master of reinforced-concrete construction, Auguste Perret. Perret's war memorial church of Notre-Dame du Raincy clearly inspired England's leading Modernist church architect, N. F. Cachemaille-Day, when he designed the Church of St Michael and All Angels, Wythenshawe, in a suburb of Manchester.

By the mid-1920s, some architects were aware of the work of Michel Roux-Spitz and of the assertively Cubist buildings of Robert Mallet-Stevens. Writing of his group of houses in Paris, Howard Robertson considered that 'Mallet-Stevens has a light touch. His houses are less austere than those of Le Corbusier, and are therefore, in a popular sense, more pleasing.' Nevertheless, they 'are expressions of the French passion for logic, and strict logic, as opposed to the broader teaching of the humanities, is apt to be a little depressing'.[72] Robertson, who had been at the Beaux-Arts and was particularly interested in French architecture, observed perceptively in 1926 that:

> The so called art nouveau, which is almost universally condemned today as an unpleasing phase of artistic expression, is largely responsible, we believe, for the very interesting developments which are just now taking place in France, and in England there will almost certainly take place a revival of the applications of the art nouveau principles with an expression so different that its parentage may at first sight appear little evident.[73]

Two years later he published Yerbury's photographs of *Examples of Modern French Architecture*, which included 'work which will be universally admitted as sanely *evolutionary* in character side by side with work which is frankly *revolutionary*'.[74] This, of course, was the work of Le Corbusier.

Charles-Édouard Jeanneret, or 'Le Corbusier' (1887–1965), was usually perceived in Britain as being French rather than Swiss. The English translation of his *Vers une Architecture* appeared in 1927 and the following year a reviewer recorded that, 'The fame of Le Corbusier . . . percolated to our islands some four years ago.'[75] Later that same year, P. M. Stratton asserted that:

> The French modernists have made so great an impression in England with their new impulse that there must surely have been room for their ideas. It is a dubious compliment to two nations to say their argument has rushed like wind into a vacuum; but at least le Corbusier's book in Mr Etchells' spirited translation has raised a storm.[76]

At first, however, Le Corbusier was known not for his buildings but for his ideas, powerfully conveyed in his polemical text and by the brilliant use of images: of ships, cars and aeroplanes juxtaposed with Greek temples. Younger British architects soon grasped the message 'that a house should be a machine and, like it, should be built efficiently'.[77] As far as John Gloag was concerned, writing in 1931,

> For over a century France has been a land that is kind to new ideas. . . . Sometimes we recognise in the artistic discoveries of France an old friend in new clothes, and recently we have been introduced to an old friend whose clothes have been removed. Nudity needs no excuse in France, but for the benefit of English decorum it is carefully explained that we are being presented to a scientific discovery, not an artistic one.[78]

For most British architects, the first encounter with this alarming new architecture came in 1925 if they visited Paris to see the *Exposition Internationale des Arts Décoratifs et Industriels Modernes*. There, by the banks of the Seine, they could seek out Le Corbusier's Pavillon de l'Esprit Nouveau and Melnikov's Soviet Pavilion, which Howard

Robertson considered an 'economic solution but looked rather like an aeroplane falling through a garage'.[79] There was also Mallet-Stevens's Pavillon du Tourism, whose De Stijl-influenced campanile would inspire a much bigger tower the following decade: Tommy Tait's tower in Bellahouston Park, Glasgow, for the 1938 Empire Exhibition. This 'odd crossing of the top-part of an upright by a few sharply projecting horizontals' was, Pevsner considered, 'a strangely aggressive motif, typically 1920 in its violence and jazziness'.[80] Most of the national pavilions in Paris were rather more accessible and sympathetic essays in the various national modern styles designed by leading national architects.

What most impressed visitors, however, were the official French pavilions and their luxurious and desirable contents. The French decorative arts were notable both for their fine, traditional craftsmanship and for the novelty of expression. Not for nothing did the 1925 Paris Expo give rise to the term 'Art Déco' to describe the new artistic spirit of the time. Even the elderly Arts and Crafts designer Henry Wilson was impressed, and wrote in the official British report that 'The Paris Exhibition, its variety, its multitudinousness, its unending vitality, its instant ever-changing appeal was a thing that no report can render. . . . It was radiant promise, to which was added much brilliant performance. It was partly realised prophecy. Everything was in bud: the germination of new ideas was visible everywhere.'[81] Looking back fourteen years later, Nikolaus Pevsner concluded that 'The Paris Exhibition of 1925 can be regarded as the fountainhead of the Modern Movement in Britain. Several of the most opposed tendencies in architecture and decoration are to be traced back to it.'[82] These he categorised as, first, *'French Florid'*, which was usually too rich and sensuous to be taken up, and, secondly, *'Jazz*, that type of vulgar jagged ornament which swamped Britain immediately after the exhibition and did not lose its appeal until the beginning of the thirties'. The Modernist architect R. A. Duncan agreed:

Unfortunately, the exhibition had the undesirable result of letting loose a flood of sensationalism, which the age, with its inherent vulgarity, has been quick to seize upon. . . . This modernist phase of New Art has become identified with places of amusement, the flashier restaurants and shops; it has been rather aptly dubbed the 'Jewish Renaissance'.[83]

'Art is becoming international,' wrote Vernon Blake in the *Architectural Review*, 'hence the idea itself of this exhibition': 'We are at the entrance of a new epoch in art as in other manifestations of human activity.'[84] Similarly, Hubert de Cronin Hastings, soon to become editor of the *Architectural Review*, was sure that it was 'quite clear that a modern expression has arrived':

> If we contemplate jazz music, French furniture and painting, Swedish architecture, dress design, interior decoration, literature, whatever way we look we see new expressive forms taking over the emotional intention of old. The process is slow, but inevitable. Convalescence begins to set in after the distemper of the war, and vitality grows. The Paris exhibition may be taken as a gesture for modern international art.[85]

This new spirit even affected the British Pavilion, despite it having no clear national identity. For many, that was a mercy; the British presence at earlier exhibitions had usually been housed in a reproduction of an Elizabethan mansion or in Tudor half-timber. As Lawrence Weaver, who had been in charge of the exhibits at the Wembley exhibition the year before, observed, 'The people who had expected to see a Jacobean house were tragically disappointed, and it is a good thing they were disappointed.'[86] What they saw instead was an eclectic structure designed by Easton & Robertson that combined an attenuated Swedish Baroque with the plain walling of Spanish Colonial; some arches were elliptical, some were polygonal, while part of the interior of the pavilion was decorated like a Gothic

British Pavilion, Paris Exposition (Easton & Robertson, 1925)

church and the restaurant overlooking the Seine was covered by a hand-painted tent roof. The young architect Frank Scarlett and the painter Marjorie Townley, who worked on the Pavilion, later recalled that the impression it made was 'predominantly ecclesiastical'.[87] The French were, on the whole, astonished: 'Why the motley-coloured plaster, the glass steeple with the galleon perched on it like a weathercock? Is this all that old Albion can bring us? A fantasy created in an opium den by a retired colonel?'[88] Hastings thought it came 'hot from the Architectural Association pantomime'.[89] This allusion to the theatrical suggests another important influence on Britain at the time: the colourful exotic glamour of Diaghilev's *Ballets Russes* and the sets and costumes by Bakst.

Hastings was not, however, being unkind to the architects of the British Pavilion. 'The peculiar interest of this design,' he concluded, 'is that it is perhaps, before everything, a product of the Architectural Association... And this is apt, for the Architectural Association is the English exponent of Modernism. It is good that its influence should begin to be felt.'[90] British architects in the 1920s were conservative, but they were cautiously becoming less insular. They clung to the belief that architecture must evolve in response to local conditions, but they increasingly felt that it was necessary to try to give expression to the technological and social changes that were transforming the country; to try to be modern. And modernity was to be found across the English Channel, as well as across the Atlantic.

The New Architecture was deliberately cosmopolitan, as old Sir Reginald Blomfield complained:

> For myself I am prejudiced enough to detest cosmopolitanism. I cannot conceive anything more dull and uninteresting than a dead level of standardised architecture, and a culture organised on mechanical lines is a contradiction in terms. I am for the hill on which I was born; French for the French, Germany for the German, England for the Englishman, and in saying this I do not for one instant mean to suggest international jealousy and hostility. Each people with a great historic past has its own tradition, its own profound and unalterable instincts, and it should pursue its destiny in accordance with those traditions without losing its regard for others and that admiration which we feel for those who maintain their self respect. In this way only can there be a real League of Nations.[91]

Amongst architects between the wars, however, this was increasingly a minority view.

CHAPTER FOUR

BRAVE NEW WORLD

———◆———

Wʜᴇɴ Eᴛᴄʜᴇʟʟs's translation of Le Corbusier's *Towards a New Architecture* appeared in 1927, the frontispiece was the thirty-two-storey Telephone Building in New York City, which had been completed the year before to the design of Ralph Walker of Voorhees, Gmelin & Walker. The message was clear: the future was high, and it already existed across the Atlantic. But it was not only Continental modernists who were enraptured by the glamour of New York and building high; British architects were similarly captivated by the New World and did their best to rebuild London in the image of New York and Chicago.

In his book *London in My Time*, published in 1934, the novelist and writer Thomas Burke suggested that:

> The first quarter of this century, indeed, may be known to history as London's American Phase, since the major part of the many and rapid changes it has suffered may be traced to America. Our tube railways we owe to America. The bulk of our entertainment is American in quality and largely in personnel. All our latest hotels

derive from American models. Our snack-bars and all-night supper stands are pirated from America. Our electric night-signs are an American idea. Our street songs are American. Our popular press models itself on American journalism, and on our bookstalls English periodicals lie smothered and half-seen under piles of American magazines. Our newest buildings, where they are not German or Swedish, are American.[1]

New standards of comfort were also American. As far as Raymond Myerscough-Walker was concerned, central heating was 'the one thing, apart from the Dolly Sisters, that we have to thank America for': 'Sensible people now take it for granted that central heating shall be laid on.'[2]

America was increasingly responsible for what was changing the Old World: through technology, through popular culture and through politics. Not only had the United States intervened decisively in the Great War in 1917, but President Woodrow Wilson had been instrumental in redrawing much of the map of Europe at Versailles, albeit with disastrous consequences. After the Armistice, as Robert Graves and Alan Hodge noted at the beginning of another war,

> The Americans now regarded themselves as the leading nation in the world, with most of the world's royal metal in their safe-deposit vaults as a proof of this, and with the indisputable glory of having decided the issue of the war, not so much by what they did as by what they threatened to do. Their national exuberance and the lead they gave in all social fashions, while withdrawing politically from co-operation in 'restoring world-order', is a leading factor in the 1918–39 period.[3]

The telephone was an American invention, as was the gramophone; and it was two Americans who had finally conquered the air in 1903. Other momentous technical innovations may have been European in genesis but they were developed on the other side of the Atlantic.

The mass-produced motor car was an American achievement, and American cars were admired for speed and reliability. Above all, perhaps, there were the movies. The cinematograph may have been first developed in France, but even before the war Hollywood had begun to dominate the film industry. German films were screened in Britain in the 1920s, but, especially after the advent of the 'talkies' in 1928, it was American films that most appealed to British audiences.

Links with America became closer, and speedier. Although in 1919 Alcock and Brown's Vickers Vimy was the first aeroplane to cross the Atlantic, and subsequent pioneering flights by Charles Lindbergh and others generated much enthusiasm, almost all visitors to the United States were obliged to travel by sea. The interwar years were the heyday of the great ocean liners, when the Atlantic was traversed by huge, comfortable and safe ships that seemed like floating cities. When illustrated in books, famous ships were often depicted beached in urban settings to give an idea of their size. Great liners like the *Queen Mary* and the *Normandie* were glamorous, practical symbols of national pride, and their design had a strong influence on architecture on land. But it was the skyscraper rather than the liner that became the principal symbol of modernity. A particularly revealing image is the 1926 painting by the architect William Walcot entitled *The Savoy As It Will Appear in the Year 2000*. In this optimistic depiction of the Thames, the Savoy is the base of a huge, hollow skyscraper into which is floating the New York–London airship.

After the war, the United States found itself comparatively rich and a creditor nation for the first time in over half a century. The situation in Britain was the reverse. The Treasury's anxiety about repaying wartime loans was responsible for the economies which dogged the building of the new British Embassy in Washington DC, first designed by Lutyens in 1924. American businesses were now investing in London and introducing new standards of comfort. A telling example was the purchase by an American consortium in 1925 of an unfinished steel frame in Piccadilly, planned as an hotel before the war by the German owner of the Curzon Hotel. Its leading figure was Harry Wardman, the Yorkshire-born contractor who went on to build the Washington Embassy. The Piccadilly building was completed in 1927 to the designs of a British firm, Messrs Tanner. The best feature of the Park Lane Hotel was the Art Deco ballroom, while Wardman ensured the hotel provided American standards of luxury and, for the first time in Britain, 'every room [was] to have a bath'.[4]

British architects had taken an interest in American architecture for some time. Unlike the Dutch and Germans, they had paid little attention paid to the domestic work of Frank Lloyd Wright; what seemed important were large urban buildings with steel frames supporting masonry architecture. J. J. Burnet had visited New York and Chicago, Charles Holden and Thomas S. Tait had also visited North America, while C. H. Reilly made the first of many visits in 1909. Immediately after the war, Robert Atkinson went to study architectural education and cinemas, Giles Scott went later to look at libraries, and Vincent Harris had crossed the Atlantic no fewer than five times by 1939. Then there was the curious case of Alfred Bossom, who went to the United States in 1903, built up a practice designing unremarkable but efficient multi-storey commercial buildings in places like Richmond, Virginia, and Houston, Texas, and finally returned home with his fortune made in 1926 to become a Conservative politician. Having steered the Architects' Registration Bill through Parliament, he was made one of the first Life Peers after retiring as MP for Maidstone.[5]

Although skyscrapers were not possible in London, owing to the London County Council's strict insistence on a height limit of eighty feet to the principal cornice, much was learned from the United States about giving coherent architectural expression to multi-storey commercial buildings. Burnet's pre-war Kodak House on Kingsway was one of the first to face intervening floors in metal, leaving the masonry-clad vertical stanchions to be read as giant columns or pilasters. This was a treatment adopted with particular panache in the interwar years by Leo Sylvester Sullivan, a founder member of London's Beaux-Arts *atelier* in 1912, for the façades of his offices in

Kodak House, Kingsway, London (John Burnet, 1911)

the City of London. Although they were *néo-Grec* in style, Sullivan gave these buildings a greater vertical emphasis than was compatible with strict Classical models, with coherent, subtle and stylish results. One of the best was the warehouse for Courtauld's in St Martin's Le Grand, built in 1924–25, where 'the close-set verticals owe much to such Chicago firms as Holabird and Roche'.[6]

One reason for the growing interest in American architecture was the campaign to establish academic schools of architecture in Britain. In the early years of the century, the Architectural Association in London and the schools of architecture in Liverpool and Glasgow were reorganised on the general model of the École des Beaux-Arts in Paris, where many Americans, a few Scots and virtually no Englishmen had been trained. In awe of French sophistication and increasingly embarrassed by the seemingly amateurish eclecticism of the past century, British architects aspired to the Grand Manner. But, as Alan Powers, the historian of Edwardian architectural education, has observed, they also responded to 'the impression that the Promised Land for architects lay over the Atlantic', where the grandest manner was to be found and Paris-trained designers were applying the historic styles of Europe to banks, office buildings and railway stations.[7]

C. H. Reilly, appointed to the Liverpool school in 1904, adopted Beaux-Arts methods at one remove and built connections with the United States, sending his best students to work in New York offices. Glasgow went one better and in that same year, 1904, invited a Beaux-Arts prize-winning Frenchman, Eugène Bourdon, to be head of a new, combined school of architecture. Bourdon's task was also to counteract the Mackintosh 'New Art' influence and to direct his students towards the academic Classicism of America, where he had briefly worked.[8] He was killed on the first day of the Battle of the Somme while fighting in the French Army, but his influence continued in Glasgow in the several big Classical steel-framed commercial buildings raised in the city in the 1920s, buildings which would not look out of place in Detroit or Montreal.

Bourdon's pupils at the Glasgow School of Architecture included A. T. Scott, who became Sir Herbert Baker's chief assistant in London, responsible in particular for the firm's large Classical banks, but the best of them was Richard W. M. Gunn, who, as a student, had expressed admiration for the Chicago buildings of Louis Sullivan. Having survived the war, Gunn became chief assistant to the prolific Glasgow architect James Miller, and was entirely responsible for the 1924 competition-winning design for the Union Bank of Scotland chief office in St Vincent Street. With its large, top-lit banking hall, double-height basement and giant order of pilasters uniting several storeys and rising to an oversailing cornice, the building was strongly influenced by York & Sawyer's Guaranty Trust Building in New York of 1913. Later, in the Commercial Bank of Scotland in Bothwell Street, built in 1934–35 after Gunn's early death, the conventional cornice was replaced by a tall attic with set-backs, giving the building that abstracted monumental feel typical of the decade and reminiscent of the work of the French-American Paul Cret.

Further along Bothwell Street are the huge premises of the Scottish Legal Assurance Society of 1927–31. This was designed by

Union Bank of Scotland, Glasgow, Scotland (Richard Gunn, 1927)

Edward G. Wylie, a pupil both of Burnet and of Bourdon, who had entered into partnership with Alexander Wright, lately returned from Canada. Other steel-framed, stone-clad American Classical buildings in the Second City of the British Empire were designed by A. Graham Henderson, the New Zealander who had taught at the Glasgow School under Bourdon and who had replaced Mackintosh in the office of Honeyman & Keppie. Henderson had won the 1914 competition for reorganising Glasgow Cross for the firm and, as executed in 1922, the Mercat Building there has a giant exedra like that at Bush House in London. Not everyone, however, was happy with Glasgow looking to America. No doubt remembering the days at the turn of the century when the city was evolving its own progressive 'New Art' manner, Mackintosh's associate, James Salmon, insisted that:

From the point of view of the creative architect, America, great as she is, is less inspiring than almost any other country.* Her architects are products of the hot-house schools of Paris, trained in rigid styles by the French architect dominie. Architecture has never been understood by the French. . . . The Americans suffer from having gone to school there instead of – playing truant.[9]

C. H. Reilly was so entranced by American Classicism that, in 1924, he published a short eulogy of McKim, Mead & White in the Ernest Benn series on 'Masters of Architecture'. The architects' skill and sophistication in adapting Italian Renaissance precedents for modern commercial use was not universally admired. 'They were the high priests of the genteel tradition in American architecture,' wrote an anonymous reviewer in the *New Statesman*:

> Compared with most modern English architecture, this American stuff is harmless enough. But a thousand McKims, Meads and Whites would not make an architectural summer . . . The trouble really is that architecture at the moment needs a genius. There is a lack, not of talent, but of inspiration. The art of building has not yet found its Cézanne or its Wagner, much less its Picasso or its Stravinsky. . . . But if the Baedeckers of the future double-star any buildings of the present age, they are, we hope, less likely to be these monuments of opulent pastiche than an occasional skyscraper, factory or block of flats, whose architect has refused to imitate past work, and has relied

---

* David Walker (1989) notes that there is a draft of a lecture among Salmon's papers at the Royal Commission on the Ancient and Historical Monuments of Scotland in which America is criticised: 'America's antediluvian ideas & want of originality is a great hindrance to architectural development. Many people have an idea that Americans are original. That shows a great error in the conception of originality. Of course they have done everything that has been done by anybody else and done it broader, thicker, deeper, higher, harder, longer and quicker but then these qualities don't make it a new thing.'

upon his knowledge of material and his feeling for mass. As an antidote to Professor Reilly we would suggest Monsieur Corbusier-Saugnier's *Vers une Architecture*.* For in spite of the author's exclamatory style and sometimes extravagant theories, it is at once more sensible and more imaginative than any other book on the modern practice of the art.[10]

Le Corbusier's polemic had yet to be translated into English; the weekly magazine was demonstrating that it was more in touch with architectural thinking than the contemporary professional papers.

Few of the Glasgow architects had actually seen the American buildings they imitated, but many of the products of the Liverpool School of Architecture certainly had; Reilly had got to know several of the leading New York architects and arranged for them to work in their offices. Students who enjoyed these six-month stints in America included E. Maxwell Fry, who went to the office of Carrère & Hastings and later recalled how, at Liverpool, 'We imbibed the Renaissance as the architecture of humanism extolled by Geoffrey Scott, but it came to us monitored by America.'[11] Liverpool, like Glasgow, was a great port city with close links to America and was the home of several shipping lines, notably Cunard and White Star. The Adelphi Hotel, rebuilt immediately before the war by Frank Atkinson for travellers embarking for or arriving from America, was self-consciously transatlantic in style. The architect who was almost entirely responsible for giving Liverpool an American air was one of Reilly's first pupils, Herbert J. Rowse. After arriving at the Liverpool school in 1906, he had worked for F. W. Simon, who opened an office in Winnipeg and took Rowse there with him. He then worked in Chicago and New York, where, he told Reilly,

---

* [The French edition supplied the author's name as Corbusier-Saugnier, the joint pseudonym of Corbusier and Amédée Ozenfant ('Saugnier'), its true collaborators. In its English translation, it was credited to Corbusier alone. RH.]

he took three months to determine whether he would stay for good on the other side with all its temptations of immediate practice – tempting partnerships being offered him – or return to England to make use of his American experience here. Wisely, I think, he determined on the latter course, and never has he had a moment's cause to regret his decision.[12]

Water Street in Liverpool, running from the town hall to the monumental Edwardian piles at Pierhead, is dominated by two large commercial blocks that might have strayed from, say, Montreal (Plate 11). Both were designed by Rowse and made his reputation; both were won in competition. That for India Buildings, for Alfred Holt & Co., owners of the Blue Funnel Line, was assessed by Giles Scott in 1924; that for Martins Bank, on the opposite side of the street, was assessed by Reilly.

The tall stone-clad bulk of both blocks is relieved by exquisite Classical detail. India Buildings boasts a vaulted arcade of shops

Adelphi Hotel, Liverpool (Frank Atkinson, 1914)

India Buildings, Liverpool (Herbert J. Rowse, 1932)

1. St Martin's Garrison Church, New Delhi, India (Arthur Shoosmith, 1930)

2. Cambridge University Library, Cambridge (Giles Gilbert Scott, 1934)

3. Scottish National War Memorial, Edinburgh, Scotland (Robert Lorimer, 1927)

4. Viceroy's House (Rashtrapati Bhavan), New Delhi, India (Edwin Lutyens, 1929)

5. Middleton Park, Middleton Stoney, Oxfordshire (Edwin Lutyens, with Robert Lutyens, 1938)

6. Arnos Grove Underground Station, London (Charles Holden; Adams, Holden & Pearson, 1932)

7. St Saviour's Church, Eltham, Greater London (N. F. Cachemaille-Day, 1933)

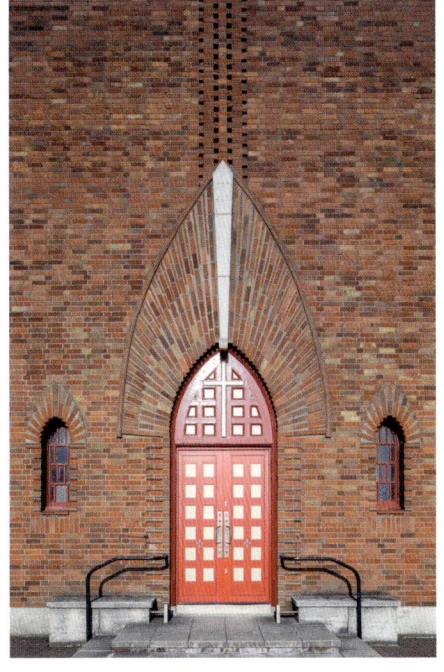

8. St Peter in Chains, Ardrossan, Scotland (Gillespie, Kidd & Coia, 1938)

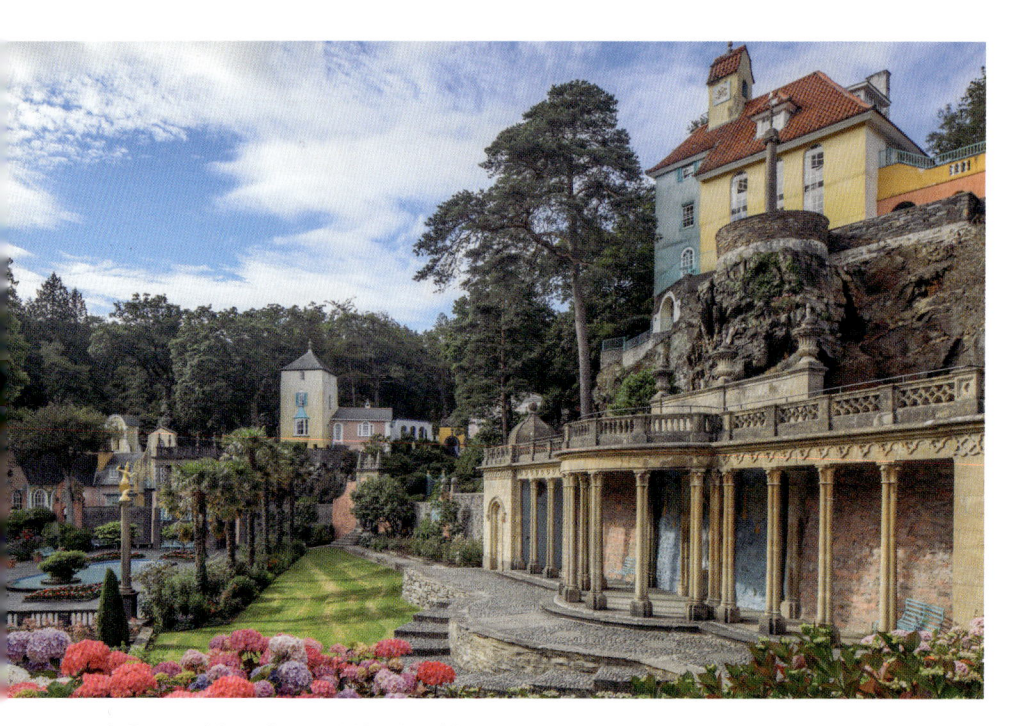

9. Portmeirion, Gwynedd, Wales (Clough Williams-Ellis, 1925–76)

10. Ideal House (formerly the National Radiator Building), Great Marlborough Street, London (Raymond Hood, 1929)

11. India Buildings, Liverpool (Herbert J. Rowse, 1932)

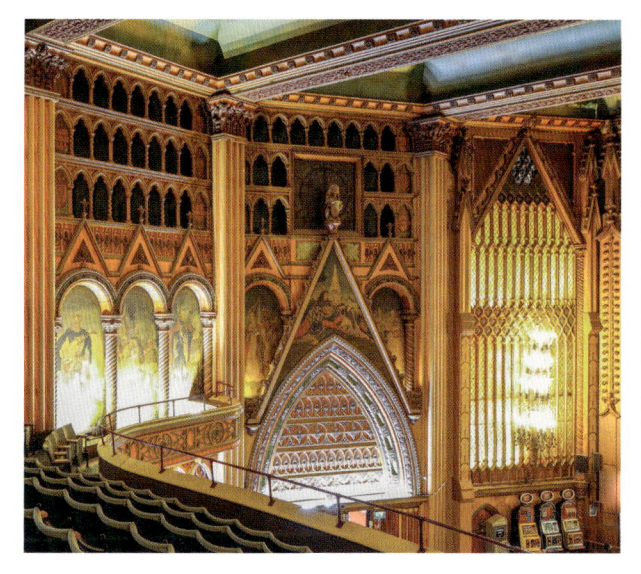

12. (*Above*) Auditorium, the former Granada Cinema, Tooting, London (Cecil Masey; interior Theodore Komisarjevsky, 1931)

13. (*Right*) Shakespeare Memorial Theatre, Stratford-upon-Avon, Warwickshire (Elisabeth Scott; Scott, Chesterton and Shepherd, 1932)

14. Marylands, Ewhurst, Surrey (Oliver Hill, 1931)

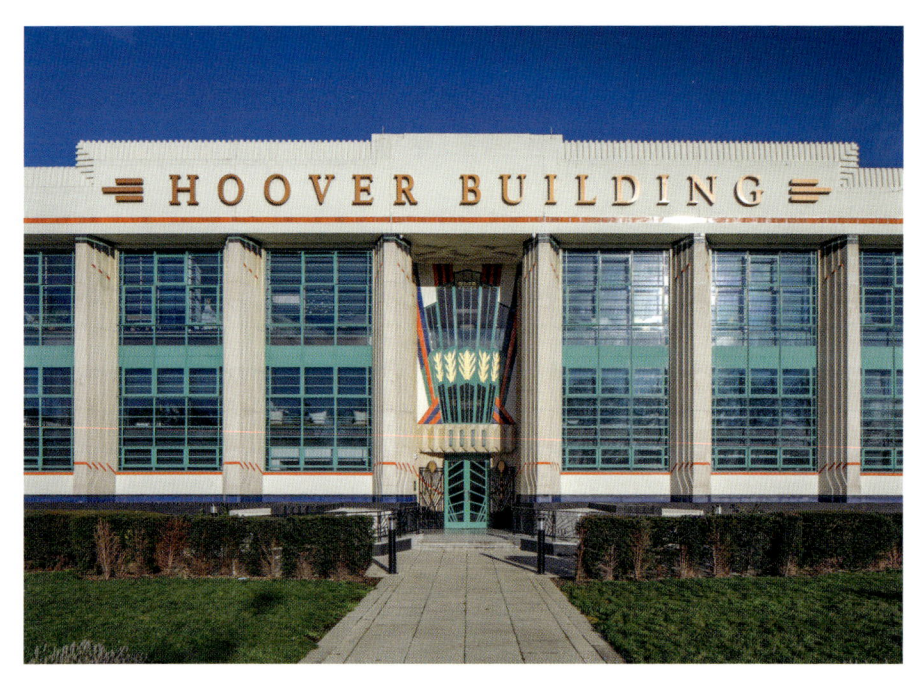

15. Hoover Factory, Perivale, Greater London (Wallis, Gilbert & Partners, 1932)

16. Carreras Cigarette Factory, Mornington Crescent, London (M. E. and O. H. Collins, with Arthur G. Porri, 1928)

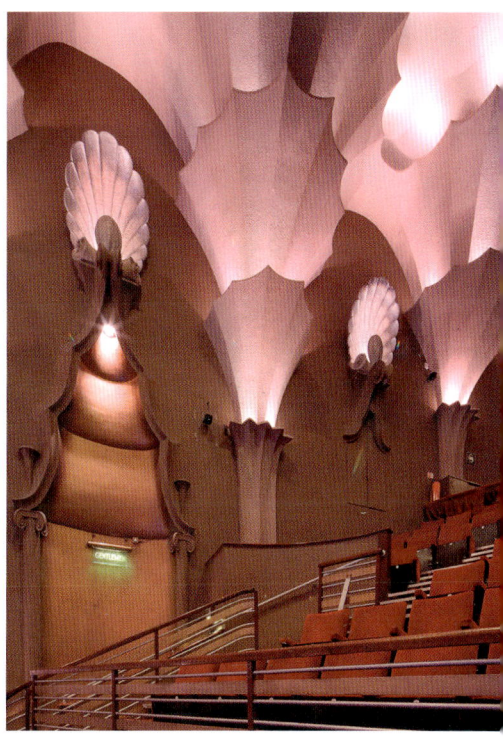

17. (*Above left*) Freemasons' Hall, Great Queen Street, London (Henry Victor Ashley and F. Winton Newman, 1933)

18. (*Above right*) New Victoria Theatre, Wilton Road, London (E. Wamsley Lewis and W. E. Trent, 1930)

19. (*Left*) Interior, *Daily Express* Building, Fleet Street, London (Robert Atkinson, 1933)

20. Yaffle Hill, Poole, Dorset (Edward Maufe, 1930)

21. Battersea Power Station, London (Giles Gilbert Scott and J. Theo Halliday, 1929–55), following reconstruction (Wilkinson Eyre, 2014–22)

running along its central axis; Martin's Bank contains a large vaulted and colonnaded banking hall of American sumptuousness. In 1930 Reilly considered that 'it will undoubtedly be the finest bank and office building in the country'.[13] A few years later, it was Goodhart-Rendel's view that:

> For tall or tallish buildings, whether set back at the top or not, the Americans have evolved a sort of neo-Roman style that has become to them an accepted symbol of high finance. This architecture or near-architecture, whichever we may decide that it is, has been brought to a pitch of rare perfection by the multiple firms of architects that supply the needs of American commerce, and has generally proved beyond the scope of architects having only English experience. That an Englishman should have produced single-handed a specimen equal to America's best is undoubtedly gratifying, although the flawless magnificence of Martins Bank at Liverpool may evoke in us admiration unmingled with affection. This building is a remarkable one, displaying great technical accomplishment on the part of its designer.[14]

By the beginning of the following decade Rowse had moved from a monumental Classicism to a modernistic style equally American in derivation. This can be seen in the series of structures he designed in connection with the construction of Queensway, the road tunnel under the Mersey that opened in 1934.

London allowed not only American architecture but authentic American architects to provide the designs. This phenomenon began in the 1880s with H. H. Richardson designing a house at Bushey, Hertfordshire, for the painter Sir Hubert von Herkomer, but, as Andrew Saint has written, this 'potent infiltration of American architectural ideas' occurred largely between 1908 and 1939, 'equivalent roughly to the period of the great liners', and was at its height in the 1920s.[15] Two important commercial buildings in London designed by Americans, Selfridges and Bush House, have

The former Martins Bank, Liverpool (Herbert J. Rowse, 1932)

already been mentioned, and we will come to Raymond Hood's Ideal House; later Bernard George would work with C. A. Wheeler of Chicago on the Derry and Toms department store of 1929–33, and C. Howard Crane, again of Chicago, would design the Earl's Court Exhibition Building of 1936–37, as well as the Gaumont cinema in Holloway. All these were large and complex projects; as Saint has observed, 'clients went to American architects for management and efficiency, not just, if at all, for aesthetics'.[16]

C. H. Reilly was himself responsible for one large American import. As he recalled in his autobiography, he was approached by the managing director of the builders Holland, Hannen & Cubitts, who had bought the Piccadilly side of William Kent's Devonshire House, abandoned by the Duke of Devonshire in 1918. 'We think that the right thing to do is to build an American apartment house upon it, costing about two millions. It is very important we should get the right American architect for the job. You, I believe, know them all.'[17] Reilly recommended his friend Thomas Hastings, formerly of Carrère & Hastings and now in partnership with Shreve & Lamb, the future architects of the Empire State Building in New York. Reilly was retained as joint architect, although he claimed that the final, executed scheme had 'little to do with me . . . except that by some strange luck my outline of the masses to Piccadilly survived throughout'.[18] The large central rectangular mass was made less dominant by lower ranges flanking the streets and the repetitive elevations were relieved by carved Classical detail. Plaster models for all carved work were sent over from New York; Hastings only visited London once.

When New Devonshire House was completed in 1926, some critics were disturbed by the flatness of the ornament and the shallowness of the window reveals because of the underlying steel frame. W. G. Newton, about to retire as editor of the *Architectural Review*, thought that 'This sense of a hesitation between two modes of expression hampers all of us who are concerned with steel framed buildings, and it will lie with this generation to find the solution.'[19] Maxwell Fry later claimed that it was this ambivalence that turned him towards the New Architecture, although in truth he was still designing stations in an American Classical manner for the Southern Railway at Ramsgate and Margate when Devonshire House was under construction. However, although Fry, like so many architects, was later anxious to rewrite his own history, his account is worth quoting to illustrate the profound change in attitudes which took place in British architecture towards the end of the 1920s:

> I stood contemplating over the hoardings the rising volume of the new Devonshire House in Piccadilly. The steel framework

Devonshire House, Piccadilly, London (Thomas Hastings, with C. H. Reilly, 1926)

had been standing there for some time in sufficient elegance, and what I saw now was a crust of stonework, heavy in intention but bared to its essentials, being hung and bolted and jointed onto the framework like so much scenery. Broad but flat-cut Florentine rustications had topped the Guinness advertisements and were joining in an elaborate cornice, with over it a frieze of fat cherubs carrying swags of fruit. Memories of New York and the School established their provenance. I knew it all like a game played out, and in those duplicating *amorini*, the last of their long line, I thought to find the cherubic face of my naughty professor playing Ariel to old man Hastings in New York and turned in a gesture of moral revulsion from everything I had been taught. That evening I sought out rolls of drawings treasured from those years of tutelage, and gazing at them, not without some fondness, I consigned them to the dustbin.[20]

The new Devonshire House was a conspicuous and expensive example of a building type imported from America which was transforming the character of the capital: the apartment block. 'The flats at Devonshire House have been modelled upon the most up-to-date designs of London, America and Paris, and every known device for the comfort and convenience of tenants has been embodied in the lay-out.'[21] London, and England, had been late in adopting the block of flats as an alternative to the terrace of houses, but after the war the commercial pressure was irresistible. The inspiration was now American rather than Continental, however. Houses and mansions gave way to multi-storey residential blocks whose red brick bulk supported on a steel frame was relieved either by touches of Classical detail or modernistic styling. Osbert Lancaster analysed the phenomenon perceptively, if pessimistically:

> Hitherto the English, almost alone among European nations, had resolutely refused to become flat-minded, but during the 'twenties and 'thirties of the present century the acute shortage of domestic servants, the sedulous apeing among all classes of everything American, the appalling rise in the rates and an increased familiarity with the works of Dr Marie Stopes* led to a wholesale abandonment of the capacious and dignified mansions which had been the pride of the upper and middle classes in Victorian times in favour of these labour-saving cliff dwellings which have done so much to ruin London's skyline.[22]

Most of this redevelopment took place in the West End of London and around Hyde Park, but other areas were completely transformed. These included Bloomsbury south of Euston Square and the north-western inner suburbs around Regent's Park. In the late 1930s, the replacement of small terrace houses in Marylebone by blocks of flats designed by Robert Atkinson in various modernistic styles provoked a mild protest in the *Architectural Review*.[23] At the same time, Lancaster complained that

---

* [Marie Stopes (1880–1958) was a pioneering advocate of birth control; she was also, as it happens, the daughter of an architect. RH.]

those residential districts such as Mayfair, which are of the greatest interest architecturally, have been ruthlessly cut up in order to make way for truncated red-brick tenement buildings, which may possibly with the addition of another thirty stories achieve a certain monumental impressiveness in the neighbourhood of Park Avenue, but which are completely unsuited to Park Lane.[24]

Such buildings were usually Classical in detail but modernistic in their massing. The transformation of the Grosvenor Estate in Mayfair was well described in 1930 by Robert Lutyens, who noted how 'New York is probably the parent of the modern movement, because that city had early to face the prospect of a growing population on an island site and the demands of "Big Business"'. After recalling that the *Daily Express* had 'recently called upon Business to "find and engage another Adam"', he asked:

> But why another? We have dozens of Adams! Together they will rebuild, not only the Grosvenor Estate, but London. Apparently shops and flats, shops and flats are the order of the day. Very well then, granted there are people to live in the flats and buy from the shops, we will have acres of shops and flats, interspersed here and there with cinemas and sublimated pubs, and (if disarmament conferences continue to foster international bitterness) a few plots reserved for suitable memorials to the next great war. And who will design all this? As though it mattered! Let one architect submit an essay in an obsolete style, another an edifice embodying his robot-cum-Hollywood dreams of human destiny, a third a Queen Anne residence on the instalment plan, elastically extended in any direction.[25]

British architects increasingly realised that what was impressive about modern American architecture was the technical daring required in the design and construction of tall buildings. 'One can hardly think of America apart from skyscrapers and one cannot think at all of skyscrapers apart from America,' argued Alfred Bossom: 'In the skyscraper America has invented and developed a wholly new and revolutionary form and type of building that is absolutely and characteristically her own. . . . It is a creation entirely original to herself and emphatically, comprehensively – if you like, stridently – American. As such it exactly expresses the spirit of her people.'[26] Even so, Bossom did not want to import this purely American building type. 'I am definitely against skyscrapers in England,' concluded the ex-architect and new Conservative MP in his 1934 book, *Building to the Skies*:

> the atmospheric conditions and the law of light are altogether against skyscrapers on English soil. Nor have we in England the raw growing towns, panting to advertise themselves, or the national psychology that delights in the new and overlooks its blatancy. Buildings suited to and admirably expressive of the Canadian and the American temperament would in England be incongruous and an irritant without the compensation of supplying any existing social or economic need.[27]

Bossom was not alone. 'The Royal Institute of British Architects has declared itself to be opposed to them,' recorded Trystan Edwards in 1924, 'and the London County Council has forbidden them on account of the difficulty in adequately safeguarding them against fire.'[28] With his concern for urban good manners, Edwards was convinced that the commercial skyscraper was 'unsociable':

> Whether it is safe or unsafe, well or badly planned, whether it truthfully expresses its construction or whether its form is decorated with every symbolic feature belonging to the historical 'styles' of architecture, whether it is Gothic or Classic, stone or concrete, plain or coloured, ugly or beautiful, the commercial skyscraper is all wrong. . . . As far as the development of civic design is concerned, the skyscraper is a cul-de-sac.[29]

A decade later, Clough Williams-Ellis and John Summerson went further. 'American architecture is famous for its skyscrapers. No other country has produced buildings of such prodigious size,' they admitted. 'But a building can be enormously high and yet not particularly beautiful; many of the largest American skyscrapers are remarkable, apart from their size, only for the stupidity and vulgarity of their design.'[30] John Gloag, similarly, was wary of Americanisation, and disturbed both by standardisation and by the general run of American building. 'The magnificent experimental genius of the United States in architecture may degenerate,' he feared:

> Already the worship of imitation has been responsible for all kinds of queer exaggerated borrowings – railway-stations that are enormous enlargements of Roman Baths, for example. . . . Will the twentieth century see a return to foolish copyism? Will American architects continue to sin in antique ways to oblige their plutocratic patrons who cannot get the ruins they 'did' during their European tours out of their systems?[31]

Even so, several attempts were made in the 1920s to build skyscrapers in London. 'There are many British architects who greatly admire the skyscraper form and would like to design skyscrapers for erection in England. Wistfully they look towards America'.[32] These even included Sir Edwin Lutyens, who tried to raise one on top of his Britannic House. This, along with Harvey Corbett's attempt to build a tower on top of Bush House, and Gordon Selfridge's attempt to enhance his eponymous department store in Oxford Street with a skyscraper by the fashionable country house architect Philip Tilden, have been mentioned.[33] In the event, no real skyscrapers were built in Britain before the Second World War. One moderately tall commercial building that was treated like a miniature skyscraper was Lutyens's Midland Bank in Manchester, which, rising from a square island site, was conventionally enhanced at the bottom and top – a rusticated ground floor and a domed pavilion roof at the summit

The former Midland Bank, Manchester (Edwin Lutyens, 1935)

– while the intervening plain walls were enhanced by set-backs.

Charles Holden was responsible for two tall buildings in London whose height and bulk reflect the influence of America. One was the conspicuous stepped stone landmark tower raised over Bloomsbury for the Senate House of London University, completed in 1937, which the LCC had initially insisted be left internally void with no floors above the eighth storey.[34] This was preceded a decade earlier by the headquarters of the Underground Group raised above St James's Park Station at 55 Broadway in 1926–29. Its cruciform plan culminated in a massive central tower, modelled with Holden's austere, rectilinear aesthetic, leading P. Morton Shand to describe the

Senate House, University of London, Malet Street, London (Charles Holden, 1937)

building as 'the Underground's skyscraper'.[35] Pedestrian routes from the surrounding streets to the station at the building's core governed the cruciform plan, but it also enabled Holden to design radiating wings of offices all enjoying light and air without overlooking lightwells. Holden succeeded in producing a conspicuously tall building that was both functional and yet romantic in its massing. The inspiration may well have been partly American; he had visited the United States, and may have been influenced by an earlier design of 1904 by Beresford Pite for an urban hospital, which, again, was American in conception.[36] However, as Charles Reilly pointed out in 1931, 'Charles Holden was a modernist thirty years ago, when the term had not been invented.'[37]

No. 55 Broadway was the first large building in London to exhibit the new spirit in architecture. The *Observer* newspaper called it 'A Cathedral of Modernity', and Morton Shand wrote how 'the Underground provides citizens of London and country cousins with a gratuitous education in the outward manifestations of the modern spirit'.[38] The public was impressed by two aspects of the design. The austere simplicity of the towering white walls of Portland stone hung on the internal steel frame made a dramatic contrast with the surrounding lower brick buildings, although, in his perspective drawing exhibited at the Royal Academy in 1927, Muirhead Bone was careful to depict his friend Holden's masterpiece as it would look in the wet, smoky London climate. The aesthetic was essentially a simplified Classicism, but simplicity seemed a rare, and economical, virtue. 'No. 55 Broadway cost much less proportionally than a second PLA or ICI building,' Shand pointed out, 'or a replica of the "new" Lloyds. It is neither "period" nor "palatial" for the excellent reason that it is erected A.D. 1928–9 and is not intended to be a spiritual home for the ghost of Lorenzo the Magnificent. But it is very imposing, because it is sincerely designed and finely massed.'[39] The second aspect of the building which attracted attention, much of it unwelcome, was the external sculpture, carved *in situ* by a group of sculptors including Jacob Epstein, Eric Gill and Henry Moore. This was possibly

55 Broadway, London (Charles Holden, 1929)

unwise, given the trouble there had been two decades before, when Holden used the young Epstein on the British Medical Association building in the Strand: the naked figures on the frieze (since mutilated) were considered too explicit. Epstein's *Rima* in Hyde Park, a memorial to the naturalist W. H. Hudson, had provoked further controversy, leading to it being tarred and feathered by reactionary artists. But Holden believed that it was the hand of the artist that raised building to Architecture. Rooted in Ruskin and the social ideals of the Arts and Crafts movement, he and his patron Frank Pick were part of an influential group that the modern historian Michael T. Saler has characterised as 'medieval modernists'.[40] Even Reilly, who had done so much to deflect English architecture from the Arts and Crafts tradition, recognised this. 'Holden's is an austere spirit,' he wrote. 'There is a fine puritanical appearance about all his structures, which however long before the War they were built, makes them fit the temper of these post-war times.'[41]

The inspiration of the American skyscraper was, however, as much Gothic as Classic, as Raymond Hood had shown when he won the international competition for the Chicago Tribune Tower in 1922. This striving for height, and to give tall structures convincing vertical expression, was admired even by a conservative Classicist like A. S. G. Butler. In his 1926 book *The Substance of Architecture*, with a foreword by Lutyens, he noted how:

In the modern commercial world ... the cost of land in large cities is so great and the competition to trade in a limited number of streets is so fierce, the matter of ground-area becomes one of vital consequence. The result, of course, is height, checked in England by law, but unchecked in America by anything except structural possibilities in steel and the new zoning regulations. Hence the startling effect of the commercial towers of New York, and the gradual evolution of a quite definite style arising from the dominant influence of this one limitation ... Given the continued opportunity, American architects may create a style which will be ranked one day with the achievements of the thirteenth and fourteenth centuries in France.[42]

Raymond Hood, who became one of the leading American architects of his time and was responsible for some of the best New York skyscrapers, also worked in London, but not in his Gothic style or on a tall building. In 1928, the year he acted as one of the international judges for the Shakespeare Memorial Theatre competition, he was asked to design the National Radiator Building on Great Marlborough Street (Plate 10). He had already designed the American Radiator Building in New York in 1924 – before the Paris Exposition, in which the use of ceramic colour decoration gave it that distinctive stylistic character which, with hindsight, can be labelled as 'Art Deco'. Something equally striking was created in London, right opposite the new half-timbered Tudor of Liberty's. Trystan Edwards called it 'The Moor of Argyle Street'.[43] The severe, rectilinear elevations, punctured by regularly spaced windows, were faced in black Swedish granite, but they rose to a multi-coloured cornice of clear Egyptian derivation while the ground-floor shop windows were given a colourful decorative edging of bronze and enamel. The underlying steel frame was neither expressed nor denied: 'If the handsome face of this building answers no questions,' Goodhart-Rendel observed, 'it also tells no lies.'[44] The decoration was Parisian 'Déco' in style, but, as Andrew Saint has observed, 'There is

Ideal House (formerly the National Radiator Building), Great Marlborough Street, London (Raymond Hood, 1929)

also a subdued whiff of Tutankhamun about the building, conveyed more by texture and *entasis* than by overt stylistic reference.'[45]

The National Radiator Building, completed in 1929, showed not only that an alternative to historic styles was possible, but that the creative spirit of America was not limited to a correct, overblown Classicism. Hood's building was influential. His English collaborator, Gordon Jeeves, who enlarged it along Argyle Street in 1935, went on to design Drage's, or Everyman House, on Oxford Street a year later, and a shiny cladding of black granite was also used for the Pantheon in Oxford Street designed for Marks & Spencer; for the Odeon cinema in Leicester Square of 1937 designed by Andrew Mather; and for many of the countless Montague Burton tailors' stores across the country designed in a distinctive vertical, Art Deco manner.

'Art Deco' is an unsatisfactory but essential term. Like 'Gothic' and 'Baroque', it was first applied as a pejorative term to describe a style which would later be regarded as characteristic and distinct. 'Art Déco' was apparently first used in 1966, in connection with an exhibition held in Paris about *Les années '25*; it was adopted by Martin Battersby in his books on *The Decorative Twenties* and *The Decorative Thirties* to describe the style which developed after about 1910 and culminated in the 1925 Paris Expo. Only at the end of the 1960s was the acute accent over the 'e' dropped, when the term began to be applied to the distinctive style of the 1930s. The terms 'Moderne', 'Modernistic' or 'Jazz Modern' were used by contemporaries to characterise the flashy, commercial manner which both Traditionalists and serious Modernists affected to despise. Osbert Lancaster's 1939 caricature of a 'Modernistic' interior in *Homes Sweet Homes* depicted a suburban lounge filled with what would now be described as commercial Art Deco furnishings. By 1968, when the journalist and historian Bevis Hillier published his pioneering guide, *Art Deco of the 20s and 30s*, it was clear that the zeitgeist of the interwar decades affected not only the decorative arts but architecture as well. Compared with the United States, there is comparatively little pure 'Deco' architecture in Britain, just as there was little 'Art Nouveau', but all styles and building types, even Classical and Tudor, were touched by this spirit. Today the term 'Art Deco' is often applied indiscriminately to characteristic buildings of the interwar decades.* Given the subsequent ubiquity and importance of a term that was, at the time, an insult and

---

* For example, Hines (2003) not only includes the Swedish-influenced RIBA building and the pure Modern Movement of Simpsons in Piccadilly, but also the stripped Classicism of Holden: the Underground building, Senate House and Arnos Grove Station.

a euphemism for cheap incoherent vulgarity, it is worth pausing to consider a definition.

Hillier argued that 'Art Deco' was the best term to describe the decorative arts objects of the interwar decades which he celebrated with a certain condescension, for they were generally felt to be vulgar and contemptible at the time:

> I would suggest this as a working definition: an assertively modern style, developing in the 1920s and reaching its high point in the thirties; it drew inspiration from various sources, including the more austere side of Art Nouveau, cubism, the Russian Ballet, American Indian art and the Bauhaus; it was a classical style in that, like neo-Classicism but unlike Rococo or Art Nouveau, it ran to symmetry rather than asymmetry, and to the rectilinear rather than the curvilinear; it responded to the demands of the machine and of new materials such as plastics, ferro-concrete and vita-glass; and its ultimate aim was to end the old conflict between art and industry, the old snobbish distinction between artist and artisan, partly by making artists adept at crafts, but still more by adapting design to the requirements of mass-production.[46]

Although Hillier was thinking more of the decorative arts than buildings, this is a definition which still generally holds good when applied to architecture. It is interesting to note how this definition corresponds with that given by Osbert Lancaster thirty years earlier to characterise the vulgar and commercial 'Modernistic' he disliked. This style he considered 'a nightmare amalgam of a variety of elements derived from several sources':

> The foundation was provided by that Jazz style which enjoyed a mercifully brief period of popularity in the immediate post-Versailles period, which was itself the fruit of a fearful union between the flashier side of Ballets Russes and a hopelessly

vulgarized version of Cubism. To this were added... a half-hearted simplicity that derived from a complete misunderstanding of the ideals of the Corbusier-Gropius school of architects and found uneasy expression in unvarnished wood and chromium plate, relentlessly misapplied.[47]

A similarly dismissive but more snobbish definition of the style had been given by John Betjeman a little earlier. '"Jazz-modern" is the product of insensitive minds,' he wrote in 1937:

> It is the decoration of art-school students. You all know it. The 'modernistic suites' to be seen in hire-purchase catalogues, the dashing milk-bars which have dispensed with the need for capital letters. ... Later a style that was neither the one nor the other, but called 'not too modern and not too traditional' was used, as it is now, for cinemas, churches and public buildings. Sir Giles Gilbert Scott is its most successful exponent.[48]

As Charlotte and Tim Benton noted at the time of the V&A exhibition in 2003, architecture is central to an inclusive view of Art Deco; thanks to the conservation movement that emerged in America in the 1970s, those buildings of the 1920s and 1930s, so frowned on at the time, have been rehabilitated.[49] What is clear from such alternative terms as 'Jazz Modern' is that, despite the 1925 Paris Expo, what we now think of as 'Art Deco' architecture was largely American in origin. A British Art Deco architecture there certainly was, however, and its inspiration came as much from Hollywood cinema as from architects and designers. In London there was Claridge's ballroom, designed in 1929 by Oswald Milne, with an interior by Basil Ionides incorporating glass by Lalique. In the same year the Savoy Theatre re-opened after Ionides had redesigned the auditorium with a painted ceiling to represent an April sky, walls of translucent gold on silver, and seats upholstered in different colours. There was also the foyer of the *Daily Express* building (Plate 19), but

Interior, Eltham Palace, Eltham, Greater London (Seely & Paget, 1935)

Interior, Eltham Palace, Eltham, Greater London (Seely & Paget, 1935)

perhaps the most sustained expression of Art Deco in England was Seely & Paget's extension to the medieval Eltham Palace.

A commission from the millionaire patrons of the arts, Stephen and Virginia Courtauld in 1933, its exquisitely detailed interiors embodied every fad and fashion of the period, including a centralised vacuum-cleaning system and heated accommodation for Mah-Jong, Virginia's pet ring-tailed lemur.

By the 1930s, the influence of America was evident beyond Central London in the suburbs and in provincial cities, and it was in the design of factories and cinemas that the most conspicuous expressions of Art Deco were to be found. The cinema was, arguably, the one new building type characteristic of the interwar decades. In 1921 there were already some 4,000 cinemas in Britain, but most were either in theatres or converted from halls or other buildings. Thousands of new, purpose-built cinemas now appeared, many accommodating audiences of between 2,000 and 3,000. In 1940, Graves and Hodge considered that the 1920s had been 'the golden age of pictures, between their first quaint beginnings and their eventual streamlining as Big Business'.[50] Similarly, Paul Rotha, author of *The Film of To-day*, published in 1931, looked back with regret to the era of the silent screen when films were not 'bolstered up with variety turns and orchestral interludes, as well as by the erection of vast palaces of luxury and atrocious vulgarity'.[51]

By the end of the 1920s America, thanks to Hollywood and the popularity of Charlie Chaplin, had come to dominate cinema. After the war, 'Even the stickiest British families seemed ready to abandon their mistrust of the cinema, if the vulgar American scene could only be replaced by a wholesome British one', but the nascent British film industry was soon defeated by American film distributors.[52] And although German cinema design had an influence on British architects, most cinema proprietors looked to America for inspiration. British cinema architects studied developments in the United States and the design of cinemas went through rapid stylistic and technical changes. Some American architects actually designed cinemas in Britain, though the results were not impressive architecturally. The Empire in Leicester Square, which could seat 3,326 when it opened in 1928, was designed by the Scottish-born Thomas W. Lamb, who had designed The Regent in New York, the first super-cinema, in 1913 and went on to design the New York Capitol, which would seat 5,300. Morton Shand was unimpressed:

> In America, which, perhaps naturally, has remained our standard model in these respects, the meaningless parade of garish glitter has likewise been carried as far as the almighty dollar can carry it. The new 'Empire' in London is the monstrous fruit of an Anglo-American collaboration between 'specialists' in cinema design'. . . . It is bad enough that the 'Empire' should be one of the most supremely *parvenu* buildings in the world. What is worse is that the enormous sum lavished on it has only helped to make this glorified gin-palace more hopelessly out of date as a cinema than that *chef-d'œuvre* of Edwardian fruitiness, the neighbouring 'Hippodrome', as a music hall.[53]

The Regent at Brighton, opened by Provincial Cinematograph Theatres in 1921, was the first 'super-cinema' in Britain of real architectural quality. Its architect was not a specialist in theatre design but that most versatile practitioner and teacher, Robert Atkinson, who had been sent by the RIBA on a fact-finding tour of the United States in 1919 to study architectural education but where he also looked at the new cinemas. The Regent was ingeniously planned to combine a fan-shaped auditorium with restaurants, bars and public spaces – all sumptuously decorated. 'However much Atkinson had benefited from American expertise in planning, he succeeded in producing a building of far greater artistic merit than any of those he had seen, and one most fully expressive of its purpose.'[54] Atkinson solved a number of problems in cinema design for the first time, notably by designing a façade with a large proscenium arch able to incorporated giant lettering and posters; 'is it not rather stupid,' he

Regent Cinema, Brighton, Sussex (Robert Atkinson, 1921; demolished 1974)

later wrote, 'to design the front of a theatre to look like a Roman temple and then cover it up with posters and moving electric signs, so that the Roman temple disappears behind paper and lamps?'[55]

The Roman theme was continued in the interior, where there were murals and decorations by accomplished artists. 'By his masterly use of brilliant and harmonious colour, inspired perhaps by the work of such artists as Bakst, Benois, and Lovat Fraser, Atkinson gave the auditorium an atmosphere of carnival gaiety, and although most of the architectural and decorative elements were derived from Roman, Italian Renaissance, or Adam sources, the total effect was entirely original.'[56] Unfortunately, long before its demolition in 1974, the interior had been altered and spoiled. Nevertheless, Walter Ison came to recall, 'with affection',

> a building which, apart from Easton and Robertson's Royal Horticultural Hall, was the only British building of its time to receive the unstinted admiration of a visiting party of Swedish architects whose standards were the works of Østberg, Tengbom and Asplund. In conclusion it must be said that very few of the many super-cinemas built in Britain deserved serious consideration as works of architectural merit and decorative art. Amongst the few, Robert Atkinson's Regent was equalled, though certainly not surpassed, by Frank Verity's Shepherd's Bush Pavilion and Wamsley Lewis's New Victoria in London.[57]

The inspiration for the Shepherd's Bush Pavilion, opened in 1923, was Roman rather than Imperial American, and the sober monumentality of its brick exterior so appealed to an architectural establishment apprehensive about theatrical vulgarity that it was awarded the RIBA's London Medal in 1924. 'Internally,' writes Richard Gray, 'Verity designed in the full glory of the Roman Empire – coffering, tripod funerary urns, stencil decoration and even fake drapery.'[58] But it was a losing battle: such were the commercial pressures imposed by the cinema chains that when Verity came to design the Plaza in

The former Pavilion Cinema, Shepherd's Bush, London (Frank Verity, 1923)

Regent Street in 1926, the American influence was clear in both the florid Palladian style and in the splayed ante-proscenium walls in the auditorium. Two years later, the Piccadilly Theatre opened as a 'showcase' for Hollywood studios. Cinema architects and cinema proprietors visited the United States to study the latest developments. George Green sent his architect, John Fairweather, across the Atlantic before he designed Green's Playhouse in Glasgow. Built in 1925–27 it could seat 4,254 customers and was the largest cinema in Europe at the time.

America was responsible for the craze which affected cinema design at the end of the 1920s: the 'atmospheric'. The first in Britain was The Lido at Golders Green, opened in 1928 and designed by W. J. King, where the interior painted by Guy Lipscombe was intended to invoke a scene on a North Italian lake. Morton Shand was particularly disgusted with this departure, both from pure decoration and functional design:

> The phrase is well suited to the nature of this nauseating stick-jaw candy, so fulsomely flavoured with the syrupy romanticism of popular novels and the 'See Naples and die' herd-nostalgia which

speeds Cook's conducted tours on their weary ways. 'Atmospherics', or 'outside-in' interiors as Mr Leathart wittily dubs them, are now reintroducing the type of 'glowing' landscape which is no longer admitted even to that home of long lost artistic causes, the Royal Academy.[59]

But even Julian Leathart, whom Shand considered 'our foremost cinema-architect', was soon guilty of having 'gone over to the enemy' when he gave his Richmond cinema of 1929 an interior like 'the courtyard of a seventeenth century Spanish nobleman's house', a lapse for which he would recant five years later.[60]

About a dozen 'atmospherics' were built in Britain, none rivalling the interiors of contemporary cinemas in cities like Los Angeles. The Regal, Marble Arch, by Clifford Aish, had an auditorium with walls decorated by Charles Muggeridge to depict woodland settings, 'while the ceiling comprised a pergola festooned with creeper and vine leaves, together with more fake foliage cascading down in front of the organ screens'. At the Astoria at Brixton, by Edward A. Stone and Thomas Somerford, with Ewen Barr, 1929–30, the interior was meant to evoke a large Italian courtyard: 'Here was literally "An Acre of Seats in a Garden of Dreams", to quote American publicity for similar creations.'[61] A few of these fantasies had Gothic interiors; several were creations on the theme of Spain, like Cecil Masey's eponymous Spanish City in the new London suburb of Northfields. In contrast to Morton Shand's snobbish disdain for such things, Richard Gray points out that, 'In the 1930s, holidays in Italy or Spain were the preserve of the rich, and these interiors were the nearest the average person was likely to get to the romantic and seductive Mediterranean shores.'[62]

'In the past,' wrote Walter Goodesmith in 1936, 'the interiors of many English cinemas have been unduly influenced by American design with a resultant display of excess ornament and an air of sumptuousness. A marked change is taking place, however, and a more logical approach to the problem is noticeable.'[63] A pioneer in

Interior details, the former Spanish City cinema, Ealing, Greater London (Cecil Masey, 1932)

Auditorium, the former Spanish City cinema, Ealing, Greater London (Cecil Masey, 1932)

this process was The Kensington in Kensington High Street, designed in 1926 by Leathart & Granger for Joseph Mears, where the façade was a sober rectilinear composition on the proscenium theme set by Atkinson in Brighton. Morton Shand admired the result: 'So uninspired, indeed, are our "Picture Palaces" – the very name seems to foredoom designers to false values – that the "Kensington Cinema" . . . till lately ranked among them as one of the more interesting and encouraging designs.'[64] And Richard Gray points out that The Kensington 'did proclaim the respectability of film in a middle-class district – an important factor when film was trying to rid itself of its fairground image'.[65]

By the 1930s, a distinct cinema style had emerged, which reflected the influences of both American and German design. The exteriors, sometimes of brick, sometimes clad in faience, were often streamlined compositions in an Art Deco manner. The interiors were more impressive, for however functional cinema planning became, the need for decoration, for a sense of occasion and luxury, was not forgotten. But the decoration was no longer historical in derivation. Walls of fibrous plaster were moulded in abstract patterns, relieved by decorative features and exotic light fittings. A good example is the Rex at Berkhamsted, designed by David Nye in 1938. Here the theme was nautical, with undulating lines on the walls to suggest waves, shell-like lights and porthole windows, while the screen was framed by a proscenium arch with wide panels of ornament and given enough curvature in the mouldings to suggest a modern Baroque. As Charlotte and Tim Benton observed, 'almost uniquely among art historical styles, some of Art Deco's most persistent meanings are to be found in fantasy and fun'.[66]

The development of the cinema style was encouraged by the successful chains which embarked on programmes of expansion and rebuilding. Each had its own staff architect – William Trent for Gaumont-British (which had amalgamated with Provincial Cinematograph Theatres), William Green for Associated British Cinemas – running a large office to cope with the amount of work.

Auditorium and (*below*) detail of wall light, Rex Cinema, Berkhamsted, Hertfordshire (David Nye, 1938)

Gaumont built 51 new cinemas during the 1930s; Associated British opened 93; meanwhile, the Odeon chain, founded by Oscar Deutsch in 1928, opened no less than 142. Its architects' office expanded from 6 to 140 staff in eighteen months. Those employed were some of the best cinema designers: Cecil Clavering, Andrew Mather, George Coles, Keith Roberts. Coles, the most versatile of cinema architects, was responsible for the Gaumont State at Kilburn, built in 1937.

Odeon Cinema, Leicester Square, London (Harry Weedon and Andrew Mather, 1937)

Interior, Odeon Cinema, Muswell Hill, London (George Coles, 1936)

This was the largest cinema in England, able to seat 4,004, and with a tower possibly reminiscent of the Empire State building in New York. The flagship Odeon in Leicester Square, with its tower faced in polished black granite, was opened the same year, designed by Weedon, Mather and Thomas Braddock. Inside, the 'sensational art-deco auditorium of ribbed fibrous plaster' had low relief figures by Raymond Britton Reviere.[67]

Not all cinema proprietors were such adventurous patrons as Oscar Deutsch. Sidney Bernstein, who commissioned the extraordinary Gothic interiors of the Granada cinemas at Tooting and Woolwich, preferred more traditional design and was generally dismissive of British cinema architecture, which, he wrote in 1936,

> has not yet reached the level of the best American and Continental design. During the past few years, the ambitious cinema proprietor, prompted by the impulse to build on the boom wave, has been responsible for many vulgar, inefficient, jerry-built cinemas that are to be found in all the prosperous districts. . . . Most cinemas decorated in the alleged modern manner already look old-fashioned. Perhaps their architects were afraid that by

taking lessons from Michelangelo, Wren, Inigo Jones and other great masters they would prove they were just passengers in an age of mediocrity.[68]

A further problem faced by cinema architects was the speed at which they were designed and built. 'Time is the essence of all building contracts, but in cinema building it is, perhaps, the most vital factor of all,' explained Julian Leathart:

> It is not overstating the urgency of this matter to describe cinema building operations as an unceasing headlong rush from the time the hoarding surrounds the vacant site to the moment when the last painter and chair-fixer are being 'shushed' out of the back door while the mayor and corporation are crossing the red carpet from their cars to the front door for the opening ceremony.[69]

In consequence, almost all cinemas were steel-framed structures within brick walls. It is this speed of construction combined with their ephemerality which still makes the cinemas of the 1920s and 1930s seem so exotic and untypical in the history of British architecture, however popular they were in their heyday (Plate 12). Such an approach to design and construction was learned from America. Perhaps a representative example is the Rex at Hayes in Kent, designed in a sort of Deco Hispano-Moresque style by Cecil Masey in 1936. Built at the end of a new shopping parade soon after the branch line from Charing Cross had been electrified by the Southern Railway and renamed The Odeon after the Second World War, it lasted not quite twenty years before being demolished in 1956 to make way for a supermarket.

There was, indeed, a certain Wild West quality about many cinemas that corresponded with many of the films shown in them. They seldom attempted 'good manners' in architecture. Often grotesquely out of scale with their surroundings, cinemas presented bare brick walls to the sides and rear, and were only given a coherent,

The former Granada Cinema, Woolwich, London (Cecil Masey and Reginald Uren, 1937)

attention-seeking façade towards the high street or main road that they faced. Even so, surrounded as they often were by half-timbered Tudor shopping parades or by ordinary suburban houses, these structures represented a taste of the modern, an alternative glamorous world. Yet the names given to these buildings were redolent neither of Hollywood nor New York, but suggested an inexplicably recondite romance of their own. As Ian Jack has written, recalling his first experience of the Ritz cinema, opened in the depressed Lancashire cotton town of Farnworth in 1927:

Had any of us heard of César Ritz and his grand hotels when we first went through its doors? No, of course not, and not for a long time after. Cinema names seemed independent of any history. They may have been intended to suggest luxury, romance, good birth and breeding, foreign parts, ancient history, and therefore to be fitting vehicles for the films shown inside them; escapist images within escapist architecture. But how many among their audiences could have connected the Hippodrome to horse racing in ancient Greece, or the Rialto to Venice, the Alhambra, Granada and Toledo to Spain, the Lido to Mediterranean bathing, the Colosseum to Rome, the Savoy to the Strand, the Odeon to Paris, the Regal to majestic behaviour? . . . Before they were anything else, they were the names of cinemas. Cinemas were what they described.[70]

The other type of proud modern structure which might be conspicuous in a suburb was the factory. In 1933, C. H. Reilly congratulated Thomas Wallis of Wallis, Gilbert & Partners 'on the fine series of factories on the Great West Road, which make all the domestic architecture, for miles around, look absurd'.[71] New factories were designed in deliberate contrast to the dark brick Victorian mills and the heavy industries associated with the depressed cities of the North. Erected for the manufacture of electrical goods and motor cars, which generated much of the prosperity of the Midlands and the South, these structures used new materials, conveyed an image of efficiency and cleanliness, and were again American in inspiration. 'The country's recovery from the Great War,' thought Wallis, 'was, to a large extent, dependent upon the ability of our industrialists to compete favourably in the world's market. To ensure this they were ready to throw aside old methods and abandon old plant, and in its place to install the most up-to-date plant at almost any cost.'[72]

Almost all these new factories were of reinforced-concrete construction. Although the French had pioneered reinforced concrete, the lead had been taken by systems developed in the United States. Even before the Great War, the Trussed Concrete Steel Company

Ltd (Truscon) was responsible for the design of industrial buildings in Britain using the Kahn system of reinforcement. The company was founded by the Kahn brothers in Detroit and opened an office in London in 1907. Albert Kahn established a reputation as the architect of modern industrial structures; Julius and Moritz Kahn were engineers; between them they evolved the 'Kahn Daylight System' for factory design, using an exposed concrete rectilinear grid of column, beam and slab which allowed the external walls to consist of large glass windows.

The young Owen Williams, who would emerge as the master of reinforced concrete at the Wembley Exhibition in 1924, had joined the British office of the Trussed Concrete Steel Company in 1912. As chief estimating engineer he was responsible for erecting the Gramophone Co. building at Hayes, Middlesex, designed by Arthur Blomfield, but the leading exponent of the system was Thomas Wallis.[73] Highly successful in the sphere of industrial design, Wallis was a slightly dubious, maverick, swashbuckling figure between the wars. According to legend, he once arrived at the editorial offices of the *Architectural Review* with a horsewhip following the publication of a satirical poem and cartoon about the flashy Deco façades of his factories.[74] In 1916, Wallis had left the Office of Works to establish his own practice, to work in collaboration with the London office of Trussed Concrete Steel. He may well have been accused of unprofessional conduct as the American company was already contracted to work for the British government. Wallis's practice was known as Wallis, Gilbert & Partners – 'Gilbert' being, apparently, a non-existent American or Canadian.[75] 'There is no doubt that we must credit America with the first conceptions of the new style of industrial buildings, with Germany a close runner-up,' Wallis told the RIBA in 1933:

> The reason for this was undoubtedly American methods of mass production, which quickly demanded the essentials of planning on the direct route principle. Their methods were soon followed in the British Isles, and I feel that whilst we can still learn from America,

they also, if they care to, can now learn from us, not only in methods of production, but also in the many details of factory design.[76]

Wallis was an assiduous self-promoter, happy to accept authorship of designs even when his firm were only executants, as for instance with the factory for British Berberg Ltd at Doncaster, an impressive composition in a pure, white, Germanic Modern manner.[77] He also succeeded in having a volume of photographs of his firm's work published under the title *Industrial Architecture* in the intriguing 'Masters of Architecture' series emanating from Geneva.* Many of the illustrations depict American-looking 'Daylight' factories that might have come from Moritz Kahn.

Wallis, Gilbert & Partners became best known for the series of nine 'Fancy' factories built between 1927 and 1935, mostly on new arterial roads out of London, which have come to be regarded as emblematic British Art Deco buildings of the 1930s. They all had dramatic show fronts, of monumental character, with coloured decorative trim that contrasted with the utilitarian reinforced-concrete structures behind. These were often criticised: after Wallis lectured to the RIBA on 'Factories' in 1933, several architects praised his work while regretting 'these veneers'. Wallis later pointed out that 'our buildings on the Great West Road have not façades [to] represent only just a veneer on them. These buildings have the administration offices on the front, and I am of the opinion that although the offices adjoin the factory, an administration office is entitled to an architectural treatment just as much as any City office.'[78] The best of them, the Firestone Factory on the Great West Road, was suddenly demolished in 1980 in anticipation of its being listed. Today, the

---

* This abstruse series of small, handsome books covered a wide range of European architects such as Siclis, Gočár, Muzio and Piacentini; British subjects included Sir John Burnet, Tait & Partners (edited by Trystan Edwards) and Philip Hepworth. According to Skinner (1997), the book devoted to Wallis, Gilbert & Partners was considered to be advertising and 'was banned by the RIBA and all copies ordered to be destroyed' (p. 17).

BRAVE NEW WORLD

Boundary piers and fence of the former Firestone Factory, Brentford, Greater London (Wallis, Gilbert & Partners, 1929)

Firestone Factory, Brentford, Greater London (Wallis, Gilbert & Partners, 1929; demolished 1980)

Canteen Building, Hoover Factory, Perivale, Greater London (Wallis, Gilbert & Partners, 1938)

most dramatic and distinctive of the surviving Fancy factories is the former Hoover Factory in Perivale, where the trabeated concrete system of construction is expressed on the entrance front as a giant vertical order within a decorative and abstracted frame, flanked by towers with unusual semi-circular corner windows, which may be of German rather than American derivation (Plate 15).* A 1935 survey of industrial architecture noted that, 'As the building is situated in a prominent position facing onto a busy highway [Western Avenue], more money was spent on the front than was strictly necessary, and it was carefully designed to create an impression which would be of favourable advertising value.'[79]

The historian and campaigner Joan Skinner has been anxious to stress, firstly, that the Firestone Factory was remarkable as a complete factory design, and not just for its spectacular Egyptian-Deco façade; but that, secondly, the American character of these Fancy factories

---

* Compare Hans Poelzig's Sulphuric Acid Factory in Lubón, Poland (1912).

has been exaggerated: 'After the severance of the early American connections, having taken what was useful from that source, Wallis, Gilbert & Partners were no longer influenced by American design. They pursued their own way, knowing their own market.'[80] However, not only were several of their clients American (notably Hoover Limited and the Firestone Tyre and Rubber Company), but these factories were perceived at the time as American. Starting on his *English Journey* in 1933, J. B. Priestley wrote how,

> After the familiar muddle of West London, the Great West Road looked very odd. Being new, it did not look English. We might have suddenly rolled into California. Or, for that matter, into one of the main avenues of the old exhibitions, like the Franco-British Exhibition of my boyhood. It was the line of new factories on each side that suggested the exhibition, for years of the West Riding have fixed for ever my idea of what a proper factory looks like; a grim blackened rectangle with a tall chimney at one corner. These decorative little buildings, all glass and concrete and chromium plate, seem to my barbaric mind to be merely playing at being factories.[81]

The American character of these factories is possibly also suggested by Michael Dugdale's contemporary satirical poem: 'Leave no space undecorated; / Hide those ugly wheels and pipes. / Cover them with noughts and crosses, / Mess them up with stars and stripes.'[82]

Some British architects realised that there was more to American architecture than tall buildings, cinemas and factories. 'The most intelligent and interesting new buildings of America are not necessarily sky-scrapers,' Williams-Ellis and Summerson pointed out in 1934, advancing the view (an argument that Nikolaus Pevsner would develop a few years later) that:

> Forty years ago America was hard at work making classical buildings which should be as impressive as anything in Europe,

old or new. The famous firm of McKim, Mead & White produced efficient designs in Greek, Roman, Renaissance, Byzantine, and several other styles, and Bertram Goodhue built beautiful Gothic churches. At the same time, another architect, Louis Sullivan, was trying to make architecture more reasonable and scientific, and less dependent upon European traditions – in fact, Modern and American. Sullivan was doing in his own country what Mackintosh, of the same period, was doing in Glasgow.[83]

The reference to Bertram Grosvenor Goodhue is interesting, for he would have a considerable posthumous influence on Britain, although not through his churches.

Goodhue died prematurely in 1924. Two years later, an exhibition of his work was held at the Architectural Association which moved Goodhart-Rendel to declare that 'the work of the late Mr Goodhue was not sufficiently known or appreciated in this country. From the English point of view it was probably the most interesting work done in America in recent years.'[84] The exhibition was opened by Giles Gilbert Scott, which was appropriate, not least since Goodhue had so admired Liverpool Cathedral, while Scott appreciated the American's freedom from academic restraints. 'I knew Goodhue intimately,' announced Scott. 'I knew him as a man and as an artist. . . . Goodhue's work was always fresh and independent. He worked in many styles and always said he was not an out-and-out Gothic architect – his views were broader than that.'[85]

Indeed, Goodhue's most influential building was not Gothic but in his own free and dynamic round-arched Classical manner; it was the big public work that came to him by competition towards the end of his life and which was completed after his death: the new State Capitol in Lincoln, Nebraska. It was a remarkable building for its dramatic domed tower and for its treatment of wall planes, with sculpture seemingly growing out of its monumental, stepped-back masses.[86] Its influence may be seen in several new British civic buildings – like those at Swansea and Southampton – where large arched openings pierce discrete cubic pavilions. It may also be detected, perhaps, in the strong vertical emphasis on the tower of Giles Scott's own Cambridge University Library (Plate 2). Not only did Scott know and admire Goodhue's work but he, together with members of the University, made a tour of American libraries in 1930 before making his final design for the Cambridge library – which was built with the help of £250,000 from the foundation financed by John D. Rockefeller, junior.[87] No wonder C. H. Reilly wrote how, after standing in one of the two interior courts with 'the great blocks of the book stacks, with their striking vertical lines rising on all sides, one cannot help being impressed. One has the same feeling among the cliffs of Fifth Avenue or 42nd Street, but here is order and balance as well as size.'[88]

There are other, exotic aspects to the Cambridge University Library which may be American in inspiration. Like Scott, undoctrinaire about style, Goodhue had also employed that simple, whitewashed round-arched manner of building, with residual Baroque detail, which the Spanish had earlier brought to California. This Spanish Colonial architecture enjoyed a revival in the early twentieth century and was often employed for expensive mansions in Hollywood and Santa Barbara. In Cambridge, its influence can be detected in the pantiled trim to the cornices below the roof planes of red-brown Lombardic tiles, and in the round-arched windows of the great Reading Room, their internal arched heads supported on attenuated corbels, although this detail, like the painted timber roof, also has a Swedish air to it. The impact of American Spanish Colonial on Britain in the 1920s and 1930s was complicated and subtle. In adding 'Spanish Super-Colonial' to his familiar menagerie of styles in 1958, Osbert Lancaster wrote how,

> In the years immediately after the first German War there raged on both sides of the Atlantic a strange enthusiasm for all things Spanish, which resulted, on one level, in the increased appreciation of the paintings of Greco and the music of de Falla and, on the other, in a rush of tortoiseshell combs on the head

and the staggering popularity of the late Rudolf Valentino in *The Four Horsemen of the Apocalypse*. In England it was confined, in its architectural manifestation, to the adoption of Curzon Street Baroque for interior decoration and a scattering of wrought-iron grilles over unsuitable façades.[89]

By this date, however, Lancaster distinguished Spanish Colonial from that other exotic style redolent of warmer climates which he had earlier categorised as 'Pseudish', when it is arguable that the two are in fact aspects of the same tribute to Mediterranean culture. In Britain, the whitewashed round-arched style derived partly from Italy and partly from Herbert Baker's revival of Cape Dutch in South Africa, where houses were given fancy-shaped gables, but there would seem to have been a Spanish Colonial, or Hollywood, element. It certainly influenced cinema design, as with the 'Spanish City' at Northfields, but a more distinguished manifestation was

'Pseudish' (Osbert Lancaster, 1938)

'Pont Street Dutch' (Osbert Lancaster, 1938)

Julian Leathart's Twickenham Cinema of 1928, whose white façade with three Spanish Baroque windows was given pantiled wings and an exotic decorative trim.

Spanish Colonial-cum-Pseudish was, however, primarily a domestic style of building. It was used by the Rome scholar Philip Hepworth in his house designs, and was reinterpreted by Oliver Hill in Marylands on Pitch Hill in Ewhurst, Surrey, where the walls below the pantiled roof are of stone (Plate 14). More typical, however, are the houses where the walls were whitewashed and the roof covered with blue or green glazed pantiles. Osbert Lancaster's 1938 definition of 'Pseudish' must be quoted:

This style, which attained great popularity both in this country and in America (where it was generally known as Spanish-colonial), is actually our old friend Pont Street Dutch with a few Stockholm trimmings and a more daring use of colour. In the most typical examples the walls are whitewashed, the roof is covered with Roman tiles in a peculiarly vehement shade of green, and the windows have been enriched with a great deal of fancy leading of a tortuous ingenuity. It was the upper-class style *par excellence* of the pre-slump years, but latterly has sunk a little in the social scale and occasional examples are now to be found alongside some of our more exclusive by-passes.... While it was essentially a country-house style and many of its greatest masterpieces are located on the sea-coast, a few examples are to be found in the more expensive suburbs of the capital and it can be studied in all its diversity in the neighbourhood of Hampstead.[90]

In Hampstead, indeed, can be found a typical expression of the style in the house in Frognal Way designed by the Suffolk architect C. H. Lay for the singer Gracie Fields. Better examples were on a larger scale. Woodfalls, at Melchet Court, Hampshire, designed by Darcy Braddell and Humphrey Deane, had a conscious South African air — except that it had a look-out tower instead of a fancy Cape Dutch gable. Ridgemead at Englefield Green, was designed in 1938 by Robert Lutyens for Captain Woolf Barnato, 'who wanted something resembling a Spanish Mission style house in California'.[91] The result was a stylish Classical house with a horizontal emphasis which Lutyens thought would be 'my spring-song and swan-song combined'.[92] Perhaps the finest and most inventive example of the style was Yaffle Hill at Poole, designed by Edward Maufe in a whitewashed round-arched style on an Edwardian 'butterfly' plan; although roofed in peacock-blue glazed tiles, it was Pseudish but without vulgarity (Plate 20). Yaffle Hill, with 'Georgian elements restated in a lucid labour-saving plan devised for maximum fresh air and sunlight', was selected by the Architecture Club in 1946 as representative of good buildings of the period 1920–1940.[93] In 1933, Christopher Hussey thought it 'unmistakably English, and unquestionably fine architecture, at the same time being both modern and functional', but it is a house which could conceivably have been built in California.[94]

An exception to the surprising neglect in Britain of the work of Frank Lloyd Wright was Williams-Ellis and Summerson's assertion, in 1934, that Wright 'became America's greatest Modern architect, and . . . has strongly influenced the architecture of Europe, especially of Holland. Lloyd Wright is the Le Corbusier of America.'[95] The only direct influence of Wright was a curiosity: a house built in his Californian concrete-block manner for a film cameraman at Hyver Hill, Barnet, in 1934–35. This was designed by a young architect, Denis Harrington, who had been to the United States on a scholarship and studied Wright's work closely.[96] When Wright visited London in 1939 to give a series of lectures at the RIBA, young radical architects were not particularly impressed by the grand old extrovert and his ideas about urban decentralisation. As Andrew Saint has written, 'for British planning intellectuals, reared on Ebenezer Howard, the garden city, and the land-reform theories of Henry George, this was old hat by the 1930s. Broadacre City, if they knew about it at all, would have appeared a visionary irrelevance; Henry Wright of Radburn fame meant more to them at this time than Frank Lloyd Wright.'[97]

20 Frognal Way, Hampstead, London (C. H. Lay, 1934)

If Wright was comparatively unknown in Britain, other American modernists did have an impact, even though their modernism was European in origin. In 1931, the Swiss-born architect William Lescaze, in partnership with George Howe in New York, was invited to work on school buildings on the Dartington Hall estate in Devon. The client was the American teacher William Curry, who had arrived that year to be the headmaster of the Foxhole Junior School.[98] The first commission was High Cross, the headmaster's house, built by Lescaze in 1931–32 in partnership with the English architect Robert Hening. Twenty years later, Pevsner described it as 'the first essay in the International Modern Style at Dartington, and one of the first in England'.[99] Lescaze went on to design other buildings at Dartington, such as the Warren Lane school of 1934–38, all of which were in marked contrast to the more traditional school buildings there. He was also responsible for a development of flat-roofed Modern houses at Churston Ferrers, Torbay.

The American influence at Dartington preceded Lescaze; the Aller Park Junior School of 1929–31 had been designed by Ides van der Gracht of the New York firm Delano & Aldrich. This was because Dartington Hall had been bought in 1925 by the American progressive educational reformers Leonard and Dorothy Elmhirst. Over the following decade, the ancient house with its medieval hall was carefully re-roofed and restored by the 'Anti-Scrape' architect William Weir.* 'It may be objected,' Pevsner commented, 'that the C14 Dartington has re-emerged almost too perfect from under the hands of the careful and wealthy restorers. The setting and the buildings certainly combine the genuine and the comfortable and liveable-in to a degree which must appear even more ideal to the American than to the sloppier British.'[100] Dartington, therefore, exemplifies both the influence of modern American ideas and its

---

* ['Anti-Scrape' was the nickname of the Society for the Protection of Ancient Buildings, originally founded by William Morris and others to oppose the drastic over-restoration, or 'scraping', of medieval architecture. RH.]

High Cross Hill House, Dartington, Devon (Lescaze & Howe, with Robert Hening, 1932)

complete antithesis: the American interest in Old England – for Dartington Hall was one of many ancient houses bought by wealthy Americans since the late nineteenth century.

This interest was not always benign. Some houses were bought to despoil as part of the trade in period rooms, which resulted in English interiors being recreated on the other side of the Atlantic. This was scarcely surprising, given what Peter Mandler has described as the 'general public's near-total indifference to the fate of the country house in the 1920s and 1930s'.[101] Perhaps the most notorious case was Sutton Scarsdale, bought in 1920 by a speculator who sold the interiors to the Philadelphia Museum of Art, leaving the Baroque pile as a gutted shell. Another was Basildon Park, whose dining room ended up in the Waldorf Astoria Hotel in New York after the 1st Lord Iliffe had sold this country house to a developer, George Ferdinando; fortunately, proposals to re-erect the whole building in America came to nothing. The timber-framed 'Olden Time' Agecroft Hall near Manchester was, however, sold, dismantled and rebuilt in Richmond, Virginia, in 1926.[102] The great estates had long been under financial pressure, exacerbated by the political unrest under Asquith's pre-war Liberal government, but such sales were also a consequence of the war; with so many heirs having been killed, higher taxation and falling land values, not a few aristocratic owners sold their estates or demolished their houses. And many were very happy to exchange a country house for a modern flat in London. As Ralph Nevill complained in 1925, 'The idea of a permanent home seems to have but slight attraction for those of the present generation well endowed with the good things of the world; in all probability the custom of making frequent trips abroad, and staying in luxuriously equipped hotels, has largely contributed to such a state of affairs.'[103]

In truth, Americans were rightly held to be more interested in the old homes of England than the natives. 'The incursion of wealthy Americans has undoubtedly saved quite a number of old English country houses,' Nevill concluded; 'nevertheless, in a number of cases, the latter have been entirely transformed, not always with happy aesthetic results.'[104] With the slow and belated growth of the conservation movement in Britain, such sales and exports were an aspect of the financial and cultural dominance of America which began to be resented in the limited circles that cared about such things. Some items eventually returned, however: after the Second World War, Sir William Burrell bought back a stone doorcase from Hornby Castle removed after the 1930 sale. It had eventually been acquired by that obsessive collector William Randolph Hearst, but – like many other objects intended for his American castles – had never been unpacked.[105] The fifteenth-century door is now built into the fabric of the Burrell Collection in Glasgow.

CHAPTER FIVE

TUTANKHAMUN

———◆———

I N 1926, THE YEAR of the General Strike, work began on a large cigarette factory for Carreras Ltd on the site of the gardens of Mornington Crescent in London.[1] Five hundred and fifty feet in length, it was constructed entirely of reinforced concrete, was one of the first factories in Britain to have air conditioning and a dust-extraction plant, and contained nine acres of floor space. What, however, most impressed the public was the front of the factory facing the Hampstead Road, for, in the centre, there was a colonnade of twelve Egyptian columns beneath the coved cornice and, flanking the temple-like entrance, were two seven-foot-high bronze seated Egyptian cats, while ten more black cats were incorporated into the façade. This Egyptian theme was continued in the plainer five-storey wings, for the concrete walls were given a batter – a pronounced backwards tilt – like an Egyptian temple. The factory was designed by M. E. and H. O. Collins, but the Egyptian styling was the responsibility of an expert: Arthur G. Porri (Plate 16).

When the factory opened in 1928, the *Architect and Building News* pondered: 'Whether the Egyptian style is that best suited for a tobacco and cigarette factory may be open to question; but there is little doubt that the "Black Cat" trademark of the owners suggested an association with Bubastis, the feline or cat-faced goddess [Bastet] and, consequently, with Ancient Egypt.'[2] That association was undoubtedly encouraged by 'Tutmania', the publicity-fuelled obsession with Ancient Egypt, provoked by the discovery of the tomb of Tutankhamun by Howard Carter and the Earl of Carnarvon six years earlier. 'Ancient Egypt suddenly became the vogue,' as Robert Graves and Alan Hodge recorded:

> Replicas of the jewellery found in the Tomb, and hieroglyphic embroideries copied from its walls, were worn on dresses; lotus-flower, serpent, and scarab ornaments in vivid colours appeared on hats. Sandy tints were popular, and gowns began to fall stiffly in the Egyptian style. Even the new model Singer sewing-machine of that year went Pharaonic, and it was seriously proposed that the Underground extension from Morden to Edgware, then under construction, should be called Tootancamden, because it passed through Tooting and Camden Town.[3]

This revival of Egyptomania affected all the arts, not least architecture. With its brilliant permanent colour on columns and cornice, what was properly called the Arcadia Works of the House of Carreras must have been the most exotic building to rise in Central London since William Bullock built his Egyptian Hall in Piccadilly just over a century earlier. There was nothing new about buildings in the Egyptian style being erected in Britain; James Stevens Curl, the historian of the Egyptian Revival, points out that the director of the Office of Works, Sir Frank Baines, could seriously propose building a colossal Egyptian pylon flanked by Egyptian temples at Hyde Park Corner as a national war memorial over two years before Howard Carter first glimpsed the glint of gold in the hidden tomb of the young Pharaoh. This was a design dismissed by Sir Thomas Graham Jackson as an 'offence against reason and good taste'.[4]

Reason and good taste were, of course, no defence against 'Tutmania'. 'Serious archaeologists were surprised that so much popular interest greeted this discovery,' Graves and Hodge noted,

> which had done no more than fill up a small gap in comparatively recent Egyptian history, while so little could be beaten up for far more interesting, ancient and beautiful discoveries in the Mesopotamian cities of Ur, Nineveh and Carchemish, and in the Indus valley. The fact was that Tutankhamen, who had succeeded his revolutionary father-in-law the Pharaoh Akhenaton, seemed somehow to embody the modernist spirit; whereas the Mesopotamians were boringly ancient.[5]

Just as Ancient Egypt had seemed so intriguingly modern after the Battle of the Nile, so, now, Egyptian art and design seemed appropriate for such modern building types as cinemas, office blocks and factories.

The Carreras Factory, now restored to its Jazz Age polychromatic glory and renamed Greater London House, seems not so much a monument of the Egyptian Revival as one of the most conspicuous examples of Art Deco architecture in London – though these two categories cannot be precisely separated. In analysing the contribution of Ancient Egypt to Art Deco, Christopher Frayling has described how the 'boy-pharaoh seemed – across the spectrum of visual culture – to be both ancient and modern at the same time': 'Modern in the sense that he died so young (between seventeen and twenty years old, Carter eventually

Exterior, Carreras Cigarette Factory, Mornington Crescent, London (M. E. and O. H. Collins, with Arthur G. Porri, 1928)

estimated, like all those young soldiers in the trenches of Flanders), and, by a very 1920s telescoping of time . . . an incarnation of the very essence of modernism.'[6]

It now seems extraordinary that the architecture of the 1920s and 1930s could ever have been written about without recourse to the irreplaceable stylistic category of 'Art Deco'.* Whether the Paris Expo of 1925 is regarded as the fulfilment or the beginning of the development, there is no doubt that a wide range of exotic ingredients can be found in the style manifested in the exhibition pavilions and their contents: the modern Russian designs of Bakst associated with Diaghilev's *Ballets Russes*; the African sculpture that was having such an influence on Cubist paintings; Chinese and Japanese art; the arts of Indo-China that were being absorbed into the sculptural treatment of Amsterdam School buildings; the buildings of the Maya and Inca civilisations in Mexico and South America that had for some time interested American designers; and – perhaps above all – the archaeological treasures of Ancient Egypt.

The debt to a variety of exotic civilisations can be seen in some of the most characteristic Art Deco buildings and their interiors, such as that of the New Victoria Cinema in London. Several cinemas had polychromatic faience-clad façades that were Egyptian in style, such as the Carlton in Islington by George Coles and the same architect's Carlton in Upton Park, East London, both of the late 1920s. Cinema architecture was often Egyptian in style; the treatment of Masonic temples invariably so, given the debt of Freemasonry to the Hermetic traditions of Ancient Egypt. Freemasons' Hall in London's

---

* Charlotte and Tim Benton, for example, the co-editors of *Art Deco 1910–1939* (published in connection with the major exhibition at the V&A in 2003), never once used the term 'Deco' in reference to 1930s architecture in the catalogue to the *Thirties* exhibition at the Hayward Gallery in 1979. Then again, that rather blinkered interpretation of the decade was almost exclusively concerned with the advent and development of Modernism (Hawkins and Hollis, 1979). I too was guilty of this, however, only referring to 'Art Deco' once – in reference to Paris – in my Introduction to the double issue of *Architectural Design* devoted to 'Britain in the Thirties', preferring to use 'jazz-modernistic' or 'moderne' (Stamp, 1979).

Freemasons' Hall, Great Queen Street, London (Henry Victor Ashley and F. Winton Newman, 1933)

Great Queen Street is modern Grecian rather than Egyptian on the exterior, but the extravagantly grand decoration of the interior spaces has an Egyptian flavour which modern commentators seem to find indistinguishable from Art Deco (Plate 17).* Nikolaus Pevsner described the exterior treatment as 'bewilderingly self-possessed', and the corner tower, facing down Long Acre, is a dominating

---

* Jay Merrick, for example, could describe the archaeologically detailed modern Americo-Grecian of the interiors, with their Egyptianising Masonic furniture and elaborate bronze doors to the Grand Temple, by Walter Gilbert, as 'a rather jolly riot of art deco' ('The Temple of Secrets', *Independent*, 11 May 2005).

composition placed on the diagonal of a clever plan on a tapering site.[7] The Classic manner, reported one contemporary journal, 'in the opinion of the patrons and their architects, was the most suitable medium, expressing the ancient traditions and dignity of Freemasonry'.[8]

A conspicuous example of the modernised Egyptian manner was the new building for the *Daily Telegraph* newspaper designed by Elcock & Sutcliffe in association with Sir John Burnet & Partners. Six giant attenuated, fluted columns rise above a projecting first floor balcony enlivened with wavy Deco detail. It was probably the influence of Thomas Tait that placed this dominant colonnade within a giant Burnettian frame below the upper storeys, ornamented with more wavy lines.[9] In analysing the design, Howard Robertson noted that 'This motif of the frame is one which many architects have employed at various periods since the days of ancient Egypt. It owes its popularity to the opportunity it affords for suggesting strength and achieving unity of effect by simple means.'[10] The monumental assertiveness of this building soon resulted in the nearby *Daily Express* reacting by cladding its own new offices in a smooth skin of glass and black Vitrolite designed by Sir Owen Williams and giving it a spectacular American-style entrance lobby, an extravagant Art Deco creation by Robert Atkinson. But it was the *Daily Telegraph* that was surely the model for the 'Megalopolitan building', the home of the *Daily Beast*, with its 'Byzantine vestibule and Sassanian lounge' in Evelyn Waugh's 1938 novel, *Scoop*.[11]

The importance of Egypt in this architectural *mélange* may be demonstrated by the ubiquity of the polygonal arch, or the square arch with stilted or corbelled corners, a characteristic Art Deco shape. It is a shape both derived from Ancient Egypt but also encouraged – particularly in industrial buildings – by the form of the steelwork in reinforced-concrete structures, when additional reinforcement is required where beams meet the supporting post. The dominance of Ancient Egyptian sources can be seen, above all, in one of the most characteristic types of Art Deco buildings in Britain: the modern

Daily Express Building, Fleet Street, London (Owen Williams, 1933)

factory. It is there in the Carreras cigarette palace, with its literal references to the goddess Bastet, but it is also present in the celebrated 'Fancy factories' of Wallis, Gilbert & Partners.

Both the Firestone Factory and the Hoover Factory had a colourful giant colonnade within a framed surround and terminated at either end by recessed pylons. It is a composition derived from Burnet's façade on the pre-war King Edward VII Galleries on the north side of the British Museum, but instead of Greek Ionic, Wallis used a modern, stylised order with coloured decoration. The Egyptian character of these show façades was emphasised by the pronounced batter of the ends of the principal decorated surround, but it was also present in the decorative symbolism. 'Despite the classical patera and guttae,' Joan Skinner writes of the Firestone Factory,

> and the emphasis of the company identity in monogrammed shields, the detail in path and doorway announce the entrance to the temple of Amun-Ra. Ram's-head sphinx, ram's horns on the heraldic device, beside the clock, on the final pedestals and the lamp standards above them, stand for Amun – the most powerful of the gods of ancient Egypt (or Zeus-Amun or Jupiter-Amun to include a conflation of Greco-Roman-Egyptian reference). The many circular motifs denote the sun and the sun god Ra. His rays burst forth in the fanlight, in the bronze filigree of the doors and again above the round face of the clock – time being eternal as the diurnal progress of the sun.[12]

Similarly, at the slightly later Hoover Factory, where the giant order was given jazzy Deco fluting, there are decorative details derived from the art of Central and North American Indians – possibly as a reference to the American origins of the company – but the principal iconographic scheme was Egyptian.

> In ancient Egypt, the confidant most close in body and second only in rank to the king was the king's fan bearer. The colourful,

Interior, Hoover Factory, Perivale, Greater London (Wallis, Gilbert & Partners, 1932)

long-poled, semi-circular fans were of vulture feathers. The vulture symbolised the goddess Mut, protector of the king. . . . The vulture and the Wedjat snake together symbolise the protectors of the 'Two Lands' of Egypt. This Egyptian symbolism comes closer to a representation of the close relationship between the Hoover parent and its first overseas base than, say, thunderbird feathers worn by an Apache chief.[13]

How seriously Wallis expected all this to be taken is not recorded.

Perhaps the *Illustrated London News* got nearer to the reality in 1933 when it described how:

> Along Western Avenue, one of the great new arterial roads leading in and out of London, the traveller will see, a few miles only from the heart of the Empire's capital, a gleaming palace in dazzling white and red, with soaring white towers, the walls almost all glass, set like a glittering gem in the midst of green lawns and gay flower-beds. With its flat roof and general design it might almost be the palace of some Oriental potentate . . . As a matter of fact, it is the new home of the Hoover Sweeper.[14]

This exoticism, so closely related to the escapism of the 'atmospheric' cinema interior and, indeed, to the fantastic, archaic film sets of, say, Cecil B. DeMille's *Cleopatra* or D. W. Griffith's *Intolerance*, was typical of the post-war decades. In the Carreras building and the Great West Road factories, as well as in faience-clad cinema

The former Willans and Robinson Factory, Queensferry, Wales (H. B. Creswell, 1901)

façades, the exoticism was suggested by colour and detail, but it was the monumental massing of new buildings that was characteristic of the period. Partially to cope with the aesthetic problem posed by new building types such as the large factory or the multi-storey building, architects adopted the massive and timeless austerity characteristic of the surviving monuments of the Ancient World. The essential ingredients of this monumentality were the elimination of most ornamental detail, unbroken wall surfaces and the pronounced slope given to vertical lines. This was a tendency already evident well before 1914. It can be seen in the brick boiler factory at Queensferry, near Chester, where the brick walls and the dominant tower were reinforced by clasping buttresses which were given a pronounced slope; the effect was at once unequivocally industrial and yet reminiscent of an Egyptian temple.*

Such monumentality can be seen in the work of the firm that would become Sir John Burnet, Tait & Lorne, which both explored new directions and yet is so representative of the interwar decades in Britain. This tendency became more evident when Burnet – whose pre-war north wing for the British Museum was the formal model for Wallis's 'fancy factories' – was joined by Thomas Tait. It can be seen in particular in Adelaide House of 1925, where the entrance is flanked by squat Doric columns within an Egyptian temple frame and the pronounced verticals rise to an oversailing coved Egyptian cornice.

This aesthetic was developed further, and abstracted further, in Summit House in Red Lion Square by P. J. Westwood and Joseph Emberton, where the treatment of the faience-clad verticals, and recessed faience panels between the windows, also owes much to Holland House, that little-noticed London wartime building by the great Dutch modernist, H. P. Berlage. At Summit House, however,

---

* H. B. Creswell's perspective of his factory design is illustrated in Stamp (1982b), where it is juxtaposed with a reconstruction of the Temple of Solomon at Jerusalem by C. Stanley Peach, the power station architect (p. 121).

Adelaide House, London Bridge, London (Sir John Burnet, Tait & Lorne, 1925)

the vertical piers are contained within a continuous flush frame and are given a definite curved batter – all rising, most significantly, *not* to an oversailing cornice but to a slightly recessed top storey. This gave the characteristic monumental or ziggurat profile of the period.

In his two illustrated volumes on *The Monumental and Commercial Architecture of Great Britain of the Present Day* published in 1928 and 1930, Dexter Morand considered that 'the question may arise as to why it was thought necessary to have "Monumental" architecture and "Commercial" architecture bound together, for it hardly seems correct to have Savage's Masonic Temple in the same place as Westwood & Emberton's Summit House.* Yet, on the other hand, it may become quite a difficult problem to know where one ends and the other begins.'[15] Monumentality, with echoes of the exotic past, was the mood of the time. This mood is reflected in the paintings and in the popular etchings by the architect-artist William Walcot, who painted Egyptian temples with impressionistic rich colour and captured the vast magnificence of Ancient Rome in the reconstructions of basilicas and baths depicted in the vague, rich chiaroscuro of etchings – while giving the same monumental qualities to new buildings in other contemporary prints. No wonder that, in his much-admired Shepherd's Bush Pavilion Cinema with its vast brick external walls, Frank Verity looked to Rome for inspiration.

But America also looked to the Ancient World. The influence of Mayan architecture on the work of Frank Lloyd Wright is clear in such buildings as the Hollyhock House in Los Angeles of 1919–21. And a similarity between Ancient Egyptian buildings and the massing of the new Devonshire House by Carrère & Hastings was noted by juxtaposing illustrations of both in one Glasgow architectural publication, to show that: 'Architects are again obtaining the most pleasing effects in large buildings as well as in houses by attention to proportions rather than by "frilly gables, nooks, and pretty-pretty roofwork".'[16] The first to identify and analyse this new monumentality as the essential aesthetic of a new architecture would seem to have been the young Robert Byron. In discussing monastic architecture in the *Architectural Review* in 1928, he saw parallels with the present and identified the underlying motive of this 'new spirit' as 'movement in mass'. 'Today,' Byron wrote,

---

* Oddly enough, neither Summit House nor Rupert Savage's Masonic Temple in Broad Street, Birmingham, of 1923–27 (now Central Television Centre) was illustrated in either of Morand's two volumes.

the new spirit may be observed in such diverse buildings as the later skyscrapers of New York, Liverpool Cathedral, the Town Hall at Stockholm, and the large block known as Adelaide House at the north end of London Bridge. . . . What, then, have all these in common, by what means is this movement in mass attained? The secret lies in uninterrupted stretches of flat, perpendicular surface; and the manipulation of perpendicular lines so that in fact or in appearance they are made to converge. Hence, therefore, the undisputed novelty of twentieth-century building. But there exist none the less two localities where a parallel style of architecture has developed and where the same abstract vigour informs buildings other than places of worship.

These were Mount Athos in Greece and Lhasa in Tibet, where, 'in comparatively modern times, have the holy men in their seclusion erected buildings to which only London and New York of the last ten years can offer parallel'.[17]

Although not himself an architect, Byron's enthusiasms conveyed in his writings are revealing about the architectural sensibilities of his time. In 1937 appeared his best-known book, *The Road to Oxiana*, which described his travels in Persia and Afghanistan. As both text and illustrations reveal, he was particularly taken with the extraordinary tall brick burial towers of northern Persia, whose simple geometrical forms and vertical emphasis seemed so reminiscent of a modern water tower. He had been drawn there, in particular, by photographs of the fluted brick tower at Gumbad-i-Kabus, which he decided was one of the great buildings of the world. In his 1932 book on *The Appreciation of Architecture*, Byron had illustrated this tower and noted that it 'exhibits the principle of vertical mobility in design carried out with that merciless severity so fashionable in modern industrial architecture'.[18] Again and again he was concerned to point out that there was, in essence, little new about the new industrial aesthetic; in illustrating an ancient brick wall at Merv, now in Turkmenistan, he noted that:

the building might almost be mistaken, at a casual glance, for a modern smelting-works instead of a medieval fortification. Not that this need imply any particular merit. But it may prove to those whose admiration for industrial forms amounts to mania that the architectural excellence in such forms (when it exists) is not so exclusively the gift of machinery as they imagine.[19]

Was it coincidence that the spiral gate-piers at Oliver Hill's modernistic Midland Hotel at Morecambe could be seen as miniature versions of the spiral minaret of the Malwiyeh mosque at Samara'a near Baghdad?[20]

Given the mood of the time and the purpose of the event, it is not surprising that the principal buildings erected for the British Empire Exhibition in 1924–25 reflected the taste both for the monumental and exotic. As at earlier exhibitions, many of the pavilions were temporary, decorative palaces of fibrous plaster designed in a variety of styles to represent the many parts of a culturally diverse Empire,

British Government Pavilion, Wembley, Greater London (Simpson & Ayrton, 1924)

but for the official buildings the old national style of Tudor brick and half-timber had been replaced by the temple forms of Egypt and Greece. 'Here it is on English soil,' commented Harry Barnes in the *Architectural Review*,

> yet housed in buildings on which Greek and Arab alone have left their print. What has become of all the art that filled England from the first William to the last Henry? How are the dominant dominated, and those who have builded this enduring Empire become the imitators of those whose empires are in the dust? It is the triumph of the temple and the mosque, the pillar and the beam. The arch is ousted, will it come again?[21]

It was as if the old Victorian battle between the arch and the lintel, between the Gothic and the Greek, between Gilbert Scott and Alexander Thomson, had at last been resolved in the Scotsman's favour.[22]

The British Government Pavilion set the imperial tone. It was a severe temple, as much Egyptian as Greek, stretched horizontally, but with two square piers instead of columns set beneath a flattened pediment and flanked by pylons and guarded by six Wembley lions. 'When Aladdin wanted a palace,' commented the *Official Guide*,

> he rubbed his lamp and the building rose overnight, complete with every detail save for the jewelling of a single window. Wembley has not been able to beat that record, but came within a reasonable distance when it built the British Government Pavilion in eight months. This Pavilion has a significance of its own that marks it as a house apart. . . . A building that compels attention, simple yet of abounding dignity, this Pavilion shelters within its ample walls many of the symbols of Empire.[23]

It was certainly rather more dignified than some of the pavilions in indigenous exotic styles representing different parts of the Empire containing such attractions as full-sized models of Australian cricketers or the Prince of Wales in Native American costume sculpted in butter.

A similar neo-Classical manner was used for the Palace of Arts, while for the exteriors of the two vast sheds which lay either side of the central avenue, the Palaces of Engineering and Industry, pediments were abandoned for pylons and piers. Designed by Sir John Simpson and Maxwell Ayrton and constructed of reinforced concrete, they presented unadorned textured concrete to the public, thus reconciling modernity with traditional monumentality. A drawing of the British Government Pavilion was used as the frontispiece to *The Pleasures of Architecture* by Clough and Amabel Williams-Ellis, who wondered 'whether the actual ferro-concrete construction with its look of almost cardboard attenuation should be distinguished or not. On the whole Mr Maxwell Ayrton compromised, leaving for example the true construction to thrill us with bridges of fairy-tale lightness and the façade of the Stadium to impress us with a fake solidity.'[24] This permanent stadium at Wembley, with its twin landmark domed towers reminiscent of New Delhi, opened in 1924 and was sited at the south end of the exhibition's central avenue. Along with all the other concrete structures, it was the achievement of the consulting engineer, Owen Williams, and the success and speed of erection of these buildings won him a knighthood at the age of thirty-four.

If the resonances of past empires were thought suitable for the official buildings at the British Empire Exhibition, so they were for the official buildings around the Empire itself. The supreme example was, of course, the new capital of India at New Delhi, designed before the war.[25] In the buildings by Lutyens, and Baker, as we have seen, imperial axial monumentality was given a dynamic quality by what Byron described as 'a faintly pyramidal principle'.[26] The dominant element, however, remained the Western Classical tradition – the language of Wren and Bernini. It was in some of the later, lesser buildings in British India that the contemporary taste for older and more exotic monumentality achieved appropriate expression. Above all, there is St Martin's Garrison Church, an extraordinary building which rises from the hot, dusty plain in the cantonments to the west of Delhi. Its massive walls of pinky-red bricks step back dramatically to enclose the interior volumes and are only occasionally pierced by windows. On axis, the profile of the building resembles a ziggurat, but from the sides the modelling of the tower leaves buttresses to suggest a Gothic church, yet the windows have round heads. A few details, like the recessed arches of the main entrance, hint at German Expressionism, or the work of modern architects like the highly influential Dutchman, W. M. Dudok, yet the overall impression is of the massive sublimity of ancient monuments (Plate 1).

This brick ziggurat was designed in 1928. Penelope Chetwode, daughter of the Commander-in-Chief of the Indian Army, recalled that it was known as 'the Cubist Church' when it opened in 1930.[27] It was both modern and traditional, an intelligent response to the heat of India and resonant with understated symbolism. Those who saw this church when new were deeply impressed, and Christopher Hussey wrote in 1931 that:

> Elemental as the conception is, it none the less has a very definite style, appropriate both to the climate and the building's purpose. Had this church been the work of a French or German architect, Europe would be flabbergasted by the magnificently simple and direct design. But since it is the work of an Englishman, it will probably never be heard of abroad.[28]

And so it was: its architect, A. G. Shoosmith, never built again after returning home to England.[29]

Shoosmith had been responsible for supervising the execution of the new Viceroy's House and Lutyens's manner is evident in the church, both in the sensibility governing the alternative set backs of the planes of brickwork and in the style of the cool, Classical interior.

'Bricks!' wrote Lutyens to Shoosmith; 'A building of one material is for some strange reason much more noble than one of many . . . The Romans did it! Why should not Britons?'[30] But Shoosmith was twenty years younger than his master; he believed that simplification had become a virtue and that 'brickwork unadorned and the stark and vital forms of reinforced concrete were capable of a new conception of beauty'.[31] This he demonstrated in his exotic, extraordinary masterpiece made of three and a half million bricks and vaults of reinforced concrete.

A similar manner, abstracting ancient monumentalism to create a style at once modern and exotic, was adopted by Austen St Barbe Harrison for his buildings erected in Palestine during the British Mandate. Harrison, who had worked briefly both for J. M. Simpson and in Lutyens's New Delhi office, chose to spend almost all of his working life abroad after he became chief architect to the Mandatory Public Works Department, although he was later associated with the design of Nuffield College, Oxford. In the ancient land of Palestine, he rose to the challenge both of reconciling old and new as well as East and West, Christian, Jew and Arab. This he achieved, above all, in his two principal buildings: the High Commissioner's Residence (1928–31) and the Palestine Archaeological Museum, now the Rockefeller Museum (1927–37), both in Jerusalem. Both buildings have axial plans which owe something to both the Beaux-Arts tradition and to old Islamic architecture; both employ a modernistic streamlined aesthetic relying on plain surfaces and shadow, using round arches and the traditional Palestine vault; both have powerful landmark towers.

Perhaps only between the wars could a British architect have responded to the imperatives of ancient religious cultures and the proximity of ancient monuments without either copying or ignoring the exotic context. The lesson of Lutyens in India and the contemporary taste for the monumental certainly helped, but the British respect for Jerusalem played a part; the insistence of the first military governor that all new buildings in the city should be built of stone resulted in Erich Mendelsohn designing some of his most impressive and appropriate works in Palestine.* Christopher Hussey described the High Commissioner's house as 'A Crusaders' Castle of Today'. The new Government House, he wrote in 1931, 'is frankly twentieth-century. But it appeals to our northern imagination because the architect, consciously or unconsciously, has made its general form remind us of the Holy Land of the Crusades, not of the Roman province of Judea nor, by some flight of fancy, of Solomon's palace.' Interestingly, Hussey compared Harrison's approach with what he knew of modern British buildings in India:

> The building is the product of a romantic modernism expressed in terms of the Near East sympathetically understood. It differs radically from the new Turkish government buildings at Angora [i.e. Ankara], designed by [Clemens] Holzmeister, in that there the Near-Eastern element has been purposely suppressed. Here native traditions have been developed and infused with Western life. The closest analogy to it is the work of another young architect, the Cantonment Church at Delhi by Mr A. G. Shoosmith. Both might be said to represent the more conciliatory and appreciative spirit that has animated imperial policy since the War.[32]

Sixty years on, modern Israeli historians have lauded Harrison's achievement, and concluded: 'It was, perhaps, in Palestine that the Empire produced its last intellectually ambitious architectural statement. . . . Within the limits of colonialism, this architecture has risen up to the moral and architectural challenge. It makes a poetic and compelling response to the complex meaning and charged landscape of the country.'[33]

---

* General Edmund Allenby, the conqueror of Jerusalem from the Turks in 1917, appointed Sir Ronald Storrs as military governor, who, at Allenby's suggestion, appointed the engineer William McLean to prepare a master plan for the city which included the stipulation that all new buildings be faced in stone.

Something of the abstract character of Shoosmith's masterpiece is evident in contemporary churches back in Britain. The long length of St Andrew's, Luton, for instance, by Sir Giles Gilbert Scott, articulated by dramatic sloping brick buttresses, is terminated by a massive west tower, whose squat proportions, upper frieze of slit windows between clasping buttresses, and hints of battlements give it the character of a Crusader castle. But the taste for the exotic and monumental is most evident in Scott's secular work. The massive tower rising in the centre of his Cambridge University Library clearly has its origins in the evolving designs for the central tower of his great cathedral in Liverpool, but the vertical modelling of the brickwork, terminating in vestigial temple porticoes just below the unusual pyramidal roof, give it the character of some Middle Eastern mausoleum as well as that of an early New York skyscraper (Plate 2). With good reason, the historian of the institution has described the evolution of Scott's design as a 'transformation from a practical library with modest classical features to the Assyrian palace which confronts us today'.[34]

St Andrew's, Luton, Bedfordshire (Giles Gilbert Scott, 1932)

This aspect of Scott's architecture is evident, above all, in the industrial buildings that established his reputation as a most versatile designer. In 1930, Scott was wheeled in as consulting architect to make acceptable the design of the controversial coal-fired electricity generating station the London Power Company was building on the south bank of the Thames near Battersea (Plate 21). The basic configuration and massing of the steel framed structure, with its four corner chimneys, had already been established by J. Theo Halliday of the Manchester architects Halliday & Agate. Scott's role was to humanise the great bulk of the building while not denying its industrial character. The chimneys, of reinforced concrete, were modelled as giant fluted columns, while the walls were faced in fine pink bricks and their massiveness tempered by high-level recessions and bands of vertical fluting. This treatment was described by contemporaries as 'jazz-modern', a term which hints at its American, Art Deco origins; in 1937 John Betjeman described the power station as 'the supreme example of the restrained jazz' in London.[35] Indeed, in the treatment of the walls, with friezes of repetitive non-historical decoration, there are echoes not only of American brick-clad skyscrapers but also the Californian houses of Frank Lloyd Wright. And these – the Hollyhock House, the Ennis House – were influenced by ancient Mayan architecture.

Even when only two chimneys of Battersea 'A' had been raised next to the busy railway viaducts out of Victoria and Waterloo, Scott's architectural treatment of the huge blank walls was much admired. 'The great Power Station at Battersea,' W. Curtis Green said in 1933, 'by the intelligent co-operation of the architect, Sir Giles Scott, with the engineers, has been transformed into something that gives pleasure by its dignity and expression of power.'[36] So successful was his industrial brick style that he soon used it again to dramatise and unify the three great irregular blocks of the Guinness brewery at Park Royal, where he worked with the consulting engineers Sir Alexander Gibb & Partners. Scott only achieved total control over the massing in his final 'temple of power'

Control Room A, Battersea Power Station, London (Giles Gilbert Scott, 1933)

at Bankside (now Tate Modern), opposite St Paul's Cathedral and the City of London. Here, all the flues were gathered into one great central campanile and the resulting symmetry, combined with a ziggurat profile and the careful modelling of the massive planes of brickwork with jazz-modern fluting, gives the great bulk of the building something of the character of a Mayan temple – as filtered through the imagination of Wright – but it was not designed until 1947.[37]

C. H. Reilly, in reviewing Scott's Battersea Power Station in 1934, began by wondering:

> What is this great romantic pile with its long, incised vertical lines and hidden windows? Is it a new cathedral by that interesting fellow up in the north, F. X. Velarde? There is certainly something of his at Blackburn rather like it. No, it cannot be that. There is a faint plume of steam from one of the towers that can hardly be incense.[38]

Velarde, Reilly's former pupil at the Liverpool School, had established a reputation for designing striking modernistic churches; his Anglican Church of St Gabriel at Blackburn, remarkable for its vaulted interior filled with chromium-plated Art Deco furnishings, indeed had a blocky brick exterior which, in its cubic abstraction, resembled nothing so much as an industrial building. Another Liverpool product whose work was strongly affected by American Art Deco was Herbert J. Rowse, who was responsible for what was perhaps the most unexpectedly sublime example of interwar British architecture: a tall brick ziggurat on the edge of the River Mersey.

In the 1920s, as we have seen, Rowse designed several large commercial buildings in Liverpool in the Classical manner more typical of New York and Chicago than London. In 1931, he was appointed architect to the Mersey Tunnel Joint Committee, and for the structures associated with this project he adopted a more modernistic style, strongly influenced by contemporary Deco buildings in the United States (although, as far as Pevsner was concerned, Rowse used 'French-1925-moderne details, with Egyptian touches').[39] The tunnel, connecting Liverpool and Birkenhead and known as Queensway, had been begun in 1925 and was, at over two miles long, the longest underwater road tunnel in the world. Architecturally, the project presented a challenge without precedent as he had to plan and design six large buildings – three on each side of the river – to house the equipment and ducts needed to ventilate the tunnel, as well as designing the tunnel entrances and associated lamp standards and toll booths. All was done in a consistent monumental manner, enhanced with Deco fluting and detail and semi-abstract integrated sculpture by Edmund C. Thompson and George T. Capstick. The tunnel entrances were originally lit by giant fluted columns, faced in black granite, rising to glazed bowls of gilded bronze, while Rowse lined the interior of the tunnel with a dado of black glass, broken every fifty yards with

Ventilation Tower, St George's Dock, Liverpool (Herbert Rowse, 1935)

Ventilation Tower, Birkenhead, Merseyside (Herbert Rowse, 1934)

vermilion fire stations.* As far as Reilly was concerned, writing soon after its opening in 1934, this was 'one of those bright, clean, lean things, where the architect beats the engineer at his own game'.[40]

Particularly impressive are the ventilation stations, carefully tucked into the existing urban fabric but dramatically distinctive in their windowless verticality. Most were faced in brick, artfully enhanced with decorative banding and fluting, as well as sculptural ornament, which gives them an exotic air. Behind Pierhead, however, where the St George's ventilation chimney was combined with administrative offices, the structure was faced in Portland stone. Here the architectural treatment is more Classical, but the detailing of the cornice-less parapets and the vertical shafts and fluting on the central chimney-tower can only be described as Art Deco.

The most impressive of all these structures, however, is the strange tower standing right by the Cheshire bank of the Mersey. This is the Woodside Ventilation Station, one of the finest and certainly one of the most dramatic examples of British architecture of its time. Vast overlapping planes of multi-coloured bricks rise from a base of horizontal brick rustication to create a ziggurat profile, culminating in the central square chimney-shaft. Detail is spare but carefully considered, and there is a central vertical feature of textured brickwork rising up the centre of the dominant central plane. The handling of the interlocking masses is masterly, the sense of scale faultless. Rowse succeeded in combining conspicuous modernity with a sense of the sublime in an unprecedented structure that echoes the ziggurats of the Maya and the brick towers of the Middle East. No wonder that in 1947 the Architecture Club put a photograph of the Woodside Ventilation Station on the front cover of its survey of the best *Recent English Architecture 1920–1940*.

That there was a connection, or at least an affinity, between monumental structures of the Ancient World and modern tall

---

* Both the tunnel interiors and the entrances have since been spoiled, with the black granite column at the Liverpool end having been removed.

buildings was certainly admitted by contemporaries. In his 1934 book *Building to the Skies*, Alfred Bossom juxtaposed an illustration of a 230-foot high ziggurat with a monumental staircase at Tikal in Guatemala with a 35-storey commercial tower designed by himself, in which 'the decorations are based on primitive American motives similar to those which inspired the Guatemalans to use such forms nearly 2,000 years ago'. In North America, Bossom explained,

> the light is particularly hard and white and the shadows uninteresting. The Mayans in Mexico accordingly evolved an architecture of simple surface decorations with no cornices but with a strong emphasis on ornamented angles to form a towering silhouette. The designers in Chicago and New York, working under identical conditions, did the same. It was almost a law of architectural necessity that the Americans in stretching their buildings skywards should come to use the same treatment of flat surfaces, set-backs and ornamented silhouettes.[41]

Whether deliberately or not, both Rowse in Liverpool and Scott in Cambridge followed ancient models when dealing with the problems presented by verticality and unusual height. The challenge was to design structures that take the eye upwards and then provide a satisfactory visual termination to this ascent. In the past, only religious monuments rose grandly above the general horizontal level in towns and cities, but now quite ordinary buildings were creeping upwards. As Robert Byron put it:

> The problem of building outside the scope of vision has existed, and has been the subject of increasing thought and refinement, throughout the history of architecture. The new problem is an extension of the old one, arising from the genius of the steel girder. . . . Metaphorically speaking, there are no limits to the heights of which steel construction is capable.[42]

There were two solutions to this aesthetic problem; that most favoured in Britain was 'in-stepping', or recessions at high level. 'In cases where in-stepping takes the form of or assists a real grouping of masses, and where that grouping is readily visible, the principle

Dorchester Hotel, Park Lane, London (Curtis Green, 1931)

is justified' (as Lutyens demonstrated). 'But to cut out little chunks and ledges at the top of every tall building is to invite confusion.' The other solution was to make the building protrude at the top, perhaps with an exaggerated projecting cornice.

It was here, Byron went on to argue, that the monumental buildings of the past could provide useful lessons:

> It is not only in Europe and America that the tall building has developed. In the mosque of Sultan Hassan at Cairo or the Gateway of Akbar at Fatehpurt Sikri; in the towering Vimanahs of Orissa, the Gopuras of Dravida, or the clumped spires of Angkor; in the convergent perpendiculars of the Potala at Lhassa or of the great Gateways at Pekin; in all these, and of innumerable others, there may be found, not a solution of the problem – for their ancillary conditions admit of no comparison with those of our streets – but a clue as to how it might be solved. The architects of these buildings knew nothing of classical or Gothic. Yet they created beauty in their own way, and in doing so made of height a servant instead of a master.[43]

Byron cited two tall modern London buildings as particular aesthetic successes. One was the Underground headquarters at St James's Park, by Charles Holden; the other was the Dorchester Hotel in Park Lane, designed by Curtis Green over a reinforced-concrete frame originally envisioned by Owen Williams. 'These have faults,' opined Byron,

> particularly the latter, whose material and ornament are so repulsive as almost completely to obscure its deeper merits; but they can be analysed, because their aim is righteous, because their architects, within the limits of site, function, and expense, have been inspired by knowledge of what has constituted architecture through the ages, by consideration for the capacities of the human eye, and above all by a desire to achieve, even if the achievement is not quite complete, the expression of growth and organic unity.[44]

Holden's multi-storey building, after following the irregular street lines at low level, rises on a cruciform plan to culminate in a central tower. The composition is symmetrical, logical, and achieves a pyramidal or ziggurat-like profile, while projecting cornices are replaced by flat string-courses. Everything tended towards a monumental simplicity.

By the beginning of the 1930s, simplified masses, pyramidal in overall form, with the appearance of inward slope to the walls and with the upper levels stepped back, had become the characteristic shape for conventional modern architecture. Holden had achieved this look a decade earlier in his work for the Imperial War Graves Commission in France and Belgium, designing stone lodge buildings of military severity with the upper level recessed. A very similar aesthetic had been adopted for his Underground stations on the Northern Line extension to Morden, where the monumental treatment of the simple, stone-faced entrances again eschewed the cornice. An analogous process can be observed in the tall, American-style Classical banks in Glasgow designed by the firm of James Miller; in the early 1920s they have proud cornices, but when the Bank of Scotland in Bothwell Street was built in 1934–35, the principal cornice had disappeared and the upper storeys were treated as a single recessed, slightly tapering mass. The aesthetic was still American, but now inspired by the ancient monuments of the Mayan civilisation.

A grossly conspicuous example of this approach to the massing of buildings was the new Shell-Mex House, designed by F. Milton Cashmore of the prolific commercial firm of Messrs Joseph and built in 1931–32 on the site of the Hotel Cecil between the Strand and the Thames. The symmetrical Portland stone-clad façade over a steel frame that rises thirteen storeys has no projections, only recessions. These increase in depth and frequency towards the summit, to create balconies and terraces and leaving a central squat tower on whose windowless wall is placed a giant clock. The whole effect is that of an Art Deco mantelpiece ornament blown up large. Contemporaries were impressed by the efficient planning of the building and by the

Shell-Mex House, The Strand, London (F. Milton Cashmore, 1932)

fact that, it '*looks* like an office building'. As for the gigantic clock, the *Architect and Building News* was impressed that it was placed 'where the more thoughtless would use a flashing sign, and serves the same purpose far better'.[45] Raymond Mortimer, writing in the more critical *Architectural Review*, while admitting that it was 'one of the best pieces of office architecture in London', wished that both architects and clients had shown more courage and produced something less Classical and monumental. Familiar as he was with

Primary Filter Building, Kempton Park Waterworks, Sunbury-on-Thames, Surrey (Henry E. Stilgoe, 1930)

the well-designed advertising material associated with Shell petrol, and knowing Emil Fahrenkamp's streamlined, metallic Shell-Haus in Berlin, he could only find this new London block 'very disappointing'.[46] What, however, is most pertinent to the theme of this chapter is that he thought that the giant clock (which housed water-tanks and lift machinery) 'spoils the Embankment façade by a monumental heaviness and vaguely Assyrian shape'.

If one characteristic building of 1930 be sought, perhaps it could be the severe, temple-like block that stands prominently near the Kempton Park racecourse next to the main road out of London to the south-west. Set on a slight mound, the staircase to its entrance rises between projecting rusticated pylons, while further, smooth pylons flank the portal itself. Above is a clean, monumental block, penetrated on the front by three tall slit windows and with more groups of three vertical openings on the longer side elevations. The smooth rendered walls display a pronounced batter, while the upper, windowless attic recedes in a series of steps to reach a flat roof. Away from the road, a ground-level wing stretches away to reach more pylonic masses. The whole composition is a masterly, powerful combination of horizontals and verticals. Yet this great suburban temple, the modern Egypto-Mayan ziggurat, is not the tomb monument of some great national figure but the primary filter building for a sewage works. Completed in 1930, it was apparently designed by H. E. Stilgoe, chief engineer to the Metropolitan Water Board – but who was the architect?*

A similar aesthetic was used to dignify another minor utilitarian building in Sheffield. The Education Department office, built in 1938, was a powerful Archaic-Classical design by Sheffield's city architect, W. G. Davies. The entrance is placed in an Egyptian-Deco frame and is surrounded by glass within another Egyptian frame which is elided both with the surrounding wall surface and the faces of the simple square piers between the regular windows. The corners are contained by massive pylons, emphasised by projecting plinths. There are no projections, only recessions, from strong plinth, to pylon, to wall, and then, by several steps to a narrow attic ornamented with Deco squares. A final antique air of sophistication is given by the narrow-and-wide pseudo-isodomic coursing of the stonework. The result is that this small, free-standing two-storey block of offices had the physical presence of an ancient temple.

The design of this Sheffield building owed much to the work of Burnet and Tait, whose enthusiasm for the tapered, stepped-back Egyptian pylon can be traced back to before the Great War. Tait was the architect involved with the design of the great Sydney Harbour Bridge, designed in 1922 and opened in 1932. For purely visual reasons, he felt that the huge bowspring steel arch of the bridge should be terminated and anchored by massive masonry piers that rose well above the roadway as flanking pylons. As may

---

* A photograph of this building was chosen as the frontispiece of the very first number of *Architecture Illustrated*, published in June 1930.

Tyne Bridge, Newcastle-upon-Tyne (R. Burns Dick, with Mott, Hay & Anderson, 1928)

be seen from construction photographs, these pylons were hollow, had no structural purpose and were added after the completion of the bridge itself. Aesthetically, however, they add much to the huge bridge's power. No wonder, therefore, that similar pylons appeared on the approaches to Newcastle's smaller version of the Sydney bridge, the Tyne Bridge of 1925–28 designed by Mott, Hay & Anderson engineers and the architect R. Burns Dick. And in Giles Gilbert Scott's first design for rebuilding Waterloo Bridge across the Thames, four tall and massive stone pylons with decorative friezes were to frame the arched masonry structure.[47]

It fell to Burnet, Tait & Lorne to create the most sophisticated example of this Egypto-American-Mayan-Deco manner – and one of the finest public buildings in interwar Britain: St Andrew's House in Edinburgh. Appropriately, it is a monumental structure, formal in style but romantic in conception, which rises from Edinburgh's own Acropolis, Calton Hill. Decades of debate about the proposal to replace the old Calton Gaol with a new public building had culminated in the attempt by the Office of Works in London to impose a symmetrical, Classical pile on this prominent site designed by its chief architect, Sir Richard Allison. Public and influential opinion resisted this threat, and in 1933 the government agreed to appoint a private architect for the project to build government offices and a residence for the Secretary of State for Scotland. The resulting building was completed shortly after the outbreak of war in 1939. As David Walker, historian of the building and the Burnet firm, has written, 'Tait was the only possible choice if yet another confrontation with the Scots was to be avoided. His appointment had a certain inevitability about it. By 1934 the practice of Burnet, Tait and Lorne, although based in London, had assumed the role of flagship to the entire Scottish architectural profession.'[48]

Tait had transformed the old and distinguished firm for so long dominated by Sir John Burnet, who had now virtually retired. Aware of the profound changes in European architecture, he had not only played a dominant role in the design of such influential buildings as Adelaide House and the Masonic Hospital at Ravenscourt Park, but had also produced a series of flat-roofed Modern houses in the late 1920s. In 1930, the firm was rejoined by the flash and Americanised Francis Lorne, who had been working for Bertram Goodhue Associates in the United States. Other talented new assistants were then recruited, some of whom had worked in other important American offices – one with Frank Lloyd Wright, and Gordon Farquhar with Raymond Hood, whose Rockefeller Centre in New York had an influence on St Andrew's House. Nevertheless, 'Tait designed everything himself, down to the smallest details':

> He drew upon the experience of Lorne, Farquhar and the others in much the same way as he drew upon the American and European books – several of them Russian – obtained for him by the bookseller Alec Tiranti. . . . But like Burnet before him, he never copied. He was an acute observer who took in the design principles of what he saw and grafted them to his own, resulting in an interpretation which was entirely personal.[49]

Towards the centre of Edinburgh, St Andrew's House presents a varied outline – as recommended by the critics of the official scheme for the site – achieved by a symmetrical composition of blocks and wings (steel-framed and stone-clad) of different heights, brilliantly composed so as to appear to be rising out of the rock. As Tait reported in 1934:

> In considering the design it was felt necessary to express the long low lying lines of the hillside without interfering with its outline or the monuments crowning its crest. In other words it will grow out of the landscape and appear to be part of it, composed in such a way that the wings gradually receding and varying in height will culminate in the central block and form one piece of sculpture work. The design is simple and sculpturesque rather than decorative but carried out with that strength and refinement expressive of present-day sentiments and also so essential to a building which is to form an addition to probably the most beautiful city in the world.[50]

The Ancient Greeks could scarcely have done better.

Towards Regent Road and Calton Hill, however, Tait presented a single, symmetrical, Classically inspired composition in which Beaux-Arts rigour was tempered with modernistic touches. The free-standing entrance piers, with built-in electric lights, are De Stijl compositions, while the long, stripped Classical wings end with curved forms, flat projecting canopies and tall glazed bays. It is in the massive raised central block that the monumental feel is strongest and Tait's ability to compose in terms of abstract geometrical masses most evident. The central block is framed by giant pylons, which are repeated, in tiers beyond tall windows bisected by massive stepped buttresses. Here the walls slope inwards, giving the central entrance block the feeling of, say, the Temple at Karnak. In this case, however, the giant order of six square piers is not placed within a frame, nor do these columns culminate in capitals to carry an entablature

St Andrew's House, Edinburgh, Scotland (Sir John Burnet, Tait & Lorne, 1939)

and cornice. Rather, they rise to become projections from the wall, breaking up into symbolic sculptured heads, carved by the Scots sculptor Sir William Reid Dick to represent Architecture, Statecraft, Health, Agriculture, Fisheries and Education. This motif, at once modernistic and archaic, may derive from Eliel Saarinen's unexecuted Parliament House design of 1908; it was soon taken up by the Dutch and by several American architects, notably Goodhue at the Nebraska State Capitol, and it appears in Tait's design for Norwich City Hall.[51]

Cornices appear on the long wings but not, significantly, on the central temple-like block. Here the emphasis is on massiveness and the sublime. Reid Dick's capital-heads are seen against a blank wall, which is then stepped back to culminate in an Attic frieze. The whole feeling is at once Modern-American and Ancient Egyptian, with a strong element of the geometrical-Mayan that so influenced Frank Lloyd Wright and Raymond Hood. Here is the supreme example in Britain of that 'new spirit' of 'movement in mass' which Robert Byron saw echoed in the temples and mausolea of the Ancient

World. Sober in colour and relying on fine materials rather than coloured cement and powdered glass, St Andrew's House presents a much more intelligent interpretation of the monuments of Ancient Egypt than the 'fancy' factories on the Great West Road. And over the entrance, instead of the symbol of the sun god Ra, is carved the heraldic arms of Scotland, flanked by giant stylised thistles on squat round columns.

Thomas Tait, like Charles Holden, declined a knighthood. 'He was not the sort of man to whom such things mattered much: although he had never studied at the Ecole itself, he had achieved the dream of every Beaux Arts-trained architect, to design a truly great Government building.'[52] For all his genuine interest in new materials and in new architectural solutions to functional problems, Tait was still concerned with perennial architectural values when it came to designing an important building which would be a permanent addition to the architectural magnificence of the Athens of the North.

CHAPTER SIX

MERRIE ENGLAND

———◆———

IN THE EARLY 1920S, an elaborate half-timbered Tudor palace rose off London's Regent Street. Constructed out of teak and oak taken from two old naval warships, together with blocks of Portland stone 'chisel-worked right from the quarry face' and hand-made roof tiles, it formed part of the new premises of Liberty & Co. Harold P. Clunn, that naïve enthusiast for any metropolitan improvement, thought that 'this building is a unique feature in the West End, and after it has been standing for about ten years will look as if it had always been there'.[1] Today, however, Tudor House looks no older than Raymond Hood's Art Deco block opposite, and certainly not more ancient than Liberty's own grand Classical concave front around the corner facing Regent Street. What may seem extraordinary is that both department store blocks – connected by a three-storey stone and timber gabled bridge – were built at the same time and designed by the same architects, Edwin T. & E. Stanley Hall.

The booklet issued by Liberty's at the opening in 1924 explained that, in the old store in Regent Street, Arthur Lasenby Liberty 'always strove to introduce a Tudor feeling'; when Nash's street was rebuilt, a compromise was effected whereby the main front was designed in the Renaissance manner insisted on by the authorities and 'a building in the style of the days of Henry VIII and Queen Elizabeth' was raised on the store's freehold land in Great Marlborough Street. 'The Tudor period is the most genuinely English period of domestic architecture,' insisted Ivor Stewart-Liberty:

> There is a glamour about the lavish and stirring days of Henry VIII and Queen Elizabeth; while the sight of red tiled gables and carved bargeboards, of hanging balconies and leaded casements, is essentially English, and brings to the mind a picture of those by-gone days when the ancient guilds of the craftsmen and the merchant adventurers displayed, in the beautiful gabled buildings of old London, the productions of their handicrafts and the treasures for which they sailed so far and endured so much.[2]

Not everyone was convinced. 'Those who hold that the contemporary buildings of a city should be civil towards each other and should dress harmoniously, with only such variations as good taste and circumstance dictate, will be disappointed,' wrote Sydney Kitson in the *Architectural Review*.[3]

Liberty's Tudor House is the most conspicuous example of a style of architecture that was immensely popular between the wars, despite the continual sneering of critics and architects. The problem with Tudor was not so much its sentimental archaism but its populist ubiquity. Adopted in modified form for the huge number of speculative new houses built between the wars for a new, upwardly mobile and more independent middle class, it almost amounted to the defining style of the period. It is therefore a type of architecture which deserves to be taken seriously, even if difficulties are presented by the hostile attitude of most contemporary literature and by the anonymity of the ordinary suburban house, which, like the Georgian terrace, is the work of a builder with a pattern book.

Liberty's Tudor House, Great Marlborough Street, London (E.T. and E. S. Hall, 1924)

Contemporary dismissals of neo-Tudor are easy to find – usually in connection with its suburban expression, 'the abominable Tudoristic villa of the By-pass road'.[4] Advertisements for Tudor suburban houses from builders' catalogues were regularly reproduced in the *Architectural Review* without comment. J. M. Richards praised Charles Holden's Underground stations in contrast to 'the worst bogus Tudor housing estates' amid which they often stood.[5] In 1934, Maxwell Fry considered that the half-timbered house 'is now an anachronism and a fairy tale for tired business men. Wilfully so.'[6] As one of those older, influential architects, M. H. Baillie Scott, complained in 1933,

Nothing can be more absurd than the conception of what is described, with a deprecating snigger, as 'Tudor' by most of its critics, who usually choose one of the worst examples of the misuse of half timber work to illustrate their remarks – for it is an article of faith with such writers that half timber is the hallmark of Tudor work![7]

The artist Paul Nash concluded in 1932 that the taste for the antique was the 'favourite flavour' of 80 per cent of the population, 'or at least is supposed to be by the builder and furniture makers': 'What is the alleged ideal home offered to dwellers in Metroland? A gabled house with bogus beams and lattice windows.'[8] A more reasonable criticism was made by John Gloag in 1934 when he asked:

Why are you, or perhaps your neighbours, living in an imitation Tudor house with stained wooden slats shoved on the front of it to make it look like what is called a half-timbered house? Those slats have nothing to do with the construction of the house. They are just applied as ornaments. The house does not look like a real half-timbered house and it never can. It has been built in quite a different way from a real Tudor house, and it has been built by people totally different from the people who lived in the sixteenth century.[9]

For Anthony Bertram, author of *The House: A Machine for Living In*,

The deal laths on Tudoresque villas are the most tremendous symbols of the architectural rottenness which has infested most people in this Middle-Ages-ridden country. Useless, meaningless, tawdry and yet costing good money, their very origin has been forgotten. . . . The man who builds a bogus Tudoresque villa or castellates his suburban home is committing a crime against truth and tradition: he is denying the history of progress, denying his own age and insulting the very thing he pretends to imitate by misusing it.

The problem was, Bertram asserted, that 'man is conservative, and most speculative builders are ignorant and stupid'.[10] But at least Gloag recognised the human impulse behind the adoption of the style when he wrote in 1938: 'I am not making a plea for the retention of those repellent, jerry-built, sham-Tudor houses that disfigure England; but I do suggest that the reason why people are happy in them, why they can take pride in them, is worth studying.'[11]

The taxonomist of the style was Osbert Lancaster. The origins of neo-Tudor, he felt, lay before the Great War in the expensive, outer-suburban houses designed in 'Wimbledon Transitional', with 'its plentiful use of pebbledash, its giddy treatment of gables and its general air of self-conscious cosiness'.[12] Inside the more expensive versions of such houses, 'the lounge-hall reaches the ultimate peak of its development': a double-height galleried space descended from the medieval baronial hall via Welby Pugin and Norman Shaw. This he termed 'Aldwych Farcical' because of its frequent adaptation into stage-sets with 'a bewildering selection of doors and French windows'.[13] Wimbledon Transitional, Lancaster wrote in 1938, 'occupies a position of peculiar importance in the history of modern British architecture, as being the connecting link between Pont Street Dutch and Art Nouveau, and such familiar modern styles as Stockbrokers Tudor and By-Pass Residential'.[14]

'Stockbrokers Tudor' (Osbert Lancaster, 1938)

Stockbrokers' Tudor has become the popular generic term for the half-timbered style widely adopted for new houses in the 1920s and 1930s. It was a style, Lancaster explained, which had gone down-market, adopted by the builders of new suburbs, so that:

> when the passer-by is a little unnerved at being suddenly confronted with a hundred and fifty accurate reproductions of Anne Hathaway's cottage, each complete with central-heating and garage, he should pause to reflect on the extraordinary fact that all over the country the latest and most scientific methods of mass-production are being utilized to turn out a stream of old oak beams, leaded window-panes and small discs of bottle-glass, all structural devices which our ancestors lost no time in abandoning as soon as an increase in wealth and knowledge enabled them to do so.[15]

Most suburban houses, whether detached or semi-detached, were not pure versions of Stockbrokers' Tudor but were hybrids with elements reflecting the influence of the Art Nouveau, Pseudish and the modernistic combined with vernacular motifs derived from great

The Mall, Surbiton, Kingston-upon-Thames (H. C. Jones & Co., c. 1932)

'By-Pass Variegated' (Osbert Lancaster, 1938)

Late Victorians such as Charles Voysey and Richard Norman Shaw. This manner Osbert Lancaster categorised as 'By-Pass Variegated'.[16]

There were two principal interrelated reasons for the popularity of Tudor architecture. The first was the long-standing interest in the domestic architecture of the late medieval period identified by Peter Mandler as that vague, romantic 'Olden Time' which merged with a national enthusiasm for Shakespeare and the Tudor monarchs. This was a romanticised view of the past, and of England, which was encouraged by the trauma of the war and the difficulties of the present. Clive Aslet quotes an officer writing home from the trenches describing how, when off-duty, 'out comes my pipe, and the latest *Country Life* from England, and I sit down in front of the dug out and read about old houses'.[17] As far as Anthony Bertram was concerned, writing in 1938 when another war was threatening,

> the popular love for the Tudor, whether genuine or bogus, is based on fear and a wish to escape. . . . These are insecure and frightening times, and I believe that economic depressions and the fear of war are the chief promoters of the Tudoresque. The insecurity of the old days was taken for granted, so it never led to this escapism, this fear of the new, this anchoring, as it were, to the past.[18]

Such escapism well pre-dated the war, however. It is surely significant that at the 1900 Paris Exposition the pavilion representing the nation that had once created the Crystal Palace was a partial replica of the early-seventeenth-century Kingston House at Bradford-on-Avon designed by Lutyens, who was also involved in the 'Shakespeare's England' exhibition held at Earl's Court in 1912. This fund-raising exercise for the Shakespeare Memorial Fund consisted of a series of replicas of historical structures.[19] After the war, enthusiasm for Shakespeare's England grew: the Shakespeare Festival at Stratford-upon-Avon, which had attracted some 14,000 in 1904, was visited by 200,000 in 1938.[20] In view of this and the popular, enduring affection for Tudor architecture – both old and new – the resolve of the judges in choosing a modern design, by a woman, in 1928 to replace the destroyed Shakespeare Memorial Theatre seems all the more remarkable.

Tudor monarchs excited popular interest, especially Elizabeth I and Henry VIII. 'The "good old days" of the Tudor dynasty appear to linger in the minds of all as an inviolable conception of ease, comfort, and peace,' complained the cinema architect Julian Leathart. 'This fantastic illusion of a period of social history notorious for its tyranny, oppression, disease, and filth is well-nigh irradicable from the minds of the Englishman and his wife. It becomes articulate with his demand for the bijou-baronial-mansion type villa as a befitting place of residence.'[21] Alexander Korda's *The Private Life of Henry VIII*, considered 'probably the most important film produced in Britain before the Second World War',[22] was released in 1933 and had considerable impact, as Ernö Goldfinger discovered when he visited Oliver Hill at home in the country.* 'I didn't think much of Hill's architecture, but he was a really nice chap,' the Hungarian modern architect recalled four decades later:

---

* The house was Valewood Farm, near Haslemere, which Hill restored and shared with Christopher Hussey. 'Swimming, preferably nude, sunbathing and surprising his guests into joining nudist frolics on the hilltops in the summer, Hill's relaxations seem as strenuous as his work' (Powers (1989), p. 24).

He lived rather grandly in the country, in Sussex.... You came into a great Tudor hall, with a dining table on a dais across the room. One was served like Henry VIII and he flung bones to the dogs. I was not so impressed by this, and soon realised that the Korda film was then showing and Oliver was modelling himself on it.[23]

When the Nun's Head pub in Nunhead, south-east London, was rebuilt in 1934 as an improbable black oak and red-brick tall-chimneyed mansion amidst shabby London stock-brick terraces, Gothic letters on the exterior made the proud if dubious claim that it was 'Licensed in the Reign of King Henry VIII'. All this perhaps confirms the truth of Osbert Lancaster's description of the Stockbrokers' Tudor style, in which he observed how:

> certain classes of the community were in a position to pass their whole lives in one long Elizabethan day-dream; spending their nights under high-pitched roofs and ancient eaves, their days in trekking from Tudor golf clubs to half-timbered cocktail bars,

The Old Nun's Head, Nunhead, London (Joseph Hill, 1934)

and their evenings in contemplating [Charles] Laughton's robust interpretation of Henry VIII amid the Jacobean plasterwork of the Gloriana Palace.[24]

The other impetus behind neo-Tudor architecture was the still potent legacy of the Victorian revival of a vernacular domestic architecture, the 'Old English' style of Norman Shaw, combined with the continuing Arts and Crafts movement. The architectural expression of the followers of Ruskin and Morris was best represented by the houses of the 1890s by C. F. A. Voysey and Edwin Lutyens. Such artfully gabled houses were characterised by the use of pegged oak timbers, roughcast wall surfaces, leaded-light casement windows in oak frames, external brick chimneybreasts, elements which were freely adopted (and modified) in the neo-Tudor smaller house of the 1920s and 1930s. In particular, that characteristic motif of the suburban house, the triangular roughcast gable placed over a curved projecting double-height bay window, came straight from houses by Voysey.

By the 1920s, the Arts and Crafts movement had become much more diffuse and popular; it had passed 'from the avant-garde out to the woolly fringe'.[25] Indeed, it was something to be sneered at. William Morris was now a joke, complained Lionel Cuffe in the *Architectural Review* in 1931. 'His designs have all been travestied, his doctrine taken all wrong. Yet Sweden can hold an exhibition, and call it one of Arts and Crafts, in London, and everyone goes to it. And it is not taken as a joke. Why are English Arts and Crafts a joke?'[26] Although no longer avant-garde, however, it can be argued that the movement was far more influential in the 1920s than it had been before the war. Institutions like the Art Workers' Guild carried on, if now rather conservative and introverted in attitude. And many other bodies and tendencies were ultimately inspired by Morris's social and cultural ideas. These included not only the Society for the Protection of Ancient Buildings and the several craft communities associated with figures like Eric Gill, but such tangential manifestations as the English Folk Dance Society founded by Cecil Sharp in 1911.

The Arts and Crafts movement was also partly responsible for that worship of age that encouraged the sham antique and the attachment of the letter 'e' to 'old'. 'In ye olde villages and ye newe imitations of ye olde villages, struggling gentlefolk are busy travestying Morris,' Lionel Cuffe complained.* 'Wherever there is an art tea shoppe and a flat home-made cake, there too will be a match-box or a flower-pot painted over in the name of Arts and Crafts.'[27] Indeed, a half-timbered, Tudor-style 'Ye Olde Tea Shoppe' seems all but emblematic of England between the Wars. At the beginning of his *English Journey* in 1933, J. B. Priestley encountered a romantic failed entrepreneur on the coach to Southampton:

'That's no good,' he told me, after a minute or two's talk about nothing.
'What isn't?'
'Tea rooms.' And he pointed to one we were passing. 'I tried it once. The wife was keen. In Kent. Good position too, on a main road. We'd everything very nice, very nice indeed. We called it the Chaucer Pilgrims – you know, Chaucer. Old style – Tudor, you know – black beams and everything.'[28]

It is surely significant that, that same year, the RIBA chose to award its Royal Gold Medal, not to a designer associated with contemporary practice, but to an antiquarian architect concerned with historic preservation: Sir Charles Peers, who had been Inspector of Ancient Monuments in the Office of Works, had restored the roof of Westminster Hall and was Consulting Architect to several medieval cathedrals.

---

* [As he might have added, 'ye' is merely an archaic typographical form of 'the', and is consequently often mispronounced as if it were same word as the old second-person singular pronoun. RH.]

A younger generation reacted against what John Betjeman called 'Antiquarian Prejudice' in 1937, in favour of the radically modern.[29] In this context, a revealing definition of what the Arts and Crafts movement had become is conveniently defined by Evelyn Waugh's scatter-gun rant against it and the narrow, middle-class enthusiasms of his father's generation:

> The detestation of 'quaintness' and 'picturesque bits' which is felt by every decently constituted Englishman, is, after all, a very insular prejudice. It has developed naturally in self-defence against arts and crafts, and the preservation of rural England, and the preservation of ancient monuments, and the transplantation of Tudor cottages, and the collection of pewter and old oak, and the reformed public house, and Ye Olde Inne and the Kynde Dragone and Ye Cheshire Cheese, Broadway, Stratford-on-Avon, folk-dancing, Nativity plays, reformed dress, free love in a cottage, glee singing, the Lyric, Hammersmith, Belloc, Ditchling, Wessex-worship, village signs, local customs, heraldry, madrigals, wassail, regional cookery, Devonshire teas, letters to *The Times* about saving timbered alms-houses from destruction, the preservation of the Welsh language, etc. It is inevitable that English taste, confronted with all these frightful menaces to its integrity, should have adopted an uncompromising attitude to anything the least tainted with ye oldeness.[30]

Waugh concluded that, 'In England, the craze for cottages and all that goes with them only began as soon as they had ceased to represent a significant part of English life.' But surely, in a Tudoresque suburb, the streets were also in perfect harmony with their inhabitants?

The Arts and Crafts movement, with its anti-industrial and anti-urban bias, continued to encourage suburban, low-density development away from city centres, and this included garden cities and garden suburbs based on town-planning principles derived from Ebenezer Howard such as Welwyn Garden City and the less ordered speculative developments that grew around railway lines and arterial roads. Another consequence was the concern with the countryside and with the preservation of picturesque rural cottages. Here the legacy of William Morris was still potent, both through the continuing Society for the Protection of Ancient Buildings and through his political and social bias in favour of the humbler vernacular dwelling and against the aristocratic mansion. In 1928, no less a person than the Prime Minister, Stanley Baldwin, chaired a conference at the Royal Society of Arts to launch an appeal for a Fund for the Preservation of Ancient Cottages. 'Nothing is more characteristic of England's countryside than the cottage homes which, for century upon century, have sheltered her sturdy sons of toil,' he announced. 'Who has not felt a thrill of admiration on catching sight of some old-world village round a bend of the road?' The threats to them included indifference and poverty, but also 'the well-meaning but thoughtless zeal for widening roads [which] has robbed us of many a native homestead, to be replaced by gimcrack bungalows with composition-tile roofs, or ill-proportioned and bedizened "villas".'[31] One result of this campaign was the acquisition of the village of West Wycombe in Buckinghamshire and its transfer to the care of the National Trust.*

Baldwin had Arts and Crafts credentials – his uncle, by marriage, had been Edward Burne-Jones and his cousin was Rudyard Kipling – and he said the right things, but he was widely denounced for hypocrisy. As Peter Mandler has written, 'Baldwin presided over a

---

* West Wycombe was the image chosen for that difficult year 1929 for his annual portentous hand-drawn card by the former skyscraper architect, and future Conservative MP, Alfred Bossom, who later wrote how he 'helped the Royal Society of Arts to acquire and restore the historic West Wycombe to its original and alluring old English charm. It so stands today . . . a monument to the little group of men and women who jointly made the effort, and when it was completed turned the village over to the permanent ownership of the nation under the direction of the National Trust. Had it not been done at this time, this delightful bit of Buckinghamshire would undoubtedly have gone to rack and ruin': see Bossom (1948).

massive roadbuilding and electrification programme that shredded the countryside. He detached his party and also his own portrayals of the English character from its aristocratic past, playing up a gentle, modest, domesticated, cottage-loving image that fitted neatly with established trends within the middle class.'[32] But there was also a deeper paradox here. The Arts and Crafts outlook that cherished the countryside and helped inspire the foundation of the Council for the Preservation of Rural England in 1926 also encouraged the low-density housing and the desire for a cottage home that threatened that same countryside with suburban or scattered development.

There were deeper forces at work here. The decade after the Great War saw a social and geographical revolution in which, to quote Mandler again, 'The withdrawal of the aristocracy from the land paved the way for the reappropriation of the countryside by urban society.'[33] The old aristocracy withdrew from many country seats partly because of the dreadful attrition of male heirs during the war but mostly because of high taxation and death duties. Many peers seem to have given up their country houses – and their grand town houses – without much regret, exchanging them for a modern flat. As Ralph Nevill complained in 1925:

> Formerly, people troubled themselves little about artistic surroundings, and provided a house was comfortable to live in, little more was required. . . . To-day the vast majority of those living even in houses of historic interest appear ready to sell or let their residence without the least feeling of regret, provided they can secure advantageous terms.[34]

Into this vacuum moved the housebuilders and speculators, catering for urban and suburban populations that wished to escape the crowded city centres and terraced houses and have a real home of their own. While the population of Britain expanded by 10 per cent between the wars, the number of houses increased by 30 per cent.[35] This process was encouraged by new suburban railways and Underground extensions as well as by bus routes, but above all by the growth in the number of private cars. There were 109,000 in 1919 and over 2 million by 1939. It was the motor car, together with the motor bus and the 'charabanc', that opened up the previously closed countryside. This went hand in hand with the popularity of bicycling and hiking. Significantly, the Youth Hostel Association was founded in 1929. Peter Mandler again: 'A much larger social constituency now discovered the England of the Arts and Crafts movement – the small, homely, farmyard country.'[36]

Not that the adherents of the Arts and Crafts movement necessarily liked the consequences of this populism. They deplored the road-side cafés, the petrol stations, the advertisements that sprang up in fields, the litter. But they did not much worry about the abandonment and demolition of so many country houses; the Arts and Crafts movement, after all, had no interest in the stately home, with its associations of social hierarchy. Despite charabanc tours and Green Line buses, country house visiting was in decline. That there was little concern for the fate of Palladian mansions is not surprising. What, however, seems extraordinary is that even the more picturesque vernacular houses, the medieval and Tudor piles that had always been popular, could be abandoned without much regret. 'Everywhere, our once beautiful country is being disfigured,' complained P. A. Barron in 1929. 'Fine old English homes are being demolished, and estates are being cut up into tiny plots upon which are erected modern villas and bungalows which are ill-proportioned, often badly built, and so ugly.'[37] While Knole and Ightham Mote remained popular, Haddon Hall was closed to the public; Montacute was nearly demolished, despite the earlier efforts of Lord Curzon to save it; Rufford Abbey was bought, stripped and abandoned by Sir Albert Ball, the former Mayor of Nottingham. At least Wollaton Hall was rescued by Nottingham Corporation and Temple Newsam by Leeds.

Evelyn Waugh's account of the fate of King's Thursday in *Decline and Fall*, published in 1928, may seem all too believable. The house, described as 'the finest piece of domestic Tudor in England', had escaped alteration and modernisation, but it 'had been built in an age when twenty servants were not an unduly extravagant establishment'. Modern servants, however, 'were less receptive than their masters to the charms of Tudor simplicity'. So, 'With rather less reluctance than might have been expected,' Lord Pastmaster decides to sell the house to his sister-in-law, Margot Beste-Chetwynde, who soon demolishes it to make way for a Modernist masterpiece by Professor Otto Silenus, a project to re-erect it in Cincinnati having come to nothing.[38] As for that other great fictional country house of the period, P. G. Wodehouse's Blandings Castle, it seems clear that it was a large rambling pile of the Olden Time.* Fortunately, Lord Emsworth was not the sort of peer to sell up and retreat to a London flat, which merely confirms that the vision of England presented by Wodehouse, the middle-class product of Dulwich College, was far from an accurate picture of contemporary aristocratic life; rather, it was an engaging caricature of a pre-war world that was disappearing without much regret, either on the part of the aristocracy or the general public. It was as if those who aspired to live in Stockbrokers' Tudor were quite uninterested in the real thing. Wodehouse, so conventional in his tastes, lived in a house he had bought in Le Touquet in Stockbrokers' Tudor, or, rather, the French equivalent, *style Normande*; designed by Pierre Drobecq, it was called Low Wood.[39]

There can be no doubt that a domestic architecture consisting of gables, tall brick chimneys and leaded-light mullioned windows remained the most popular style for new houses, at least during the first decade after the Armistice. Although many of the most

---

* That is how it was imagined by Osbert Lancaster in his series of 'Great Houses of Fiction Revisited', drawn for the 'Destruction of the Country House' exhibition at the Victoria and Albert Museum in 1975 and published in Lancaster (1978). Murphy (1986) quotes Wodehouse recalling in 1971 that 'Blandings was a sort of mixture of places I remembered' (p. 219) and suggests it was a combination of Corsham Court and Sudely Castle (p. 221).

talented Arts and Crafts architects had long abandoned the rustic, half-timbered manner for a more sophisticated Classical style, the taste for domestic Tudor remained strong. A majority of the houses illustrated in the first post-war edition of Lawrence Weaver's *Small Country Houses of Today* were in the half-timbered, tile-hung vernacular manner, while even in Patrick Abercrombie's 1939 'panoramic survey', *The Book of the Modern House*, the style was well represented. In the chapter on 'The Suburban House', H. C. Bradshaw wrote of 'those houses which may be described as of the *rustic* or *informal country* type':

> In these the architect has been content to follow the time-honoured methods and forms which have developed in the various parts of rural England. . . . Its wide popular appeal is bound up with the Englishman's inherent love of the country and, in its proper interpretation, it implies, and indeed necessitates, the survival of the best standards of traditional building.[40]

Some architects simply carried on the glorious Edwardian domestic tradition, merely making allowances for higher building costs. M. H. Baillie Scott continued as before, building comfortable, well-planned, vernacular houses, now in partnership with his former assistant A. Edgar Beresford, and had built enough by 1933 to publish a second edition of the book of his work, *Houses and Gardens*. Wychden at Seal, Kent, was built in 1931–32 and has great sweeps of tiled roofs and prominent brick chimneys, tile-hung triangular gables and areas of timber and plaster 'to give value to the tones of bricks and tiles'.[41] Church Rate Corner at Cambridge (1925) is a more austere composition of similar elements, eschewing brick and tile for smooth rendered surfaces. It is reminiscent of Baillie Scott's work of around 1900, which had established his reputation as an advanced designer, while these later houses have been generally ignored. They were, perhaps, slightly influenced by Lutyens but no diminution of quality and care is, however, evident; by holding fast to his Arts and Crafts

Church Rate Corner, Cambridge (M. H. Baillie Scott, 1925)

ideals while the world changed around him, Baillie Scott moved from being progressive to reactionary. He and/or Beresford could write in 1933:

> Instead of that uninspiring and rather tiresome slogan, 'Fitness for purpose', which any pigsty can fulfil, let him rather inscribe, on his banners, 'England, Home and Beauty'. Instead of turning his back on the splendid work of his fathers, let him find inspiration in the buildings which have given us the precious heritage of rural England. He need not go to Sweden.[42]

Edwin Lutyens was also prepared to abandon the 'High Game' and to return to the vernacular manner that had made his reputation. One of his last houses, Halnaker, near Chichester (1936–38), was for an old client, Reginald McKenna of the Midland Bank, and is a simplified, austere composition of the vernacular elements he liked to play with. A few years earlier he had carried out a final commission for Edward Hudson, the founder of *Country Life*, for whom he restored and added a music room to Plumpton Place.

Here, the new big oak mullioned and transomed windows make a rectilinear composition quite as abstract and modern as that in any contemporary Functionalist house, but carried out in more sympathetic materials. 'There is wit and may be humour in the use of materials,' Lutyens said in 1932:

> I enjoy all construction, and the steel girder with its petticoat of concrete is a most useful ally in the ever recurring advent of difficulty. . . . But I crave for soft thick noiseless walls of hand-made brick and lime, the deep light reflecting reveals, the double floors, easy stairways, and doorways never less than 1 ft. 6 ins. from a corner. The waste of space, which unwittingly creates that most valuable asset, a gain of space.[43]

Many younger domestic architects were in thrall to Lutyens's example, not least Oliver Hill. But Hill could produce vernacular houses with a distinct character of their own. On the Kintyre peninsular opposite the Isle of Arran, he created a country house soon after the war whose sophisticated ruggedness responded to the Scottish landscape (Plate 23). Built of local stone, with its great sweeps of roof covered in stone slates, the massive walls of Cour are pierced only by horizontal bands of small, round-arched windows with stone mullions. More typical, however, were his houses in the Home Counties, which had thatched roofs and wobbly elm weatherboarding, and which, in their exaggerated domestic imagery, may possibly have owed something to the vernacular Expressionist work of Vorkink & Wormser and other Dutch architects (t'Reigersnest near Rotterdam, for example).[44]

The most interesting was Cock Rock, built by the sea at Croyde in 1925–26 with a deliberately 'rambling plan and silhouette'.[45] Even more austere and rugged were the handful of houses built in England by John A. Campbell, an independent-minded architect in the Arts and Crafts tradition who had earlier practised in Germany. Campbell's houses were built of whitewashed rubble-stone, which

Cock Rock, Croyde, Devon (Oliver Hill, 1925–26)

gave them an air of simplicity that might have been a response to contemporary Modernism, but which also derived from the earlier work of Arts and Crafts architects like Baillie Scott.

As Alan Powers has argued, the work of this sophisticated architect bridged the gulf between so-called Modernism and Traditionalism. Writing of Birchens Spring in Beaconsfield, completed in 1938, with its plain white surfaces, simple geometrical forms and continuous bands of fenestration, Christopher Hussey thought: 'There is about its outward aspect a boldness, and yet a sensitiveness, and a feeling for the substance of the building, that calls to mind the best elements in our heritage of building craftsmanship.'[46] The Arts and Crafts tradition could still flourish without becoming mawkish or twee. 'To aim consciously at achieving "style",' wrote Campbell,

> is to follow a will o' the wisp, for the pursuit of 'style' is like the pursuit of happiness: both must necessarily lead to disappointment and failure. . . . I wish all architects were practical builders. The trouble with architects is that they often regard themselves as gentlemen and not as tradesmen, and especially is this so to-day when it is the architectural colleges that produce them.[47]

Drummers Yard (formerly Birchens Spring), Beaconsfield, Buckinghamshire (John Campbell, 1938)

Campbell designed three houses at Chapel Point, a promontory at Mevagissey, Cornwall, after 1933, whose construction by direct labour he supervised personally as they were 'intended to demonstrate that it need not be any more expensive to build a traditional-looking house out of local stone than it was to build a standard . . . bungalow of the kind that so disfigured the Cornish coastline'.[48] The house built for himself at Chapel Point was included in the Architecture Club's selection of *Recent English Architecture 1920–1940* as a 'notably picturesque demonstration of contemporary use of traditional methods and materials for regional, especially seaside, architecture'.[49] Also included among the domestic examples of representative good architecture were Coleton Fishacre, another rugged stone Arts and Crafts house designed by Oswald P. Milne, and Ashcombe Tower, also in Devon, designed by Brian O'Rorke, considered to be a 'modern version of regional tradition' in what might be described as simplified Tudor.[50] It is, however, significant that by 1947 no overtly half-timbered house was considered representative.

Restoration of Baylin's Farm, Beaconsfield, Buckinghamshire (Forbes & Tate, 1920)

More literal expressions of Stockbrokers' Tudor continued to be built throughout the 1920s and 1930s. Forbes & Tate designed Baylin's Farm at Beaconsfield with tile-hung gables, brick chimneys and visible half-timber (Plate 24). This firm was also responsible for 'A Thatched House' overlooking Harewood Downs golf course. Thatch continued to be employed as an authentically vernacular and traditional roofing material, despite its inflammability. Clough Williams-Ellis, indeed, used it on Cold Blow at Oare, and on other houses which cannot be described as Tudor. Sydney R. Jones was another architect practised in neo-Tudor and adept at designing small houses in it. For such an architect, these enthusiasms were a natural continuation of the Arts and Crafts movement.

One firm that produced neo-Tudor domestic architecture of high quality was that of G. Blair Imrie and T. G. Angell. With its long lines and generous-hipped gable ends, The Slip, built by the coast at Bosham in Sussex, was designed by Imrie & Angell in the style of a Wealden manor farm in which 'the house-walling is of flint and brick, with the first floor tile hung; old tiles on the roof and straightforward

The Slip, Bosham, Sussex (Imrie & Angell, 1913)

timber work introduced on the entrance side'.[51] This house had a built-in garage and an open verandah overlooking the sea. Imrie & Angell also designed smaller dwellings, and two of their new houses at Esher were included in R. Randal Phillips's compilation of *Houses for Moderate Means*, first published in 1936. 'On every side we see new houses springing up. It is a time of widespread building. Unhappily also it is a time of widespread spoliation,' Phillips began. These offending buildings had 'been put up by speculative builders and estate firms':

> In the midst of all this nondescript profusion, here and there we come across houses that commend themselves, seemly-looking houses, built of sound materials, and not tricked out with sham half-timber, foolish windows and ponderous porches; and it will be found that these form part of estate development where competent architects have been employed, or they are houses built by such architects for individual owners.[52]

In Hammels, a large house for the Oxford Professor of Horticulture at Boars Hill in Oxfordshire completed in 1923, however, Imrie & Angell did not just rely on good, sound materials to create a traditional, homely effect; the basic structure was a disused barn moved from Herefordshire to make a double-height living room. And here we meet that element in Stockbrokers' Tudor which has done so much to bring the style into disrepute: the attempt to create an effect of great age by using recycled materials such as oak beams. In his article in *Country Life* on Hammels, R. Randal Phillips insisted that this design was the result of economy and a desire to save the structure from being sawn up to make fake antique furniture and that, 'in re-creating it, no attempt was made in that "picturesqueness" which is a foible of some modern architecture'. But the fact was that the sentimental re-erection of old barns and old timber-framed houses had been going on for some time and for that purpose. Even Lutyens had been guilty, having created Great Dixter at Northiam, Sussex,

Hammels, Boars Hill, Oxfordshire (Imrie & Angell, 1923; destroyed by fire 1973)

by adding a timber-framed house transported from Benenden to a restored fifteenth-century house, and rebuilding a Tudor house from Ipswich at Ashby St Ledgers.

That the taste for Tudor was classless is suggested by the fact that, in the mid-1920s, the Prince of Wales rented Small Downs House at Sandwich, Kent, as a summer residence. This neo-Tudor house had been built in 1914 by C. H. Biddulph-Pinchard, who re-used old bricks from two demolished houses in Dover. A photograph of the house in the *Architectural Review* so horrified the young Anglophile Danish architect Steen Eiler Rasmussen, on his first visit to England in 1927, that he was moved to complain that:

> New materials have been sedulously avoided: the beams come from broken-up old ships, the stonework from even older ruins. High-quality craftsmen have taken pains to build the walls out of plumb, as if they had been put up by primitive people without any technical skills. . . . A building like this tells us nothing about England's proverbial conservatism. The Prince's summer retreat has no more to do with tradition than an American film.[53]

Small Downs House, Sandwich, Kent (C. H. Biddulph-Pinchard, 1914)

Nor was it just foreigners and modernists who were shocked by this approach. Crusty old Sir Reginald Blomfield, in his rant against *Modernismus*, complained about 'the craze for old buildings, which insisted that all new buildings must reproduce buildings of the past as closely and literally as photographs allowed, with the result of a steady and successful practice of fakes culminating in the wholesale removal of genuine buildings in England and their re-erection on the other side of the Atlantic'. This 'enemy to living architecture' he blamed on the Romantic movement.[54]

C. H. Biddulph-Pinchard evidently specialised in this sort of thing. After the war, he built Little Garth at Syresham, Northamptonshire, out of an old stone barn and an old brewhouse. 'With the old tiles, therefore,' it was explained in 1924, 'and the oak half-timbering, and the rich and mellow colour of the stone, the whole building has assumed the appearance of great age. But there is no faking of materials.'[55] The use of old materials to give instant patina betrayed the Arts and Crafts belief in the honest and straightforward traditional use of materials. This contrasting approach was well expressed by Gertrude Jekyll in describing Munstead Wood (Plate 22), the house built for her by the young Edwin Lutyens almost thirty years earlier:

> it does not stare with newness; it is not new in any way that is disquieting to the eye; it is neither raw nor callow. On the contrary, it almost gives the impression of a comfortable maturity of something like a couple of hundred years. And yet there is nothing sham-old about it; it is not trumped-up with any specious or fashionable devices of spurious antiquity; there is no pretending to be anything that it is not – no affectation whatever.[56]

More and more, however, it was the 'sham-old' approach that prevailed. It seems particularly to have been favoured by amateur architects with a passion for Tudor. Major Kenneth Hutchinson, for instance, built Bradley Lodge at Stratford-upon-Avon with timbers from

Bradley Hall, a half-timbered Elizabethan house which had stood near Dudley. And what was left over he used to build new houses in nearby Tudor Close.[57] The doyen of such amateurs was George Abraham Crawley, who, despite a complete lack of professional training, established himself as an architect and decorator in New York before the war, where he was assisted by Alfred Bossom. At the same time he restored Crowhurst Place near Lingfield for himself and, after he was obliged to sell it, enlarged the ancient house further for Consuelo, Duchess of Marlborough.

After the war, Crawley reconstructed and enlarged two old houses in Surrey using old materials to create a convincing ancient effect. One was Crowhurst Place, the other Old Surrey Hall, completed after Crawley's death in 1926 by the Arts and Crafts architect Walter Godfrey. These 'crazy fairy-tale restorations' found unlikely admirers in Nikolaus Pevsner and Ian Nairn, who, despite their

Crowhurst Place, Lingfield, Surrey (George Abraham Crawley and Walter Godfrey, 1926)

commitment to the Modern Movement, included these buildings in the *Buildings of England* guide to Surrey as 'living proof that any style, if taken far enough and sincerely enough, will produce worthwhile architecture'.[58] Old Surrey Hall, with its garage made from an old barn, was built of old timbers, bricks and stone with such duplicitous skill that its real history is almost impossible to read. 'The result is indescribable, imitation carried to the point of genius,' wrote Ian Nairn, who was able to enter into the spirit of the thing and appreciate it as a valid product of its time.[59]

What Aslet has described as 'the most extreme – and most successful – of all Tudor taste country houses', Bailiffscourt in Sussex, was also the creation of an amateur, Amyas Phillips, who preferred to describe himself as an 'antiquarian'.[60] Created between 1927 and 1933 for Lady Moyne, Bailiffscourt incorporated a real, ancient chapel but was otherwise new, built of old stones from a demolished farmhouse with details from medieval buildings. Inside, the rooms were lined ('panelled is not the word') with rough, blackened wood. The result was as much medieval as Tudor in style, and seems almost like a realisation of an etching by F. L. Griggs, especially after other old buildings, including a fifteenth-century gatehouse from nearby

Bailiffscourt, Chichester, Sussex (Amyas Phillips, 1933)

in Sussex and a seventeenth-century half-timbered house from Old Basing in Hampshire, were re-erected round about. The result was at once real and fake, serious and absurd; in its essential escapism it was certainly a typical product of its time. As Clive Aslet has written, 'if the houses of the Modern Movement were built for occupants living their "little time of sunshine" between two wars, Bailiffscourt and other Tudor taste country houses are equally products of a generation that was too impatient to allow time to take its course. Even age had to be instant.'[61]

Fantasies like Bailiffscourt and Old Surrey Hall were not just the creations of the very wealthy. That the re-use of old beams and weathered masonry to create an instant effect of age was widespread is suggested by the contents of an extraordinary book published in 1929, *The House Desirable* by P. A. Barron. Much of the book consists of useful advice for couples who wished to build their own homes, but the essential message of the text was immediately conveyed by the frontispiece. This is a photograph of Ellens at Rudgwick, Surrey, 'a fine example of a modern house built in such manner that it has

Ellens, Rudgwick, Surrey (Maurice Webb, 1925)

the appearance of age. The roof is of mossy Horsham stone obtained from old houses and barns which had been demolished.'[62] After all, as Barron told his readers, 'Though you appreciate the advantages and comforts of modern houses, you may feel that with regard to beauty, they cannot be compared with those which have been aged by passing centuries.'[63] Hence 'the present popularity of lattice windows, or leaded lights, as they are called', he continued: 'They do not obstruct the view so much as might be supposed, but they make a room look cosy.... Big panes of plate glass do not give this snug appearance, and a room fitted with windows of this type may look cheerless in winter-time.'[64]

Ellens had been designed by Maurice Webb and largely completed in 1914. In his chapter on 'New "Old" Houses', Barron further explained that much of the oak 'used in the construction of the new building was... obtained from old barns':

> The Horsham stone of which the roof is composed came from ruined farm-houses and outbuildings, and it was necessary to ransack Sussex in order to find a sufficient quantity.... The appearance of age is, to some extent, due to the fact that the perfectly straight lines of new walls and roofs have been avoided. In some parts walls and timbers were placed deliberately 'out of truth'.[65]

Maurice Webb was a well-established architect, the son of Sir Aston Webb and a future Vice-President of the RIBA, but most of the designers whose work Barron admired were rather less well known, and several were builders rather than architects.* One was Reginald F. Wells, who had trained as a sculptor and practised as a potter

---

* 'I was considered by some to exert an evil influence,' recalled Howard Robertson, 'and was once tackled in the Arts Club – happily after lunch – by the late Maurice Webb, at that time Chairman of the RIBA Board of Architectural Education. He accused me of pernicious and corrupting influence on the general body of students through publicising modern trends, and in that way of doing a disservice to the architectural profession' (H. Robertson (1962), p. 855).

before taking up architecture in 1925. At Chiltington Common, near Pulborough on the South Downs, his company, Tiles and Potteries Ltd, built some thirty 'lovable little cottage homes', mostly 'for Londoners who like to spend their week-ends in the country'. Almost all these houses were thatched, and Barron admired how 'Mr Wells designed car homes of the same style as the cottages, with harmonious results'.[66]

Amongst the other developments Barron singled out for praise was the proposed building of 300 houses on the Titsey Estate north of New Oxted in Surrey, where 'the prevailing style is Tudor, though here and there one may find a Georgian house of gracious proportions'. As for New Oxted itself, built around the railway station away from the old village of Oxted:

> if you passed through in a car, and were not informed that the half-timbered shops and business buildings had been erected during the last few years, you would never guess the truth. You would carry away an impression of quaint gables, weather-worn oak, lattice windows, and doorways enriched by carvings. You would remember it only as one of the most charming of England's old-world villages.[67]

Most of the buildings here were the work of L. J. Williams of J. I. Williams & Son of Oxted (Plate 25), a firm that had been involved in restorations at Compton Wynyates and at Ockwells, as well as working at Old Surrey Hall for George Crawley. And then there was Tudor Close at Rottingdean near Brighton, a three-sided court of seven houses created by The South Coast Land and Resort Co. Designed by yet another amateur enthusiast and restorer, A. Caplin, it was built in 1924–28 out of old oak timbers from broken-up ships and old barns, recycled bricks and flint and 'mossy tiles', which, combined with fanciful and inventive new oak carvings, resulted in a wildly picturesque composition or, rather, as a contemporary put it, 'perfect representations of the wonderfully artistic and fascinatingly romantic

Tudor Close, Rottingdean, Sussex (A. Caplin, 1928; G. K. Green, 1937)

houses of the Tudor period'.[68] As far as Barron was concerned, 'you will find it very hard to believe that the buildings were not erected in the distant days of Henry VIII, or Queen Elizabeth'.[69] Such glamour evidently appealed to Hollywood; soon converted into an hotel by the architect G. K. Green, Tudor Close became a favourite with the likes of Bette Davis and Cary Grant (Plate 28).[70]

The hero of Barron's *The House Desirable* was Blunden Shadbolt, an architect who specialised in 'New "Old" Houses' of extreme irregularity, even laying roof tiles on wobbly chicken wire to create an effect of weathered age. His masterpiece was Smugglers' Way in the New Forest, begun in 1925, a wildly irregular gabled composition of timber and brick, roofed with both tile and thatch. Such effects were not easy to achieve, as Barron explained:

Workmen have to be trained to forget all their conventional ideas. At first it seems to them that they are asked to do everything as badly as possible. Instead of laying perfectly even courses of brick of uniform colour, they have to use bricks which do not match, and to lay them crookedly, 'any which way', as I have heard them say. Chipped bricks, or broken bricks, which they have been taught to discard, must be built in with the sound ones. Timbers which are crooked, and so weatherworn that they look unsound, are chosen especially for prominent positions, and nice, clean wood, smooth and straight, is only used in places where it cannot be seen.[71]

Perhaps the high point of Shadbolt's career was when he created a house at the 1924 *Daily Mail* Ideal Home exhibition which was built of timbers salvaged from the Old Friar House at Horley and roofed in tiles which, apparently, still had moss growing on them. After a hundred thousand visitors, including George V, had passed through

Pond Cottage, Pinner, Middlesex (Blunden Shadbolt, 1926)

Brooklyn Cottage, Salfords, Surrey (Blunden Shadbolt, 1934)

it, this house was re-erected as Monk's Rest in Pinner, Middlesex.* Also to be found in Pinner was Pond Cottage, built by Shadbolt out of old oak, tiles and brick, in which 'one of the peculiarities of the plan is that the rooms are of irregular shape; instead of having four straight walls, they have many nooks and corners which produce uncommon and pleasing effects'.[72] No wonder, perhaps, that in 1939 the residents of Pinner petitioned the London Passenger Transport Board that a proposed new station building on the Metropolitan Line 'should conform to the medieval character of the village'.[73]

Such an approach to modern domestic architecture may well seem ludicrous, but in exaggerating the elements of Tudor vernacular

---

* A plaque on the front garden wall proclaims, in Gothic lettering, 'Ye Olde Friars House Horley / once a rest house for weary travellers / Built circa 1400 / Dismantled and reconstructed at / The Ideal Home Exhibition 1924 / Finally rebuilt at Pinner Hill 1926 / Overseen by the architect Blunden Shadbolt / Opened by King George V / Now known as Monks Rest'.

Meads, Dippenhall, Surrey (Harold Falkner, 1935)

Burles House, Dippenhall, Surrey (Harold Falkner, 1937)

architecture, Shadbolt not only indulged in a mannerism that satisfied the taste of his time but also displayed an inventiveness that verged on true originality. The same can be said of the creations of Harold Falkner, the ageing Arts and Crafts architect, who, in his native Farnham in Surrey, used neo-Georgian to harmonise with the town he loved but on his own land at Dippenhall built vernacular fantasies. In the words of Falkner's modern biographer, these nine houses, slowly created between 1920 and the architect's death in 1963, 'were structurally unsound; they did not comply with building regulations; their internal layout was unsatisfactory; they failed to appeal to buyers. Despite all this, they are works of genius [and] a triumph of architectural salvage.'[74] Like Shadbolt, 'Wanting the houses to look old, [Falkner] not only used old bricks and timbers, but went out of his way to make modern materials look old – kicking bricks, deliberately pointing them badly, doing internal work with rusty nails and very rough plaster, getting his men to walk up and down new staircases in their heaviest boots.'[75] The first writer to see the point of these wobbly vernacular fantasies was Nicholas Taylor, who, in 1968, denied they were born of 'flattery of pastoral-comical stockbrokerly yearnings':

> They were much more nearly a physical embodiment of the dreams of a king of perspectivists: the crooked lines, the hairy textures, the paradoxes of scale. At a time of paper architecture, when the applause of an Academy private view mattered more than the actual performance on a Surrey hillside, only Falkner had the perverse integrity actually to build his perspectives.[76]

Then there was Ernest Trobridge, the Belfast-born enthusiast for 'Compressed Green Wood Construction'.[77] Trobridge argued that the use of freshly cut elm for modular framed structures, roofed with thatch, was an economical and practical solution to the post-war housing problem. Although the withdrawal of government housing subsidies undermined his proposed development of timber houses

45 Buck Lane, Kingsbury, Middlesex (Ernest Trobridge, 1927)

at Kingsbury, Middlesex, the success of his Elm House at the 1920 Ideal Home Exhibition led to many individual commissions. Most are in Kingsbury, where elm weatherboarding, extravagant brick chimneys, seemingly arbitrary patterns of half-timbering, bedroom windows peering like eyes from under undulating sweeps of thatch, and the occasional use of masonry battlements proclaim the authorship of this single-minded and eccentric designer. These buildings seem comparable with, if anything, the wilder outbursts of contemporary Dutch Expressionism, yet Trobridge both satisfied contemporary conventional aspirations for domestic architecture and displayed ingenious individuality in the composition of elevations and interior spaces. His semi-detached castles in Kingsbury, built in 1927, with their faceted window surrounds and sculptural forms, may well reflect the influence of the architecture of Rudolf Steiner.[78] Ian Nairn long ago remarked on the 'much wilder details that would not be out of place in Gaudí's Barcelona. Like most true follies, more than a joke and more than a whim: a real expression of the dreams of individuality which sent people flocking here in the 1920s along with the Underground.'[79] Trobridge's masterpiece, since destroyed, was the Hotel Ozonia, a wild composition of shaggy thatch and wobbly elm weatherboarding built on Canvey Island, Essex, in 1936–38 with self-catering apartments for East Enders to take cheap holidays.

Trobridge also applied his licentiously free Tudor style of half-timber and brick-nogging to blocks of flats in Kingsbury, also built in the 1930s. Textured, picturesque neo-Tudor may have been a style with rural domestic associations, but it was a style used for buildings in the town as well as in the country. In Chelsea, Darcy Braddell and Humphrey Deane designed a number of terraces of houses in a streamlined Tudor style whose charm comes from the use of a rough, mellow red brick. The style was also used for blocks of flats. The three blocks at the corner of Finchley Road and Hendon Way in north-west London are a curious example. Here the top storeys and projecting gabled bays are given the half-timbered treatment in contrast to red brick walls. A blue plaque on Vernon Court announces

Hanger Hill Garden Estate, Ealing, Greater London (Douglas H. Smith, 1936)

that this was for a time the home of the record-breaking aviatrix Amy Johnson, confirming that there was no necessary connection between an enthusiasm for new, fast machines and a taste for Functionalist architecture.

One of the largest and most consistent Tudor developments was a combination of terraced houses and flats. The Hanger Hill Garden Estate was built in 1928–36 on the site of Acton Aerodrome. The terraces of houses are in the tradition of earlier garden suburbs except that they are more overtly Tudor in style, with much half-timbering. Variety was given to the groups of houses by some having gables, in pairs, but more remarkable are the three-storey blocks of flats, arranged around grassed courts. These are superbly detailed compositions of brick, tile and timber with the elements used in such a way as not to pretend that they are ancient manor houses, while the end pavilions are witty and scholarly essays in traditional half-timbering. The Hanger Hill Garden Estate is one of the finest residential developments of its type: varied, imaginative and conspicuously well-constructed and detailed; that it is less well-known than other garden suburbs can only reflect the widespread prejudice against the Tudor style when built after 1914.

When, in 1954, Nikolaus Pevsner described the pinky-red brick Fisher Building, designed for Queens' College, Cambridge, by George C. Drinkwater in 1935, as 'looking exactly like a friendly block of flats at, say, Pinner', he was at least prepared to concede that its 'Tudor style is not positively offensive'.[80] The style had been chosen to harmonise with the real Tudor red-brick buildings of the college, and university structures were one of the building types where, for particular reasons, Tudor was generally thought appropriate.

Few at the time would have agreed with J. M. Richards when he said, 'To imitate antique styles because we are building in a University town or Cathedral city is an insult to the very architecture we hold in such respect.'[81] Elsewhere in Cambridge, Lutyens demonstrated how the style could be adopted with sophistication and wit rather than with pedantic antiquarianism. In 1928, Magdalene College launched an appeal for a grand three-sided new court to be named after the late Master, the writer A. C. Benson. This would have swept away both the ancient buildings along Magdalene Street and part of

Fisher Building, Queens' College, Cambridge (George C. Drinkwater, 1936)

Mallory Court, an adaptation of existing buildings by the architect Harry Redfern named after the celebrated mountaineer.

In the event, the economic depression after 1929 ensured that only one side of the scheme was built. Lutyens had written that, 'Architecturally, it is proposed to keep the buildings traditional and in sympathy with the old stone building that contains Pepys' Library,' and his building relies for effect on calm horizontality and the use of fine materials: hand-made red bricks above a base of Wealden stone with flush timber-framed windows.[82] The *Architects' Journal* found that the 'details show Sir Edwin Lutyens's familiar but ever-astonishing versatility in the use of traditional forms', and particular delight was taken in the individual treatment of the staircases, each with a different pattern of carefully crafted and pegged panelling, balustrades and newel posts, to enable, so tradition relates, drunken undergraduates to feel their way back to their own rooms at night.[83] The Arts and Crafts movement was alive and well here.

Lutyens was also responsible for one building in Oxford: Campion Hall for the Society of Jesus. This was thanks to the patronage of the Master, Martin D'Arcy. The residential wing of the buildings, completed in 1936, is in an abstracted Tudor style but what tells on the confined exterior are the plain walls of rubble-stone, so typical of interwar Oxford. Inside, the barrel-vaulted chapel is lit by clever light-fittings reminiscent of cardinals' hats and has a *baldacchino* in the apse which uses the Delhi order; the pews rest on an undulating base painted bright red in contrast to the black and white marble floor; elsewhere, the timberwork of the staircases was pegged together. 'Every detail,' Father D'Arcy was pleased to find, 'came out of Lutyens' fertile brain,' and, as Geoffrey Tyack has written, 'like Baker, he never lost sight of his Arts and Crafts upbringing, and it was this aspect of his genius which came to the fore at Campion Hall'.[84]

Sir Herbert Baker had already completed Rhodes House in Oxford, arguably that flawed architect's most successful creation in England. Rhodes House was built in 1926–29 to accommodate the scholars endowed under the will of that thuggish imperialist graduate

Rhodes House, Oxford (Herbert Baker, 1929)

of Oriel College, Cecil Rhodes. The only possible architect was Baker, his protégé in South Africa,* who later wrote how 'no work that fortune brought me gave me greater satisfaction than that of building the Oxford Home of the Spirit of my first patron and friend'.[85] As in his beautiful war memorial cloister for Winchester College, Baker succeeded in combining the Classical and the vernacular, the cool and sophisticated with the rough and rustic, thus emphasising that the Arts and Crafts tradition was not a style but an attitude. Facing south across the gardens towards the old buildings of Wadham College, Rhodes House is designed in a sympathetic Elizabethan

---

* Baker later published *Cecil Rhodes by his Architect* (Oxford University Press, 1934).

or Tudor style with a large central oriel between projecting wings, but towards the street it presents a Pantheon-like domed rotunda and a deep Ionic entrance portico. This, Baker hoped, 'is surely not out of place in the seat of classical scholarship. There is, I feel, some magic influence under a dome, and I hoped that this high note of impressiveness in the vestibule would arrest the attention of all who entered there.'[86]

The other public spaces in Rhodes House achieve a fusion of the Classical and the medieval, with its great hall, Milner Hall, having an arched-braced open timber roof above a gallery supported on Tuscan columns. Everywhere the craftsmanship is superb, and Baker revelled in that literal symbolism which Lutyens eschewed: there are texts cut in fine lettering, heraldic devices and sculptured details referring to Rhodes's life and interests, to create rich, comfortable interiors using exotic timbers reminiscent of Baker's earlier work in South Africa. 'Nowhere in Oxford is the spirit of the Arts and Crafts movement more pervasively present.' Inextricably redolent of attitudes and of an Empire that have long passed, Rhodes House may now seem a problematic building, but it is certainly one of the finest as well as one of the most evocative creations of its period.

Sir Giles Scott also built in a modernised Tudor Gothic style in Oxford between the wars, but in smooth ashlar rather than Bladon rubble, the stone used on his dominatingly unassertive New Bodleian Library building. This was because his task was to continue, in suitably simplified forms, the St Swithun's Buildings at Magdalen College by Bodley & Garner of 1880–84. He was also obliged to use the Tudor style for another educational building in South London, where he acted as 'associated architect' with Gordon & Viner. This was the William Booth Memorial College in Denmark Hill, completed for the Salvation Army in 1928. Scott's involvement is proclaimed by the soaring sophistication of the landmark brick tower – a domesticated version of his design for Liverpool Cathedral. 'It was the desire of the building-owners that the style should be Tudor,' explained the *Architect and Building News*, 'but it could scarcely be imagined that

Interior, William Booth Memorial College, Denmark Hill, London (Giles Scott, 1928)

an architect of such vigorous creative instinct as Sir Giles Gilbert Scott could be content with a mere transcript of decorative *motifs* derived from a past age. What we see here is in reality a twentieth-century building which in a few comparatively unimportant details is reminiscent of the Tudor style.'[87]

Neo-Tudor, whether 'Modern Tudor' or more literal interpretations of the style, was often adopted for educational buildings because of its association with ancient Oxbridge collegiate architecture. Sometimes there were more specific reasons for using it. An unlikely essay in neo-Tudor was the cinema auditorium designed by W. E. Trent for the Gaumont in Salisbury. But here the style was chosen for specific reasons: the surviving fifteenth-century hall of John Halle, which had been restored and given a half-timbered façade by Welby Pugin in 1834, was adapted as the cinema foyer and the 'architects decided that a break from this early halle to a theatre designed and treated in the modern manner

Everyman Cinema (formerly New Kinema), Oxted, Surrey (Murrell & Piggott, with R. S. Cockrill, 1930)

would be too abrupt and hard'.[88] Tudor normally represented introverted domesticity, however, and so was unsuitable for the cinema, a building intended to stand out and symbolise glamour and modernity; the odd exceptions included the New Kinema at Oxted, built in 1930.

The Tudor style was even used for a church, although with a modern aesthetic. The Church of the Holy Cross was built in Greenford, Middlesex, in 1939. The old, medieval church had become too small once the village had been overwhelmed by the suburbs of London, but rather than enlarge it, Albert Richardson designed a new church to sit alongside. With its low brick walls, massive roof and continuous clerestory of leaded-light windows, it is like a big, streamlined barn, and inside, the space is like an old moot hall, with the roof supported on a massive structure of lengths of pine bolted together. Here was the Arts and Crafts movement brought up to date, to make a building with appropriately rural, vernacular overtones. For golf clubs, however, Tudor was compulsory. Even the firm of Sir John Burnet adopted half-timber and red brick for the Hampstead Golf Club House, in which 'The lower walls are in multi-coloured red bricks. Adzed, stained and limed pine has been used in the gable in conjunction with limed plaster. The roof is covered with antique brown tiles.'[89]

Between the wars, the public house (or, rather, the 'inn') was inextricably associated with the Tudor revival. Anthony Bertram complained in 1938 that, 'although people are beginning to accept new design in their cinemas, theatres, and pleasure parks, they do not seem to be ready for it in their pubs. . . . And the pub, of course, is one of those traditional things, and so there is the demand for the old familiar form.'[90] There were two reasons for this. One was the popularity of the style itself, because many of the most accessible manifestations were the old inns of England. After a century of desuetude, the old coaching inns began to enjoy a revival with the advent of touring, first by bicycle and then by motor car. Numerous books appeared in the 1920s and 1930s on the old inns of England, notably those by A. E. Richardson (the second edition featuring a foreword by Lutyens) and Thomas Burke.[91] And if such inns, after centuries of change, did not look Tudor enough, they could always be restored. A good example was the King's Arms at Amersham, Buckinghamshire, restored by the doyen of pub architects, E. B. Musman. The timber structure had been Georgianised and then crudely Tudorised. All that was removed, and the architect 'introduced an entirely new gable',

> founded on the two genuine ones; and has 'Tudorized' all doors and windows, with the result that we now have the sham and the genuine cheek by jowl, with some detriment to the latter. The perfunctory nailing on of creosoted boards in the earlier 'restoration' was so naïve that it would have deceived no one, but the more recent changes have been done with such scholarship that they will inevitably confuse future generations, and even bring the authentic work of the fifteenth century under suspicion.[92]

The second reason, intimately linked with the first, was the campaign to reform the public house in response to the growing political power of the temperance movement in the later nineteenth century and the threat of total prohibition. The response of the brewers was to broaden the facilities offered by the public house, to enable them to provide food as well as drink in the hope of attracting women and families into a male preserve, and so to replace the image of the hard-drinking Victorian pub with that of the traditional hostelry, the inn – what one author called 'the transformation of the beershop and gin palace into the New Public-house'.[93] Architecture was crucial, and the history of the reformed public house can be traced back to Norman Shaw's Tabard at Bedford Park of 1880 and to such examples as the Red Lion at King's Heath, Birmingham, of 1903–04, designed by C. E. Bateman on the model of the famous Angel Inn at Grantham.[94] Such an aesthetic, in conscious reaction to the perceived vulgarity and ostentation of the Late Victorian urban pub, was encouraged by the enthusiasms of the Arts and Crafts movement, with its preference for the village

The Cumberland Inn, Carlisle, Cumbria (Harry Redfern, 1930)

rather than the city and its reverence for districts like the Cotswolds, full of ancient gabled and thatched inns.

The threat of greater state control over public houses was real. Soon after the outbreak of hostilities in 1914, opening hours were restricted to help the war effort and the strength of beer was reduced. In 1916, anxious to maintain the production of munitions in areas where the only entertainment for the workforce was drinking, pubs and breweries in several areas were taken into state control. The most important of these was an area of some 500 square miles in and around Carlisle. Many existing pubs were closed; waiter service and food was provided to discourage 'perpendicular drinking', and the surviving houses rendered less commercial and vulgar in character. The 'Carlisle Experiment' lasted until 1972; in the first few decades new public houses were erected, almost all to the design of the Arts and Crafts architect Harry Redfern. Some were Georgian in style but most were neo-vernacular or Tudor. A good example is the Cumberland Inn, built in 1928–30, which has a gabled stone façade with mullioned and transomed windows and a central oriel.

Not all drinkers found these tasteful evocations of old coaching inns congenial. Redfern's first attempt, the conversion of an old post office into the Gretna Tavern in 1916, was a failure, mainly because he chose to paint the bleak interior battleship grey. In 1919 a party of journalists from London visited the reformed Carlisle pubs, and while the man from the *Daily Mail* thought one village pub was 'as cheerful as a morgue', the reporter from the *Star* thought that 'some of the better-class houses ... remind one of an arts and crafts exhibition'.[95] This was an apt comment, for the Arts and Crafts movement continued to inspire the design of most new public houses. In 1941, the aged C. R. Ashbee considered 'the reformed English pub to be one of the greatest achievements of modern democracy, and it is good to note how the Guild Idea has ... helped in the achievement'.[96] This was written in his memoir of the accomplished pub architect and expert Basil Oliver, who was Master of the Art Workers' Guild for 1932.

Oliver was a significant figure. The son of a Suffolk brewer, his practice involved the restoration of historic buildings as well as the designing of new pubs.[97] He had acted as assistant to Redfern in the early days of the Carlisle Experiment, along with C. R. Mackintosh's collaborator on the Buchanan Street tearoom, the Glasgow designer George Walton. In 1932, Oliver lectured to the RIBA on English inns, publishing his text as a pamphlet on *The Modern Public House* in 1934, with a foreword by Lutyens. In 1947, this was expanded as *The Renaissance of the English Public House*, a book which catalogued and illustrated most of the significant new public houses built during the interwar decades and charted the changes which had led to more civilised drinking.

Oliver was principally concerned with the planning and design of improved pubs and had little to say about style, although in his chapter on 'Untraditional Design and All That' he argued that:

> it is entirely unconstructional, and the purest make-believe, merely to face a building of the present day with ... framing, and it is a still greater offence when the sham 'veneer' is made up of nothing more than one-inch creosoted boards applied to the exterior. All architects know this kind of thing is wrong, yet some of them are unable to resist the pressure of their clients to do it.[98]

Most of his illustrations, however, depicted new pubs in a neo-vernacular or vaguely Tudor style and both his frontispiece and dust-jacket illustrated the Drum Inn at Cockington, a grand, thatched evocation of Merrie England designed by no less than Lutyens himself, in the centre of an ideal (if unfinished) traditional village near Torquay. Oliver was strongly influenced by the Drum Inn when he came to rebuild the Red Lion at Grantchester near Cambridge in 1938–39. An unpretentious old village pub and its thatched cottage neighbour were replaced by a huge new inn-cum-roadhouse, twice as tall and roofed in thatch. Murals in the Garden Room by E. M. Dinkel illustrated Rupert Brooke's poem 'The Old Vicarage, Grantchester', and outside, as a free-standing inn-sign, a red lion was carved by Joseph Armitage.

The Drum Inn, Cockington, Devon (Edwin Lutyens, 1935)

In the event, the temperance movement was less of a threat by the 1930s. Social changes and new attractions like the cinema resulted in less business for breweries, who declined in number from 3,650 in 1914 to 885 in 1939. The number of pubs declined, encouraged by magistrates closing city-centre houses and their being replaced by large new inns or roadhouses in the suburbs.[99] In 1935, in their optimistic celebration of *The Good New Days*, Marjorie and C. H. B. Quennell were sure that 'drunkenness became very much more prevalent in Victorian times than it is now', and the Carlisle Experiment and Redfern's building campaign had much to do with this improved state of affairs: 'This work has been of great importance, not only to Carlisle, but because it helped reformers everywhere. The good work begun in the War is being continued in peacetime. The pub, in fact, has become respectable,* and there are now as well pleasant roadhouses where young folk can dance and swim.'[100]

Such roadhouses sprang up on prominent sites on the new arterial roads out of London. Some were neo-Georgian in style, such as the Myllet Arms at Perivale, by E. B. Musman; some modernistic, like Musman's Comet Inn on the Great North Road at Hatfield. But a majority would seem to have been vaguely Tudor in style. An extraordinary example is Musman's Berkeley Arms on the Bath Road at Cranford, Middlesex, with its round towers and conical roofs on the corners, reminiscent of a French, or Scottish, chateau (Plate 27). The finest examples, however, are to be found not around London but around Birmingham; magistrates pioneered the Birmingham Surrender Scheme, whereby brewers were permitted to build new premises in the suburbs in return for the suppression of licences in the city centre. The result was 'the most ambitious and earliest

---

* The Quennells illustrated this improvement with a set of contrasting images: a rumbustious Victorian pub, the World Turned Upside Down in the Old Kent Road, as it was rebuilt in bland, modernistic neo-Georgian; and 'Waiting for father to come out. An East-End public-house', contrasted with 'Ready for anyone to go in. The new milk bar in Fleet Street'.

The Black Horse, Northfield, Birmingham (Bateman & Bateman, 1930)

rebuildings in all England', further encouraged by the Bishop of Birmingham urging on the chairman of the City of Birmingham Licensing Justices the model of 'a German beer garden, where there was no reflection on a man, or his wife and children, if they were seen going in and coming out'.[101] Thanks also to the enlightened architectural policy of the brewers, Mitchells & Butlers in particular, magnificent brick or stone Tudor roadhouses were built on main roads in Birmingham's suburbs.

The finest, largest and most astonishing example is the Black Horse at Northfield, Birmingham, designed in 1929 by Francis Goldsborough of Bateman & Bateman for John Davenport & Sons brewery. The building closely resembles a sixteenth-century country house; towards the road it presents a series of projecting gabled bays, all in black and white half-timber, while towards the garden, with its long stone and timber pergola, timber and plaster alternate with brown Cotswold rubble-stone buildings with mullioned and transomed windows and leaded lights. 'This surely must be one of the most sumptuous inns in the district, if not in England,'* thought Basil Oliver: 'Here are quite separate and self-contained service bars, even with their own cellarage, at the far end of the bowling green, more especially for charabanc parties which need not thus invade and congest the licensed rooms of the house.'[102]

'We trundled along at no great pace down pleasant roads, decorated here and there by the presence of huge new gaudy pubs,' recorded J. B. Priestley as he approached Birmingham by bus in 1933:

> These pubs are a marked feature of this Midlands landscape. Some of them have been admirably designed and built; others have been inspired by the idea of Merrie England, popular in the neighbourhood of Los Angeles. But whether comely or hideous, they must all have cost a pot of money, proving that the brewers – and they seemed to be all owned by brewers – still have great confidence in their products. At every place, however, I noticed that some attempt had been made to enlarge the usual attractions of the beer-house; some had bowling greens, some advertised their food, others their music.[103]

A feature of many of these cheerful evocations of Tudor England is a double-height hall, with open timber roof. A good example is the former Henekey's in High Holborn, built in 1923–24 and now called The Cittie of Yorke. Lined on one side by giant vats above a long bar counter and on the other by enclosed timber booths behind a timber arcade, this was the drinker's answer to Liberty's nearby Tudor House. But some of the most extraordinary examples are to be found in, of all places, the Regency town of Brighton. On the west side of the Steyne is the King and Queen Hotel, a large inn with an open courtyard behind a façade of randomly textured rough brickwork and patches of stone – that treatment, so typical of the period, which

---

* It has also been described as 'one of the largest examples of "brewers' Tudor" ever built' (Brandwood, Davison and Slaughter (2004), p. 80).

suggests great age. Inside, there are rustic oak beams. Typically, while the old pub on the site once had figures of King George III and Queen Charlotte on the façade, in the rebuilding, carried out in 1931–32, Henry VIII and Anne Boleyn were represented instead. This 'gorgeous flight of architectural imagination', as it was called at the time,[104] may seem alien among stuccoed terraces but perhaps is no more exotic than the Prince Regent's Pavilion. And then there is the New Ship Inn of 1933–34, whose stone Tudor façade with a 'portcullis gateway' and projecting half-timbered gables, filled with brick nogging, evokes a Brighton centuries older than the Regency. Inside, there is a large wide galleried hall with an open timber roof and, on each side, 'old world galleries with recesses where privacy may be obtained, and that all-important "deal" may be discussed'.[105] It is a vision of the Middle Ages which equals anything attempted by Pugin or Norman Shaw in their houses.

Such hostelries were no doubt popular with those antique-loving myopic motorists beloved by P. A. Barron, who were so easily fooled by half-timbered shopping parades. As far as Anthony Bertram was concerned,

> the Tudor pub is the supreme form of escape. But what fantastic situations it leads to. We dash out from the city in our sports models and are helped to park them by a gentleman in medieval costume. We go into a low-beamed bar where an electric fire winks merrily in the old inglenook and where we drink our cocktails surrounded by a display of Tudor tankards – not for use.

Bertram at least recognised that such places were popular, as the desire to escape was deeply rooted in his time. 'Isn't this the very symptom of the disease of our epoch, its fear of itself, its romantic hunger for a purely imaginary ideal of the good old days?'[106]

It is in the ordinary suburban house, built in its millions, that the power of the Tudor architectural ideal was strongest – hence the unceasing abuse of it by the architectural profession. Few with access to the printed page had a good word to say for these buildings. One who did was J. B. Priestley, who in 1927 wrote: 'A few more of these houses and this place will no longer charm the eye; a great many more of them and it will be hideous.' On the other hand, 'We should be content to make the whole country hideous if we know for certain that by doing so we could also make the people in it moderately happy.'[107]

At least the architect Julian Leathart understood why such houses became ubiquitous. 'It is fashionable to hurl abuse at the speculative house builder,' he wrote at the end of the 1930s,

> and it is, without dispute, to his appalling vulgarity and ignorance that the despoliation of town and countryside during the last twenty years is attributable. But the jerry builder has fulfilled a public demand, and, in the sacred name of private enterprise, his depredations have been allowed to go unchecked by either Government or local authority. He has built a degraded version of a recognized English style of architecture, and his best-sellers have been those houses which conform to the half-timbered Tudor style.[108]

A foreign observer, Rasmussen, understood the anti-urban impulse that lay behind these houses, writing in 1934 that 'people do not want to live in street houses any longer, they want a *Cottage* which must be situated in a small garden of its own. A Tudor house with old oak beams looking as if it had been inherited from the great-great-grandparents is a good seller.'[109] What is certain is that, for millions of families, the spec-built suburban house, with its neo-Tudor details, its false half-timbering, tile-hung gables, bay-windows and rough-cast walls, represented an image of home, of freedom and domesticity, for millions of families able and willing to afford a down payment and the mortgage instalments.

Yet, although numerous studies have been written about the advent and the impact of the New Architecture in Britain, very little has been published since on the extraordinary phenomenon of the millions of houses in new suburbs built so rapidly and efficiently in the 1920s and 1930s, developments which continue to define the essence of Britain. And while there have been studies published about the pattern of suburban developments and on the influence of transport, economics and official planning policies on the shape of the new suburbs, very little has appeared on the design of the houses themselves.* Indeed, almost the only serious modern study of the interwar suburban house is a remarkable book emanating from the Department of Architecture at the then Oxford Polytechnic and published in 1981. Written by Paul Oliver, Ian Davis and Ian Bentley, *Dunroamin: The Suburban Semi and its Enemies* was a product of rare research questioning the values and hegemony of the Modern Movement and the importance of the vaunted professional architect, while suggesting that the interwar housing boom might have some lessons for the present.

'Dunroamin' was the generic name given to the interwar, privately owned suburban house. The authors of this book took the design of the suburban house seriously, understanding that free individuals bought houses with fake half-timber and tile-hung gables because they represented home and security. Their book recognises that the suburb was a product of 'dream-builders': 'This recognition, that there were deeper issues in the aspiration of families for their homes than strict physical criteria, was totally lost on most architects and writers. Few were able to grasp the significance of the dreams, associational imagery . . . or the symbols of the suburb.'[110] It is not necessary to accept the argument that, what with the 'swelling bosom of the bay windows combined to communicate maternal warmth'

---

* For notable exceptions, see Alan Jackson (1973); Ward and Ward (1978); and *Little Palaces: The Suburban House in North London, 1919–1939* (London: Middlesex Polytechnic, 1987), revised as *Little Palaces: House and Home in the Inter-War Suburbs* (London: Middlesex University Press, 2003), with a foreword by Christopher Frayling ('this little book has a big purpose: to save the suburban house, and its inhabitants, from the enormous condescension of history').

and the more mannered front door recesses resembling genital orifices, 'the home was a woman', to agree about the importance of architectural imagery. 'What the new Dunroaminer sought was an imagery that spoke of home, of family and of individualism. Modernists were prepared to clad their brickwork in render that appeared to be concrete for the sake of the new architecture projected; the Dunroaminer saw no incongruity in having his home clad in the symbols of domesticity.'[111]

The private house owner did not want to buy a house in the Modern style as that was, deliberately, reminiscent of the factory, which for them, had no attractive associations. Nor would he choose a neo-Georgian house, for that style, in its tasteful, reticent uniformity favoured by architects, was pejoratively redolent of local authority housing, of the Council house. Sir Leslie Scott, KC, of the Council for the Preservation of Rural England, regretfully acknowledged in 1936 that:

> there has been a revolt against the artistically good simplicity of the well-designed Council house. This reaction has manifested itself in a demand for the kind of house which is an abomination; a house which is bought just because its exterior is so different from the decent exterior of the Council house that the casual observer must see at a glance that its owner is *not* living in a Council house – it may even have been chosen in the belief that people will think it has cost more. There is probably thus an element of snobbery in the mental attitude.

There was certainly a great deal of snobbery in this supercilious lawyer's false sympathy for the builder whose 'potential customers insist on indulging their false taste for sham Tudor houses'.[112] Well did Paul Oliver conclude that:

> Refusing to admit that the semis of Dunroamin had any positive values, architectural writers considered the houses and their collective layout as mindless examples of non-design. Yet

Dunroamin has great design consistency, which was unwittingly acknowledged by the fact that its *extreme* consistency was itself a source of criticism and of the frequent assertions of monotony.... In their arguments for the new, 'clean-and-decent' design it seems that architects considered that the forms and plain, undecorated, white surfaces of Modern Movement buildings were value-free. That they were as controlled by concepts of style, as loaded with the imagery of boat-decks and machines as Dunroamin was of cottages and Jacobean details, was never admitted. Modern Movement imagery spoke of clinical efficiency as Dunroamin spoke of domesticity.[113]

The problem faced by the authors of *Dunroamin* – as by the historian today – is the comparative absence of contemporary publications dealing with the ordinary suburban house from an architectural point of view. Not only did most critics despise such buildings, but they were seldom connected with the name of an architect. Unless there is a local history or study of a particular suburb or development – as there is, for example, of the genteel neo-Tudor 'garden suburb' at Petts Wood – the historian must rely on advertisements and catalogues and brochures issued by the building firms themselves.[114]

One informative and revealing source is *House Building 1934–1936*, published by the National Federation of Building Trades Employers. Illustrated by the architect and perspectivist Raymond Myerscough-Walker, this contained articles on the housing and planning acts, on house purchase, tax and mortgages, and interviews with three successful commercial house builders. It also contained contributions by architects who were clearly anxious to have a role in this lucrative activity. 'We are most desirous of encouraging the co-operation of architects in the building of houses for sale,' insisted the builder, J. Laing, which suggests that this was unusual. 'For this purpose we have set aside one of our estates, and architects are in competition in regard to house plans.'[115] But even Gordon Allen, an experienced domestic architect, could not help being snooty about the average suburban house:

> What the average purchaser wants as regards the elevation of his house is a question of psychology rather than of art. He is probably uncertain, although much influenced by a pleasing exterior. His judgement has been affected by being told that the fussy villa is evidence of bad taste, and also by his experience that houses spattered with 'features' are restless in appearance and expensive in upkeep. It is safe to say he desires his home to be different from his neighbour's, and, above all, unlike the municipal house, owing to his sense of social dignity. In many instances the 'modernist' elevation, with its freshness and 'breadth', appeals to him a good deal.[116]

The evidence of most suburbs suggests otherwise.

Gordon Allen had won the *Daily Mail* Prize for the best £1,500 house in 1927, with Donald McMorran as runner-up, and his design was erected at the Ideal Home Exhibition that year. All the designs entered, for both the £1,500 house and the £850 house, were reproduced in *The Daily Mail Ideal Houses* book, but, as the assessors were architects, a high proportion were partly or wholly neo-Georgian in style, and so not representative of what was actually in the exhibition. 'It is a happy coincidence that as this book goes to press, the Prime Minister, Mr Stanley Baldwin, is supporting a movement with the object of recovering the spirit of ancient English cottage architecture,' wrote the editors. 'Here . . . is expressed the very ideal for which for many years The *Daily Mail* has worked through the medium of the Ideal Home Exhibition annually held at Olympia, London, W.'[117] On the cover was a photograph of the 1926 exhibition with, in the foreground, the 'Tibbenham Tudor House'. 'Tibbenham Houses have combined old-time charm with modern utility,' ran the advertisement for the Tibbenham Construction Co. Ltd. 'They are constructed with a solid oak framing like the old Sussex farmhouses

'Tibbenham Tudor House', Northgate, Middlesex (Frederick Tibbenham, with Stanley Hamp, 1921)

which today stand foursquare to the winds with a sturdiness that is a tribute to the method and a beauty which redounds to the credit of our forefathers.' Other representative advertisements include one for Maple & Co., reproducing the design of the half-timbered 'Maple's House' erected at the exhibition, and the butterfly-plan 'Suntrap House' erected by the Potters Bar Estate – another half-timbered design with leaded-light windows.

Architects were conspicuous by their absence in the many catalogues issued by builders. Indeed, in that issued by the Universal Housing Co., Ltd, of Rickmansworth, customers were offered a complete specification and plans for approval so that, 'in this way we save you architects' fees – a considerable item'. Yet architects were clearly responsible for the designs of the many half-timbered neo-Tudor houses illustrated. In a catalogue issued by Comben & Wakeling, Ltd, eight different types of semi-detached house were offered on the Sudbury Court and St Augustine's Estates in North Wembley. All were explicitly or vaguely neo-Tudor in style, and the types must, at some stage, have been drawn out by or at least approved by an architect. At Petts Wood, for instance, the streets were laid out and the builders' plans vetted by Leonard Culliford, who also designed some houses (Plate 26).[118] It is noticeable how often the word 'Tudor' was adopted.* In the guide to *London and Suburbs, Old and New*, published in about 1933, builders' advertisements appear between the pages describing 'many of the best residential suburbs of London'. These included one for the Gunnersbury Avenue Estate, Ealing – Tudor Way and Carbery Avenue: 'Only a few plots on this very popular Estate are now left, and if a house of distinction in the Tudor style appeals to you, come along without further delay.' Readers were also invited to inspect 'Tudor Style Houses of distinction' erected by the Tudor Building Co., of Tudor Avenue, Worcester Park, Surrey, on the Tudor Estate: 'An unique high-class estate in a splendid situation, every house devoted to the true Tudor Style, constructed by experts', where a freehold semi-detached house cost £895 and a detached £1,200.[119]

Suburbs containing such houses grew around Liverpool, Manchester and Birmingham and most large cities. In London, they are particularly associated with 'Metro-land', the name given by the Metropolitan Railway to developments it promoted along its long, newly electrified tentacle from Baker Street Station through Middlesex and into deepest Buckinghamshire. *Metro-land* was also the name given to the promotional guidebooks published every year by the company from 1915 until 1932, after which the Metropolitan Railway was absorbed by the London Passenger Transport Board. Readers of the 'House Seekers Section' in the 1932 edition were informed of how 'fortunate' it was 'for prospective purchasers that the large, new residential estates at Wembley Park, Northwick Park, Pinner, Rickmansworth, Amersham and Rayners Lane (for Harrow Garden Village), Eastcote, Ruislip and Hillingdon, on the Uxbridge Section, are controlled by such an organisation as the Metropolitan

---

* In the 2002 *London A-to-Z*, seventy-seven separate addresses are listed with the word 'Tudor': Tudor Avenue, Tudor Close, Tudor Court, Tudor Drive, Tudor Gardens, and so on.

Station Square, Petts Wood, Greater London (Basil Scruby and Leonard Culliford, 1930)

Railway Country Estates, Ltd'.[120] By that date, however, the activities of other developers were undermining the exclusive character intended by the company, whose 'publicity photographs of Metroland showed tree-sheltered homesteads of ineffable distinction, sometimes with thatched roofs'.[121]

New suburban streets, lined with a rich variety of examples of Stockbrokers' Tudor or By-Pass Variegated, were being laid out all round London, however. There are particularly fine specimens, for instance, in Petts Wood, to the south-east, which grew around a new station which the Southern Railway opened in 1928 on land provided and with money offered by the developer, Basil Scruby.

By 1930, forty-five builders were active in Petts Wood, but Scruby remained firmly in control of the planning. The result was a consistent neo-Tudor suburb, with some imaginative variations. The new town centre was also Tudor, with the new shops laid out around Station Square faced in red-brick and timber, and in 1935 the Daylight Inn rose in the middle, designed in extravagant Tudor by Sidney Clarke of Leigh-on-Sea to be in stylistic harmony.[122]

Great Thrift, Petts Wood, Greater London (Noel Rees, c. 1930)

Hayes was another characteristic example. The old Kentish village had been connected with Charing Cross by a branch line opened in 1882, whose electrification in 1926 seems to have been the catalyst for a decade of intensive development. Hayes Place was demolished in 1933, despite its association with two great prime ministers (William Pitt the Elder died there, and Pitt the Younger was born there), and by 1938 the Hayes Place Garden Estate, laid out and built by Henry Boot & Sons, Ltd, was nearing completion. The Southern Railway rebuilt the station in 1933–35 on a new Station Approach, at one end of which was the Rex cinema, opened in 1936, and at the other, the New Inn, rebuilt in 1935 in grand half-timbered and Cotswold stone Tudor by the Birmingham architects Bateman & Bateman. In between, new ranges of shopping parade were erected: some neo-Georgian, one in a curious modernistic style, but most in half-timbered neo-Tudor. And right opposite the new modernistic station entrance, a richly carved group of Tudor shops housed the local estate agent. 'It is an original piece of building,' one sympathetic observer commented. 'One day, it will be in the picture books of Old England.'[123]

The Daylight Inn, Petts Wood, Greater London (Sidney Clarke, 1935)

From here, to the north, east and west, stretched new residential streets. Some were formed entirely of detached houses; others all of semi-detached pairs. Architectural writers may have sneered at such houses, but as designs they are worth taking seriously. H. C. Bradshaw, the Liverpool-trained Secretary of the Royal Fine Art Commission, may have thought they lacked the 'beauty which the monotonous planning of the speculative builder, in spite of his efforts to create variety by such means as false gables, sham half-timbering, pebble-dash walls and assorted shapes in bay windows, cannot hope to achieve', but such streets are no more monotonous than those planned by the heirs of the Arts and Crafts movement in garden suburbs or, indeed, than the Georgian terraces that the Victorians found so intolerably boring.[124] Variety was introduced by alternating several different designs or by reversing the plans. In Sandiland Crescent, Hayes, for instance, several different types repeat: one with a half-timbered central bay, flanked by sloping roofs; one an asymmetrical rough-cast bay with a bay window under a hipped gable; and one with a central brick chimneybreast rising from ground level – Gothic functionalism in the tradition of Pugin and Norman Shaw.

These suburban houses owed much to the designs for small and cheap cottages made decades earlier by Arts and Crafts architects like Baillie Scott, but a new, standard type had evolved from the typical gabled 'Queen Anne' urban terrace. Gone were the projecting back extensions characteristic of the terraced house; instead these houses were compactly planned, usually with the dining room next to the kitchen at the back (perhaps connected by a serving hatch) and three bedrooms upstairs. The authors of *Dunroamin* also emphasise the cleverness of the composition of the standard semi-detached pair, in which elements like the hipped roofs and the two distinct bay windows 'emphasised the separateness of the *pair* of semis', while 'other design features developed to display the importance of the individual house *within* the pair' – like the front doors being placed at the sides.[125]

As for the stylistic references, these are in a long and distinguished tradition stretching back to John Nash. The vernacular tile hanging can perhaps be traced back to Shaw, and Voysey's triangular gable and double-height curved bay was the latest variation on a well-established theme in English domestic architecture; the more mannered window forms, canted bays corbelled out, or corner windows, or the occasional vaguely Art Nouveau small projecting oriel, probably derived from Voysey, Mackintosh and, before them, Norman Shaw.[126] What is self-evident is that all the elements constituted a distinct style, characteristic of its time. Indeed, it can be argued that not only was Tudor the most popular and ubiquitous style in architecture between the wars, but the neo-Tudor suburban house, in all its many manifestations, constituted the first universal, generally accepted manner of building since the Georgian domestic style of the eighteenth century. Such was the achievement of suburbia.

It was, of course, almost an article of faith amongst architects and critics that despite the manifest failings of Modern houses, these anonymous neo-Tudor houses were 'jerry-built'. Standards may well have fallen since the turn of the century, and the Quennells were sure that, 'Since the War of 1914–18 the quality of building has deteriorated.'[127] There were certainly many cases of defective building and infringement of the bye-laws, often ending up in court.[128] Rasmussen lamented that the 'simple, plain and modern houses of the eighteenth century have been replaced by the badly built semi-detached houses of the twentieth century, houses provided with half timber work, gables and projecting bays, small crooked porches and twisting roofs'.[129] Even so, most houses were not badly constructed. In 1939, the architect Stanley Ramsey admitted to 'a shrewd suspicion that much of the criticism of "Jerry building" is, in effect, the "wish being father to the thought" – finding these houses so unpleasant to look at, one is apt to jump to the conclusion that they must of necessity be badly built'.[130] Nevertheless, in 1937 Betjeman could claim to have heard 'of the bay window of a modern Tudor house lifted by a storm from its setting and flung over the opposite house-tops while the family in the parlour was at Sunday dinner'; he insisted that 'the luckless occupants' of such houses 'will find themselves in a few years' time saddled with a slum'.[131] The following year, Osbert Lancaster lamented 'that so much ingenuity should have been wasted on streets and estates which will inevitably become the slums of the future'.[132]

Far from being a slum, the suburban semi continues to perform its role as house and home, but few have acknowledged its success. One who did, having changed his mind about the suburbs, his vision widened by being in Egypt during another world war, was J. M. Richards, who in 1946 published *The Castles on the Ground*. Illustrated by John Piper, this was a celebration of the romance and virtues of the English suburb as it had developed since the early nineteenth century:

> We well know the epithets used to revile the modern suburb – 'Jerrybethan', and the rest – and the scornful finger that gets pointed at spec-builder's Tudor with its half-inch boards nailed flat to the wall in imitation of oak timbering, though perhaps we should not criticize so fiercely the architectural idiom the suburb has adopted as its own if we understood the instincts and ideals it aims to satisfy, and how well, judged by its own standards, it often

succeeds in doing so. . . . . If democracy means anything, it means deciding – for a change – to pay some attention to the expressed preference of the majority, to what people themselves want, not what we think they ought to want.[133]

Much good did it do him. Richards later recalled how the 'book was scorned by my contemporaries as either an irrelevant eccentricity or a betrayal of the forward-looking ideas of the Modern Movement, to which the suburbs were supposed to be the absolute antithesis'.[134] The subject was soon dropped.

In vain did Richards point out the huge number of houses built between the wars, such that 'the suburban environment determines the style in which – for good or ill – modern England lives'.[135] In 1979, in the major exhibition mounted at the Hayward Gallery entitled *Thirties: British Art and Design Before the War*, architecture was almost entirely represented by the familiar icons of the Modern Movement. 'Speculative Housing' was treated as a sub-section of 'Architecture: A Spectrum of Styles' and consisted of photographs of Rectory Gardens, Edgware, a development of semi-modernistic semis that was scarcely typical. As Paul Oliver noted at the end of *Dunroamin*, one of these was a family photograph taken outside No. 81 Kingsway, Coney Hall, entitled 'The Promise of Suburban Bliss' and captioned, with no further explanation: 'Victims of the Thirties building boom. The Borders family outside their jerry-built house, aptly named *Insanity*.'* As he equally aptly concluded, 'Fifty years after, the Establishment of architects and critics clings tenaciously to its clichés.'[136] Another quarter-century – and more – has passed since, but neo-Tudor is still sneered at while the great estates of interwar suburbia, varied, distinctive and representative, remain largely unexplored.

---

* In Hawkins and Hollis's exhibition catalogue, *Thirties: British Art and Design before the War* (1979), a photograph of one of these Edgware semis was reproduced next to similar 'superior semi-detached homes, Becontree Estate', which, being the work of the London County Council, was not speculative housing. The photograph of the Borders family was not included.

CHAPTER SEVEN

NEW GEORGIANS

———◆———

'ONE HARDLY KNOWS whether to laugh or to cry on seeing a modernistic architecture imported into London, which is far less suitable to the spirit of the age than the Georgian houses of about 1800.'[1] Such was the reaction of Steen Eiler Rasmussen, the Anglophile Danish architect, when writing *London: The Unique City* in 1934. Many native architects agreed with him, except that they wished to base a modern architecture on the detail of the architecture of 1800 rather than on its essential spirit. 'Neo-Georgian', an often rather crude revival and development of the Georgian tradition, was certainly one of the dominant approaches to design at the time. Others wished to learn only from the simplicity and fine proportions of the best Late Georgian urbanism. Nevertheless, a fusion of these two approaches occurred, resulting in a streamlined or modernistic Georgian that was a characteristic style of the interwar decades.

'There are two styles in England which are the basis of domestic design,' explained Raymond Myerscough-Walker in *Choosing a Modern House*. These were the Tudor and the Georgian, and to illustrate the latter he chose a rendered brick house in Cambridge designed by Harold Tomlinson: 'This house is typical of the Georgian tradition; it is symmetrical, its proportions are classical; and it is altogether more ordered than the medieval work which was romantic in its outlook rather than orderly, and where asymmetry happened as a matter of course, according to the simple desires of the people of that time.'[2] The key word was 'ordered'. As Myerscough-Walker recognised, the Elizabethan and Tudor, 'in their variety of forms', were still popular. He might have added that the Georgian mainly appealed to architects, for it was the association between Georgian urbanity and planned council housing that made so many English people opt for the romance of Tudor. A decade earlier, R. Randal Phillips had prefaced his *Country Life* book on *Small Family Houses* with a photograph of a 'Late Georgian Example' at Petersham. 'It may be just as right,' he argued, 'to build a house of the old English sort, in half-timber and plaster, with latticed windows and moulded brick stacks, as to build a four-square house of Georgian type, with sash windows and a trellis porch or hooded entry. The one is no more right or wrong than the other.' Even so, he continued, 'whereas the Georgian type is a purely formal one . . . the other can only be successful if it is done in a thorough-going way, with no make-believe about it.'[3]

The taste for neo-Georgian well pre-dated the accession of another King George in 1910. As early as the 1890s, Arts and Crafts vernacular was evolving into something more formal in response to the recognition that the domestic Classicism of Wren and the Georgian country rectory belonged to a valid English tradition. This change can be found in the work of Ernest Newton, Reginald Blomfield and, above all, of Edwin Lutyens before 1914. Also before the Great War, admiration for the ordinary Georgian had extended forwards into the Regency. This can be seen in the book on *London Houses from 1660 to 1820* by A. E. Richardson and his partner, C. Lovett Gill, published in 1911, and in the teaching and practice of Charles Reilly at the Liverpool School of Architecture. The supreme example of this is the redevelopment of the Duchy of Cornwall

Estate in Kennington by Stanley Adshead and Reilly's pupil Stanley C. Ramsey, opened by the Prince of Wales in 1914. The wheel of taste had turned full circle and the elegant urbanity of the Regency terrace was being revived.

This was a refined, self-conscious style favoured by the Architectural Association in London as well as Reilly's Liverpool School. At the AA the Principal was that versatile designer Robert Atkinson, who added to the school's new premises in Bedford Square an extension in a spare, rational Late Georgian industrial manner and then created a library, with the school's war memorial, in an elegant Regency style. Atkinson also rescued Percy Lodge, a Late Georgian house at East Sheen, for his own residence, and then built an estate of new brick houses in a similar style on part of the grounds. Reilly thought this 'little colony of houses for artists . . . one of the pleasantest development schemes I have seen'.[4] No wonder that Osbert Lancaster identified a sub-species of the neo-Georgian as 'Architectural Association (or Beggars' Opera) Georgian', which was 'distinctive by its invincible refinement'.[5]

Percy Lodge, East Sheen Richmond-upon-Thames (1740; restored Robert Atkinson, 1924)

After the war, the repetitive, orderly simplicity of the Late Georgian was widely seen as the basis for the development of a modern national architecture. Abstracted simplicity, combined with order, proportion and discipline, was what appealed. 'The period of domestic architecture from which of all others we have most to learn is the Georgian,' argued Trystan Edwards in 1924. 'The essential modernity of the "Georgian" style should be widely recognised. . . . Is it not obvious that an architectural movement which seeks to imbue modern buildings with something of the same spirit is worthy of support?'[6] And to rebuff critics who might suggest that adopting a style 'distinguished by certain qualities of restraint and cohesion' would be mere revivalism, Edwards suggested calling it 'urban' rather than 'Georgian'.

Writing in that same year, 1924, in his populist tract on *Everyday Architecture*, the proselytising former official architect Manning Robertson considered that:

> Already an immense improvement is visible, and a 'Twentieth-century Style' is being evolved. The necessity for economy is forcing us into honest expression, and the new style, although based upon past tradition and especially upon Georgian work, is not a mere copy, but bears the stamp of the present day; we are in fact continuing the sequence of English architecture from the point where it was rudely interrupted by the industrial materialism of the last century. More and more we rely for our effects upon good plain brick and tile work, of pleasing texture and varied colour, and upon the elusive quality of proportion emphasised by the play of shadows. Pretentious so-called 'ornamentation', expensive in first cost and upkeep, is disappearing, and there are ample signs that we shall once more find small buildings – houses and shops – of a beauty comparable to the eighteenth-century work we all admire.[7]

As an example of this evolving style of 'severe simplicity dependent for its beauty upon proportion', Robertson illustrated the new Ministry of Pensions building at Acton, designed by the Office of

Works architect, J. G. West, describing it as 'a prodigious structure without ornament or nonsense, imposing in its simplicity'.[8]

That this huge, remorselessly repetitive and boring neo-Georgian warehouse was so much admired says much about the aesthetic preferences of the time. The contemporary taste for Hack Kampmann's plain barrack-like Police Headquarters in Copenhagen was similar. Clough Williams-Ellis could even describe it as great architecture, comparable with Wren's Chelsea Hospital.[9] As Goodhart-Rendel observed less than a decade later, with characteristic objectivity:

> A curious symptom of the utilitarianism becoming fashionable in the nineteen-twenties may be detected in the extravagant praise accorded to the offices of the Ministry of Pensions at Acton at the time of their building. In the design of these offices it is difficult now to see any particular merit other than that of discretion, of keeping out of trouble. The proportions of the windows are not noticeably well adjusted, the design of the doorways pretends but fails to be expressive, there is nothing particularly good about the cornice, and nothing else that can be remarked at all.[10]

Even so, its salaried architect went on to become Sir James West in 1936.

Contemporary publications responded to this fashionable utilitarianism by illustrating useful and elegant precedents for a modern, severe brick neo-Georgian architecture. 'Exemplars of Architecture' were regularly published in the pages of the *Architects' Journal*, with photographs and measured drawings of the details of Georgian buildings. The photographer F. R. Yerbury published his own photographs of *Georgian Details of Domestic Architecture* in 1926 and the prolific Albert Richardson was responsible for several books which concentrated on Georgian buildings. Smart and cosmopolitan students were also aware of the influential *Um 1800*, compiled by Paul Mebes, illustrating vernacular Biedermeier architecture in North Europe.

Professor Richardson was a key figure in the development of a modern Georgian architecture, as a teacher at the Bartlett School and as a writer, but also as a practising architect. During his long career, circumstances required that he evolve from a progressive, modern Classicist into the reactionary President of the RA and grand old 'Last of the Georgians'. What was consistent was his delight in and deep knowledge of Georgian England and, in addition to his architectural studies, he somehow found the time to write a rich and entertaining book on life in *Georgian England*, published in 1931. John Summerson recalled him as his teacher, 'a picturesque character with an air of genius about him, a bit of an actor . . . He had an extraordinary knowledge of eighteenth- and nineteenth-century classicism and talked about it as if it was living architecture, which for him it was. He was a practising classicist himself, and a good one.'[11]

Richardson's magnificent book, *Monumental Classic Architecture*, published in 1914, had encouraged the revival of appreciation of Late Georgian Classicism. In the 1920s he was still a progressive figure, anxious to adapt the Classical lessons of the past to the modern steel-framed commercial building. This he achieved, supremely, in Leith House on Gresham Street, where the frame was expressed below the recognisable cornice as a rectilinear grid of stone, abstracted but elegant, and still governed by Classical principles. '*It is structure and structure alone that will provide the germ of a new style,*' insisted Richardson. 'The genius of the English race will find a method of dealing with the situation; *there must be no insane diversion or pursuit of novelty.*'[12] There was certainly no pursuit of novelty in Richardson's domestic buildings, which were more pedantically Georgian, especially those on the Duchy of Cornwall Estate in the West of England where, like Adshead and Ramsey in Kennington, he looked to Regency models.

Georgian was the style chosen for a large number of country houses, and almost the inevitable choice for the new London town house. Writing in 1951, Lionel Brett considered that the development,

Leith House, Gresham Street, City of London (A. E. Richardson, 1926)

or rediscovery, of the small house was the 'outstanding contribution' of British architecture between the wars: 'The intimacy and charm of the small house, which had vanished with the Regency villa, were recaptured by the neo-Georgians of the 'twenties, and it was partly the likeable character of these frankly derivative brick houses with their white sash windows which delayed the full acceptance of the modern house in the 'thirties.'[13] Indeed, the frontispiece of Patrick

Stockgrove Park House, Leighton Buzzard, Buckinghamshire (W. Curtis Green, 1938)

Abercrombie's 1939 compilation, *The Book of the Modern House*, was a perspective by P. D. Hepworth of the garden front of Ratton Wood in Sussex, a symmetrical seven-bay brick neo-Georgian house with a central pedimented doorcase designed by the Arts and Crafts architect Sir Guy Dawber. Earlier, another former Arts and Crafts architect, Curtis Green, had designed Stockgrove Park in the Chilterns, a large, modern Georgian pile with wings enclosing an entrance courtyard and shutters on the Georgian sashes facing the gardens.

Oswald P. Milne, a former pupil of Lutyens, was adept in the style; in the international survey of modern architecture published by the Dutch architect J. G. Wattjes in 1927, two of the three houses by Milne which were illustrated were in a free Georgian manner.[14] Then there was that elegant and fashionable figure Darcy Braddell, who, with his partner Humphrey Deane, was responsible for Barleys at Offham in Sussex, a subtly asymmetrical but slightly pompous composition that was described in the Architecture Club's selection of *Recent English Architecture 1920–1940* as a 'Fastidious modern handling of Georgian tradition producing a simple elegance in harmony with the downland site'.[15] Another, similar example of their country house work was Corbett Place in Hampshire. And Swinbrook House – so often disparaged in the vast literature by or about his daughters, the Mitford sisters – which was designed (with the 1st Lord Redesdale) by Guy Dawber as a family seat to replace the financially insupportable Batsford, was also neo-Georgian. With this style, it would seem to have been difficult to go wrong, even though a certain stiff dullness often seems to have resulted from trying to avoid the inescapable influence of the great Lutyens in handling the Classical language.

Mount Harry House (formerly Barleys), Offham, Sussex (Braddell & Deane, 1936)

'They are all over England,' claimed Evelyn Waugh in 1938,

> these models of civilized buildings, and of late years we have been turning to them again in our convalescence from the post-war Corbusier plague that has passed over us... We are again thinking of stone and brick and timber that will mellow and richen with age, and we have instinctively turned to the school in which our fathers excelled.[16]

Architects and clients were returning to Classical models, and particularly to Late Georgian ones. This was true of a number of younger architects, some of whom had decided to reject Modernism. One was Raymond Erith, who, in rebuilding Great House at Dedham, Essex, that same year displayed a deep admiration for the simplicity of the Regency and of Soane's work in particular. As Alan Powers has written, 'Many advocates of Modernism had claimed since the 1920s that Regency represented the last good period of architecture in Britain, and that all modern architecture needed to do was to pick up its threads, but none had done so as literally as Erith, supported by a fanatical attention to details such as the precise scrolling of the Ionic volutes.'[17] Others included the partnership of John Seely and Paul Paget, who, at Templewood in Norfolk, created a grand Classical bungalow that was theatrical in character, not to say camp. Rather larger, and duller, was Great Swifts at Cranbrook, Kent, designed by Geddes Hyslop for Major Victor Cazalet in 1938.

With these country houses of the late 1930s, generally inspired by Late Georgian precedents, and with remodellings of older houses, one can, Alan Powers suggests, 'almost recognise a "George VI" style of tightly buttoned Neo-Georgian emerging from the pages of *Country Life* at this time'.[18] One house, Godmersham Park in Kent, as remodelled by Walter Sarel, was painted by Rex Whistler, an artist whose whimsical evocations of the eighteenth century have a distinct character of their own which might well represent any such 'George VI' style. Often his graphics, book illustrations and murals have a

Godmersham Park, Godmersham, Kent (1732; remodelled Walter Sarel, 1935)

melancholy air, suggesting that Georgian civilisation was a distant dream, substantial though so much neo-Georgian architecture may have been. This is particularly true of his illustrations for *The Last of Uptake* by Simon Harcourt-Smith published in 1942, a contrived elegiac story about the fate of an imaginary English Palladian country house.

The new town house (which meant the London town house, because 'in the provinces town houses have not been built for more than half a century') was almost inevitably neo-Georgian.[19] Most were of brick externally, responding to the urban character of Mayfair and the West End. Some town houses, however, responded to the tradition begun by John Nash, being faced in painted stucco. A particularly fine example of this manner was Vernon House in Trafalgar Square, rebuilt as Chelsea Square after 1928. This is a detached town house with a tall pantiled roof, pedimented centrepiece and integrated flanking walls, by the ubiquitous and versatile Oliver Hill, and it still stands out as distinct from the more conventional neo-Georgian houses by Braddell & Deane around the square. One contemporary architect-historian considered that, 'If twentieth-century classicism is thought to be worthy of consideration, Hill's Vernon House . . . shows it at its best.'[20]

Hill designed other town houses which, in their Georgian manner in pink and grey bricks, owed much to pre-war examples by Lutyens. One is Wilbraham House, near Sloane Square (1922–23). Hill also designed two others close to Smith Square, both confusingly called Gayfere House, for the same client, the politician Wilfrid Ashley. In neither did the sober Georgian style of the façades continue inside. In the first, a single town house built in 1926, Hill created a drawing room covered in gold leaf and a fantastic 'undersea' bathroom. In the second, in fact a development of four houses designed in 1929, Hill worked closely with the decorator, who was Mrs Wilfrid Ashley and who wanted to 'let the Twentieth Century be responsible for its own style of architecture and interior decoration' and 'relied largely upon the use of marble, glass and steel – materials that do not want renewing and that should only be used boldly'.[21] The result was an imaginative Art Deco treatment using a great deal of mirror glass and with ideas taken from the Regency and from Lutyens.[22]

Interior, Gayfere House, Smith Square, London (Oliver Hill, 1929)

The interiors of Gayfere House have been mentioned here, despite being so radically different from conventional Georgian rooms, because such experiments were typical of their time; in the hands of refined designers, what can only loosely be called 'Art Deco' evolved into a style which Lancaster brilliantly categorised as 'Vogue Regency'. Neo-Regency interiors had been created in the 1920s and earlier by a few collectors and designers with advanced taste. There was the playwright Edward Knoblock who, with the help of the architect Maxwell Ayrton, restored the Beach House at Worthing in 1918–21 as a setting for furniture once owned by the designer Thomas Hope and acquired from the sale at his home, The Deepdene, in 1917. Other collectors of Regency furniture were architects – H. S. Goodhart-Rendel, Lord Gerald Wellesley, A. E. Richardson, Giles Gilbert Scott – who all created London interiors to display them. Some of these Regency revival interiors were described by Christopher Hussey in an article on 'Four Regency Houses' published in *Country Life* in 1931. As Hussey argued:

> It is this kinship between Regency and modern taste (the product of similar social conditions) that is the real cause of the imputation of audacity to modern 'Regency bucks'. . . . It must always be remembered that Regency was the last recognisable style that furniture designers employed before the great *débâcle* of Victorianism. It is thus one of the natural points for departure into the future, and quite the best.[23]

Another – curious – example was the studio for radio talks created in the new BBC building by the decorator Dorothy Warren Trotter, which contained a Regency armchair (for the speaker) that had belonged to the novelist Arnold Bennett.[24]

Such interiors, in which contemporary ideas and fashionable colours were combined with the Regency style in an eclectic, but refined manner, were what Lancaster meant by 'Vogue Regency'. Certainly the refined elegance and imaginative, exotic detail of

Regency chairs and sofas was close in spirit to the best design of a century later. 'Luckily,' he noted, 'the furniture of the Regency period possesses in an exceptional degree the quality of adaptability – it "goes" as well with a strapping pink nude by Picasso as with the less generously proportioned nymphs of David or Etty. And a Recamier sofa is in no way embarrassed by the close proximity of a rug by Marion Dorn.'[25] And, as Lancaster wisely concluded, reiterating what was almost a mantra of the time among designers and commentators:

> To-day the more sensible of modern architects realize that the desperate attempt to find a contemporary style can only succeed if the search starts at the point where Soane left off. . . . So long, therefore, as no attempt is made to follow the will-o'-the-wisp of period accuracy, Vogue Regency remains as suitable a style as any for a period in describing which the phrase Transitional, it is now apparent, is the grossest of understatement.[26]

The attempt to pick up the pieces left behind by the Georgians was not confined to domestic architecture. One of Lancaster's principal styles was 'Bankers Georgian', which, he thought, 'always preserves something of the air of a Metro-Goldwyn-Mayer production of the *School for Scandal*; a certain restlessness arising from the knowledge that no expense is to be spared, but at the same time refinement must be the watchword'.[27] Certainly a large number of neo-Georgian banks were built in the 1920s and 1930s. The best are branch banks in the suburbs or the provinces, where simple brick Georgian façades convey the necessary air of security and status. In Central London, the banks tended to put on grander airs, often employing an expressed order and even an engaged portico, resulting in buildings lacking the domesticated grace of the true Georgian.

At the end of the 1930s, J. M. Richards complained that still 'our civic life prefers to clothe itself in Georgian dress, with fashionable trimmings imported from Sweden or elsewhere'.[28] In more modestly sized towns, that expression was less grand than the Grand Manner.

At Worthing, for instance, either side of the central Ionic portico, the elevations of the Town Hall are plain neo-Georgian, in brick. At Cambridge, the same architect, C. Cowles-Voysey, did without a portico on the new Guildhall and presented to the marketplace a plain modernised Georgian façade of brick above a stone plinth. A more modest neo-Georgian expression was perfect for a more modest civic building type: the public library. A good example, though unfinished, is that at Colchester, interesting in part because it was designed in 1936 by Marshall Sisson, a young architect who had rejected Modernism and adopted a traditional English style. In London, the south side of Euston Square was – scandalously – built over with a series of neo-Georgian red-brick buildings, the new Post Office next to St Pancras New Church not differing significantly in expression from Hubert Lidbetter's Friends House a little further along. Schools, similarly, were often designed in a more rustic expression of the Georgian manner. The first of Henry Morris's Cambridgeshire village colleges, for example, designed at Sawston by H. H. Dunn, is a handsome single-storey brick building with elegant fenestration inspired by Regency precedents.

That the Georgian, in its widest sense, was now identified with England in the official mind was confirmed by the design chosen for the new British Embassy in Washington DC, a building achieved in the teeth of savage demands for economy by the Treasury. Lutyens's appointment was initially opposed because of his reputation for extravagance, but he was supported by Sir Lionel Earle, Permanent Secretary at HM Office of Works and Public Buildings, who argued that 'to get a really fine and well-designed building by one of the most prominent architects of the day ... would pay the State on high grounds of policy, inasmuch as America would appreciate the actions of the British government'.[29] Lutyens planned what was essentially two buildings: a Chancery facing Massachusetts Avenue, and an Embassy placed at a right angle to it and on a higher level, overlooking gardens, but connected via the Ambassador's study placed on axis on a bridge over a *porte cochère* for arriving guests. The style was that of

British Embassy, Washington DC, USA, July 1930 (Edwin Lutyens, 1930)

Wren, in brick, with 'chimneys', as Lutyens wrote, 'as impressive as those which stand as sentinels on the roofs of Chelsea Hospital' – but given a distinct American character.[30] As the chairman of the Commission for Fine Art noted with approval, Lutyens's drawings 'seem to be a happy expression of a style of architecture which the Fathers of the Republic brought overseas with them'.[31]

The Embassy was eventually completed in 1930 but with functional and structural problems that were partly owing to the economies imposed; George Lansbury, First Commissioner of Works, admitted in Parliament that 'certain minor alterations and additions have had to be authorised, as it was found that the standard of economy originally adopted had been too drastic'.[32] Difficulties also resulted from the decision to accept an unrealistically low tender from the British-born developer, who sought prestige from the commission. Harry Wardman had bought the old Legation in Washington from the government and found the site for the new Embassy. He had an interest in the Park Lane Hotel in London, but a dubious reputation in Washington. Although once successful, he suffered severely during the economic depression following the stock market collapse in October 1929. By the end of the following year his business had failed and he was unable to pay the sub-contractors working on the Embassy. However, as the local 'associated architect' on the job, Frederick H. Brooke, reminded Lutyens and the British government, 'While he had funds, he was more than liberal in all adjustments of expense. Even if the building is not perfect, has not the British Nation gotten its money's worth?'[33]

Post Office, Sherborne, Dorset (Archibald Bulloch, HM Office of Works, 1928)

Had the Treasury had its way, the new Embassy in Washington would have been a rather less sophisticated essay in neo-Georgian designed by the Office of Works. Indeed, so much official architecture was built in this manner between the wars that Osbert Lancaster identified 'Office of Works Queen Anne' as a style related to but distinct from 'Bankers Georgian'.[34] This is not to say that such buildings were necessarily standardised or mediocre, but they certainly could be predictable and repetitive. The Office of Works seldom favoured styles other than Georgian, and it was applied to official buildings almost regardless of function. The style was even used for the administrative and residential buildings required at the military airfields constructed or upgraded in the late 1930s as the shadow of war grew darker. The imagery of aeroplanes may have had a strong influence on Modernist architecture, but it would be a profound mistake to assume that buildings actually associated with flight were necessarily streamlined and planar. The authentic contemporary architectural background to the first Hurricanes and

Beech Grove Hall, RAF Manby, Lincolnshire (Archibald Bulloch, 1937; damaged by fire 2019)

Spitfires delivered to Fighter Command in the late 1930s is a range of plain brick buildings, sometimes later coated in camouflage paint, articulated by regularly spaced Georgian sash windows. A good and typical example is the officers' mess and single officers' quarters at Beech Grove Hall, Manby, Lincolnshire, of 1937 by Archibald Bulloch of the Office of Works. Well might 'Air Force Neo-Georgian' be identified as yet another sub-species, and when the Royal Air Force required a grander architectural statement to be made for the main buildings at its large new training college at Cranwell, built in 1929–33, the style was supercharged into Wrennian Baroque by J. G. West, complete with a tower that also acted as an illuminated beacon.*

Office of Works architects took great care both over details and over adapting the domestic expression of the Classical style

---

* 'RAF Neo-Georgian' was the term Roderick Gradidge used to me; the traces of brown and green wartime camouflage paint can often be detected on surviving examples.

to particular locations, at least when they were not isolated behind wire fences. This was particularly true of the public offices, sorting offices and telephone exchanges required by the Post Office: buildings which, by their nature, deserved that degree of sobriety and the air of authority conveyed by the Georgian style. On them, the 'GR' monogram, indicating erection in the reigns of George V or VI, seems seamless with a New Georgian style. It was a restrained expression, in contrast, say, to the inventive but assertive modern manner adopted for so many of the smart contemporary new post offices erected for Mussolini.

In the *Architectural Review* for October 1930, P. Morton Shand published a survey of recent Post Offices and Telephone Exchanges designed by such architects as D. N. Dyke, J. H. Markham and E. Cropper under the Chief Architect to the Office of Works, Sir Richard Allison. 'The governments of foreign countries,' he pointed out,

> avail themselves of every architectural opportunity to remind their citizens that, as the local headquarters of a department of state, enjoying all the authority and prerogatives pertaining thereto, a post office is a monumental symbol of the fact that they are governed. In Great Britain, on the other hand, our aversion to bureaucracy is such that its appearance is made as deliberately domestic as possible.

As an apostle of Modernism, Shand could not but be critical of the conservatism of these buildings while admitting their real merits:

> The able young architects employed by the Office of Works are so impeccably gentlemanly in their architectural manners that one feels they must have been personally selected by Mr Trystan Edwards. Everything they design is in perfect harmony with the English scene of the day before yesterday, which we are frantically seeking to persuade ourselves is likewise that of today.[35]

Sophisticated, restrained neo-Georgian post offices can be found in almost every town and city in Britain. In the old Kentish town of Cranbrook, for instance, a vernacular Georgian style was adopted with a bow-fronted shop window, while in Bath the Post Office, designed by A. Bulloch, was Palladian, faced in Bath stone, and was selected by the Architecture Club for praise as a 'building that worthily maintains the architectural tradition of its setting'.[36] Shand inevitably concluded that, 'in spite of an undeniably high general level of academic excellence, there is a certain rather supine tameness about the cultural urbanity of these charming little buildings, a complete lack of that robust vitality and adventurous spirit symptomatic of an era which, in other countries, has already proclaimed itself as one of radical departures from conventional design'.[37] A few years later even Anthony Bertram admitted that 'the Post Office and the Ministry of Labour are trying to do good work, though they too often timidly base their designs on the eighteenth century'.[38]

There was one expression of the Classical design commissioned by the General Post Office for which even P. Morton Shand had unqualified praise; these were the new telephone kiosks which had begun to appear on the streets of London, but they were designed not by the Office of Works but by a distinguished private architect: 'Sir Giles Gilbert Scott's very dignified steel [sic] cabinets are by far the best street telephone boxes that any country can boast of.'[39] The story of their advent is revealing about both contemporary tastes and attitudes to design in the public realm. The first 'public call offices' had been authorised by the Postmaster General in 1884, and in 1912 the General Post Office took over the control of almost all the national telephone network. In an attempt to achieve standardisation, the GPO's own Kiosk No.1 design went into production, but it was widely criticised for being ugly and old-fashioned, and some London boroughs refused permission for any to be erected. A competition organised by the Metropolitan Boroughs Joint Standing Committee that same year failed to secure a satisfactory design. A new design produced by the office of the Engineer-in-Chief of the GPO was

K2 Telephone Box, Liverpool (*left*) and (*right*) K6 Telephone Box, London (Giles Gilbert Scott, 1926 and 1935)

condemned by the RIBA, the Town Planning Institute and the Royal Academy.[40]

In the following year, 1924, the Royal Fine Art Commission was established to advise on such questions of public amenity, and one of its first tasks was to organise a new competition to find a satisfactory design for a public telephone kiosk. A limited competition was recommended, and Sir John Burnet, Sir Robert Lorimer and Scott himself were invited to submit designs to join that proposed by the Birmingham Civic Society, in reinforced concrete, and the GPO's own wretched alternative. Full-sized models of each were erected for public inspection behind the National Gallery. The following year, the Commission announced that Scott's design was the 'most suitable for erection in busy thoroughfares of large towns'.[41] Slightly modified, it went into production as Kiosk No. 2 and received almost universal praise. Less fussy than the other designs submitted, it was essentially a solid, elegant and practical miniature building, made of cast-iron with a teak door. The inspiration was certainly Classical, but precedents were intelligently digested; the domed top was possibly Soanian, the fluting around the doors fashionably '*néo-Grec*' (or Soanian), while the proportions and pattern of the glazing bars were pure Georgian.

Scott produced several other kiosk designs, including the reinforced-concrete K3, but the most often used was the K6, or Jubilee Kiosk, adopted in 1935 for erection all over Britain, both in towns and in the country. This was smaller, simpler and significantly different from the K2; the Grecian fluting was eliminated while the vertical glazing bars were moved to leave wider central panes, giving a more modern character: 'A modernistic touch, not over-emphasized, is introduced by the horizontal glazing scheme and this feature furnishes a remarkably free view from the inside of the kiosk.'[42] This design, for long familiar in the landscape and still identified as a symbol of Britain, was perhaps the single most impressive and successful example of British industrial design.* It was not officially superseded until 1968 and was one product of the 1930s that secured general approval. The attempt by British Telecom after 1985 to replace all the kiosks provoked widespread public protest, resulting in the statutory listing of many examples.†

It may seem surprising that the architect of Liverpool Cathedral, trained as an articled pupil of a Gothic church architect, should have displayed such accomplishment in adapting the Classical language for a utilitarian purpose, but Scott was as versatile in style as he was resourceful. He had tried the fashionable *néo-Grec* before the Great War, and in the 1920s adopted a refined neo-Georgian style for several secular commissions.‡ The first was the Memorial Court for Clare College, Cambridge, begun in 1922, where the residential ranges were

---

* The only competitor, at least in terms of elegance and refinement, is the neo-Classical police call box designed for Edinburgh in 1931–33 by the City Architect Ebenezer J. Macrae, and his assistants A. Rollo and J. A. Tweedie.

† [As Chairman of the Twentieth Century Society, Gavin was active in the campaign to save them. His book *Telephone Boxes* was published in 1989. RH.]

‡ As for example, 129 Grosvenor Road, Pimlico, a *néo-Grec* bungalow with an open atrium filled with neo-Regency furniture designed for the Hon. Arthur Stanley, MP, designed in 1913 by both Giles and Adrian Gilbert Scott.

Memorial Court, Clare College, Cambridge (Giles Gilbert Scott, 1924)

designed in a Georgian manner, faced in silver-grey brick, but broken by the central, axial war memorial arch in the *néo-Grec* style, its unity achieved by an intermittent double-height order. Goodhart-Rendel later observed, rather cattily, that Memorial Court 'was very much to the taste of its time and received loud applause'.[43] A similar style, again in brick, was used for the Deneke Building for Lady Margaret Hall, Oxford, and more imaginatively for Whitelands College, Putney (1929–31), where Georgian fenestration was adapted to a composition with pergolas and tiers of open terraces.

Scott's real affection for a Late Georgian style was confirmed by its use for his own house in Clarendon Place, Bayswater, built in 1924–25. As at Clare, the exterior was faced in silver-grey bricks, but between the wings the first floor was recessed to allow a terrace above the central entrance. Inside, an imaginative and refined treatment was remarkable for the use of colour and materials, as the *Architectural Review* noted: 'for colour he uses the oatmeal of the woodwork, and pale blue greens and black, and enriches them by the Mediterranean tint of a carpet, the jade and gold of a lamp, or here and there the sherry gloss of an old veneer. In all it is a work of great charm and distinction, modest and soberly rich.'[44] Charles Reilly thought that:

> Like the work at Clare College, while following the fine tradition of English domestic work in the simplicity and restfulness of its general lines, and in the character of its fenestration, Chester House, as it is called, is not only full of novel and interesting planning... but of the modern spirit in both its detail and absence of detail.[45]

The house was awarded the RIBA London Architectural Medal in 1927. A similar manner was used by Scott's younger brother Adrian for his own house in Frognal, Hampstead, which was praised by his neighbour Reginald Blomfield as 'one instance of a house which is quite modern, quite excellent, and that might have been designed either by a Modernist (in the right sense) or a Traditionalist'.[46]

That the Georgian was seen as urban and urbane was demonstrated by its adoption for a majority of city public housing

Chester House, Clarendon Place, London (Giles Gilbert Scott, 1925)

East Dulwich Estate, East Dulwich, Greater London (LCC Architects Department, 1937)

schemes between the wars. It was the treatment used for a majority of the many slum-clearance developments of 'block dwellings' pursued by the London County Council. Access to individual flats was usually by continuous balconies placed at the rear, while public open spaces and street façades were given a repetitive Georgian form. 'In the architectural treatment of the buildings the aim has been to maintain an appearance of domesticity whilst keeping within the bounds of economy,' the LCC explained.[47] A typical, large-scale example is the East Dulwich Estate on Dog Kennel Hill, built in 1931–37 under the direction of G. Topham Forrest, Architect to the Council. This consisted of 896 dwellings in 25 blocks, each with four-storey façades with regular, identical tiers of Georgian sashes, but enlivened by occasional polygonal bays breaking forward; a fifth storey was housed in the steep pantiled roof rising behind the simple parapet and behind simple unmoulded tall brick chimneys.

This was a style that had evolved from the Edwardian tenement blocks that used the red-brick 'Queen Anne' manner of Norman

Shaw and Philip Webb. J. M. Richards complained that, although such 'Typical official architecture ... is most competent technically',

> the Council has taken the safe route of adopting for nearly all its buildings a modified Georgian style. Large blocks of flats ... look particularly absurd when small Georgian-paned windows, tiled roofs, cornices and cupolas, all of which are adapted from small country buildings of the seventeenth and eighteenth centuries, are piled up into towering structures five or more storeys high.[48]

This was unfair, as the LCC's architects did not try to make the blocks look like houses; cornices were usually eliminated, and the necessarily regular windows were large and practical. In fact, a sensible large-scale urban brick style had evolved, based on the module of the timber Georgian sash window; such buildings have weathered rather better than the Modern Movement flats, with metal windows, that Richards extolled. Surprisingly perhaps, his colleague Nikolaus Pevsner, in discussing modern British architecture, could admire these LCC flats, 'which one can hardly call Neo-Georgian or anything but truly contemporary, although any demonstrative breach with tradition is carefully avoided'.[49] And Lancaster included 'L.C.C. Residential' in *Pillar to Post*, depicting a building identical in outline and fenestration to the preceding 'Park Lane Residential', noting of such working-class flats that 'they too look like pickle-factories, but quite good pickle-factories; not, it must be admitted, owing to any particular skill on the part of the architect, but solely to the fact that there has not been sufficient money to waste on Portland stone facings and other decorative trimmings'.[50]

Rather more sophisticated and playful than the LCC style was the treatment adopted by G. Grey Wornum and Louis de Soissons for the large development in Wandsworth built by Larkhall Estate Ltd in 1926–31. Balconies were placed on the outside of the blocks, leaving free neo-Georgian façades, articulated with projecting bays, to face internal courts, or gardens. Interest was given by using the occasional

Larkhall Estate, Lambeth, London (Louis de Soissons and G. Grey Wornum, 1931)

Palladian window as well as standard Georgian sashes, and an exotic touch was given by little metal canopies – Swedish-style – being placed over some of the upper windows. Ceramic relief medallions further humanised these intelligent modern adaptations of Georgian motifs. In a 1931 profile of Wornum, Reilly wrote that the 'great Larkhall scheme, which he and de Soissons have carried out together, is in my opinion the finest piece of middle-class housing this generation has produced'.[51] Sir Theodore Chambers, the chairman of Welwyn Garden City Ltd (who was probably responsible for de Soissons' appointment), claimed that the housing was 'within the range of a very large class of people in London for whom little or nothing has been done since the war, and consequently the demand is very keen'.[52]

It was de Soissons who demonstrated that an urbane Georgian manner could also be made suitable for housing in less dense and more open settings. In the LCC's 'cottage estates' of the 1920s, like the vast developments at Becontree and Downham, the Georgian sash was conventional but used in the more vernacular, Arts and Crafts style typical of the pre-war garden suburbs. At Welwyn Garden City, however, a more grammatical and consistent neo-Georgian style was applied almost universally. The experiment of a second garden city in Hertfordshire, straddling the main line of what would (in 1923) become the London & North Eastern Railway, was the creation of the original apologist for garden cities, Ebenezer Howard, who had inspired the first one founded at Letchworth in 1902. Welwyn Garden City Ltd was formed in 1920, and the proposed development of rural farmland to house a population of 50,000 at no more than twelve houses to an acre was intended to overcome the mistakes made at Letchworth. The incomplete and unfocused development of the first garden city, in a simplified cottage style, was not to be repeated.

The Welwyn company having failed to find a satisfactory architect and planner, the RIBA recommended Louis de Soissons, who was entirely responsible for the plan and architectural character of the venture as it developed over the following forty years. Born in Canada, the son of a Pole who had adopted a French aristocratic name, de

Soissons had been educated at the École des Beaux-Arts in Paris. He was not in sympathy with the architecture of Letchworth and, like so many of his contemporaries, preferred the formality and discipline of the Classical tradition. As architect to the Duchy of Cornwall in Kennington, he continued the style and approach set by Adshead and Ramsey. And whereas the general texture of Letchworth was given by roughcast gables and casement windows, that of Welwyn was to be of fine red brick and white-painted Georgian sashes.

The difference between the two Hertfordshire garden cities was explained by Frederick Osborn, the disciple of Howard and an apostle of new towns, who was involved in the creation of Welwyn. In a letter written to the American Lewis Mumford in 1943, complaining about the 'pseudo-sociology' of urban modernist critics of the perceived aesthetic and social conservatism of the garden city, he noted:

> Welwyn happens to be built mainly in an honest and functional continuation of the Hertfordshire tradition, with life and freshness of detail, and the use of the local brick was economically and structurally entirely justified – indeed inescapable unless one wanted to be funny just for the sake of being funny. Letchworth, begun in 1904, was of course in the Morris-Voysey-Barry Parker current, and its use of fletton brick covered with cement plaster was dictated by the conditions over the whole region within reach of the Peterborough brickfields.[53]

Although de Soissons himself wrote down little about his ideas, his son recalled that he 'took as the main architectural style for the garden city, the red-brick Hertfordshire Georgian that abounded in Welwyn, Hatfield, St Albans and Hertford. . . . He talked often of the importance of adapting Georgian proportions and principles to modern living requirements, not only to houses and public buildings, but shops and offices.'[54] In the 1920s this was very much a conventional view.

The success of Welwyn Garden City resulted both from de Soissons' determination to exercise architectural control and his flexibility. He produced a general plan that was both formal and informal, with a wide axial space in the centre and, in the suburbs, a varied and intricate pattern of curving streets and culs-de-sac. An important principle was that all buildings, whether domestic or public, should be good to look at all the way round. De Soissons designed many houses himself; others were designed by C. H. James and Arthur Kenyon. They varied in size and arrangement, some cheaper, experimental models having indeed flat roofs instead of hipped pantiled roofs, but all maintained a style of Georgian domestic formality surrounded by lawns and trees. R. L. Reiss, a director of Welwyn Garden City Ltd, recorded in the *Architectural Review* in 1927 that 1,600 houses had so far been built, mostly in carefully planned groups: 'This has

26 Guessens Road, Welwyn Garden City, Hertfordshire (Louis de Soissons, with Arthur Kenyon, C. Murray Hennell and C. H. James, 1925)

Parkway, Welwyn Garden City, Hertfordshire (Louis de Soissons, 1924)

secured a degree of harmony in the street architecture such as has not been achieved anywhere in this country since the construction of modern Bath.'[55] De Soissons was, however, pragmatic and adaptable; the building he designed for Shredded Wheat, completed on the opposite side of the railway in 1925, was of reinforced concrete in the American daylight factory manner, dominated by a tall grain silo. He was also happy with the few flat-roofed houses designed in the 1930s by Paul Mauger and Eugene Kent. Images of modernity and of Georgian domesticity could co-exist.

The public buildings which eventually rose along the central axis, Parkway, and the cross-axis, Howardsgate, were all designed in a modern Georgian style. De Soissons himself was responsible for the Welwyn Stores, a large block with ground-floor shops and a stripped Classical portico, built in 1938–39. The Council Offices were designed by C. G. Elsom and H. Stone, who won a competition held in 1936. The most interesting building, however, was the Welwyn Theatre, opened in 1928 and since demolished. Designed by de Soissons with A. W. Kenyon, it had a carefully proportioned seven-bay neo-Georgian façade in brick, with a low-pitched pantiled roof hidden behind a recessed parapet. The interior, however, was completely different. As the building was intended for use both as a theatre and as a cinema, the auditorium and foyers were given an exotic Deco treatment with a Swedish Baroque flavour. The interior walls were broken by canopied recesses filled with faceted mirrors, while the safety curtain was painted by Miriam Wornum. A contemporary description suggests an effect far removed from Georgian restraint; there were 'undulating as well as zigzag bands' on the walls, 'and the colours follow one another in quick succession – first ultramarine, through chocolate, orange, lemon, putty-colour, Vandyke brown, grey and cinnamon to a green-blue. . . . The doors each side of the stage are green with blue architraves, and the front of the stage itself has alternate bands of blue and chocolate.'[56]

The exterior of the Welwyn Theatre was typical of what was becoming a conventional modern style amongst architects. It was an architecture rooted in tradition, made of good materials, clearly English and able to adapt to modern ideas and methods while avoiding the dangerous and fallible excesses of Continental modernism. Simplification was the key, resulting in what Charles Reilly described in 1935 as 'that kind of nudist Georgian so popular at the moment'.[57] Such an architecture was often rather dull, but it seemed to justify that widespread conviction, at least among architects, that a modern style could be developed from where the Late Georgians left off. Only a few more thoughtful and broad-minded practitioners appreciated that those inconvenient intervening Victorians also provided some lessons for a modern expression of new structural systems.

Modern Georgian was often allowed to be more modern than Georgian. This was particularly true of the work of Murray Easton and Howard Robertson, cautiously experimental but rooted in the Classical tradition. The exterior of the administration block in front of their influential Royal Horticultural Hall is best characterised as modernised Georgian, while their Metropolitan Water Board laboratories in Finsbury, by Stanley Hall and Easton & Robertson, relies on Georgian principles for effect. In Cambridge, their St Michael's Court for Gonville and Caius College presents a regularly spaced but modernistic, horizontally proportioned façade towards the marketplace, while the internal elevation has Georgian windows. It is a more intelligent design than Edward Maufe's attempt at a modernistic compromise between Georgian and Tudor at St John's College, where brick ranges with regularly spaced but horizontally proportioned metal windows fail to respect the surrounding ancient streets.

St Michael's Court, Cambridge (Stanley Hall and Easton & Robertson, 1937)

Kingsmere House ('The King's House'), Burhill, Surrey (C. Beresford Marshall, 1936)

That modernised Georgian had become conventional, if not representative of the general state of architectural thinking, by the mid-1930s was confirmed by its choice for The King's House, intended as a Silver Jubilee gift to King George V by the Royal Warrant Holders in 1935. The large suburban house at Burhill in Surrey was the work of Beresford Marshall, whose design had been chosen by the King in a limited competition among architects nominated by Sir Giles Gilbert Scott as President of the RIBA. Built of brick with a pantiled roof, it presented symmetrical elevations to both entrance court and garden. Such detail as there was, in the doorcases and cornice, was Classical, although the interior was treated in a modernistic, Deco manner. Despite the royal connection with the enterprise, this house is unlikely to have reflected the taste of the King or of either of his sons who would, in turn, succeed him the following year.

Of all the many attempts at fusing a modern sensibility with Classical elegance, one of the most successful was Gribloch at Kippen in Stirlingshire, a house designed in 1937 by the young Basil Spence. The stylish interiors were Vogue Regency, but authentic Regency was not far away in the exterior elevations; well-proportioned windows were regularly spaced, and a vestigial cornice projected from the copings over the roughcast walls. Alan Powers has argued that 'the shallow curve of the entrance front at Gribloch, terminating in a balconied bow window, with smooth, white painted surfaces, was directly inspired by the Regency'.[58] Gribloch was a house praised by Reginald Turnor in his 1952 study of *The Smaller English House* as suggesting the way forward for domestic architecture:

> For, although unmistakably a building of the modern movement, with its almost flat copper-covered roof and clean white surfaces, it possesses all the purely architectural virtues of composition, punctuation, and – dare one say it? – taste. It is the sort of house which might have been designed in the mid-nineteenth century if there had been no Battle of the Styles.[59]

Many commentators realised that the Modern Movement itself had, if not roots in, then at least resonances with, the Classical tradition.

Gribloch House, Kippen, Stirlingshire (Basil Spence, 1939)

In his book *London: The Unique City*, Rasmussen reiterated the visual argument by juxtaposing photographs of a stuccoed Regency house in Downshire Hill, Hampstead, with a modern house of a century later at Am Rupenhorn in Berlin designed by the Gebrüder Luckhardt, the curved cast-iron covered balcony of the one nicely echoing the sleek curved projections in reinforced concrete of the other. In so many Late Georgian London houses, he noted, 'we meet tendencies which are well known to us from the "Modernism" of latter days'. Namely:

> standardization of houses, simplicity of forms, cylindrical bay windows and balconies, perfectly bare walls without even a cornice . . . flat roofs, windows which during the whole period became larger and larger in order to get as much glass-area and as thin bars as possible . . . Also we meet an inclination to use the newest technical wonders, the most modern materials, and to use colours in order to make it all look clear and precise.[60]

The English architect Clifford Holliday could write in 1939 that there 'is a curious resemblance between the modern house as a slowly evolving type and the houses of the Georgian period'.[61]

Perhaps the most sophisticated and intelligent modern development of the Georgian tradition was the terrace of three houses overlooking Hampstead Heath, designed and built by the Hungarian modernist Ernö Goldfinger in 1938–40. Although the cleverly planned interiors owed little to tradition, the exterior elevations were unified by planes of London stock brickwork and by a consistent proportional system. Small cottages had stood on the site on Willow Road, and Goldfinger countered the opposition of the Hampstead Preservation Society by arguing that his design was in harmony with the Georgian houses of Downshire Hill. Like other foreigners such as Rasmussen and his mentor, Adolf Loos, Goldfinger greatly admired the Georgian urban architecture of London for its uniform, practical reticence. As he later recalled:

1–3 Willow Road, Hampstead, London (Ernö Goldfinger, 1940)

The great contribution of England is Georgian. But hardly had I time to look at it [than] they were pulling it down. There is absolutely no respect for architecture in England. My first office in London was in No. 7 Bedford Square, on the east side which belonged to the British Museum. You know, they wanted to pull it down. When I was there we got notices.* Ignorant vandals – unbelievable![62]

Goldfinger's recollection was correct, and echoed the contemporary exasperation of Robert Byron: 'that an institution devoted to the diffusion of knowledge can contemplate an act of this description is a phenomenon so far removed from the canons of civilized behaviour that it seems at times as if the English were really as mad, as gross and as intolerant of art and culture as their foreign detractors pretend.'[63]

It may seem strange that despite an increasingly educated admiration for Georgian architecture between the wars, much of authentic Georgian London was allowed to disappear at the

---

* According to Goldfinger, this was in 1937–38.

same time. Unfortunately, Georgian architecture was not generally held in high regard while the necessity for redevelopment seemed unarguable. As Douglas Goldring explained when the Georgian Group was launched in 1937:

> Many people who never give architecture a thought are fully conscious of amenities and resent their destruction. But undoubtedly the delusion still persists that because a Georgian house, street, square or terrace cannot be described as 'ancient', therefore its demolition cannot be opposed on architectural grounds, however much it may be regretted for reasons of sentiment. And 'sentiment', as Big Business is never tired of telling us, must not be allowed to impede the march of 'progress'.[64]

Pressure for rebuilding came from the changed economic circumstances after the war, the rise in demand for flats and the increasing destructive demands of the motor car. Georgian country houses would seem to have fared no better or no worse than mansions of earlier date, but in the capital it was the legacy of the eighteenth century that proved to be peculiarly vulnerable.

Cities constantly change, of course, as older buildings are replaced, but in the 1920s and 1930s it was not just the ordinary buildings of Georgian London that disappeared but some of the very best. Little could be done to prevent this. Legislation to protect historic buildings and monuments had come later in Britain than in many other European countries, and it was only concerned with architecture built before 1714: the end of the reign of Queen Anne and the limit of the purview of the Royal Commission on Historical Monuments. The Society for the Protection of Ancient Buildings had been founded in 1877 but it tended still to reflect the anti-Classical outlook of its founder, William Morris. Popular opinion generally regarded only the medieval and Tudor as truly historic, a taste so vividly expressed in contemporary suburban architecture. The resulting destruction is as much a part of British architectural history between the wars as the taste for new neo-Georgian architecture.

While Harold P. Clunn, the uncritical enthusiast for progress who dismissed those opposed to the destruction of Rennie's Waterloo Bridge as 'short-sighted fanatics',[65] may have been an extreme case, the same attitudes were reflected in *Robinson in England*, the English nationalist novel published in 1937 by the poet, playwright and biographer of Morris, John Drinkwater. 'Every town has got to move with the times,' insisted the hero of the book, 'whether they're intelligent or vulgar':

> I think the ideal city is one that is never afraid of the present, and yet preserves enough of its past intact to remind the citizens, as the preacher says, of the famous men and their fathers that begat them. When they pulled down John Nash's Regent Street, something very charming was taken away from London. But it was something that Nelson never saw and already even you don't miss . . . But you can't talk like that about Westminster Abbey or the Tower of London. Such things are witnesses of history to one age after another, secure above the wish or the convenience of any. It's a pity they have to rebuild the Adelphi . . . but on the whole it is inevitable. But no one can ever lay hands on Westminster or the Tower with that plea.[66]

No wonder Robert Byron complained, that same year, that the 'attitude of the Englishman to art is extremely conventional':

> Painting he knows is an art, because he is told so. He is not told that architecture is an art; on the contrary, thanks to the brutish ignorance of Church, Government and speculators, he is strongly encouraged to believe that it is not. Some pieces of architecture, he is allowed to believe, are worth preserving; but if they are, it is not by any means on account of their value as works of art. The value of architecture in England, according to official and ecclesiastical

standards, varies in proportion to 1, its antiquity, 2, its quaintness, and 3, its holiness. By these standards, a bit of the old Roman wall is of more importance than Nash's Regent Street, and one ruined pointed arch than all Wren's churches put together.[67]

Churches by the revered Sir Christopher Wren could well have been the first casualties of the changed climate after the war. In 1919, as if to celebrate the peace, a report issued by the Bishop of London proposed the closure of nineteen City of London churches – by Wren, Hawksmoor and others – thus accelerating the process of selling valuable sites to fund the building of new churches in the suburbs. In the event, however, only one church perished under this proposal: St Katherine Coleman, eighteenth-century, and not by Wren, whose fittings were re-erected in St Catherine's, Hammersmith (the remarkable steel-framed new church designed by Robert Atkinson and built in 1922–23). Thanks to the efforts of the London Society, opinion for once grew articulate, and the scheme was quashed by Parliament on a petition from the Corporation of London.[68] The Church had drawn in its claws, but in the following decade it would show them again.

The next victim was Nash's Regent Street, after the Crown's ninety-nine-year leases expired, but as oil-painted stucco was being replaced on a larger scale by Portland stone hung on steel frames, it had few defenders. But it was not just Regent Street that proved to be frail. The possibility of building larger volumes on the same plot; the growing demand for flats rather than houses, as well as other commercial pressures; the increasingly importunate demands of the growing numbers of motorists: all put pressure on the Georgian fabric of the West End of London, including the great aristocratic town houses which articulated its pattern of streets.

In 1908, the historian E. Beresford Chancellor published *The Private Palaces of London, Past and Present*, a lavish celebration of 'those splendid mansions that still remain, and which are not only among the proudest possessions of London, but, in some sense, one

22. Munstead Wood, Godalming, Surrey (Edwin Lutyens, 1897)

23. Cour House, Kintyre, Scotland (Oliver Hill, 1922)

24. (*Above*) MacDonald Gill, painting of Baylin's Farm, Beaconsfield, Buckinghamshire (Forbes & Tate, 1920)

25. (*Right*) The former Westminster Bank, Oxted, Surrey (L. J. Williams and A. B. Williams, 1929)

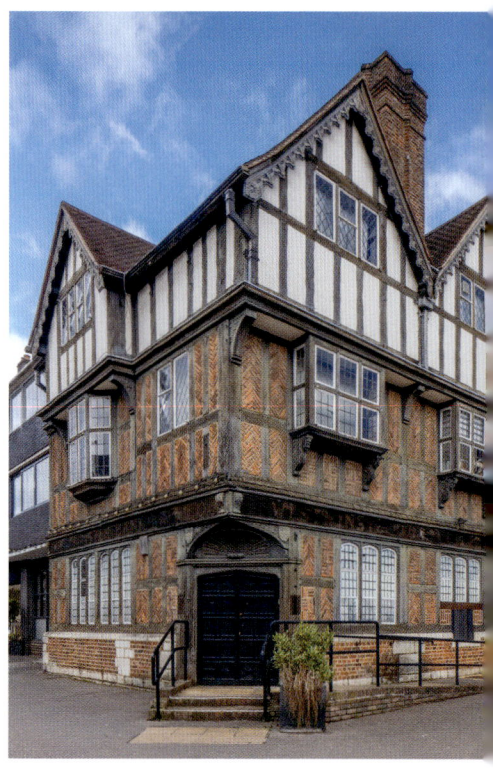

26. Petts Wood Road, Petts Wood, Greater London (Basil Scruby and Leonard Culliford, 1929)

27. The former Berkeley Arms Hotel, Cranford, Middlesex (E. B. Musman, 1932)

28. Tudor Close, Rottingdean, Sussex (A. Caplin, 1928; G. K. Green, 1937)

29. St Matthew's Roman Catholic Church, Clubmoor, Liverpool (F. X. Velarde, 1930)

30. St Mary the Virgin, Wellingborough, Northamptonshire (Ninian Comper, 1904–31)

31. Reredos, St Monica's, Bootle, Liverpool (F. X. Velarde; angel reliefs by W. L. Stevenson, 1937)

32. Alterations to Finella, Cambridge (Raymond McGrath, for Mansfield Forbes, 1929)

33. Boots, D10 ('Wets' Building), Beeston, Nottinghamshire (Owen Williams, 1932)

34. Midland Hotel, Morecambe, Lancashire (Oliver Hill, 1933), following renovation (Avanti Architects, 2008)

35. The Sun House, Hampstead, London (E. Maxwell Fry, 1935)

36. 66 Frognal, Hampstead, London (Connell, Ward & Lucas, 1938)

37. Highpoint One and Highpoint Two, Highgate, London (Berthold Lubetkin and Tecton, 1935 and 1938)

38. Liverpool Anglican Cathedral, Liverpool (Giles Gilbert Scott, 1901–78)

of the glories of the country'.[69] These mansions could have survived, even if their aristocratic owners had removed to more convenient flats. But already Chancellor saw clouds on the horizon:

> We have seen how many of those great houses which our forefathers erected with such loving care and at such vast expense, and each of which no doubt they considered *aere perennius*, have passed away, and how heavily 'Time's destroying hand' has dealt with them. What then are we to suppose will be the fate of some of those which to-day would seem to be armed so as to defy Time? Some we know are held on leasehold tenure, and when their time has run, may be ruthlessly demolished; others stand proudly in the midst of ever-changing conditions of building development; will they be, in their turn, attacked, and if so – what then?[70]

Indeed they were attacked, and most perished between the two world wars.

The first to go was Devonshire House in Piccadilly; 'a romantic place. The romance that hung about the old house was that of mystery and gloom. Dark walls hid it from the outside world; there was no more than a glimpse of it to be seen through the gates.'[71] Its treasures had already been evacuated to Chatsworth after the death of the 8th Duke of Devonshire in 1908 and the whole site was acquired in 1918 by the builders, Holland & Hannen and Cubitts. The house, with its severe brick façade by William Kent, was eventually demolished in 1924. The Piccadilly end of the site was then covered by the new steel-framed Devonshire House, 'a typical American apartment house' by Thomas Hastings whose mixed reception has already been discussed.[72] The loss to London was not just of a fine Georgian building. Until the mid-1920s there was a continuous, if private, open space running the whole way from Piccadilly to Berkeley Square, with the grounds of Devonshire House separated from the gardens of Lansdowne House by a pedestrian passage. By the mid-1930s, the latter open space was built over as well, while Lansdowne House, the mansion designed by Robert Adam for the Earl of Shelburne, was mutilated and partly demolished.

Perhaps the saddest loss was Dorchester House, the Italianate palace in Park Lane designed by Lewis Vulliamy for the collector R. S. Holford. Even Harold Clunn admitted that it was 'a magnificent mansion, probably second to none in the metropolis'.[73] Its splendour was recalled by Shane Leslie in his memoir of the Victorian writer Augustus Hare:

> London was beset by great Houses, most of which have disappeared into service flats. Before Societies for the Destruction of Beautiful Buildings had gutted Mayfair, London could offer the attractions of a classical City. A glimpse of the most beautiful of perished buildings, Dorchester House, survives in a few words: 'the staircase is that of an old Genoese Palace and was one blaze of colour and the broad landings behind the alabaster balustrades were filled with people sitting or leaning over as in old Venetian pictures'.[74]

For a time it had been occupied by the Shah of Persia; later it was the residence of the American Ambassador.

Dorchester House could have been saved: there was a proposal that it become the Italian Embassy, while Lady Beecham campaigned for it to be a centre for opera and Shakespeare. But the site was acquired by the Gordon Hotels Company and it was demolished in 1929; fortunately the great chimneypieces by Alfred Stevens found their way into museums. At least Dorchester House was replaced by a reasonably distinguished building, the Dorchester Hotel, designed by W. Curtis Green over a concrete structure by Sir Owen Williams. The same could not be said for Chesterfield House on Great Stanhope Street. Designed by Isaac Ware in 1748 for the Earl of Chesterfield and with splendid Rococo interiors, it became the London residence of George V's daughter, the Princess Royal, and her husband, the Earl of Harewood, in the early 1930s. This, however, did not prevent its

Norfolk House, St James's Square, London (Matthew Brettingham, 1752; demolished 1938)

demolition in 1937 and its replacement by a mediocre, modernistic ten-storey block of flats by P. V. Burnett and Cecil Eprile.

The last of the great private palaces to perish before the Second World War was Norfolk House, the magnificent mansion in St James's Square, built by Matthew Brettingham in 1748–52. It was already doomed when the Georgian Group was founded; the 16th Duke of Norfolk had long wanted to sell it and he eventually did so, secretly, to the developer Rudolph Palumbo via an intermediary.* Plans for a neo-Georgian block of offices to replace it by Gunton & Gunton were approved by the London County Council in 1937. The Dowager Duchess had been abroad when her London home was sold and was furious at her son's devious behaviour, joining the Georgian Group and wondering, 'would it be possible for the society to save Norfolk House from being pulled down?'[75] But the

---

* 'This mansion has recently been put up for sale and it seems probable that its site will eventually be covered with modern flats and business premises' (Clunn (1932), p. 191).

new society could do little when the name of its new owner was unknown; as Byron complained in the *New Statesman and Nation*, 'When *noblesse* ceases to oblige, it is not surprising that *richesse* should do likewise. The law not only condones the speculator; it protects him with anonymity.'[76] After a sale that took just three days, Norfolk House was demolished in 1938. The redevelopment made Palumbo's fortune; all the Georgian Group could salvage was the music room, which is now in the Victoria and Albert Museum.

It was not only grand private houses that were vulnerable; distinguished public buildings were also demolished. The worst case was the rebuilding of the Bank of England after 1924. There is no doubt that the agglomerative single-storey development of offices and banking halls north of Threadneedle Street within the blank screen walls designed by Sir John Soane was inefficient and inadequate; the answer, adopted by the Bank after the Second World War, was to find additional accommodation on another site rather than to destroy the magnificent interiors by Sir Robert Taylor and Soane, whose appearance was recorded in the series of photographs by F. R. Yerbury published in 1930.[77] Their destruction was required by the massive superstructure raised on the site, designed by Sir Herbert Baker, assisted by F. W. Troup. Clunn may have considered that the building of this 'raised palace surrounded by a fortress' was 'the greatest event which has taken place in the rebuilding of London during the last hundred years',* but, along with the controversy surrounding the design of South Africa House in Trafalgar Square, the rebuilding damned Baker's reputation with posterity.[78]

Baker's appointment was announced in 1921; the Arts and Crafts architect F. W. Troup had already† been working for the Bank.[79]

---

* He had earlier opined that 'the skyscraper which is to arise from the ruins of the old building will form one of the most imposing landmarks of this great Metropolis, and may well be the pride and glory of patriotic Londoners when the new building becomes an accomplished fact' (Clunn (1927), pp. 35–6).

† In 1917–20 Troup converted St Luke's Hospital in Old Street into a new printing works for the Bank.

'Long and sympathetic study,' Baker claimed, 'has been given to the determination of the extent to which the more valuable portions of the old building of the Bank of England could be retained.'[80] In the event, however, few of the top-lit vaulted and domed halls he claimed to admire were preserved. The first protests came in 1923, when the Trustees of Sir John Soane's Museum sent a letter to *The Times* complaining that the large Corinthian portico Baker proposed to build above the existing Threadneedle Street entrance was 'quite alien to the spirit of Soane's design'.[81] The work of destruction began in 1924, and two years later the Curator of the Soane Museum, A. T. Bolton, supported by his Trustees, objected to Baker's proposal to alter Soane's screen wall and his Tivoli Corner. Although Baker responded that there was no reason why the strange attic of the Tivoli Corner could not be retained, when it was adapted as a pedestrian passage in 1933 Soane's attic was replaced by an effete dome. Troup disassociated himself from this arbitrary alteration, and the Society for the Protection of Ancient Buildings expressed 'its regret that the

Bank of England, Threadneedle Street, City of London (John Soane, 1788–1827; reconstruction, Herbert Baker, 1921–39)

The former Foundling Hospital school, Berkhamsted, Hertfordshire (John M. Sheppard, 1935)

Directors of the Bank of England should have thought fit to alter the work of so great a master'.[82] There seems no reason to disagree with Pevsner's conclusion that Baker's rebuilding of the Bank was 'the worst individual loss suffered by London architecture in the first half of the C20'.[83]

Another distinguished but architecturally less sophisticated London institution completely disappeared at the same time. The plain brick buildings of the Foundling Hospital in Lamb's Conduit Fields in Bloomsbury were designed by Theodore Jacobsen and completed in 1747. By the early twentieth century, it was thought desirable to move the children to a more salubrious site in the country, leaving the future of the hospital's buildings and grounds uncertain. A proposal to make it the nucleus of London University having foundered, the fifty-six-acre site was sold in 1926 to a property developer, James White, who then proposed to move the Covent Garden fruit and vegetable market there, but this was strongly opposed by the London County Council and other local authorities.[84] The Foundling Hospital school moved first to Redhill, and then, in 1935, to new neo-Georgian buildings at Berkhamsted designed by John Mortimer Sheppard. The original Georgian buildings in Bloomsbury were demolished but the grounds were saved by public subscription with some help from Lord Rothermere, and in 1936 Coram's Fields re-opened, appropriately, as a playground for children, with a Classical pavilion in the centre, designed by L. H. Bucknell.

At least the grounds of the Foundling Hospital were preserved as a public amenity. Other London open spaces were built over. This was possible because, an attempt by the London County Council in 1905 to prevent London squares, burial grounds and other open spaces being developed having met with massive opposition from landowners, the resulting Act of Parliament of 1906 only protected a limited number of gardens where agreement had been reached with landlords. The consequence was that in the 1920s the gardens of Mornington Crescent became the site of the Carreras cigarette factory, and Endsleigh Gardens, on the south side of Euston Square, was acquired by the Society of Friends and other interests, leaving the noble Grecian portico of New St Pancras Church facing a modern neo-Georgian façade rather than overlooking grass and trees. Had the proposal to move the Covent Garden market to Bloomsbury been realised, Brunswick and Mecklenburgh Squares would have disappeared as well. In 1927, the London Society warned that 'there is grave danger threatening very many of our square gardens and open spaces, and it is within the power of Londoners to take steps to secure these gardens and squares as permanent sources of sunlight and fresh air for the population'.[85]

The longest running London conservation battle between the wars concerned Waterloo Bridge, whose fate became involved with the contemporary plan to rebuild the Charing Cross Bridge.[86] But whereas the Victorian bridge into Charing Cross Station was a metal girder railway structure about whose ugliness there was universal agreement, the noble Doric bridge of granite with elliptical arches designed by John Rennie and opened in 1817 was recognised as a structure of rare sophistication and beauty. Needless to say, while the hated Hungerford railway bridge remained in position, Rennie's masterpiece was destroyed. The great Italian sculptor Antonio Canova had described Waterloo Bridge as 'the noblest bridge in the world', and in 1932 John Betjeman noted in the *Architectural Review*:

> That it is the best bridge in London, such varied opinions as those of Canova, Sir Reginald Blomfield, E. Maxwell Fry, Frederick Etchells, the Royal Commission of Fine Arts, Sir Edwin Lutyens, most Royal Academicians, almost all modern artists, and the RIBA, have gone to support. Even the architect-designate for the new bridge, Sir Giles Gilbert Scott, has publicly praised its beauty.[87]

The name of W. R. Lethaby might also have been added, as he considered that 'Waterloo Bridge is the most representative monument after St Paul's Cathedral. The two buildings symbolize the metropolitan City of the Empire and should be regarded as sacred works of art to be maintained as they were built.'[88]

The problem was that the rebuilding of old London Bridge and the construction of the Victoria Embankment resulted in increased tidal flow which scoured away the foundations of Waterloo Bridge. By 1923, subsidence of some of the piers was noticeable and repairs carried out by the LCC made matters worse. The Society for the Protection of Ancient Buildings (SPAB) called in H. Dalrymple-Hay, engineer to the London Underground railways, who demonstrated that it was practical to underpin and repair the bridge, but the LCC denied that this was possible. In 1926, a Royal Commission recommended the preservation and repair of Rennie's structure, and Sir Reginald Blomfield attempted to demonstrate how it could be widened sympathetically. The LCC, however, really wanted a much wider bridge, over which tramlines could be laid. Naturally Harold Clunn, concerned solely with traffic and expense, agreed, insisting that 'Every Londoner who has the future welfare of this great metropolis at heart should raise his voice in vigorous protest against this wanton piece of extravagance. Waterloo Bridge has no claim, on historical grounds, to be retained.'[89] In 1932, Giles Gilbert Scott and the engineers Rendel, Palmer & Tritton were commissioned by the LCC to design a replacement bridge.

Old Waterloo Bridge could possibly have survived had it been agreed to replace the Hungerford railway bridge with a wide new road bridge to take the traffic demanded by the LCC. Pulling back the railway terminus to Waterloo had been recommended by the LCC as early as 1891 and, after the war, a new war memorial bridge at Charing Cross was proposed by the architects Reginald Blomfield and Aston Webb and the politician John Burns.[90] In 1926 William Walcot prepared a remarkable design for a combined double-decker road and rail bridge at Charing Cross, but most proposals were for a road bridge combined with a replanned South Bank with the existing railway terminating at Waterloo, as recommended by the Royal Commission on Cross-River Traffic in 1928.[91] A scheme for this, promoted by the LCC and the Southern Railway the following year, with Lutyens as consultant for the proposed new buildings, engendered much squabbling between knighted architects, and resulted in the famous architect's resignation from the RIBA and the Bill for a new bridge being defeated in Parliament.

Even so, the ever-optimistic Clunn could claim in 1932 that, 'By universal consent Charing Cross Bridge is now doomed and, whatever the present difficulties, its destruction will play a most important part in the reconstruction of London.'[92] But the Southern Railway could not afford to do away with the railway bridge, and it was 'the best bridge London ever had' that was sacrificed to the growth of road traffic – despite the decision of the House of Commons. In 1934, the first stone of the old Waterloo Bridge was removed by Herbert Morrison, leader of the Labour-controlled LCC; the new bridge, a structure of reinforced concrete clad in stone, was begun in 1937 and opened in 1942, but without Scott's attendant Egyptian pylons. Despite the austere merits of the new structure, the demolition of

Rennie's magnificent bridge was a shabby business; Robert Byron later concluded that 'it was lost not because of any demonstrable need for a new bridge, but because the Labour majority on the London County Council, interested only in flouting the Conservative majority in the House of Commons – which had tried for once to save a national monument – made the destruction of the bridge an article of political faith'.[93]

The final catalyst to the creation of a body to defend Georgian London from such utilitarianism was the threat to two of the finest set pieces of Georgian domestic design. The first was the Adelphi, the development of terraced houses between the Strand and the Thames designed and built by the Adam Brothers in the 1770s. Despite its historical associations, famous former residents and manifest architectural distinction, there was nothing to be done when in 1933 the central part was sold to a speculator and proposed for demolition. 'Of its usefulness for the next two hundred years or so there can be no doubt,' complained A. E. Richardson. 'Of what advantage would be newer and taller buildings on the site, to darken the street?'[94] The SPAB protested, but privately, and Douglas Goldring did his best to stir up public opposition in the pages of weekly journals. All in vain: the whole block between Adelphi Terrace and John Adam Street came down, so that the Royal Society of Arts in its purpose-built home by Robert Adam found itself facing a much taller block of commercial offices designed in a crude American Deco manner by Stanley Hamp. As so often was the case, the whole process was shrouded in secrecy. For Robert Byron, it seemed 'hardly conceivable that a transaction of such importance to the imperial capital – a transaction which indirectly had to receive the assent of Parliament – can really be kept hid from the light of the twentieth century'. Only in 1938 was he able to 'disclose the identity of the original profit-maker on the Adelphi. It was the Earl of Ellesmere who played the middleman in a transaction that obliterated one of London's most notable eighteenth-century monuments.'[95]

The second was Carlton House Terrace, the two magnificent stuccoed ranges of grand houses designed by Nash towards the end of his life. In this case, the owner was known and the press took a more active role in opposition. In 1932 it was rumoured that the Commissioners for Crown Lands proposed to redevelop the sites of the two terraces. What was certain was that the lease of No. 4 Carlton Gardens, a corner house at the back of the western terrace, had been sold. The house was demolished and the design submitted for its replacement was for a much larger building, which was clearly part of a scheme for replacing the whole of Carlton House Terrace. The architect of this, to his shame, was old Sir Reginald Blomfield, thereby ruining his reputation as a defender of London's monuments. Byron took up the fight in the pages of *Country Life*, and in early 1933 J. M. Richards organised a campaign in the *Architectural Review*, quoting both informed public opinion and Blomfield's recent public criticisms of the design for the new South Africa House in Trafalgar Square to expose his hypocrisy.[96] The cause was then taken up in *The Times*.[97] J. C. Squire, poet, writer and editor of *The London Mercury*, who had founded the Architecture Club in 1921, convened a defence committee, and the following year a Private Member's Bill in the House of Commons called for reform of the Commission for Crown Lands (who enjoyed privileged exemption from the 1932 Town and Country Planning Act) and for public consultation over the future of Carlton House Terrace. The Commissioners retreated, apparently owing to the intervention of the King himself, and Carlton House Terrace was safe – for the moment.

The Carlton House Terrace defence committee helped prepare the way for the Georgian Group. The group's real founder was the journalist and writer Douglas Goldring, who since 1932 had been calling in the pages of the *New Statesman and Nation* for the establishment of a Vigilance Committee 'charged with the duty of giving the public full warning in advance of proposed demolition of buildings which it is in the national interest to preserve'.[98] In 1936 he published a book about various architectural scandals, entitled *Pot Luck in England*. Goldring had become exasperated with the attitude and antiquarian prejudice of the SPAB and felt that a new society was needed to defend Georgian London. 'The Georgian Group, for better or worse, is just as much a product of my own brain as any of the novels, poems or travel books I have published in the past thirty years,' he later claimed, in a letter to the secretary of the SPAB. After the destruction of the Adelphi, he went on, 'I appealed in various letters to the press and in my books, for others, more influential than myself, to form a society to protect Georgian architecture and town planning. No one followed up my suggestion and, to my great annoyance, I found that if I wanted this done I should have to do it myself.'[99]

Goldring discussed the idea with, among others, John Summerson, as well as with Philip and Dorothy Trotter, founders of the Londoners' League. He was then introduced to Lord Derwent, who was preparing the motion he introduced in the House of Lords in December 1936 suggesting that the Royal Commission should prepare a list of important buildings dating from up to 1830. This generated much publicity about the threats to Georgian buildings. Worried about the proliferation of concerned societies, Lord Esher, chairman of the SPAB, wrote to Derwent suggesting that a new pressure group might be more effective if it operated under the wing of the established society. The result was that the Georgian Group of the Society for the Protection of Ancient Buildings officially came into existence in April 1937, with Derwent as chairman and Goldring as honorary secretary.[100] Many influential architects joined the committee: Richardson, Goodhart-Rendel, Clough Williams-Ellis, Trystan Edwards, Frederick Etchells and, not least, Sir Edwin Lutyens. Then there were the journalists and writers, several of them associated with the fashionable young literary set: Summerson, Betjeman, Christopher Hussey, Osbert Sitwell, Sir Kenneth Clark, Lord Berners, Eddie Sackville-West, James Lees-Milne. Indeed, the Georgian Group soon became rather grand, as well as smart. By 1939 it could boast 33 peers among its 400 or so members. This led to problems. There was tension with the SPAB, which seemed dowdy and old-fashioned, and which tried, in vain, to curb the more sensational campaigning methods used by its new branch. And there was conflict between Derwent and the irascible Goldring, who had no experience of running a society and who lasted less than a year as Hon Sec.

It was Robert Byron as deputy chairman who made the new society a force to be reckoned with. Fearless, pugnacious and incisive, he was a master of invective, a talent which he now used to further the Georgian Group, having recommended that it adopt a different tone to the SPAB. Byron wrote the article for the *Architectural Review* for May 1937 entitled 'How We Celebrate the Coronation', which has already been quoted.* Simultaneously published as a pamphlet, it effectively constituted the caustic manifesto for the Georgian Group:

> The Church; the Civil Service; the Judicial Committee of the Privy Council; the hereditary landlords; the political parties; the London County Council; the local councils; the great business firms; the motorists; the heads of the national Museum – all are indicted, some with more cause than others, because of some more decency might have been hoped for, but all on the same charge. These, in the year of the coronation, 1937, are responsible for the ruin of London, for our humiliation before visitors, and for destroying without hope of recompense many of the nation's most treasured possessions; and they will answer for it by the censure of posterity.[101]

Many were offended by Byron's language. One was Dorothy Trotter,† the gallery owner, interior decorator, and co-founder of the

---

* The Coronation of George VI took place on 12 May 1937.

† A niece of Lady Ottoline Morrell, Dorothy Warren had already made her name as a designer and decorator before opening the Warren Gallery in 1927; one of her first exhibitions was of carvings and drawings by the then unknown Henry Moore. She married Philip Trotter in November 1928. A few years later she designed the neo-Regency talks studio in the new BBC building.

Londoners' League, whose address was 'The Mutilated House, Maida Vale', because the other half of the handsome Regency semi-detached pair in which she and her husband lived had been replaced with a block of flats, despite the protests of Lutyens and Richardson, among others.[102] 'This pamphlet scandalised and disgusted many besides myself,' she complained to the SPAB, particularly because of 'its irrelevant unbalanced anti-clericalism'. 'Doubtless the pamphlet is a sure seller in cocktail party circles,' she elsewhere sneered, 'if requested by the socialite intelligentsia and wealthy leisured United-frontites where bishop-baiting is all the rage.'[103] This seems sad from a woman who, eight years earlier, had provoked scandal by exhibiting the erotic paintings of D. H. Lawrence before they were seized by the police.[104]

There was certainly much for the Georgian Group to campaign about. Some threatened buildings were in provincial cities or the countryside, but most were in London. One was the Pantheon in Oxford Street. James Wyatt's celebrated exhibition hall had long disappeared, but its stone façade survived on a building in which,

The Pantheon, Oxford Street, London (Robert Lutyens, 1938)

for a time, the architects Mendelsohn & Chermayeff had their office. It was now to be replaced by a new shop for Messrs Marks & Spencer, with a façade of black granite designed by Robert Lutyens. The Georgian Group argued that the old façade could be re-erected elsewhere, and Israel Sieff, head of M&S, agreed, even offering £200 for that purpose. Then Edward James offered to take it, and in 1938 his architect Christopher Nicholson prepared a scheme for using it as the front of a new brick country house to be built on the West Dean estate.[105] When the war came, Edward James departed for the safer side of the Atlantic, and the stones of Wyatt's façade were discarded.

Another, more difficult case was that of the Euston Arch, the magnificent Doric *propylaeum* by Hardwick erected in 1837 to announce the terminus of the London & Birmingham Railway. A century later, the London, Midland & Scottish Railway announced ambitious plans to rebuild the muddle that Euston Station had become. The architect was Percy Thomas, then President of the RIBA, who, having been sent to the United States to see the latest railway stations and hotels there,* came up with a design for a massive hotel with flanking office wings in a stripped Classical style with American Deco overtones.[106] Realising it required the removal of Hardwick's 'Arch' as well as the destruction of his noble Great Hall, the Georgian Group argued that the arch could be re-erected closer to the Euston Road, and although Thomas insisted that it could not be moved 'without smashing it to bits', the chairman of the LMS, Sir Josiah Stamp, indicated there was hope of saving it.[107] Albert Richardson and Lord Gerald Wellesley then had a positive meeting with the railway company's architects, but financial stringency led to the postponement of the rebuilding at the end of 1938. It was left to the nationalised railways after the war finally to do away with the greatest monument of the Railway Age.

---

* After a lecture on 'Railway Stations' by A. E. Richardson, reported in the *Builder* (28 April 1939), Thomas cited the new stations in Cincinnati and Philadelphia (p. 792).

Most of the threats countered by the Georgian Group concerned Georgian domestic architecture, however. There were the humble stuccoed houses of Munster Square, for instance, and, further north beyond Regent's Park, the even humbler terraces of Portland Town, which were the concern of the Londoners' League as they were replaced by blocks of modern flats, many designed by Robert Atkinson and his partner Alexander Anderson.[108] But some of the major set pieces of Georgian urban planning were also under threat, not least the east side of Bedford Square. The two three-sided squares flanking Coram's Fields, Brunswick Square and Mecklenburgh Square, were also in danger. So topical was the matter that, in January 1938, the BBC organised a radio programme entitled 'Farewell Brunswick Square' in which Robert Byron and John Summerson debated the preservation of Georgian London with W. Craven-Ellis, MP, and W. Stanley Edgson, an estate agent. The usual arguments about the necessity of slum clearance, modernisation and the importance of the building industry were aired, while Summerson argued that preservation should be considered an aspect of town-planning and needed to be conducted in a systematic manner. It was in this debate that Byron delivered his powerful, eloquent defence of the cultural value of the plain urban buildings so many still dismissed as unimportant; 'it's only Georgian architecture that really *suits* London,' he insisted:

> The Georgian style commemorates a great period, when English taste and English political ideas had suddenly become the admiration of Europe. And it corresponds, almost to the point of dinginess, with our national character. Its reserve and dislike of outward show, its reliance on the virtue and dignity of proportions only, and its rare bursts of exquisite detail, all express as no other style has ever done that indifference to self-advertisement, that quiet assumption of our own worth, and that sudden vein of lyric affection, which have given us our part in civilisation. These are exactly the characteristics that London *ought* to express.[109]

'I thought Edgson had a pleasant and companionable way with him,' Byron wrote to Summerson the day after the broadcast. 'As for Ellis – I can only wonder he isn't in prison.'[110]

Mecklenburgh Square, with its stuccoed Soanian end-pieces by Joseph Kay, was threatened principally by a plan by the Dominion Students' Hall Trust to replace the southern side with the second phase of a vaguely neo-Georgian hostel called London House. Of the already executed first portion on Guildford Street, Byron succinctly remarked: 'It was designed by Sir Herbert Baker, and other than this comment is hardly necessary.'[111] To publicise the threat to Mecklenburgh Square, the group held a Georgian ball in its gardens in July 1938, with decorations by Oliver Messel. It was hoped to repeat this success but, the following year, the gardens were unavailable so the ball was held instead at Osterley Park at the invitation of the Earl of Jersey. As for Mecklenburgh Square, in the end Baker had a posthumous triumph over the terraced houses on the south side, while of the Georgian terraces of Brunswick Square not a brick remains today.

The Georgian Group generated most publicity with its defence of the terrace of Georgian houses in Abingdon Street opposite the New Palace of Westminster, which were facing a two-pronged attack. The first was the project to erect a memorial to the late King George V in the centre of an enlarged open space in the precincts of Westminster Abbey. This required the demolition of the stone-fronted houses by John Vardy which closed the southward vista down Old Palace Yard, as well as the first two of the brick houses around the corner in Abingdon Street. As for the memorial, it was to be a Gothic canopy designed by Sir Giles Gilbert Scott enclosing a statue of the late king by William Reid Dick. The sponsor was a committee known as the Lord Mayor's Committee, supported by Cosmo Gordon Lang, Archbishop of Canterbury. With that passion for clearing open spaces and opening up vistas, however pointless, which characterises twentieth-century English taste, it was then decided to sweep away the rest of Abingdon Street, but two freeholders declined to oblige to part with their houses. Byron exposed the futility of this clearance, not necessarily required for the erection of the memorial, when he wrote how, as a result:

> out of its now decent oblivion there emerges a thing called the Jewel House, an octagonal structure quaintly restored in the last century, but Gothic and therefore righteous. What crimes King George ever committed to deserve a memorial so horrifying to its subscribers, so opposed to public interest, and so provocative of lasting execration, is a mystery to which the Primate may hold the solution but which can only fill the man in the street with a still deeper distaste at the interference of his National Church in matters which do not concern it.[112]

The second part of the attack came later when the Ecclesiastical Commissioners 'saw a convenient opportunity for profitable speculation where the Memorial Committee had failed'. Announcing that the Abingdon Street houses which they owned, and had tried to redevelop back in 1933, were structurally unsound, they submitted to the London County Council designs for two blocks of offices in the neo-Georgian style to go on the site. These were the work of E. G. Culpin, who, as Byron pointed out, 'chances to be the present chairman of the London County Council and whose plans, therefore, will have to pass the withering test of his own approval'. But the Group's counter-strategy was effective. They opened a special office in one of the privately owned Abingdon Street houses to collect signatures for a petition against the whole scheme. Nancy Mitford apparently threatened to chain herself to the railings to resist demolition, an early example of conservation direct action. These tactics worked: after only two days the Memorial Committee announced it would proceed no further and, eventually, Scott produced a more modest scheme, no longer Gothic but influenced by Lutyens, with a statue of George V, by Reid Dick, on a tall pedestal, unveiled in 1947. But as with the Euston Arch it was ultimately a hollow victory:

bomb damage resulted in the demolition of several houses in 1943 and after the war the rest were cleared, exposing the deeply unimpressive Jewel House. Only the stone-fronted houses by Vardy survive.

There was one threatened building about which the Georgian Group could do nothing, even though it was designed by Wren. The Bishop of London had begun to show his claws again and, in 1936, selected All Hallows, Lombard Street, for demolition. This was the fourth attempt made to close the church, the grounds this time being the partial settlement of the east wall.[113] The Judicial Committee of the Privy Council supported the decision, which meant that, in 1938, the church was taken down and the site sold to Barclay's Bank for a building designed by Byron's *bête noire*, Sir Herbert Baker. There was, however, a positive outcome to this vandalism; a new suburban church with the same dedication was built with the proceeds and incorporating some of the fabric of the old church. All Hallows, Twickenham, was designed, yet again, by Robert Atkinson and built in 1939–40. Although the tower of the Wren church was re-erected, the new building did not attempt to reproduce the form of the original. It was the interior, in the spirit of Wren, with simple arched windows, a brick exterior and a plastered interior with passage aisles and a coffered vaulted ceiling, in which the rescued reredos, pulpit and other fittings look at home. Wren's tower was placed right by Chertsey Road and connected to the church by a cloister containing

Interior, All Hallows Church, Twickenham, Richmond-upon-Thames (Robert Atkinson, 1940)

salvaged monuments. On the opposite side of an entrance court thus created, Atkinson placed a new vicarage designed in a modern Georgian manner. The whole would be a distinguished conception even without the Wren artefacts.

If the Bishop of London had waited a year or two, the Luftwaffe could have done his work for him. But when German bombs, rather than the Church of England, the Duke of Norfolk or the University of London, destroyed distinguished English Renaissance buildings, it was vandalism rather than the inevitable march of progress. 'On the whole, the struggle was worth it,' wrote Douglas Goldring in 1940, despite his struggles with the Georgian Group having brought him 'to the verge of what rich people call "a nervous breakdown"'. 'If Nazi bombs do not destroy what the private speculator has so far spared, future generations may have reason to be grateful that the Georgian Group came into existence and rescued for them a portion of their heritage.'[114] Robert Byron had stepped down as deputy chairman the previous year; a year later he was dead. Had he lived, he would surely have prevented certain more traditional architects in the group trying to use its influence to promote a modern Georgian architecture. J. M. Richards later recalled his misgivings, as a Modernist, that 'its aims might be confused with those of the neo-Georgian architects, who dominated the more conservative end of the profession in the 1930s'.[115] In the 1930s, however, despite a shared admiration for Georgian principles, there was a clear, if paradoxical, distinction between those who wished to preserve authentic Georgian buildings as cultural monuments and useful structures, and those who wished to build a modern Georgian world. As Herbert Read once notoriously observed, 'In the back of every dying civilization sticks a bloody Doric column.'[116]

CHAPTER EIGHT

MODERN GOTHIC

———◆———

Bishop Winnington-Ingram's horrifying proposal to demolish nineteen churches in the City of London had, behind its brazen vandalism, a serious and positive purpose. As in the nineteenth century under the 1860 Union of Benefices Act, the sale of valuable sites helped to pay for new churches in the expanding suburbs. The removal of All Hallows paid for the new church in Twickenham with the same dedication, and contributed to the funding of Albert Richardson's Holy Cross, Greenford, as well as All Saints, Queensbury; St Olave's, Mitcham; and the Ascension, Pollards Hill. All Hallows, Twickenham, is one of the better churches of the interwar period, demonstrating a resourceful respect for tradition while reflecting a strong contemporary character. If churches are seldom considered to be the dominant building type of the 1920s and 1930s, they nevertheless include some of the most representative and the most interesting buildings of the interwar years. A very large number of new places of worship were built to serve the new suburbs: some 270 Anglican churches alone were built between 1930 and 1945, a quarter of them in the suburbs of London. In one diocese, Southwark, a 'Twenty-Five Churches Fund' was launched in 1925, and by 1934 twenty had been built.[1] The Anglican churches described in the two volumes published by the Incorporated Church Building Society – *New Churches Illustrated* of 1936 and *Fifty Modern Churches* of 1947 – were mostly designed by distinguished members of the architectural profession. Indeed, some architects were known, above all, for their churches: Edward Maufe, Sir Charles Nicholson, J. Harold Gibbons, J. N. Comper, F. C. Eden, N. F. Cachemaille-Day, F. X. Velarde, Bernard Miller and, not least, Sir Giles Gilbert Scott.[2]

The interwar church is particularly instructive as a building type; vital traditions inherited from the nineteenth century were reinterpreted with great sophistication while being strongly influenced by contemporary work on the Continent. If there is none that can really be described as an unequivocal expression of the Modern Movement, there are many churches of the period that triumphantly achieved the desired compromise between tradition and modernity. 'In the building of churches,' Maufe argued in a lecture on 'Modern Church Architecture' in 1934, 'I think it is now generally recognised that we must look both to the past and to the present; our churches should not be merely reproductions in the manner of some previous style which happens to be fashionable. A copy is never the real thing.'[3] But, as Maufe also recognised, 'English churches perhaps suffer a little from sentimentalism', and a majority of the new churches were, to a greater or lesser degree, designed in the Gothic tradition, reflecting how deep and ineradicable is the association in England between Gothic and Christianity. But not all.

Atkinson won the limited competition to design All Hallows, Twickenham, probably because of his earlier success with re-using the Georgian pulpit and other old fittings in St Catherine's, Hammersmith – the positive outcome of the destruction of St Katherine Coleman. This building, raised in the centre of the London County Council's Old Oak Common estate in a mere six months in 1923, had the curious distinction of being the first steel-framed church in the country. Externally, however, it was faced in brick in a simple Early Christian, or Romanesque, style. Inside, the wide aisle-less nave and narrower chancel were covered by a smooth vault of fibrous plaster. Itself a product of destruction, St Catherine's would become one of the very few interwar architectural casualties of the next war, when, despite the survival of its steel frame, it was demolished after being hit by a stray German bomb in 1940.

St Catherine's, Hammersmith, was the representative church of the 1920s. Its simplicity greatly appealed to contemporary taste, which was in strong reaction against the decorative richness of the nineteenth century. A view of its interior illustrating an article in

Interior, St Catherine's, Hammersmith, London (Robert Atkinson, 1923)

an Anglo-Catholic newspaper by the young John Betjeman was revealingly entitled 'Away with Knick-knacks!', although the black-and-white photographs are misleading as the pews were painted blue and the ciborium was orange and blue-green.[4] Uncluttered interiors and plain plasterwork were generally favoured for contemporary church design, while the almost astylar, round-arched Early Christian or Romanesque manner of the brick exterior represented an acceptable alternative to Gothic. It was a fashionable style that can be traced back to the round-arched austerity in London stocks of C. H. Reilly's Edwardian church in Dalston and, before that, to the Byzantine of J. F. Bentley's Westminster Cathedral. This round-arched manner was a style particularly favoured by the non-Established churches and it was also adopted by the Christian Scientists. Herbert Baker's red brick Christian Science Church in Marsham Street, Westminster, with its vaulted spaces and clever planning, is a representative example, as well as one of that architect's best English works.

Interior, Ninth Church of Christ Scientist (Christian Science Church), Westminster, London (Herbert Baker, 1930)

Church of Our Lady and St Alphege, Bath, Somerset (Giles Gilbert Scott, 1929)

Ever since the completion of the structure of Bentley's seminal cathedral in 1903, the use of a Byzantine, Romanesque or Early Christian style had been encouraged by Roman Catholics. The church of St Alphege, built on a basilican model in the suburbs of Bath in the 1920s, is a particularly distinguished example. Inspired by the church of S. Maria in Cosmedin in Rome, it was Giles Gilbert

Scott's first essay in the Romanesque style. Much of its architectural effect relies on the beauty of the unbroken plain walling of local rough stone laid with coarse flush pointing. Internally the walls are carried on columns with elaborate carved capitals, while at the east end is a modern interpretation of an Early Christian *baldacchino* in gilded oak. The Italian character of the interior is enhanced by the pattern of the floor, which looks as if it is made of *pietra dura* but in fact is of small pieces of linoleum. Unfortunately, the campanile that Scott planned was never built. Soon after, Scott built another Italianate round-arched church in Ashford, Middlesex, where the exterior brick-faced walls are unbroken by buttresses, as he made them slope slightly inwards to counteract the thrust of the timber roof. It was one of his favourite works.

Several particularly distinguished neo-Romanesque churches were built in the suburbs of Liverpool. St Matthew's, Clubmoor, was designed by Francis Xavier Velarde, a local Roman Catholic architect who had been a protégé of C. H. Reilly. Built of brick rather than stone, its wide interior is dominated by another free-standing *baldacchino* which, in style, like much of the more experimental church furniture of the period, is redolent of contemporary cinema design (Plate 29). Of the Clubmoor church, Goodhart-Rendel wrote: 'Few modern churches can shew any furniture in the same class with the original and delightful baldacchino over the high altar, a baldacchino whose design is traditional enough only to throw into strong relief the originality of its treatment in detail.'[5] Anglicans could also employ the round-arched style. St Columba's, Anfield, by Bernard Miller, was of grey brick externally, where the flanking walls, pierced by tall round-headed windows, rise in stages to a high chancel, above which a bellcote rises flush with the brickwork. Internally, the walls and round arches were faced in plaster. Miller was also the architect of St Christopher's, Norris Green, where, internally, transverse arches of a stilted elliptical profile frame an extraordinary Deco-cum-Baroque reredos.

Occasionally, the exterior of these cool, round-arched buildings would be rendered and whitewashed, making the style seem more like the American vogue for Spanish Colonial – an ecclesiastical expression of Osbert Lancaster's 'Pseudish'. A good example is St Francis's in Bournemouth, an Anglican church by J. Harold Gibbons, where round-arched passage aisles are cut through shallow lateral arched openings off a barrel-vaulted nave, all rendered in white cement, and the interior is dominated by a free-standing ciborium with a Lady Chapel placed beyond. St George's at Wash Common outside Newbury is another essay in this manner, but more Italian-looking in whitewashed brick. Designed by F. C. Eden, it was eventually finished by Stephen Dykes Bower. An impressive example of this simple round-arched style, designed for an appropriate climate, is St Andrew's Scottish war memorial church in Jerusalem by A. Clifford Holliday, a powerful composition in an Early Christian manner which hints at the Art Deco.

Great Chapel, Society of the Sacred Mission, Newark-on-Trent, Nottinghamshire (Currey & Thompson, 1928)

Another powerful essay in neo-Romanesque – internally, if not externally – was a chapel built for the Catholic wing of the Church of England. Designed for the Society of the Sacred Mission at Kelham, near Newark-on-Trent, by Currey & Thompson, this was a simple structure of brick, domed and vaulted in concrete, enclosing a centralised space lit dramatically by shafts of light from small windows. The effect was enhanced by a massive brick arch which supported a Rood modelled by the sculptor, Charles Sargeant Jagger.* Nevertheless,

---

* The building is no longer a chapel and the figures from the Rood are now in the church of St John the Divine, Kennington, London.

Interior, Society of the Sacred Mission, Newark-on-Trent, Nottinghamshire (Currey & Thompson, 1928)

the choice of a simplified Byzantine style may seem surprising for this chapel as the Victorian building to which it was annexed was a vigorous work in High Victorian Gothic by Sir Gilbert Scott.

Gothic never went out of fashion in church architecture, and the Gothic Revival carried on triumphantly well into the twentieth century, notably so in the hands of Sir Gilbert's grandson, Giles Gilbert Scott. Edward Maufe was another who was not afraid to use the pointed arch. 'I am one of those who has consistently believed that we in England always have had a living church-building tradition,' he announced in his 1934 lecture:

> even throughout the Gothic Revival it is there. In spite of many of those churches being almost museum specimens, yet we have beautiful examples right through the Revival and up to our

own time. The pity is that so few people now can receive the message of those architects; we are blinded by ornament, become unfashionable; we cannot see the wood for the trees, nor the trees for the leaves. There are Butterfield, Burges, Street and Norman Shaw, but above all there is G. G. Scott and the development of his influence in Bodley, and particularly Temple Moore.[6]

It is remarkable that the general reaction against all things Victorian did not wholly operate in the church sphere. This was partly because Anglo-Catholicism, which was at its most influential in the interwar years, was intimately connected with the Victorian Gothic Revival. This may explain why, as an act of piety, St Andrew's, Wells Street, Marylebone, a building of 1845, was rebuilt stone by stone in the new suburb of Kingsbury in 1933–34 by W. A. Forsyth, complete with its High Victorian furnishings. And if the work of Street and Butterfield was often regarded as strident and ugly, the less assertive and more elegant Gothic of Late Victorian architects like G. F. Bodley and Temple Moore was still admired. Particularly influential in terms of its spare Late Gothic style was the church of St Agnes in Kennington, South London,* designed in 1874 by Giles Scott's tragic father, G. G. Scott, junior.[7] This church, completed by Scott's co-adjutor Temple Moore, was cited as late as 1924, half a century later, by Charles Marriott in his book on *Modern English Architecture* as an example of 'the treatment of the style we call "modern"'.[8] Similarly, Bodley's refined Late Gothic work was imitated long after his death in 1907, although Goodhart-Rendel complained that the principal legacy of his school was his favourite Decorated window tracery remaining 'like the grin of the Cheshire cat'.[9]

---

* In a letter to the author of 27 August 1974, Sir John Summerson described the impression of its interior as 'one of space and light – and of delicious unaffected simplicity – "anti-Victorian" . . . Yes, St Agnes was a great loss – perhaps, with St John, Red Lion Square and St Alban Holborn, the greatest war-time loss of Gothic Revival buildings.'

Interior, St Agnes, Kennington, London (G. G. Scott, junior, 1874)

To a remarkable extent, the basic form of the typical twentieth-century Anglican church was established in the 1870s, when Bodley, Scott and J. D. Sedding led a reaction against the Continentally inspired 'vigorous style' of the preceding generation of Goths, in favour of Gothic that was English and late, Decorated and Perpendicular.[10] The plan of St Augustine's, Pendlebury, by Bodley and Garner, with its continuous space from west to the altar at the east end unbroken by any chancel arch and its internal buttresses pierced by narrow passage aisles, remained conventional at least until the Second World War. It was used by Cachemaille-Day in his celebrated Modernist church in Eltham. The same architects' more usual plan of wide aisles and a generous chancel also lingered. Well might John Betjeman complain that:

> a new church in what is called the 'modern style' is often no different in its plan and construction from the dullest Victorian church in brick; the effect is 'unusual' but not truly modern, and is obtained by mouldings and shapes and colours which are the result of indigestion after a visit to Stockholm Town Hall and the *neue Baukunst* of Germany. This is 'modernistic'.[11]

Despite a violent reaction against 'High Victorian Gothic', the Gothic Revival continued as a creative force into the 1920s and 1930s. Although there had been changes in style and emphasis, with the heavy mid-Victorian manner being succeeded by the refinement of Late English Gothic in the 1870s and then given an Art Nouveau flourish after the turn of the century, there were important continuities. One was that quality encouraged by Ruskin and which Charles Booth had characterised as the 'bare style': that emphasis on unbroken wall planes to create a sublime effect of mass and height. Whatever their interior finishes, many of the churches of the interwar years were faced externally in brick and achieve a similar monumental character. The qualities of the best urban churches by Street or Butterfield are echoed in, for instance, the suburban churches of N. F. Cachemaille-Day, such as the Church of the Epiphany, Gipton, Leeds, or St Nicholas's, Burnage, Manchester, while the influence of the fortified brick cathedral at Albi which inspired so many Victorian and Edwardian church architects can be traced in the exterior of his Expressionist concrete framed church in Eltham, as well as at Giles Scott's great cathedral at Liverpool. 'It is interesting to note,' Cachemaille-Day wrote in 1933, 'how tenacious is the Gothic tradition in this country, and it is likely that a new interpretation of ecclesiastical architecture in England will still have a certain Gothic flavour, even when all actual Gothic details have disappeared.'[12]

Giles Scott's master had been his father's pupil, Temple Moore, who died in 1920 leaving some of his finest works, such as St Wilfrid's, Harrogate, to be completed by his son-in-law, Leslie Moore. In 1928, H. S. Goodhart-Rendel celebrated the genius of Temple Moore in a lecture in which he recognised that while his slightly archaeological Gothic belonged to a past age, 'To object unconditionally to a style is unworthy of rational criticism, style is only a language, and can of itself neither mar nor make the beauty of what it conveys.'[13] This lecture was followed by a debate, the report of which remains a key document in understanding the later Gothic Revival and confirmed the continuing influence of George Gilbert Scott, junior. On that occasion, Beresford Pite announced: 'The work of Temple Moore is rather distressing to some of us, because we cannot imagine what is to come after. It seems as if he summed up and completed the theory of the Gothic Revival.'

There were several active survivors from the Edwardian years still building churches in the interwar decades, such as Sir Walter

St Wilfrid's, Harrogate, Yorkshire (Temple Moore and Leslie Moore, 1927)

Tapper, who had been Bodley's chief assistant and whose debt to that master is evident in the church of the Annunciation, Marble Arch, of 1914. After the war, Tapper's work became more austere, but he was also responsible for the richly decorative metal screens in the manner of Spanish *reja*s in the transepts of York Minster. There was Sir Charles Nicholson, a scholarly and self-effacing church architect who skilfully enlarged medieval parish churches in Chelmsford and Portsmouth when they were elevated to cathedral status. There was Temple Moore's pupil, J. Harold Gibbons, whose church of St Mary, in the London suburb of Kenton, developed several Late Victorian ideas in planning but manifests idiosyncrasies peculiar to the architect. And there was E. C. Shearman, who showed remarkable originality in his St Silas's, Kentish Town, just before the Great War, and then repeated the formula when he came to design St Francis's, Isleworth, on the Great West Road, some two decades later. The near-identical churches by Shearman all employ the same purple bricks and have angular, almost Expressionist detailing; inside, wide naves with passage aisles are covered by unusual timber roofs.

And then there was J. Ninian Comper. This former pupil of Bodley was a very influential designer in the interwar decades despite his age; he was born in 1864, and remained the darling of the Anglo-Catholic wing of the Church of England until his death in 1960. Comper's early work continued the Late Gothic manner of Bodley and 'Middle Scott', but at St Mary's, Wellingborough, begun in 1904 but not completed until 1931, he introduced Classical forms to achieve an Anglicised fusion between Northern Europe and the Mediterranean (Plate 30). This exquisitely beautiful church was also remarkable for having the high altar brought forward from the east wall so that, owing to the generous provision of aisles, as many worshippers as possible could be brought around it. This eclectic combination of Gothic and Classical characterised his works of the interwar years, such as the chapel at the convent in London Colney and the church of St Philip at Cosham, Portsmouth.

St Mary the Virgin, Wellingborough, Northamptonshire (Ninian Comper, 1930)

Comper was a deeply conservative figure, eloquently dismissive of modernistic experiments in church design and antipathetic to the culture of the post-war years. What is extraordinary, therefore, is that it was he, almost alone among ecclesiastical architects, who came to be admired by a much younger generation. In 1939 an article about his work by John Betjeman was published in the *Architectural Review*, whose pages were by then almost exclusively devoted to buildings of the Modern Movement. The previous year, the editor of the *Architectural Review*, H. de Cronin Hastings, and J. M. Richards had been sufficiently intrigued to go and see St Cyprian's, Clarence Gate, of 1902, which Dell & Wainwright later photographed: 'Marx [Richards] and I went together to Comper's church in Baker Street to make sure you were mad,' wrote Hastings to Betjeman. 'To our surprise – to our inexpressible surprise – we discovered it was absolutely lovely. Not everyone's cup of vodka, perhaps, but indubitably the work of an architect – with a remarkable feeling of space and clarity of planning; qualities which, you and I know so well, are practically non-existent today under whatever disguise the pseudo-architect presents himself.'[14]

Comper was asked to design a cathedral for the Episcopal Church of Scotland in his native Aberdeen; this could well have been built had not the Wall Street Crash cut off the necessary American funding. Elsewhere in Scotland, the Gothic carried on, notably in the hands of another Edwardian survivor, Sir Robert Lorimer.

Several of his churches, like the early work of his compatriot, Comper, look to Scottish Late Gothic precedents, which are evident in his great Gothic shrine on the top of Edinburgh Castle, the Scottish National War Memorial (Plate 3). Lorimer's pupil, Leslie G. Thomson, continued with a Late Gothic manner, but with a wide rectangular internal space with narrow passage aisles, at the Reid Memorial Church in Edinburgh of 1928. St John's Renfield Church in Glasgow by James Taylor Thomson was exactly contemporary and very similar in style and plan. For Andrew Drummond, author of *The Church Architecture of Protestantism*, published in 1934, there were 'signs of the emergence of a more creative Gothic in [these] two new churches designed for urban congregations at considerable cost';[15] he detected the influence of modern American Gothic and the work of Cram and Goodhue. Taylor Thomson had, indeed, once worked for Bertram Grosvenor Goodhue, whose University Chapel at Chicago Drummond considered 'the creation of something new in the language of Gothic'.[16]

Giles Scott's colossal Anglican cathedral, slowly emerging on the Liverpool skyline, was the creation of the church architect who was most influential and most respected between the wars (Plate 38). He had won the competition in 1903 at the age of twenty-two, and this stupendous building, which he completely redesigned in 1910, giving it a single, massive central tower, provided a continuous, romantic background to his varied and busy professional life. Scott's pre-war churches at Sheringham and Northfleet anticipated the monumental Classicising of his personal Gothic style which came to characterise the great church rising above the Mersey. The tower at Northfleet, completed during the war, is almost a prototype for Liverpool. 'One sees this magnificent tower when coming up the Thames,' wrote Maufe, 'and one feels proud that foreigners can see it on their approach to London. To my mind, it is one of the best towers which have ever been built.'[17]

Amongst several churches Scott designed in the 1920s, the war memorial chapel at Charterhouse School, Godalming, was particularly remarkable for the originality of treatment of medieval themes. In this great rock of a building, Scott repeated and elongated his favourite flush transept motif, allowing light to enter the solemn interior from hidden sources. Scott was a master in the handling of traditional building materials and in the manipulation of natural light. At St Francis's Church at Terriers, a suburb of High Wycombe, there is no west window, no east window and no clerestory windows – just bare walls of beautiful knapped flint. Inside, light pours down from the tower which heralds the chancel; in the words of Nikolaus Pevsner, 'a procession of light is accomplished which is emotionally very effective'.[18] As Scott himself explained, 'lighting is one of the most important features of a church from the point of view of producing an atmosphere conducive to worship, and for that reason I like to keep the glass out of sight to a certain extent, and not to have too glaring a light in the eyes of the worshippers'.[19]

In Scott's hands, the reassuringly familiar Gothic was reinterpreted with sophistication and subtlety, as could be seen at the centrally planned brick church at Golders Green, with its dominating pitched roofs; at the Roman Catholic Cathedral at Oban, with its powerful west tower of pink granite; and in the long, streamlined brick-faced church at Luton, with its rugged west tower and internal progression of transverse pointed arches containing passage aisles. Scott seldom repeated himself. 'His work is always most imaginative and stimulating,' wrote Cachemaille-Day, 'but his own personality always seems to dominate, whatever the particular style he chooses.'[20] Sometimes, as at the Roman Catholic church in Bath or the exquisitely furnished brick chapel he designed for Lady Margaret Hall, Oxford, the style he chose was Early Christian or Byzantine; most of his churches were essentially modern Gothic in style, but he never repeated himself.

In 1924 the choir of the Anglican Cathedral in Liverpool was consecrated. Later that day King George V knighted its architect, aged only forty-four. With the completion of the first major portion of Scott's masterpiece, 'the Diocese, and indeed the whole country,

Interior, Chapel, Lady Margaret Hall, Oxford (Giles Gilbert Scott, 1933)

suddenly woke up to the realisation that there had been growing up almost unnoticed in its midst a Cathedral, which in size and beauty was worthy to be compared with the greatest churches of the middle ages'.[21] Here was powerful new home-grown architecture to encourage the architectural profession after the years of doubt and uncertainty that had followed the Great War. Although this massive fragment built of Runcorn red sandstone was Gothic in style, it was like no ancient cathedral; it was at once traditional and modern as well as romantic and original.

No wonder that Scott was asked to design many more churches, both Anglican and Roman Catholic, and commissions for secular buildings followed: for university buildings, for great libraries, and for remodelling an electric generating station by the Thames, often using the same approach. Hence C. H. Reilly's meditation on the 'great romantic pile' of Battersea Power Station in 1934 that might be 'a new cathedral by that interesting church fellow up in the north, F. X. Velarde'.[22] Reilly was thinking of St Gabriel's Church in Blackburn, a church whose austere blocky brick exterior took its aesthetic from modern industrial architecture while its rough plastered and barrel vaulted interior was enlivened by an elaborate Art Deco reredos and lit by pendant lamps worthy of a contemporary cinema interior.[23]

Scott may have continued the Gothic Revival into the twentieth century, but at Liverpool and elsewhere he interpreted tradition with resourceful originality of detail and form. Other ecclesiastical architects showed a keen awareness of striking new church buildings in Continental Europe and experimented within the constraints imposed by liturgical conventions and parochial expectations; as Maufe wrote, 'the Church cannot stand outside contemporary thought – she is there to point the way of life, and it is obvious that she can gain from, just as she gives to, our new knowledge.'[24] Several designers used centralised plans and responded to that demand for a closer involvement by the laity loosely categorised as the Liturgical Movement, which began in Belgium before the First World War and became most conspicuous in new Roman Catholic churches in Germany and Switzerland. Strangely, perhaps, one of the most conservative of British church designers was thinking on similar lines.

Comper's importance as a church planner stemmed from his writings and from his executed designs, the most significant of which was St Philip's at Cosham, built in an interwar suburb of Portsmouth in 1935–38. Externally it is Gothic, in brick, almost mean in its abstraction; inside, white plaster Corinthian columns support white plaster Gothic vaults, all in fact constructed around a steel frame to create two wide aisles, but the interior is dominated by a burnished gold ciborium over the high altar, brought a whole bay forward from the east wall. Comper wrote that 'St Philip's is the most complete and most obvious blending of the Greek and the Gothic. And,' he insisted, 'there is no claim of the invention of a new style; for a similar combination was found in past centuries. But, in so far as I

Interior, St Philip's, Cosham, Portsmouth, Hampshire (Ninian Comper, 1938)

am aware, there is nothing exactly like St Philip's.'[25] As Anthony Symondson has written, this church was Comper's 'legacy to the future': 'It was the fulfilment of his quest for beauty and liturgical planning on rational principles; a church that was essentially modern yet indebted to the unfolding development of the catholic tradition as it had evolved from Constantine to the twentieth century.'[26]

The completion of St Philip's stimulated the revival of interest in the elderly architect's work, partly because its simplicity and the combination of white and gold corresponded with contemporary taste. And it continues to be admired. For Peter Hammond, writing in 1960, this curious building bore

> little resemblance to anything that the man in the street is likely to associate with functional architecture. Yet there is no church built in this country since the beginning of the century which is so perfectly fitted to its purpose. It is the work of an architect for whom architecture is essentially the handmaid of the liturgy, and Christian tradition something far more vital than a storehouse of precedents and historic detail... The church of St Philip provides a conclusive answer to those who assert that to bring the altar forward, into the midst of the people, must involve the sacrifice of mystery.[27]

Hammond's praise of Comper is all the more telling as he was writing in favour of a genuinely modern architecture responding to the exigencies of the Liturgical Movement and was impatient with almost all more traditional churches built before the Second World War. As far as he was concerned, the 'only churches which show signs of original thought, so far as the plan is concerned, are the John Keble Church, at Mill Hill, by D. F. Martin-Smith, Sir Ninian Comper's church at Cosham, and two churches, one at Wythenshawe, the other at Sunderland, by N. F. Cachemaille-Day'.[28] All these were Anglican churches; elsewhere Hammond cited two 'exceptional' centrally planned Roman Catholic churches. One was the Church of the First

Interior, St Peter's, Gorleston-on-Sea, Norfolk (Eric Gill, 1939)

Martyrs, at Bradford, built in 1935 and designed to an octagonal plan with a central altar by J. H. Langtry-Langton. The other was 'one of the most courageous essays in planning for liturgy that the 'thirties produced'.[29] This was St Peter's at Gorleston, next to Great Yarmouth, and it was designed by the sculptor Eric Gill – who had originally trained as an architect. Outside, the cruciform building is in simplified Gothic in red brick; inside, smooth white Gothic arches interlock around the crossing where stands the altar.* 'The only thing about it to write home,' Gill thought, 'is the fact that it will have a central altar. Everything springs from that – the plan grows from that & the outside is simply the result of the inside.'[30]

The John Keble Church at Mill Hill was the result of a competition held in 1934. It still had the altar placed against the east wall of the wide sanctuary, but the choir was placed in the body of the nave,

---

* The Church of St Louis at Vincennes by Droz and Marrast had a central space formed by interlocking Gothic arches, but here the altar was still placed far to the east (Roulin (1947), pp. 215–16).

which is wider than it is long. Without the support of intervening columns creating aisles, this span was covered with a flat roof using the 'Diagrid' system of reinforced-concrete beams. Architecturally, however, the expression of this congregational plan is disappointing, with the exterior a rather pedestrian composition of rectangular brick masses surmounted by a simplistic modernistic lantern. Perhaps it was of this sort of church that Comper was thinking when he complained that 'it is the pretentiousness of these modernistic churches which is unforgivable. Their architecture expresses the self-satisfaction which has produced them.'[31]

Much more sophisticated and powerful are the churches of Cachemaille-Day, who was in partnership with Herbert Welsh and Felix Lander until 1935. In planning terms, his most remarkable church was that cited by Hammond: St Michael's at Wythenshawe outside Manchester. Built in 1937, its centralised eight-pointed star-shaped plan was that of two superimposed rectangles at forty-five degrees, and the Diagrid reinforced-concrete flat roof is supported on six thin concrete piers which create a necessary longitudinal emphasis within

St Michael and All Angels, Manchester (N. F. Cachemaille-Day, 1937)

the centralised space. The architects' original intention was to have a free-standing altar but the Bishop of Manchester insisted it be pushed back to a more conventional position within one of the glazed points of the star. The exterior of the church, faced in purple brick, has a monumental presence in a flat, characterless suburb, and the huge windows have tracery of intersecting arches made of brick and concrete. These are reminiscent of Anatole de Baudot's pioneering concrete church, Saint-Jean de Montmartre in Paris, as well as of Auguste Perret's concrete churches, but Cachemaille-Day insisted his principal sources of inspiration for this revolutionary building were medieval and English: the Octagon at Ely and Henry VII's Chapel at Westminster.

Cachemaille-Day's churches were successful because, while open to new ideas, he appreciated the cultural and emotional necessity of symbolism and historical resonances in church architecture. For him, church buildings were much more than machines for worshipping in. In ecclesiastical architecture, he argued:

> Something else is necessary, and that something else is not discovered through logic alone. This is clearly realised when it is remembered that there are many people who are forced to admire the clean and heroic lines of many modern buildings, perhaps seen to especial advantage abroad rather than in this country, but who can find in them no response to their emotional life and consequently return with relief to ancient buildings, or at least to modern buildings carried out in historic style.[32]

While using modern materials, therefore, and while experimenting with new shapes and types of plan derived from developments in Continental Europe, Cachemaille-Day recognised that the traditional forms of English churches had an emotional power which could still be used to advantage.

The ideas of the Liturgical Movement within parts of the Roman Catholic Church were introduced to Britain in Fr Gabriel Hebert's

Interior, Notre-Dame du Raincy, France (Auguste and Gustave Perret; stained glass by Maurice Denis, 1923)

1935 book *Liturgy and Society*, but the remarkable new churches built on the Continent were already familiar to architects from illustrations in the weekly journals or the illustrated books of F. R. Yerbury. Although the neo-Romanesque churches by Paul Tournon were the most influential French models for Roman Catholic architects, the best known was the war memorial church at Le Raincy outside Paris, built by the pioneering master of reinforced-concrete construction, Auguste Perret. Often described as a Sainte-Chapelle in concrete, it had a remarkable west tower and belfry that owed nothing directly to historical precedent. Inside, the frequently reproduced black-and-white photographs revealed that the walls were formed of pierced concrete blocks independent of the structural frame, but not that the openings were filled with stained glass which bathed the grey concrete in glorious colour.

Very different was the Högalid Church in Stockholm by Ivar Tengbom, an example of that 'Swedish Grace' which had such a profound influence on British designers. In the church sphere this

Högalid Church, Stockholm, Sweden (Ivar Tengbom, 1933)

was manifested in the taste for muted colours and limed oak, both evident in this tall, spare Lutheran church built during the First World War. Elsewhere in Scandinavia, the Grundtvig's Church in Copenhagen, designed just before the war by P. V. Jensen-Klint, was in the Nordic brick Gothic tradition, but what impressed visitors was the extraordinary tripartite stepped west front resembling a giant organ. For all its literal religious symbolism, such Expressionism in brick was seldom attempted in Britain, nor did the Continental tradition of expressive, rational brickwork demonstrated by the French architect-monk, Paul Bellot, at Quarr Abbey on the Isle of Wight find British followers, perhaps with the exception of E. C. Shearman. For wilful, experimental modernity, no church in Britain could equal the astonishing Roman Catholic church in Cork erected in 1927–31 to the design of the Chicago architect Barry Byrne. 'Expressionist' seems the only term to describe its serrated concrete walls with a figure of Christ the King integrated into the angular porches and its inventive wide polygonal plan. 'The interior design is so arranged that all of the lines will appear to lead to the altar,' the architect wrote to the client. 'I sincerely regard this as my best building.'[33] But it remained an aberration. Perhaps its only real peer is the remarkable synagogue built at Dollis Hill by the engineer Owen Williams in 1936–38, where the form of both walls and the roof form are jagged corrugations of planes of reinforced concrete, while the shapes of the window openings were based on the Star of David and the seven-branched candelabrum.

Most self-consciously new churches in Britain tended to show a debt to the powerful new architecture to be found in Weimar Germany. As Andrew Drummond wrote in 1934: 'The fact that the focus of architectural interest has shifted from London and Paris to Holland, Germany and Scandinavia, may lead us to ask whether these countries are not making significant experiments in ecclesiastical as in civil and domestic architecture.'[34] The most radical and experimental designer of new Lutheran churches in Germany was Otto Bartning. His Stahlkirche ('steel church'), shown in 1928 at the *Pressa* exhibition

Rundkirche, Essen, Germany (Otto Bartning, 1930)

in Cologne, rose above a concrete base and had a radiating, centralised plan based on the parabola. Walls of coloured glass filled the wide spaces between the vertical steel stanchions. Bartning's Rundkirche ('round church') of 1930, at Essen, was entirely constructed of reinforced concrete. Such austere rationalism was too much even for a Scot like Drummond, who found Bartning's churches to have 'a cold and unattractive office-like appearance which completely lack[s]

St Kamillus Church and Asthma Hospital, Mönchengladbach, Germany (Dominikus Böhm, 1928)

the sense of Christian Fellowship and the "Numinous"'.[35] Less stark were the churches of the Hamburg Expressionist Fritz Höger, whose Evangelical church in the Hohenzollernplatz in Berlin of 1929–30 used tightly pointed transverse arches internally, its outside faced in brick with vertical fluting.

The greatest of Roman Catholic architects in Germany was Dominikus Böhm, although his work was less well known in Britain than that of Bartning or Höger. Böhm's war memorial church at Neu-Ulm of 1926–27 combined Expressionistic Gothic with rugged masonry forms, while the elliptical arch was employed at the church at Mainz-Bischofsheim of 1924–26 and at the remarkable radially planned church of 1930–33 at Cologne-Riehl. Böhm enjoyed the texture of planes of traditional masonry or brickwork and often used arches. Much more austere were the churches of Rudolf Schwarz

Corpus Christi Church, Aachen, Germany (Rudolf Schwarz, 1930)

inspired by the ideas of the Liturgical Movement, such as Corpus Christi at Aachen of 1928–30 with its searingly simple white exterior, while in Switzerland, Karl Moser developed the ideas of Perret into something more monumental and solid in the concrete Antoniuskirche in Basel of 1925–31.

Knowledge of these striking new Continental churches is evident in the work of the more progressive British church architects. For instance, at A. W. Kenyon's St Alban's, North Harrow, the tall square campanile, with its shallow arched openings at the summit, derives either from Höger's rather more subtle tower in Berlin or Böhm's at Cologne, while the curious tall thin arched windows with stepped haunches – a characteristic motif of the time – came from Ostberg's hugely influential Stockholm Town Hall. The elliptical arches used by Bernard Miller at his church at Norris Green, Liverpool, or by Seely

St Alban's, North Harrow, Middlesex (Arthur W. Kenyon, 1936)

Interior, St Christopher's, Norris Green, Liverpool (Bernard Miller, 1932)

Interior, St Faith's, Lee-on-the-Solent, Hampshire (Seely & Paget, 1933)

& Paget at Lee-on-the-Solent may well derive from Böhm's work, although possibly American Art Deco may have been influential here; there was also the precedent of Wahlman's Engelbrekt church in Stockholm (1906–14). Similarly, the rough-plastered tight Gothic transverse arches used by Höger and Böhm may explain the fashion for this device in English churches of the interwar years. On the other hand, wide transverse arches of reinforced concrete, faced in stone, were used before the war by E. S. Prior in his experimental concrete church at Roker, Sunderland. At St Wilfrid's, Halton, in the suburbs of Leeds, a truly original work by Randall Wells of 1937–39, with stylised Gothic forms and austere external stonework, would seem to have been a most intelligent development of the native Arts and Crafts tradition.

In the best modern churches, a formal expression reflecting the use of reinforced-concrete construction is enhanced by a wide range of well-digested influences, even if the planning of these buildings is usually comparatively conservative. St Christopher's, Withington, Manchester, by Bernard Miller, for instance, was an austere cubic building with a symmetrical, monumental south façade. A massive central tower rose above a wide side entrance, with the walls stepping inwards. A similar square tower, but asymmetrically sited, gave monumentality to the exterior of St Gabriel's, Blackburn, by F. X. Velarde, like Miller a product of the Liverpool School under Reilly. Later, writing about churches by the two brilliant former students whose careers he promoted, Reilly argued: 'Without being in any sense bizarre, like many of the new French and German churches, theirs seem to me both reverent and inspiring.'[36] But daring and experiment could go too far, and serious problems with the flat, asphalted reinforced-concrete roofs eventually resulted in the mutilation of Velarde's Anglican masterpiece and the total demolition of Miller's.

Most of Velarde's work was for the Roman Catholic Church. Perhaps his most remarkable church was St Monica's in Bootle, of 1936–37. It was given a strong presence by a massive rectilinear tower

St Monica's, Bootle, Liverpool (F. X. Velarde; sculptor Herbert Tyson Smith, 1937)

facing the street and concealing the practical pitched roof behind. The repetitive round-arched windows that pierce the walls hint at another exotic influence: the abstracted monumental architecture of Fascist Italy and the churches of Marcello Piacentini. Internally, the brick piers – which emerge externally as buttresses above the aisles – are penetrated by round arched openings, but what dominates is the extraordinary reredos on the east wall (Plate 31). Behind a hanging canopy, flattened angels in relief climb up a zigzag pattern of rectangular panels, with a vertical emphasis given by thin gilded pilaster strips rising to the almost flat ceiling. At the Blackburn church the jazzy reredos decorated with ribs of stainless steel was painted in 'two tones of brilliant red' and the internal flush doors were painted 'a bright peacock blue'.[37] About St Gabriel's, Reilly decided that: 'The inside, together with its electroliers, is derived, perhaps a little too directly, from the Högalid church. It is sweet and curved and kindly, with a beautifully lit altar in the distance, but it is not the inside the outside would lead one to expect.'[38]

An Italian flavour is also detectable in the modern work of the principal Roman Catholic architect working in Scotland, Jack Coia, who seems to have learned from Velarde the effectiveness of placing a massive wide western tower, in brick, on the street elevation of his churches, concealing the section of the building behind. At St Columbkille's in Rutherglen, the smooth plastered walls of the interior are pierced by Romanesque arches and end in an apse surrounding a ciborium which is as much Deco as Early Christian in inspiration; at St Columba's, Maryhill, the interior is dominated by transverse arches of Gothic profile. Coia was asked to design the Roman Catholic Pavilion at the 1938 Glasgow Empire Exhibition and, under the influence of Thomas Tait, used prefabricated asbestos panels on a structural frame to erect a clean, white box with an apse that rose higher than the nave. At this time, Coia was in partnership with T. Warnett Kennedy, who may have been largely responsible for St Peter in Chains at Ardrossan, where a campanile indebted to Stockholm Town Hall accompanies textured decorative brickwork perhaps deriving from Dutch Expressionism (Plate 8).

Many contemporaries were unhappy with these modernistic churches, so heavily indebted to buildings in Continental Europe. The complaint was often made that they looked more like factories and industrial buildings, while the novelty of their interiors seemed closely related to fashions in the interior design of cinemas. Some architects worried that such modernistic buildings failed to convey that sense of the familiar and shared Andrew Drummond's concern that there was nothing of the 'numinous' quality that conservative churchgoers found in Gothic. Maufe, for instance, was certain that 'we must get something more fundamental than fashion. In the cinema we may perhaps be forgiven for pandering to this jade, of talking glibly of features being "amusing", but I still think that in churches we should aim at the eternal.'[39]

Only a few architects were strongly influenced by these Continental experiments. 'Many queer buildings,' observed Goodhart-Rendel in his account of the churches of the 1930s, 'arose on the Continent after first war':

> experimental churches in France, ferocious churches in Germany and Austria, whimsical churches in Italy and Scandinavia. All of these have been copiously illustrated in the architectural press, and have been proposed by some for imitation in this country. The English church architect, however, while not disdaining to borrow from here or anywhere little bits that tickle his fancy, has in the main been unable and perhaps unwilling to embark on strange adventures. He has, in fact, usually gone on producing the sort of building he has been producing for some time; gentle more or less Romanesque simplicities with a great deal of whitewash inside and a nice touch of pure colour at the high altar.[40]

The same could be said of the many churches which might be described as gentle and more or less Gothic simplicities, like those by Edward Maufe. In 1932 Maufe won the competition for a new

Interior and detail, Cathedral Church of the Holy Spirit (Guildford Cathedral), Guildford, Surrey (Edward Maufe, 1936–65)

Anglican cathedral at Guildford. The result, tastefully modernistic and not completed until 1965, is impressive internally owing to the vistas afforded past the simplified white Gothic arcades, but externally the massing of the brick-faced walls seems bland. As Maufe claimed, 'Churches must not strike the eye with finality; we should not see everything at once – there should be a certain mystery – there should be spaces in which the imagination can play.'[41]

Maufe believed in a very English compromise between tradition and modernity. He designed two churches in London in simplified Gothic, as well as the somewhat absurd Religious Broadcasting Studio in Broadcasting House which was in modernistic Early Christian. His best church was St Thomas's, Hanwell, with sculpture by Eric Gill forming part of the west wheel window. Inside, simplified Gothic vaults spring from internal buttresses which are pierced by passage aisles, creating a space, defined by surfaces of rough white plaster, which seems at once modern and yet reassuringly traditional.

St Thomas the Apostle, Hanwell, Greater London (Edward Maufe, 1934)

Reilly thought the interior was inspired by Tengbom's church in Stockholm but was 'more angular and Gothic',

> and thereby draws a stronger appeal to tradition. . . . Indeed, in this interior of a not very large and not very expensive suburban church, Maufe, without a moulding or ornament of any kind, has achieved, so it seems to me, that combined solemnity and sense of upward striving which is of the very essence of great Gothic architecture.[42]

The best church architects of the period demonstrated an ability to develop the Gothic Revival tradition imaginatively to achieve a conspicuous but rational, intelligent modernity in expression. This was true of some of the churches of Giles Scott, such as St Andrew's, Luton, where there is a powerfully rugged and massive west tower terminating its length and the interior is articulated by transverse arches pierced by passage aisles and expressed externally as buttresses enlivened with careful 'nogging' of the beautiful brickwork facing. It was certainly true of Goodhart-Rendel himself, who in his churches paid respect to the Victorian Goths he so admired. 'Even the best Gothic detail nowadays has to be used very sparingly,' he observed, 'and as it were in inverted commas. It has ceased to have any constructional significance for us, and has become a stage property of religion.'[43]

The intelligence and sensitivity of Goodhart-Rendel's handling of traditional forms can be seen at St Wilfrid's, Brighton, a distinguished addition to the town's stock of fine Victorian churches.[44] Externally, the brick masses are subtly modelled without literal historical references; inside most surfaces were of concrete, with the position of walls, floor and ceiling determined by a section based on the twelve-sided shape of the old threepenny-bit coin.* 'Vaults having curved surfaces,' the architect later explained,

---

* St Wilfrid's has now been converted into flats following a public inquiry held in the early 1980s at which the Thirties Society opposed the proposal.

The former St Wilfrid's, Brighton, Sussex (H. S. Goodhart-Rendel, 1934), now flats

are natural only to construction in brick, stone or concrete without reinforcement; once metal is introduced into a fire-resisting ceiling, whether in the form of large members or small reinforcements, the logical form of a ceiling is extremely unlikely to be curved. Over the roof of [St Michael's], built in 1932, a ferro-concrete ceiling has been constructed whose shape consists of five sides of a dodecagon ... The only arches in this building are those that carry brick facing over small spans, for which purpose it was found that the old way of building was actually the cheapest and most convenient.[45]

Goodhart-Rendel's brick church at Hounslow was designed in a similar style but to a very different plan. Possibly inspired by Gill's church at Gorleston, it is centrally planned, but the interlocking segmental brick arches that define the central space are of round rather than pointed profile.

An ability to develop the Gothic was true even of A. E. Richardson, who, despite his predilection for rational neo-Classicism,

Church of the Holy Cross (extension to foregrounded medieval church), Greenford, Middlesex (A. E. Richardson, 1939)

modernised the Tudor vernacular in the new church of the Holy Cross at Greenford, designed like a streamlined barn to sit beside the medieval original. The horizontality of both roof planes and the clerestory of timber and leaded lights governs the form of the exterior, while inside, the space is dominated by the structure of massive timbers of Oregon pine, bolted together.

Above all, it was true of that most intelligent and resourceful modern church architect, N. F. Cachemaille-Day, whose churches at Gipton and Burnage reinterpreted the ideas of the great Victorians in terms of new materials. At Burnage, the apsidal end faces the street, the great curve of brick containing vestries below and an elevated Lady Chapel above reached by steps either side of the high altar: a slightly theatrical modernity is combined with brilliant planning and a monumental resonance appropriate for the building's purpose. 'Avoid the unusual for its own sake,' Cachemaille-Day wrote in 1933; 'being rooted in a tradition evolving naturally' was the best way of avoiding 'the self-consciousness which is apparent in so much modern art'.[46] With its flat roof,

Church of the Epiphany, Gipton, Leeds (N. F. Cachemaille-Day, 1938)

St Nicholas, Manchester (N. F. Cachemaille-Day, 1932)

intimidating massing and vertical emphasis, Cachemaille-Day's church of St Saviour in Eltham might seem his most conspicuously modern, yet its monumental, sublime brick exterior was surely inspired by the fortified brick cathedral at Albi (Plate 7). Synthesis was the aim, and this was most notably achieved by Lutyens's assistant, Shoosmith, in the monumental church for the military cantonments at Delhi. So many of the tendencies evident in British church architecture of the time were combined and resolved here with artistic success.

Surprisingly, for all the contemporary enthusiasm for Wren and the architecture of the Georgians, few new churches in Britain were designed in a pure Classical style. Nevertheless, a strong taste for the Classical manifested itself in the design of church furnishings, although these often elided in style with the Early Christian manner of so many new buildings. This Classicism was a product of a profound reaction against the Gothic Revival, with many extreme Anglo-Catholic clergy, in particular, tiring of the attempt to develop an English Catholic tradition and naïvely attempting to make their churches look more like the Roman Catholic ones they had seen in Southern Europe, stuffed with Baroque furnishings.

The desire to go 'Back to Baroque' was an extreme response to the general reaction against the Victorian age after the turn of the new century. It was promoted, in particular, by the Anglo-Catholic Society of SS. Peter and Paul (SSPP), founded in 1911, but the society's aims were to be seen not so much in new buildings but in transforming older Gothic ones. A number of fine Victorian churches were ruthlessly transformed, their red brick walls whitewashed to serve as a background to elaborate gilded neo-Baroque fittings. One conspicuous victim was Butterfield's St Augustine's, Queen's Gate, London, where the polychromatic interior was whitened in 1928 as a suitable setting for an extraordinary flattened Southern Baroque reredos designed by Martin Travers. As Peter Anson wrote:

> The Back to Baroque movement was contemporary with a similar change in domestic *décor*. Osbert Lancaster points out 'Curzon Street Baroque', which set the tone in house furnishings towards the end of the First World War, always had a markedly ecclesiastical note . . . There is a theatrical quality about most of these furnishings. They look best under artificial light, like stage scenery.[47]

Well might Peter Anson warn of the 'danger to-day that we may feel the urge to tamper with perfectly good work erected between 1850 and 1900 just because it has ceased to be fashionable'.[48] Only Goodhart-Rendel seemed to be able to treat Victorian Gothic churches with understanding and respect, as he demonstrated when he enlarged St Mary's on Bourne Street, London, in a modern red brick Gothic manner with hints both of William Burges and Continental Expressionism.

Travers, a former pupil of Comper, became the main artistic protégé of the SSPP. A versatile and enterprising draughtsman, designer and architect, he specialised in running up elaborate altars out of the cheapest of materials. He also designed a few buildings, in collaboration with T. F. W. Grant. The most convincing was the Church of the Good Shepherd, Carshalton, built in 1929–30. Inside, the rectangular space was covered by a plaster barrel vault of complex Baroque section; outside, despite the presence of a bellcote, the meanness of the whitewashed brick walls made the church look more like a small provincial cinema.[49] Travers's church does not compare well with St Alphage's at Hendon, a church of roughly the same date by Charles Nicholas and J. E. Dixon-Spain, where the basilican interior with passage aisles is impressively roofed by a plaster vault above cross beams resting on console brackets.

Had the twentieth century followed a different course, one of the most impressive churches of the period would have been entirely Classical. Indeed, it would have been not only one of the largest but one of the finest monumental buildings in the world; as it is, its extraordinarily accomplished and complex design remains 'the very greatest building that was never built!'[50] Lutyens's conception for Liverpool Roman Catholic cathedral was revealed in the magnificent model by John B. Thorp exhibited at the Royal Academy in 1934. The foundation stone had been laid the previous year, but when work stopped in 1941 only part of the crypt had been constructed. But the crypt alone, as finally opened in 1958, is one of the finest churches of its time, in which Lutyens's ability to handle architectural form

Crypt, Liverpool Metropolitan
Roman Catholic Cathedral, Liverpool
(Edwin Lutyens, 1933–58)

as elemental, abstract sculpture is supremely demonstrated. When Lutyens died, on New Year's Day 1944, drawings of his cathedral had been placed around his bed. He had thought it would take two centuries to achieve. In the event, Lutyens's design was abandoned, and after a dismal interlude with a miserable, cut-down Classical design by Giles Scott's brother Adrian, Frederick Gibberd's coarse parody of Oscar Niemeyer's circular cathedral for Brasilia was opened in 1967.

The Anglicans had won Liverpool's battle of the cathedrals, for although Gilbert Scott's last and most dramatic design of 1942 for the west end of his building was not carried out, it was essentially completed in 1978. When Scott abandoned his original design and the cathedral authorities accepted his monumental and classicised interpretation of Gothic in 1910, he had imposed the obligation of symmetry on posterity. With the central tower finished, the nave simply had to be built to balance the mass of the choir; the composition would have looked ridiculous if changed or left incomplete.

Scott had first submitted his 'Design for a Twentieth Century Cathedral' in 1901 and the building that was dedicated some eighty years later is surely one of the most magnificent architectural creations of the century. After the choir was dedicated in 1924, work on it proceeded continuously, with Scott constantly revising his design for the great central tower until he placed the last pinnacle on its summit in 1942. 'It may be bold to date the death of the Gothic Revival within the years in which the central tower of the Cathedral Church of Christ at Liverpool (1925) was beginning to rise, and yet that date appears certain,' wrote Goodhart-Rendel. 'Perhaps the tremendous

Bell Tower, Liverpool Anglican Cathedral, Liverpool (Giles Gilbert Scott, 1901–78)

tower that now crowns this great building may become of romantic architecture the venerated last resting-place.'[51]

But Goodhart-Rendel was, for once, wrong. At the beginning of the twenty-first century, a Perpendicular Gothic tower rose above Bury St Edmunds Cathedral to complete the design for enlarging

Liverpool Anglican Cathedral, Liverpool (Giles Gilbert Scott, 1901–78)

the medieval building prepared by Stephen Dykes Bower, whose first church, at Hockerill near Bishop's Stortford, had been built in 1936 and was, of course, Gothic. But this is a rather tame and derivative design compared with the soaring vigour of Giles Scott's tower in Liverpool – the city's principal landmark. It was a design rooted in precedent and yet modern in its interpretation of the style, for Scott succeeded in making Gothic his own, expressive language. As Charles Reilly, a close observer of the whole project, put it in 1929, 'A rather hard linear style of building has been softened and broadened into something again approaching the classical. He has thereby given new life to Gothic architecture, if Gothic is now the right name.'[52] The huge and continuing popular success of Scott's masterpiece affirmed the continuing importance of church architecture and of building to last.

CHAPTER NINE

THE SHAPE OF THINGS TO COME

'A NEW METHOD OF DESIGN is incredible, simply because it is not feasible,' insisted the *Country Life* writer Lawrence Weaver in 1922. 'We had our misfortunes a few years ago in that pursuit, but even before the war the "New Art" which pleased Germany and Austria so vastly was "dead and damned" in Great Britain.'[1] Weaver was soon proved wrong, of course, although it took some time for Continental modernism to have an impact on conservative Britain. The rise of this new architecture in public consciousness may easily be traced. By 1928 it was well enough known to be satirised by Evelyn Waugh in *Decline and Fall* and, that same year, Frederick Etchells, the translator of Le Corbusier, could write: 'The modern movement in architecture which has been so pronounced a feature in the post-war life of Europe has touched this country but little; but it is evident that the attempts to meet new conditions and in the use of modern materials and methods have aroused a great interest among us.'[2]

By 1933, the ideological battle between 'Traditionalists' and 'Modernists' was the theme of the Presidential Address at the RIBA and the subject of a debate printed in the BBC's journal, *The Listener*. In 1937, the Museum of Modern Art in New York could devote an exhibition to 'Modern Architecture in England' and there were enough examples built (forty-nine) for the architect F. R. S. Yorke to fill a book devoted to *The Modern House in England*.* When the outbreak of the Second World War brought building to a halt, this new method of design, the New Architecture, had caught the public imagination – or at least that of those who informed it. Soon after that war, the future Lord Esher looked back to the modernism of the 1930s and maintained that:

> It was the most sudden and complete architectural revolution ever known, and seemed in England even more sudden because we had seen none of its early development. It seemed to spring fully armed from the head of Gropius and Mendelssohn [*sic*] during their short stay in this country. It was a splendid cause to live and die for, and when it sank in the tidal wave of 1940 it was still pure and unalloyed by any trace of provincialism.[3]

Modern architecture was not a style, its partisans insisted, but a product of the spirit of the age, a means of transforming society. This story can therefore be seen as the slow but inevitable triumph of the architectural expression of the twentieth century, of a new age. Indeed, this has been the conventional way of interpreting the 1920s and 1930s. As John Summerson put it in 1959:

> It seems natural writing about the past thirty years of English architecture, to write as if the only things worth bothering

---

* 'In 1934,' the author explained, 'when *The Modern House* was first published, it was difficult to find material to fill the fourteen pages devoted in this book to English Examples. Within a little more than two years there were enough modern houses in this country to provide material for a double number of the *Architectural Review*, and now, within three years, it is possible to produce a book devoted to English houses only' (Yorke (1937), p. 16).

about were the local initiation, progress and achievements of the 'modern movement'. Historically, this is evidently lop-sided; but also, historically, it would be extremely difficult to write about the architecture of the period as if it could all be evaluated in much the same way. It cannot be. In architecture, as in poetry and sculpture, there has been a wide and deep gulf between the moderns and those who are vaguely and rather misleadingly described as traditionalists.[4]

A gulf was certainly there but, over half a century later, it does not seem as wide as it once did, nor do the certainties of that Modern Movement seem transcendent. Not only is it now possible to assess both traditional and modern buildings of the period by the same architectural criteria, but there were many architects deserving of respect who, with a greater or lesser degree of success, attempted to straddle the gulf.

Instead of the architecture of the period being examined in terms of polarised categories, it can now be seen to be more of a spectrum, with ideas and motifs from Continental modernism being gradually adopted for a wide range of buildings as time passed. There certainly was an architecture of the Modern Movement – that 'International Style' – as the Americans, Henry-Russell Hitchcock and Philip Johnson, labelled it in 1932 – which was defined by the propaganda of its adherents and by the distinctive reinforced-concrete, flat-roofed aesthetic sympathetically caricatured by Osbert Lancaster as the 'Twentieth-Century Functional' style. This was, as one partisan critic put it, 'the work of those who have been able entirely to throw over bondage to Georgianism and the fading influence of the Stockholm Town Hall and belong to the international school of which Le Corbusier is evangelist-in-chief'.[5] However, Nikolaus Pevsner, in his unpublished 1939 survey of 'The Modern Movement', could also include such buildings as the bow-windowed modernistic blocks of flats by Atkinson & Alexander north of Regent's Park, the horizontally streamlined Comet Inn at Hatfield by E. B. Musman, and the stripped-Classical Piccadilly Line stations by Adams, Holden & Pearson – all built of brick – as examples of 'the specifically British approach to the Modern Movement in some of its implications'.[6]

It was, nevertheless, the Functional style, or the 'Ultra-Modern', 'a style of which any thoughtless disparagement is to be heartily deplored', 'as a means rather than an end', which became the concern of both the propagandists of Modernism and its critics.[7] Pevsner insisted that 'this new style of the twentieth century' was to become universal, as it was 'a genuine style as opposed to a passing fashion'.[8] However, the significance of the phenomenon should not be measured by the associated rhetoric. Even in 1939, this new architecture represented only a small proportion of new British architecture as a whole, and those forty-nine flat-roofed houses, for all their conspicuous modernity, might well seem to recede in importance in the wider context of the four million new homes built between the wars. As J. M. Richards admitted, in his *Introduction to Modern Architecture*:

> To-day the most urgent problem before the modern architect in England is not one of perfecting his ideas in theory, but one of getting opportunities to put his theories into practice. For the optimistic statement . . . that England is now the headquarters of modern architecture, though not untrue, does not mean even that any considerable proportion of the new architecture in England is what we have been calling modern. A walk down any city street that has been the scene of recent building activity will show a strange mixture of style.[9]

Nor had modernism in general really won over the wider public. As John Summerson privately admitted in 1940, 'I think modern architecture will have to beat a retreat, simply because the public can't understand it, never will, and hates it like poison.'[10]

The uncomfortable fact was that the New Architecture was only really acceptable for particular building types (factories, health-centres and places for entertainment, as well as houses) and in particular places. The building of ultra-modern houses met with strong opposition from many local authorities and, on the whole, the pioneering manifestations of the British Modern Movement are to be found in what might be described as fringe conditions: by the seaside or in zoos or in peculiar locations. It should also be borne in mind that if England had become 'the headquarters of modern architecture' by the end of the 1930s, this was not so much due to the achievements of native designers but largely to the presence of several talented designers born overseas in parts of the British Empire, powerfully augmented by the galaxy of experienced Continental architects who found homes and refuge across the Channel during the first half of the decade.

The new conditions which gave rise to this conspicuously new architecture were social as well as structural. One in particular was the desire for more sunlight, considered to be essential for health and enabled by developments in the manufacture of plate glass. 'The sunlight cult, already powerful on the Continent, is still embryonic in England, where climate and the vestigial respectability that still denotes our Victorian ancestry check its development,' wrote John Gloag in 1931:

> Nevertheless, many people unconnected with medical work are now actively conscious of the therapeutic benefits of natural ultra-violet radiation conferred by sunlight and all unobstructed daylight. . . . This latter tendency has been accelerated by the invention of glass that admits a large proportion of the ultra-violet rays in daylight, and the modern window may continue to expand for health as in the Gothic churches it expanded for holiness.[11]

A decade later, Julian Leathart could write how:

> During the last quarter of a century the mode of living has tended to change; this change has been brought about by the increased pace and tension of life, and the advance of the science of hygiene.

> It may be said that, physically speaking, there is now a more healthy outlook to-day than in pre-war times. No longer is fresh air associated solely with chilling draughts, no longer is a healthy, vigorous body regarded as a manifestation of an undesirable paganism, and considered to be slightly indecent – the age of the vapours and the discreetly draped piano leg has gone for good.[12]

This cult of the sun, of the hygienic, of the physical, was certainly exploited in the New Architecture. As Osbert Lancaster noted in his caricature of 'Twentieth-Century Functional', 'the new architects could seldom resist making a house fit for purposes such as sun-bathing, which the English climate and environment frequently rendered impossible of fulfilment'.[13] The desire for more sunlight in buildings,* however, was certainly not confined to Modern Movement architects but was an aspect of the spirit of the age. It was associated with the new scientific, hygienic attitude to life, and went with libertarian fashions introduced from Weimar Germany: sun-bathing, nudism and hiking. As Robert Graves and Alan Hodge described in *The Long Week-End*:

> Sun-bathing had originally been found useful in Germany to cure children of 'deficiency diseases' caused by the British blockade and by the severities of the post-war years. It had now become a general cure-all, in disregard of its stupefying effect on the minds of most of its addicts, and the warning of doctors that long exposure to the sun's rays weakened the resistance of the skin to infection.[14]

In truth, a large, counterbalanced timber Georgian sash window could let in as much light, and air, as a sliding pane of plate glass framed in metal, and was, in many ways, more practical. A belief in

---

* When Lancaster illustrated the equivalent 'Functional' interior the following year for *Homes Sweet Homes*, he took care to draw heavy rain falling on the terrace visible through the big picture-window.

the healthiness of fresh air, in contrast to the perceived 'stuffiness' of Victorian interiors, was shared by Traditionalists and Modernists alike. Outdoor sleeping porches were a common feature of Arts and Crafts houses before the Great War, and even Sir Giles Scott included one in his own modern neo-Regency house in Bayswater in the 1920s. Some went further, and responded to the cult of fresh air by advocating open-air schools for 'delicate' children, even in the winter.* As for schools whose buildings had walls as well as roofs and floors, their architecture, often neo-Georgian in style, reflected these priorities. Emphasis was placed on the provision of light and air. In the years just before the Second World War, the Modern Movement began to influence the design of schools, although, as one accomplished school architect later concluded, 'the change mainly took the form of a revolt against the Neo-Georgian treatment as such, and amounted to little more than the exchange of one architectural style for another'.[15] Denis Clarke Hall, who won the competition for an ideal school organised by the *News Chronicle* newspaper in 1937, designed the impressive Richmond Girls' High School in Yorkshire. Yet, as Alan Powers has written, in discussing the social purpose of Modernism:

> Modernists believed that their way of building alone would achieve the best results, but a non-partisan comparison between, say, the neo-Georgian Sawston Village College† near Cambridge of 1930 and Walter Gropius's Impington of ten years later showed that the programme had not changed in essence, and that while the spacious, informal layout of Impington produced tangible benefits in such skilled hands, Sawston, practically speaking, was nearly as good.[16]

---

* There were 155 such schools in England and Scotland just before the Second World War (see Brian Cathcart, 'School's Out', *Independent on Sunday* magazine, 23 January 2005).

† Sawston was designed by H. H. Dunn, Cambridgeshire County Architect, for the educational reformer Henry Morris, who later commissioned Impington Village College.

Sawston Village College, Sawston, Cambridgeshire (H. H. Dunn, 1930)

The contemporary emphasis on health, fitness and exercise had another architectural consequence in the building of many new swimming pools. 'The sudden popularity of swimming, the result of a tidal wave of mass-suggestion,' opined the *Architectural Review* in 1932, 'created an apparently insatiable demand for what stalwart Victorian pioneers used to call "bathing facilities" both under cover and in the open air. Concrete provides the most economic and satisfying material for all types of waterside and underwater construction.'[17] Many indoor pools were covered by a roof with stepped bands of glazing supported by reinforced-concrete transverse paraboloid arches, an industrial form popularised by its use for the Royal Horticultural Halls in London. One good example is the public swimming baths in Northampton which opened in 1936. It is significant that the celebrated Pioneer Health Centre in Peckham, that experiment in human biology designed by the engineer Owen Williams in reinforced concrete, had its facilities grouped around a central swimming pool. Many local authorities also built open-air pools or lidos. The buildings surrounding such pools were sometimes

Classical but often Modernistic in style, with the structural and sculptural possibilities of reinforced concrete exploited in tall and elaborate diving stages.[18] The Modern Movement was but one, albeit distinct and coherent, manifestation of the spirit of the age.

Behind all this lay a profound reaction against the Victorian Age, a perceived touchstone for darkness, dirt, clutter, oppression, prudery and any other possible vice. But the principal reason for the adoption and development of a new architecture, self-consciously divorced from tradition, was the deep trauma of the Great War. As Raymond McGrath reflected twenty years after the outbreak of hostilities, the loss to architecture in terms of individuals was incalculable, but the effect on those who survived was manifested partly in that 'burning desire for sunlight and clean air and clean thought'.[19] Not only did the war divide the Victorian and Edwardian ages from the present, it discredited the old ways and split the generations. 'The war years had left little of the old tradition,' R. A. Duncan found, as an instructor at the Architectural Association in 1918. 'Continuity had been broken, and it all had to begin again at the beginning.' As for the intake who had returned from the trenches, they were different. 'Doctrinaire ideas could not be rammed down the throats of these students. They might listen respectfully, but they acquired no beliefs in the old faiths.'[20]

They rebelled against Goodhart-Rendel's attempt to reintroduce a Beaux-Arts model of education at the AA. No wonder that they became committed to an architecture that promised to transform society:

> Only through a knowledge of how social relations operate can we work effectively for change, recognising the forces that are pitted against change, and the forces that fly off unproductively at a tangent. And only the knowledge of the necessity of change, of how we may attain it, and of the technical and human liberation that it can open up for society, can give us the pattern for our action in the future, and the faith and energy to continue.[21]

Many older architects sympathised. 'The accusation against the modern style that it is revolutionary may best be met by admitting that it is *meant* to be revolutionary,' wrote Julian Leathart:

> Why should architecture be considered inviolable to the ever-changing conditions of modern life? Why should it be detached from the reality of existence and be doomed to remain the agency through which is transferred the past into the future in fixed and immutable form to mislead posterity? If it is to mirror the social conditions of its age, as have all past epoch-making architectural styles, it *must* change.[22]

The experience of the war, combined with rapid scientific and technological advances and the disturbing experience of economic depression after 1929, lay behind the widespread conviction that society had changed and was still changing, radically and irreversibly; that existing institutions and methods were failing; that modern life was unstable and dynamic. This was an outlook manifested by an architecturally conservative commentator such as Harold P. Clunn, as well as by Modernists such as R. A. Duncan in his messianic 1933 tract, *The Architecture of a New Era*. 'There is to-day a searching of hearts and minds,' he concluded, 'and in spite of the uncertainty, there are many who believe that we stand at the threshold of a new era of progress, peace and prosperity.'[23] 'The art of building has its roots in contemporary economic, producing and social conditions,' insisted F. R. S. Yorke:

> The majority of present-day towns and buildings appear as travesties of the towns and buildings of former times, but . . . there has been a revolution in the conditions that give rise to the forms of architecture. If the buildings have, in spite of such changes, old faces, these must be spurious and their architectural expression an anachronism.[24]

As for Pevsner, he was convinced that he was living in 'a century the precision of which leaves less space for self-expression than did any period before', and that it was 'the creative energy of this world in which we live and work and which we want to master, a world of science and technique, of speed and danger, of hard struggles and no personal security, that is glorified in Gropius's architecture'.[25]

Walter Gropius, who came to England in 1934, was born in 1883. Any architect of his generation had grown up in a very different world. By the time he had reached the age of forty he had not only experienced a devastating world war but had seen the advent of the motor car, the aeroplane, the telephone, electric light and power, the radio and the cinema, as well as the machine gun, the submarine and the tank. And now even television was being talked of. The mass-ownership of cars was opening up the countryside, encouraging the growth of suburbs and the rebuilding of older city centres; air travel was developing rapidly and becoming safe and almost conventional, while the very nature of social relations was being transformed by the comparative liberation of newly enfranchised women. 'If in 1913 I had suddenly been transported through time to 1938,' wrote John Gloag in his foreword to Hugh Casson's 'Handy Guide to Contemporary Architecture', 'I should have imagined that I had travelled at least a century into the future, for the change in the scale and character of London streets and buildings, the shape of the vehicles and the rarity of the horse, would have made the present seem like some remote fantasy by H. G. Wells.'[26] No wonder many architects were excited by new possibilities while others became alarmed and defensive.

In 1927, in an article on 'Modern Decoration', Grey Wornum listed 'some of the factors in our mode of life today' which were transforming the nature of domestic architecture:

- Reduction of servant labour.
- Smaller meals, smaller kitchens, smaller homes. Large open spaces.

- More daylight, better night light.
- Better heating, ventilation, sanitation.
- Discredit of dust-collecting features.
- Improved fire prevention.
- More freedom of the sexes.
- Drawing room accessible to all, for smoking, drinking and recreation.
- Generally a more communal sense, less desire for privacy.
- Abolition of heavily-curtained windows, high garden walls, and long useless corridors.
- Then there is the strain of living itself.
- More noise, more speed, more mechanical occupation.

These factors create a desire for as little burden of possession as possible. They demand the dramatic for diversion, and the extremely simple for repose.[27]

Such was the gradual but radical change since the calmer days of the Victorians and Edwardians, against the perceived clutter and stuffiness with which the modern world was so often and so tediously contrasted.

Twelve years on, Oliver Hill usefully summarised the effect that new materials and methods of construction had had on architecture:

Within the last two decades the demands of modern life and the invention and scope of modern industry have completely changed methods of building, and enable us to cover immense spans with slender supports and cantilever our façades with freedom and economy. . . .

We can place the windows of each room independently, wherever the aspect or view dictates, long, sliding, landscape-embracing windows of convenient height which tend towards reposeful horizontality. Supports, being concentrated at certain points, have freed our walls from supporting loads, and their function is merely that of enclosing screens to admit or exclude light and air.

The new materials, the product of the engineer, chemist and machine – concrete, steel, glass, rubber, cork, asbestos, plyboard, plastics and the metallic alloys having cleanable and durable surfaces – each with its own intrinsic beauty of colour and texture, needing no embellishment, provide the forms we use. The requirements of to-day and the profound influence of the machine-made article which makes for precision, have been utilized by sensitive designers and compound the new aesthetic. Clarification of purpose, the elimination of the inessential and disencumbrance from the pomposities of the past are the keynotes of the contemporary house.[28]

F. R. S. Yorke naturally agreed: 'Concrete, steel, glass, rubber, cork, and modern metallic alloys, which neither rust nor oxidise, all have their own beauty, their own colour and their own texture; and these qualities, with the new forms, compound the new aesthetic.'[29]

The principal structural innovations which had transformed architecture were the steel frame and reinforced-concrete construction. These, of course, were not exclusively associated with the Modern Movement. Intelligent architects had for decades been concerned with the honest expression of the steel frame and had sought ways to reconcile its structural geometry with traditional architectural languages. Smith & Brewer and A. E. Richardson, in particular, sought to adapt the Classical language to create a rectilinear, trabeated style of masonry treatment, with a careful hierarchy of vertical and horizontal elements reflecting columns and cornices, which did not deny the existence of the underlying grid of steel. Other architects relied on a more Gothic treatment, stressing the verticals. As for reinforced concrete, its formal possibilities seemed almost infinite, but the search for its rational expression was complicated by the fact that many pioneering buildings whose bare walls and horizontal lines suggested an aesthetic generated by concrete were actually constructed of rendered brickwork and so were not 'honest' at all.

'The horizontal motif may perhaps arise from a certain sense of horizontal movement in everyday life – rapid transit, a constant outward growth, a movement to include in one's orbit distant things and places,' Howard Robertson suggested in his book on *Modern Architectural Design*:

> A sense of amplitude is conveyed by long horizontal sweeps; and this is in remote, but nevertheless definite, accord with the presence on the modern mental horizon of big ideas and wider understanding... In the same way, continuous vertical lines have their architectural devotees. They soar, they suggest unchecked and swift movement; above all, in the same way as long horizontals, they convey the impression of continuity, and hence of unity.[30]

On their architectural tour of Northern Europe in 1930 in search of useful ideas for adoption on the London Underground system, Frank Pick, Charles Holden and W. P. N. Edwards found that both the vertical and the horizontal were stressed by modern Continental designers. 'The steel skeleton and reinforced concrete frame,' concluded Edwards, 'introduced entirely new factors, requiring a radical re-orientation of our attitude to architecture and, to some extent, postulating the evolution of a new style':

> Nor is this entirely unexpected. All the great styles – Greek, Byzantine and Gothic – were largely the result of the discovery of a new constructive principle, and now that we in our turn have discovered a new principle of structure, it seems reasonable to suppose that it will to some extent require, and ultimately produce, a new style.[31]

But Edwards also appreciated that no definitive solutions had yet been produced: 'One fact only seems certain. The architects of the new order have almost unanimously rejected traditional forms of ornament and decoration. But in their place there seems to be yet no common agreement as to what is the most appropriate treatment for the covering of the steel or ferro-concrete frame.'[32] More cautious Modernists realised that there would have to be more to any new style than pure structural expression. Howard Robertson wondered what was actually meant by the word 'honesty' in an architectural context:

> Is it honest to expose stanchions, girders, and rivets to the corrosion of the atmosphere, for the sake of showing that they exist? Is it dishonest to clothe them in a protective veneer of stone or brick or terra-cotta, thus complying with the practical requirements of maintenance and incidentally with the building code? Is it necessary in building to show complicated details and joints, any more than it is necessary to abolish the bonnet of the motor car in order that the passer-by may see the motor and all its adjuncts?[33]

As far as H. S. Goodhart-Rendel was concerned, 'No true architect can become the slave of stanchions and girders,' and he denied that 'any design revealing construction is intrinsically better than any other in which construction has to be guessed at'.[34]

Goodhart-Rendel, wisest of critics and most learned of architects, was certainly no conservative traditionalist. In his Hay's Wharf offices overlooking the Thames near London Bridge, he attempted to provide a solution to the problem of structural expression in a modern commercial building. The result, built in 1930–31, is a most stylish and representative building of the period which has been categorised as Deco but also hailed as a pioneering British Modern Movement achievement. Forty years on, it was selected by Pevsner as one of the first batch of interwar buildings to be listed. More recently, Alan Powers has written that at Hay's Wharf, 'Goodhart-Rendel answered the challenge of Modernism by rationalizing the

St Olaf House, Hay's Wharf, London (H. S. Goodhart-Rendel, 1931)

frame construction and cladding, and reinventing ornament from basic geometry in a version of Art Deco derived from medieval Gothic.'[35] The architect himself explained how 'the enclosed storeys had to be raised over an open car-park, and an attempt has been made to reconcile this necessity with an architectural expression of stability by shaping the stanchion casings so as to suggest that they are threaded through the structure like posts through a scaffold'.[36] The faceting and fluting of the horizontal bands of fenestration both acknowledged Modernist precedents and provided a further decorative effect. Once, when asked what style the building was in, Goodhart-Rendel replied that it was in the 'Early French Gothic style' – a perversely cryptic remark that (as Alan Powers plausibly suggests) may refer to the French rationalist tradition associated with Viollet-le-Duc, as manifested by the ascending pattern of windows reflecting the interior disposition of a staircase.[37]

Steel and concrete may have been instrumental in the development of Modern Architecture but such forms of construction, first developed towards the end of the previous century, were not essential for it. The material which had most impact on the new style was glass. 'The Glass Age Arrives,' announced the manufacturers Pilkington Brothers in 1934. Glass, of course, was scarcely new, and it can be argued that the advent of plate glass had had a much greater impact on the architecture of the preceding century, but this advertisement cited the different types of glass which could be used on an 'imaginary residential tower'.[38] Glass technology was certainly making rapid advances and glass was now available in larger sheets than ever before, while it could also be coloured as 'Vitrolite'. Masonry façades could now be made to appear to float above continuous shop windows of plate glass, while the picture window adopted for houses broke with the conventions of both Tudor and Georgian. Framed construction could allow buildings to be completely sheathed in glass, as with the spectacular black Vitrolite and clear glass-clad new offices for the *Daily Express* newspaper in Fleet Street, or, a few years later, the Peter Jones store in Sloane Square.

'It is etched, sand-blasted and engraved,' enthused Raymond Myerscough-Walker in describing the new materials available to the architect. 'Brilliant cutting and colour sprayed. Shop fronts are becoming symphonies in glass, and in Fleet Street we are treated with a modern newspaper office exuding a twentieth-century ostentation in black glass.'[39] Glass seemed the answer to almost every architectural problem, while expressing the spirit of the age. Perhaps it was rather unkind of Julian Leathart to point out that:

> Now that machine-manufacturing processes have been developed so that glass is both cheap and obtainable in large sizes, there no longer remains the vestige of a reason for perpetuating the undersized glass pane and window opening. So much can be acknowledged. The entirely glazed wall which is an accentuated expression of the freedom in planning arising from the concrete constructional system, needs more justification than this, however. Of all building materials, glass offers the least resistance to thermal and sound penetration, and the glazed opening which stretches from wall to wall and from ceiling to ceiling ensures frigid indoor temperatures in winter and torrid heat in summer.[40]

The properties and possibilities of glass were celebrated in the lavishly illustrated book on *Glass in Architecture and Decoration* published in 1937 and compiled by Raymond McGrath and A. C. Frost. 'Glass has,' they wrote, 'reached a point where even its remarkable versatility almost ceases to astonish. It has reached the point where its absence is more noticeable than its presence. It has arrived.'[41] McGrath was one of the first architects to exploit the decorative possibilities not just of glass but the many new laminates, plywoods, plastics, wallboards and new metals available to the profession.[42] This he did first inside an early Victorian villa in Cambridge, creating a famous interior which – exactly halfway between the two world wars – became a catalyst for change. In 1927 this house, renamed Finella, had been leased by Mansfield Forbes, a charismatic don who, as a Fellow of Clare College, had been instrumental in Sir Giles Scott's appointment to design Memorial Court. In that same year, Forbes had met McGrath, a young Australian architect and designer, and persuaded him to come to Cambridge to do research on 'Modern Entertainment Architecture'. This dissertation was never completed, as McGrath and Forbes became absorbed by the creation of Finella the following year.

The house was notable for its imaginative use of glass and other new, bright materials. 'A clean modernity of pure line and plane and clear tones of colour is the sole key of her architecture; light and the overlooked beauty of metal and glass make up the rest,' wrote Frost, McGrath's brother-in-law, in the *Architectural Review*.[43] 'The hall was roofed with green glass,' McGrath himself later wrote,

> its walls covered with metal leaf, and the floor done in a polished black mixed substance of wood powder and asbestos. At the far end the wall was completely covered with gold-leaf glass through which there was a door opening into the south of two rooms joined by folding copper doors. Glass of different sorts and colours was used in the room for meals, the coat-room off the hall, and the three bath-rooms. All this glass was designed in relation to the lighting, and between them they gave the house a feeling of clear space and delicate colouring by night and by day.[44]

The interiors at Finella might today seem as much Art Deco as Modern, but the house deserves its celebrity because of the stimulus it gave to realising the New Architecture in Britain (Plate 32). It was experienced by a surprising number of visitors – 30,000 by 1932, according to one reckoning.[45] Its admirers included many influential figures. Forbes enjoyed entertaining and his house was designed as a meeting place, which, as McGrath wrote in 1934, 'in its short history has certainly seen the birth of a number of new ideas and important organizations'.[46] It also launched McGrath's own career. It was, however, Sir Giles Scott who recommended McGrath to Sir John Reith, the high-minded Director-General of the British Broadcasting Corporation.[47]

The BBC had been founded in 1922 as a company licensed by the Postmaster-General to regularise and develop the new medium of radio. In 1928 it had acquired an awkward site in Langham Place, originally proposed for an hotel, from a syndicate which also supplied the architect Lt-Col G. Val Myer. Thanks to McGrath, however, the interiors of the big Portland stone battleship which rose next to John Nash's All Souls' Church were very different in character

Broadcasting House, Portland Place, London (G. Val Myer, 1932)

from the rather incoherent Classical-Deco elevations and public spaces designed by Myer. In 1930 – the year McGrath won the competition for an apartment for an imaginary client, organised by the *Architectural Review*[48] – he was asked to co-ordinate the interior design and brought in like-minded modern designers: Wells Coates and Serge Chermayeff. Responding to purely functional briefs and using plywoods, plastics, fabric and tubular steel, the three created striking and stylish colourful interiors for broadcasting that were widely publicised, the first case of public patronage for unashamedly modern design. As Robert Byron wrote in the special issue of the *Architectural Review* devoted to the BBC building:

> To see a great public corporation making some effort, however belated, to use the real talent available in this country has become a rare spectacle and one for which . . . it is impossible not to be grateful. Owing to the conscious antagonism between Traditionalism and Modernism which prevails at the present time, and to the issue of false but none the less influential morality

which by some obscure English means have become involved in it, the action of the BBC in employing specifically Modernist decorators has been a courageous one.[49]

Windowless, soundproofed and insulated from the outside by a peripheral corridor, the BBC studios could not exploit the possibilities of glass, but McGrath's enthusiasm for the material did not wane, and it culminated in *Glass in Architecture and Decoration*. This magnificent book not only promoted the innovative use of glass in modern buildings but also contributed to what became the myth of the Crystal Palace as the one worthwhile and progressive example of architecture in the backward-looking Victorian Age. Photographs of Joseph Paxton's vast glazed structure on the summit of Sydenham Hill showed it as it looked before its tragic destruction by fire in 1936. And a poignant photograph of the ruin was used as the frontispiece of the Museum of Modern Art's book on *Modern Architecture in England*. It had been, wrote Henry-Russell Hitchcock, 'the most prophetic monument of the mid-nineteenth century, a monument

Interior, Broadcasting House, Portland Place, London (Raymond McGrath, Wells Coates and Serge Chermayeff, 1932)

often hailed with pardonable exaggeration as the first modern building'.[50] It was the building Erich Mendelsohn had asked to see when he first came to England. 'Let's Build Another One!' argued John Betjeman immediately after the fire:*

> It is an emblem of all that was best in the great Victorian age, when England was prosperous and full of hope: when she was bolder than she is now. Remember, too, that though the Crystal Palace was built in 1851, it is still the most modern building in the country. There would be nothing sentimental in rebuilding this greatest of Victorian cathedrals.[51]

An architecture of glass opened up another dramatic possibility owing to the development of another new technology, that of electric lighting. Here was another manifest aspect of modernity. Not only was electric light becoming more powerful and adaptable, but it also allowed exterior illumination from within. No longer were buildings to be conceived in terms of the highlights and shadows cast by the sun, since, as R. A. Duncan put it, 'the night effect of a building artificially illuminated becomes almost as important as the normal daylight appearance'.[52] In 1931, the *Architectural Review* carried an article on 'The Architecture of Night' because 'Cinemas, theatres and public houses, whose duty it is to attract the crowds in streets after dark, have found it necessary to make use of a new architecture – the architecture of artificial light' (although, in truth, this was something achieved in the nineteenth century by the gas-lit 'gin palace').[53]

'London at night is no longer lapped in sullen brooding,' found Thomas Burke. 'It shines. It is a proud and burnished London, dressed for social life. Throughout its centre it offers white avenues, all of light, and elsewhere are caverns and recesses of gold and diamond.... Much of the modern brilliance is due not only to municipal operators

---

* I am grateful to Jan Piggott for this reference.

but to the advertisers and their night-signs' – which tended to distress some austere Modernists.[54] This was seized on by the more intelligent designers. To make them beacons by night as well as by day, Charles Holden designed large London Underground symbols, internally lit, to enhance the new stations on the Piccadilly Line, and Osterley Station had a strange pinnacle, partly formed of glass blocks rising above its tower which became illuminated at night. Electric lighting was fully integrated into the architecture. The master of this was Oliver P. Bernard, who, at the Strand Palace Hotel, created balustrades of glass enclosing electric lighting and illuminated glass columns, lit from within.

Electricity was an essential ingredient for both Art Deco and Modernist architecture. Owen Williams at the *Daily Express* in Fleet Street succeeded in combining the two. At night, electric light illuminated the bands of clear glass between the areas of black Vitrolite,* while more subtle lighting made Atkinson's spectacular exotic Art Deco entrance hall seem all the more extraordinary when seen from Fleet Street. But at Williams's other, similar, glass buildings for the *Daily Express* in Manchester and Glasgow, the electric lighting made visible to night-time passers-by the working printing presses within. The function of the building was made manifest, and the function was industrial; machines were celebrated in a mechanistic architecture. Functionalism aspired to the efficiency displayed by machines whose form was governed solely by function, although, to be fair, no serious modern architect ever maintained that functionalism alone was enough – architecture was an art as well.[55] Even so, as Alan Powers has written, 'For some, one feels, Modernism represented an easy solution to the hard thinking required for understanding the complexity of combining form and content in architecture. The answer could be simply to leave the content out and focus on "efficiency".'[56]

---

* According to Andrew Saint, it was Bertram Gallannaugh of Ellis & Clarke who was 'said to have suggested and certainly detailed the cladding of black vitrolite and glass' (Saint (2007), p. 264).

Images of mechanical efficiency were horribly seductive, however. 'It is perhaps interesting to compare architecture with other structures which our age has produced,' argued the modernist Joseph Emberton, somewhat simplistically, in 1933:

> Take, for example, the aeroplane, motor-car, liner or omnibus, for it seems to me that a building is as much a machine to work in, or to live in, as these are for transport. These have all produced beautiful – or, at least, satisfactory – forms, without much thought having been given to aesthetic effect. In many cases the quality of beauty is directly related to efficiency.[57]

F. R. S. Yorke preached a similar message, maintaining: 'It is significant that the modern aesthetic of architecture is born elsewhere than in the ateliers of architects. It is born in factories and laboratories, in places where new things for daily use, without precedent, are created; where tradition has no influence, and there is no aesthetic prejudice.'[58] And Anthony Bertram, in his book on *Design*, was quite clear about 'what a house ought to be – a common-sense thing fulfilling practical needs, like a fountain-pen, a bicycle or a telephone'. It should also have beauty, 'not the beauty of the past, but a new beauty, a new pattern expressing the new rhythm of life'.[59] And in his introduction to his translation of Le Corbusier's *Towards a New Architecture*, Frederick Etchells was anxious to demonstrate that such ideas were already in the air, quoting an advertisement in the *Architects' Journal* in 1925 that claimed: 'The modern hospital is a triumph of the elimination of the detrimental and the unessential. Because of its absolute fitness to purpose, its operation theatre – like the engine room of an ocean liner – is one of the most perfect rooms in the world.'[60]

The equation of architectural purpose with simplicity and efficiency had a long history, stretching back through W. R. Lethaby and the Arts and Crafts movement into the previous century, but the principal origin of such commonplace thinking was Le Corbusier, who claimed that engineers were now producing the best and most efficient architecture and postulated his notorious aphorism that 'The house is a machine for living in'. After 1927, when his polemic became available in English, the British architect could read how:

> We must create the mass-production spirit.
> The spirit of constructing mass-production houses.
> The spirit of living in mass-production houses.
> The spirit of conceiving mass-production houses.
> If we eliminate from our hearts and minds all dead concepts in regard to the houses and look at the question from a critical and objective point of view, we shall arrive at the 'House-Machine', the mass-production house, healthy (and morally so too) and beautiful in the way that the working tools and instruments which accompany our existence are beautiful.[61]

But the message was clear even without the text because of the brilliant use of illustrations: photographs of grain-silos, ocean liners and aeroplanes, and of motor cars juxtaposed tellingly with Ancient Greek temples.

It was not only Arts and Crafts architects, ideologically opposed to the values of mass-production, who argued against this modernist simplification. The fallacy that architecture is but engineering was attacked by, amongst others, John Gloag, who argued in 1931 that Le Corbusier, 'Like a true modern . . . cannot see beyond the machines that were created for service and not for adoration. "We claim, in the name of the steamship, of the airplane, and of the motor-car, the right to health, logic, daring, harmony, perfection." Why not claim the right in the name of man?'[62]

A subtly telling analysis of functionalist machine worship was offered by Goodhart-Rendel in 1934:

> Now nobody much minds how grandfather used to go on, but father's little follies generally seem to us particularly pitiful. When father liked his little bit of fluff he was dooming us inevitably to

the sentimental starkness of our present fancy. Moreover his little bit of fluff was perhaps rather cheap fluff; the poor man had not time to make a careful choice. Starkness on the other hand is too negative often to give its perpetrator away. I have called starkness 'sentimental' a few lines back because it seems to me obvious that what the young man of to-day feels for aeroplanes and reinforced concrete is just as emotionally irrational as what the young man of yesterday used to feel for farm-carts and hand-wrought oak. Both feelings have been earnestly but unconvincingly 'rationalised' – in the psycho-analyst's sense of that term; aeroplanes and reinforced concrete being made to express an Age of Progress and what not, and farm-carts and oak bringing us socialist News from Nowhere. I do not think that either of the two theories thus brought into being has any lasting validity, but I think that the sentiment that gave them birth has been aesthetically productive of much for which we can be grateful.[63]

A notable, and brutal, deflation of 'this most mischievous fallacy' came from old Sir Reginald Blomfield, who, curiously, advised on the design of the National Grid's standard electricity pylon, and who wrote in his sharp attack on *Modernismus*:

That some forms of mechanical construction have an accidental beauty of their own under certain conditions, one may readily admit; a great liner, for example, coming towards one on a sunlit sea, or the fine thin lines of steel construction, such as cranes or electric towers and the like; but change the mechanical object and the argument falls to pieces. Big Bertha, for example, could drop a shell into Paris from a range of thirty miles, undoubtedly efficient but unspeakably ugly. The engine of a French express can do its seventy or eighty miles an hour, or whatever is asked of it in the way of traction, but it is about as unsightly and squalid an object as it would be possible to find.[64]

Blomfield was, of course, an avowed enemy of Modernism, but even sympathetic observers, like Aldous Huxley, could find the mechanistic, functional imagery of Modernism tiresome, complaining that, 'to dine off an operating table, to loll in a dentist's chair – this is not my ideal of domestic bliss'.[65]

But, for younger architects, there was no resisting the seductive images presented by Le Corbusier. Not only did architects aspire to the clean efficiency of machines in their work, but many of their creations came, whether consciously or unconsciously, to imitate the forms of certain machines – indirectly confirming, perhaps, that architecture remained concerned with form and not just with pure function. There were two, in particular, that were presented in numerous photographs in *Towards a New Architecture*: ships and aeroplanes. Le Corbusier wrote that 'our daring and masterly constructors of steamships produce palaces in comparison with which cathedrals are tiny things', so it is not surprising, perhaps, that many white-painted Modern Movement houses look like the upper decks or the bridge of the Cunard Line's *Aquitania* or the SS *France*, with horizontal lines, cantilevered-out sun-decks and open galleried

Marine Court, St Leonards-on-Sea, Sussex (Dalgleish & Pullen, 1938)

corridors.⁶⁶ On a more naïve level, there was the widespread fashion for the round porthole window and the open metal stair ascending to an upper deck; both can be found at Oliver Hill's 'Landfall' at Poole, on the Dorset coast. Some buildings managed to resemble entire ships: Marine Court at St Leonards by Dalgleish & Pullen, with its long horizontal balconies and rounded end, might well seem like a large liner beached on the Sussex shore. Given the naïveté of much of this mechanistic imagery, no wonder, perhaps, that Evelyn Waugh could ridicule the whole modernist vogue, noting how,

> From Tromso to Angora the horrible little architects crept about – curly-headed, horn-spectacled, volubly explaining their 'machines for living'. Villas like sewage farms, mansions like half-submerged Channel steamers, offices like vast beehives and cucumber frames sprang around their feet, furnished with electric fires that blistered the ankles, windows that blinded the eyes, patent 'sound-proof' partitions which resounded with the rattle of a hundred typewriters and the buzzing of a thousand telephones.⁶⁷

As for aeroplanes, what is the familiar trope of a thin reinforced-concrete slab raised up on thin metal columns, or, as he termed them, pilotis, other than a tectonic translation of the strutted wings of the numerous large biplanes – and triplanes – that Le Corbusier illustrated? 'The lesson of the airplane lies in the logic which governed the statement of the problem and its realisation. The problem of the house has not yet been stated.'⁶⁸ Unlike trains and ships, aeroplanes were an entirely new, constantly developing product of the twentieth century and they naturally captured the imagination of young, modern architects. In 1932, Raymond McGrath prepared a design for Rudderbar, a combined house and hangar to be built next to Hanworth aerodrome near London for the racing driver and aviatrix Mrs Victor Bruce, one of the many intrepid female pilots who attracted publicity for their exploits between the wars. The brief was fantastic:

The airwoman owner was to make an attempt at a new record for keeping in the air a longest time. At the start of the flight the first brick was to be dropped from the air. The building was then to be put up as quickly as possible so that when she came down at the end of her flight she was to be able to put her machine away and go into the house waiting ready for her.[69]

Alas, it was never built. As for Le Corbusier himself, his love-affair with aviation resulted in his compiling *Aircraft*, a book of images of flight, for a series called *The New Vision* published in English in 1935, with the epigraph *'L'avion accuse . . .*'; 'The airplane, advance guard of the conquering armies of the New Age, the airplane arouses our energies and our faith.'[70]

In 1937, the RIBA organised an exhibition on *Aircraft and Airways*. 'The conquest of the air deserves its monuments,' wrote the President, Percy Thomas, in his introduction to the catalogue, 'and what could be more appropriate than that these should form the buildings which serve that achievement?'[71] London's first commercial airport, at Croydon, had terminal buildings and an hotel in a rather

Speke Airport, Liverpool (Edward Bloomfield, 1937)

stodgy Classical manner, but by the 1930s new airport buildings, such as that at Shoreham and the circular 'beehive' at Gatwick, were efficiently designed in a clean, modern manner.[72] The buildings at the largest and best civil airport built in Britain between the wars, at Speke outside Liverpool, were Art Deco in style. Built in 1935–37 and designed by Edward Bloomfield for Albert D. Jenkins, surveyor to Liverpool Corporation, the terminal building was faced in brick, had a curved plan and a tall central control tower.[73]

Others were designed to appear more literally aerodynamic. The terminal building at Birmingham airport (1939), by Graham Dawbarn of Norman & Dawbarn, sprouted cantilevered concrete wings on either side, but the finest combination of the New Architecture and aeroplane imagery was achieved at Ramsgate by David Pleydell-Bouverie. The administration building for this small municipal airport consisted of one single concrete and hollow roof slab supported on steel columns, to allow part of the glazed non-load bearing perimeter wall to be movable. As the oversailing roof canopy tapered towards the extremities, and as the central control tower raising above resembled a cockpit, Graham Dawbarn praised it for its 'enviable lightness and grace' and noted that when 'seen on plan from the air, it has a resemblance to an aeroplane in flight'.[74] This most stylish and elegant building disappeared at the end of the 1960s, but the photograph of it by Dell & Wainwright, taken from under the wing of a parked high-winged airliner, survives as one of the most telling and arresting images of British architecture of the time.*

Machines date far more quickly than buildings, which emphasises the flaws in the mechanistic fallacy. Just as the cars Le Corbusier parked outside his villas soon looked old-fashioned, so the biplane ceased to be a relevant model for the Modern aesthetic. By the mid-1930s, the biplane was being replaced by sleek, streamlined monoplanes, but here again the machine had a profound influence on architecture. Streamlining was much in vogue, and the aesthetic

---

* The aeroplane was a Short 16 Scion Junior six-seater of 1934; see Stamp (2003).

of the clean shapes with horizontal fluting found on Reginald Mitchell's Supermarine S.6B racing seaplane, or on Nigel Gresley's record-breaking 'Silver Jubilee' steam trains on the London & North Eastern Railway, was also applied to architecture.

'The automobile is not disguised as a stage-coach, at increased expense and reduced efficiency,' explained F. R. S. Yorke. 'The specialist is allowed to dictate, and we have become accustomed to the lines that follow a logical arrangement of components; in fact we find the new forms evolved by streamlining singularly attractive. In this direction we pride ourselves on being modern.'[75] Goodhart-Rendel, typically, considered that this exaggeration of horizontality had produced 'buildings that can be described according to taste either as noble streamline compositions or as imitation railway accidents made of piled-up Pullman cars'.[76] Streamlined modernism was certainly applied to railway buildings as well as to other structures concerned with transport, like petrol filling stations. In the 1930s, the Southern Railway adopted this style for modernised stations such as those at Richmond, Wimbledon and Surbiton, all ostensibly designed by the company's chief architect, J. R. Scott.* Other examples are on the company's then newly electrified branch line to Chessington South, opened in 1938–39. The chief architects to the other members of the 'Big Four' railway companies – W. H. Hamlyn for the London, Midland & Scottish, and P. A. Culverhouse for the Great Western Railway – also flirted with the modernistic in the 1930s.

Streamlining was not just applied to transport and utilitarian buildings. 'Horizontality of a kind less exaggerated and more rational is the ruling characteristic of the block of flats called "Mount Royal" which in the year 1934 made a surprising arrival in Oxford Street,' recorded Goodhart-Rendel. 'The striping of this building is just the architect's fun; it is purely decorative and

---

* In fact almost certainly not designed by the elderly and conservative Scott, but by junior assistants hired by Maxwell Fry: see Fry's recollections of working for Scott in Stamp (2004b), pp. 31–4; examples of these stations are illustrated in Buck (1992).

Mount Royal, Marble Arch, London (Sir John Burnet, Tait & Lorne, 1934)

arises from no necessity.'[77] Designed by Sir John Burnet, Tait & Lorne, it occupied a complete urban block. Above a ground floor of shops, the continuous façade which curved around the corners was layered, with red bands of brickwork containing regularly spaced metal windows alternating with bands of yellow brick, and the upper layers stepping back. Behind this styling was an experiment in modular planning, for the flats were organised on a standard repeating unit. As far as the critic in the *Architectural Review* was concerned, this 'Mass-Produced Shelter' was 'an efficient piece of machinery': 'Whether this is a fit way of providing shelter for Man, who is in the habit of regarding himself as half divine; whether it is "good for architecture" or bad for civilization, the fact remains that there are people who find the convenience and economy of this mode of life attractive.'[78]

So often, in Continental examples, horizontality was achieved by layers of glass alternating with bands of smooth rendered masonry. 'Britain has as a rule disregarded this extremist solution and preferred to counterbalance the horizontal sweep by vertical posts at frequent intervals,' wrote Pevsner in his 1939 survey of modern British architecture. 'This toning-down of the Continental motif may even go so far as the reintroduction within the horizontal band of solid wall between individual windows.'[79] As a German immigrant, Pevsner was often thought to want to import Continental modernism wholesale, but in this unpublished article he was concerned to identify and extol a specifically British Modern Movement. 'On the whole it can safely be said that spatial movement is not what British architects wish to express in their buildings,' he concluded.[80] This was undoubtedly true, although he felt able to praise the house in Hampstead built in the style of Mies van der Rohe by that architectural chameleon, Oliver Hill, who 'has now chosen brick to express that keen sense of spatial joy which goes through all his houses in whatever phantastic disguise it may have appeared in the past'.[81] One very British characteristic, he thought, was the widespread use of traditional brickwork. Another was the predilection for the projecting semi-circular bay. This could be glazed, enclosing a staircase, as in many Continental buildings, or it could be formed of a vertical succession of bay windows on several floors of a block of flats, as in those designed by Atkinson & Alexander. This motif was far from new, 'but, as Mr Atkinson incorporates it into his compositions, it becomes an integral part of a whole so entirely English that it could never be mistaken for anything else'.[82]

These tendencies all came together in what might be regarded as one of the quintessential British buildings of the 1930s: the Comet Inn on the Great North Road at Hatfield. Considered by Pevsner to be 'one of the earliest inns in England, built in the style of the C20, without borrowings from the past', it was designed by the doyen of roadhouse architects, E. B. Musman, and opened in 1936.[83] The composition was one of horizontal masses and in the centre was a projecting glazed semi-circular bay, with a smaller recessed concentric bay placed above, while lateral ground-floor curved bays gave the appearance of wings on plan. It was architecture that reflected speed, designed as it was for passing motor traffic

The Comet Inn, Hatfield, Hertfordshire (E. B. Musman, 1936)

and built on a new by-pass close to the De Havilland aerodrome. Indeed, the name 'Comet' was that of the DH.88 twin-engined monoplane in which, in 1934, C. W. A. Scott and Campbell Black had won the England-to-Australia air race, and a model of this streamlined racing aeroplane was placed in front of the building, mounted on a strange totem-pole carved by Eric Kennington to illustrate different methods of flight. 'The more one examines this clever building the greater grows one's respect for its architect,' wrote Basil Oliver,[84] and, indeed, it secured almost universal praise.* Julian Leathart thought it 'a thoroughly sound example of design in the modern romantic manner, and ... practically and architecturally an outstanding achievement', while for Pevsner it was 'easily the best designed pub in Britain'.[85]

Even so, the Comet is not a pure example of what its partisans considered 'Modern'. Its horizontal styling was characteristic

---

* The Comet Inn has since been altered, the plan having been changed and more windows placed in the blank areas of walling around the lavatories, while the thin lantern on top has disappeared.

of much Modern architecture, but also of what was often defined as '*moderne*' (rather than 'modernistic'), despite Pevsner's broad-minded attempt in 1939 to demonstrate that the several approaches to modern design overlapped. There was nevertheless a wide gulf between the modern and what was usually dismissed as 'modernistic' (and would often, today, be described as Art Deco). For many critics, committed as they were to a social programme, the modernistic was vulgar and commercial. 'Novelty is not an architectural quality,' wrote J. M. Richards, wisely, 'and commerce, in the pursuit of novelty, is apt not to discriminate between the genuine and the false; so architecture, though it owes a debt to commerce for its spirit of enterprise, also owes to commerce the worst examples of "modernistic" design.' Presumably referring to the Art Deco premises lately erected by Burton's, he concluded: 'One can imagine nothing uglier than the recent structures put up by, for example, mass-production tailors.'[86] For Anthony Bertram, 'The modernistic is bogus modern, as the Tudoristic is bogus Tudor.' And when it came to domestic architecture, 'what the modernistic builder does is build an old-fashioned villa with the old-fashioned plan in the old-fashioned way, and then he "streamlines" it, tacking on his modern features just as the Tudoristic builder tacks on his bogus beams.'[87] Thus did the Modern Movement attempt to define its avant-garde credentials and distance itself from popular taste.

The story of the introduction of genuine Modern architecture into Britain has been told countless times and need only be summarised here. Although a number of flat-roofed houses were built immediately before and after the Great War, the first prominent example was an unashamed foreign import: a house by the great German designer Peter Behrens. This was New Ways in Wellingborough Road, Northampton, the first truly Modern Movement building in Britain, commissioned in 1924. The client was the engineer and model railway manufacturer Wenman Bassett-Lowke, who, a decade earlier, had commissioned C. R. Mackintosh to transform the interior of his Late Georgian brick terraced house in the city centre. The interiors

Front and rear, New Ways, Northampton (Peter Behrens, 1926)

Mackintosh produced, with their severely geometrical detailing, may have been partly German in inspiration, while anticipating Art Deco, but they were hardly known at the time.[88]

There was a certain historical justice to Bassett-Lowke's patronage of Behrens. In his 1937 book, F. R. S. Yorke wrote that New Ways 'was probably the first manifestation of the new manner that had already arrived from the Continent', but went on to observe that:

> the struggle for a departure from revivalism, the acceptance of the machine by the artist, and the freeing of the plan that made such an architecture possible, had been made in this country towards the beginning of the century, by such men as Mackintosh, C. F. A. Voysey, Edgar Wood, and George Walton, following, each in his own way, the pioneer work of William Morris.[89]

He was thus reiterating an argument that had been aired by P. Morton Shand in his 'Scenario for a Human Drama' in the pages of the *Architectural Review* and which had been sanctified by Pevsner in his book *Pioneers of the Modern Movement from William Morris to Walter Gropius* published the previous year. Others, less exclusively committed to Modernism, agreed, with Patrick Abercrombie writing in 1939 of 'irruptive tendencies' before 1914:

> Mackintosh with his unrestrained fantasy in Glasgow; Edgar Wood with his flat roofs in Lancashire; Baillie Scott with his more determined return to folk art; Voysey with his own special originality – these men were outside the general trend; they were anathema in the Schools; but they set fire to continental thought, which was either shackled in a much stricter classicism than ours in France or Italy, or groping in a false romanticism in Germany and Austria. The horrible epidemic of Art Nouveau soon passed, and Modernist design sprang into being after the gap of the War, sobered by the need for larger masses of strictly economic building.

Our Mackintosh-Wood-Scott-Voysey offspring returned to these shores with a foreign intonation: it upset the orderly development of our neo-Georgian tradition, hence this new period of Transition through which we are passing.[90]

Behrens's New Ways was remarkable in style, but not at all remarkable in its plan or in the handling of space. Illustrated in the *Architectural Review* and elsewhere, it was, however, influential. The projecting V-shaped window in the centre of the entrance façade – a feature which might seem as much Art Deco as Modern – reappeared in the flat-roofed houses designed by Thomas Tait in Silver End, the progressive model village in Essex laid out after 1926 around the Crittall Works, the factory producing the standardised metal windows that became an essential component of the new style. The classically trained younger partner of the great Sir John Burnet, Tait was open to new ideas. The resulting buildings were intelligent compromises, like his house at Newbury: monumental but flat-roofed, with rendered walls and, again, that V-shaped window. Tait was also responsible for the £1,750 concrete house exhibited at the 1928 *Daily Mail* Ideal Home Exhibition, a severe, heavy, brick-shaped building with a long first-floor balcony. John Gloag thought it resembled 'some vast, overwhelming exhibit of Empire produce – Australian butter* for example'.[91] This was not, however, the first 'modern' house to be placed before the house-buying public. That honour lay with R. A. Duncan's 'House of the Future', exhibited at Olympia the previous year.

Behrens and New Ways were clearly the models for the fictional King's Thursday, designed by Professor Otto Silenus for Lady Metroland, in Evelyn Waugh's *Decline and Fall*, published in 1928.[92] Silenus, the fictional young German architect who had been in Moscow and at the Bauhaus and who designs the new King's Thursday, pronounces

---

* Tait's was one of two prize-winning houses in a competition promoted by the Portland Cement Selling & Distribution Co. Life-size human sculptures in butter had been shown in both the Australian and Canadian Pavilions at the Wembley Exhibition in 1924.

on the 'problem of architecture'. It is, he announces, 'the problem of all art – the elimination of the human element from the consideration of form. The only perfect building must be the factory, because that is built to house machines, not men. I do not think it is possible for domestic architecture to be beautiful, but I am doing my best.' 'I think that he's a man worth watching,' notes the earnest Arthur Potts, just down from Oxford. 'He's got right away from Corbusier, anyway.'[93] 'And if, by then, few in England had much idea who Le Corbusier was and even fewer what he was up to,' Summerson observed some three decades later, 'it made all the more exciting the notion that he could be got away from.'[94] Enterprising young architects had been able to obtain *Vers une Architecture* in the foreign newspaper shops in Charlotte Street and after 1927 in Etchells's English translation. Corbusier's *Urbanisme* followed, as *The City of To-morrow*, two years later. 'It was talk that counted and there was a sense of anticipation,' Summerson went on. 'A good many young men bought themselves black hats and discovered that architects were, or should be, "intellectuals". They had been "gentlemen and scholars" for too long.'

Etchells had the distinction of designing the first Modern building erected in London. Completed in 1930, it was for Crawford's Advertising and was conspicuous for its horizontal bands of fenestration between plain bands of masonry supported on stainless steel mullions. But Etchells was too intelligent and independent-minded to remain part of the Modernist faction in the architectural profession; he later became more interested in church architecture, liturgy and conservation, and delighted in ridiculing the pomposities of the profession. Etchells belonged to the generation who had served in the trenches and who experimented with the new style. Another was the versatile Oliver Hill, who, having designed suave houses in Tudor, Georgian and Pseudish, was inspired by seeing Asplund's work at the 1930 Stockholm exhibition and happy to try something new. His houses, such as Holthanger at Wentworth in Surrey, have a dynamic presence assisted by curves on plan and prominent horizontals. However, with their flat roofs and large windows enclosing staircases, they were more than usually prone to the problems suffered by so many Modernist designs. At Hill's first modern house, Joldwynds, of 1931–32, the external render fell off in places while the clients found the hard surfaces of the interior uncomfortable. Having pursued their architect for compensation, they sold Joldwynds and built another house close by. Hill was undeterred and went on to design a whole estate of Modernist houses at Frinton-on-Sea in Essex. The flat-roofed houses did not sell so well, however, and his grand plans for the area remained incomplete. Perhaps his most successful house in this idiom was at Poole in Dorset. Like so many of these houses which exploited the aesthetic of reinforced concrete, Landfall was built of rendered brick in 1936–38, its modern image enhanced by generous open verandahs, porthole windows and a gravity-defying sweeping external staircase.

Hill was responsible for one of the first larger, institutional buildings in the new style to capture the public imagination: the Midland Hotel at Morecambe (Plate 34). Built partly as a public

Interior, café, Midland Hotel, Morecambe, Lancashire (Oliver Hill; mural (recreated), Eric Ravilious, 1933)

Interior, Midland Hotel, Morecambe, Lancashire (Oliver Hill; mural, Eric Gill, 1933)

relations exercise by the London Midland & Scottish Railway (LMS) to encourage the holiday industry at a time of economic depression, it opened to much acclaim in 1933. The building was undoubtedly stylish: its horizontality emphasised by projecting cornices, its long length curved along the seafront. 'It rises like a great white ship, gracefully curved,' extolled Lord Clonmore in the *Architectural Review*.[95] Hill was also anxious to embellish his creation with modern works of art. Eric Gill was responsible for the sea horses high above the entrance, the ceiling mural over the circular staircase, the carved stone relief of Nausicaa welcoming Odysseus in the entrance lounge, and the pictorial map of the Lancashire coast in the children's room, while Eric Ravilious painted a mural in the circular café at one end. Unfortunately, this soon fell victim to the endemic damp.

Although Hill did much to promote Modernism, he was such a stylistic chameleon that the more doctrinaire Modernists regarded him with a degree of suspicion. The Midland Hotel was a compromise between popular Modernistic and Modern, but perhaps that was its strength. 'I have made it my business to keep in touch with the best Continental work of this kind,' Hill told the LMS, 'and I feel that you have here an unique opportunity of building the first really modern hotel in this country.'[96] Similarly dependent on new buildings on the Continent was the work of Joseph Emberton, who moved from a monumental Deco manner derived from his time with Burnet & Tait to embracing the Modern Movement. This was first evident in his streamlined cement façade for the Olympia Exhibition building in London, designed in 1930. However, there is evidence that the progressive designs that emanated from his office were the work of younger assistants, among whom there was a rapid turnover.

Emberton exploited the possibilities of the steel frame in his Royal Corinthian Yacht Club at Burnham-on-Crouch in Essex, completed in 1931, which has generous projecting balconies overlooking the water and the staircases expressed externally as sloping window bands. He went on to design a series of buildings, or structures, at the Pleasure Beach in Blackpool, emphasising perhaps that the Modern

Casino, Blackpool Pleasure Beach, Blackpool (Joseph Emberton, 1939)

Movement was acceptable in peripheral conditions. Originally intended to be Lancashire's answer to Coney Island, the Pleasure Beach was redeveloped in the 1930s, with Emberton brought in to create 'a unified modern design'. Alan Powers comments that the resulting buildings 'are a unique example in Britain of modern architecture and mass culture meeting on equal terms'.[97] With their use of pictorial imagery, machinery and coloured light, they are also examples of the contemporary phenomenon of what has been called 'Form Follows Fun'.[98] The entrance to the Casino, for instance, with its tall spiral staircase rising to an elevated viewing platform, can be read as a giant stylised gin and tonic with a straw in it.*

Other younger British architects converted to Modernism included: H.C. Hughes of Cambridge, who designed the Mond Workshop and Laboratory in Cambridge for the physicist Ernest Rutherford; the Rome Scholar Marshall Sisson; Frederick Gibberd, whose principal work before the Second World War was Pullman Court at Streatham, a development of five-storey reinforced-concrete blocks of flats; and the architectural perspectivist Raymond Myerscough-Walker, who designed a remarkable house at Nottingham on a semi-circular plan. But the most important were E. Maxwell Fry and F. R. S. Yorke. Although he designed a handful of rectilinear flat-roofed concrete houses, Yorke is probably more significant as a propagandist for the New Architecture, assembling several collections of examples, British and foreign, which were published by the Architectural Press: *The Modern House* (1934), *The Modern House in England* (1937) and (with Frederick Gibberd) *The Modern Flat* (1937), as well as (with Colin Penn) *A Key to Modern Architecture* (1939).

Maxwell Fry was responsible, both alone and with his sometime partner, Walter Gropius, for some of the most impressive modern buildings of the 1930s. A product of Charles Reilly's Liverpool

---

* Rosemary Ind, however, sees the circular form not as a giant slice of lemon but as a wheel, to 'invite comparison with pit-head machinery [as] a compliment to holidaying miners' (Ind (1983), p. 39).

School of Architecture who had worked briefly in New York, Fry's conversion to the new way of building may be described, with a certain compression of the chronology, as an epitome. He designed several private houses. The Sun House in Hampstead, with its generous thin balconies and wide bands of plate-glass windows, all raised up over a garage, proclaimed the aspirations of the modern by its very name and was built entirely of reinforced-concrete construction (Plate 35). 'As with all revolutionary movements you had to make a noticeable break with the past,' Fry himself later recalled. 'Concrete was a vehicle of release. It was used without a great deal of knowledge but with a great deal of courage. Sometimes it was an unsuitable material . . . but with its canopies and wide span windows it could not have been done any other way.'[99] A similar house, Miramonte at Kingston, became 'a classic image of Modernism in the 1930s'.[100]

It was much to Fry's credit that he also became seriously interested in social architecture, an essential element of the theoretical stance of Modernism. He was responsible for Sassoon House in Peckham, next to Owen Williams's Pioneer Health Centre, and then, with the housing 'consultant' and expert Elizabeth Denby, he designed Kensal House, an experimental and promotional development of sixty-eight working-class flats off Ladbroke Grove in West London, for the Gas, Light & Coke Company. Fry was successful in an internal competition among the team of architects acting as consultants by exploiting the circular site of a gasholder, and he introduced a telling curve into one long block of flats to make a dynamic composition which could well have been built in Berlin during the previous decade. As far as Denby was concerned, Kensal House was 'the first "urban village" to be built in Britain. It is an experiment in rehousing families from slum areas.'[101] Fry later recalled how 'joyfully we set to work to build no ordinary block of flats but a community in action, with social rooms, workshop, a corner shop, with larger flats, better balconies, even a separate drying balcony, and in my disused gasholder hollow a nursery school, one of the first of such buildings, swinging around the curve left for us to play with'.[102]

Kensal House, Ladbroke Grove, London (E. Maxwell Fry, with Elizabeth Denby and G. Grey Wornum, 1936)

Kensal House was built in 1933–36. Writing in 1959, Summerson reflected that 1927 was the crucial year when a general opinion coalesced 'that such a thing as a "modern movement" existed'. Even so, 'Nothing of substantial importance in the new spirit was built here before 1933.'[103] But this is to ignore the first strikingly modern house that caught the imagination of the public. High and Over was designed in 1929 in open countryside on the top of a hill near Amersham in Buckinghamshire. The client was the Classical archaeologist Professor Bernard Ashmole, the retiring director of the British School at Rome; the architect was Amyas Connell, one of Ashmole's students, who had cut short his three-year scholarship to establish himself as an architect. The house was remarkable in every way. Built with a reinforced-concrete frame with rendered brick and block infill, the contractor having been unable to carry out the intended concrete construction using movable steel shuttering, it had a Y-shaped plan with three rectilinear wings radiating from a hexagonal central hall – according to the architect, 'a well organised centralised and nuclear plan, similar to many buildings of the

Renaissance'.[104] The elevations were careful studies in symmetry and asymmetry; walls were rendered flat white; windows were wide rectangles; and the flat roof was partially covered by a flat canopy. The house was to some extent an intelligent compromise, of tradition with modernity, with the new aesthetic of De Stijl applied to an Edwardian butterfly-plan.

Amersham Rural District Council made it clear that it only approved the plans 'with the greatest reluctance' because they could not find anything to which a legal objection could be made, but objections were made to the separate application for the detached concrete water tower which added to the drama of the composition.[105] This was the first of many battles that modern architects had to fight with conservative local authorities who, claiming to reflect the feelings of local communities, insisted on traditional materials. A few years later, in 1933, a Modern design by Connell and his partners was opposed by Ruislip-Northwood Urban District Council, whose members could 'see nothing in the planning which would render it necessary that it should be treated in this fashion which is not new but of Continental origin':[106]

High and Over, Amersham, Buckinghamshire (Amyas Connell, 1931)

We are satisfied that, despite full publicity for all discoverable examples in the technical Press, there is in fact little work of this character being built in this country and if, as appears likely, it becomes unfashionable the isolated examples are likely to prove unacceptable to tenants and may even become derelict, to the disadvantage of surrounding property.*

Others regarded High and Over more favourably. There was even an enthusiastic article in *Country Life*, written by Christopher Hussey, who thought that there was 'nothing in its clean level lines nor in its whiteness that does not harmonise with the rolling chalk uplands'.[107] There was even a Pathétone Weekly film made about this new 'Ultra Modern House'. 'Today, we dream of houses open to the sun and air, embodying everything modern science can offer,' reads its opening caption. 'Such a dream house has come to reality on a hilltop at Amersham, Buckinghamshire,' the narrator then announces.[108]

One significant fact about the young architect of High and Over was that he was born in New Zealand. Amyas Connell was one of several outsiders who were either from remote parts of the British Empire or from Continental Europe who encouraged the development of the Modern Movement in Britain. Without them, there would have been little built of any consequence by the end of the 1930s for commentators such as Henry-Russell Hitchcock to notice and praise. They were all significant members of MARS (the Modern Architectural Research Group), which was the British wing of CIAM (the Congrès Internationaux d'Architecture Moderne), the propagandist committee to which the leading Modernist figures on the Continent belonged. The MARS Group was founded in 1933 and John Summerson, who was a member, later noticed that of the principal figures only Maxwell Fry had

---

* That such attitudes still linger was unpleasantly demonstrated by Runnymede District Council approving the (illegal) demolition of the (listed) Greenside by Connell, Ward & Lucas in 2003.

Interior, High and Over, Amersham, Buckinghamshire (Amyas Connell, 1931)

been born and trained in England. 'We didn't think this important at the time, but one can see now that it was. These people had a detachment, sharper ambition, a fresher outlook than the average English architect. Also, of course, they hadn't got the Englishman's acute and sterilising sense of class.'[109]

Connell had arrived in Britain from New Zealand in 1924 together with his friend and fellow architect Basil Ward. They later became partners, along with the Englishman Colin Lucas, as Connell, Ward & Lucas, a practice that was responsible for some of the best and most controversial Modern Movement buildings of the decade. One was the house in Hampstead, 66 Frognal, whose design met with objections from local residents, notably Sir Reginald Blomfield, as well as Hampstead Council and the London County Council (Plate 36).* Ultimately the client, the solicitor Geoffrey Walford, took the case to the High Court, and won. An invitation to an opening party at the house in 1939 quoted the opinion of one Member of Parliament that it was 'one of the greatest pieces of vandalism ever perpetrated in London'.[110] Another house, called New Farm, among other names, near Haslemere in Surrey, had one of the most remarkable plans of any Modern Movement house. Built in 1932–33 with four-inch reinforced-concrete walls, the design had a completely irregular radiating plan. 'Viewed from the air,' Raymond McGrath wrote, 'viewed from any angle some judges say, [it] is more like an invention by Picasso than a house. High and Over has a suggestion about it of Roman building, but [this] is unlike any house,† Roman, Renaissance or English.'[111] Surprisingly, the client was a seventy-two-year old financier, Sir Arthur Lowes Dickinson. Even so, the local authority insisted on a screen of lime trees to protect passers-by from seeing this shocking new building.

McGrath, born in Australia, arrived in Britain in 1926. After designing Finella for Mansfield Forbes and co-ordinating the team responsible for the new studios inside the BBC building, he went on to design a remarkable house in Surrey, St Anne's Hill, on the site of a villa once owned by Charles James Fox. Another Modernist from

---

* [66 Frognal is now listed Grade II*. RH.]

† [It is in fact, in its radical relation of plan to site, very much like the house built by John Nash for Uvedale Price in 1791–94, which was considered similarly scandalous at the time. RH.]

the Antipodes, George Checkley, a New Zealander who studied at the Liverpool School, designed a handful of Modern Movement houses in Cambridge before devoting himself to teaching. And then there was Wells Coates, perhaps the most glamorous figure in the world of the MARS Group, of which he was effectively the founder. Coates was born in Tokyo to Canadian parents, and then studied engineering in Vancouver before ending up in London in the early 1920s. Journalist and versatile designer of shop interiors and wireless sets, Coates was not a trained architect, yet he was responsible for one of the most iconic buildings of the 1930s: the Isokon flats in Lawn Road, Hampstead.

This block, containing twenty-two 'minimum dwellings' with fitted furniture, was the brainchild of Jack Pritchard, salesman for the Venesta Plywood Company. 'Isokon' stood for Isometric Unit Construction.* After several false starts and changes of plan, work began on the block, constructed of reinforced concrete throughout, in 1933. Long and thin, with its horizontality enhanced by long projecting balconies which dramatically terminated with diagonal flights of stairs, the Isokon flats presented a compelling image of modernity and attracted much attention.

Isokon flats, Hampstead, London (Wells Coates, 1934)

Having been 'designed with special reference to the circumstances of the bachelor or young married professional

---

* In his largely unpublished memoir, Berthold Lubetkin recalled how, 'One way or another, I arrived here and was introduced to a swaggering architect called Wells Coates, who was in the process of charming the wife of Jack Pritchard in order to obtain her husband's approval of his lousy sketch scheme for the Lawn Road flats' (Lubetkin (1993), p. 72).

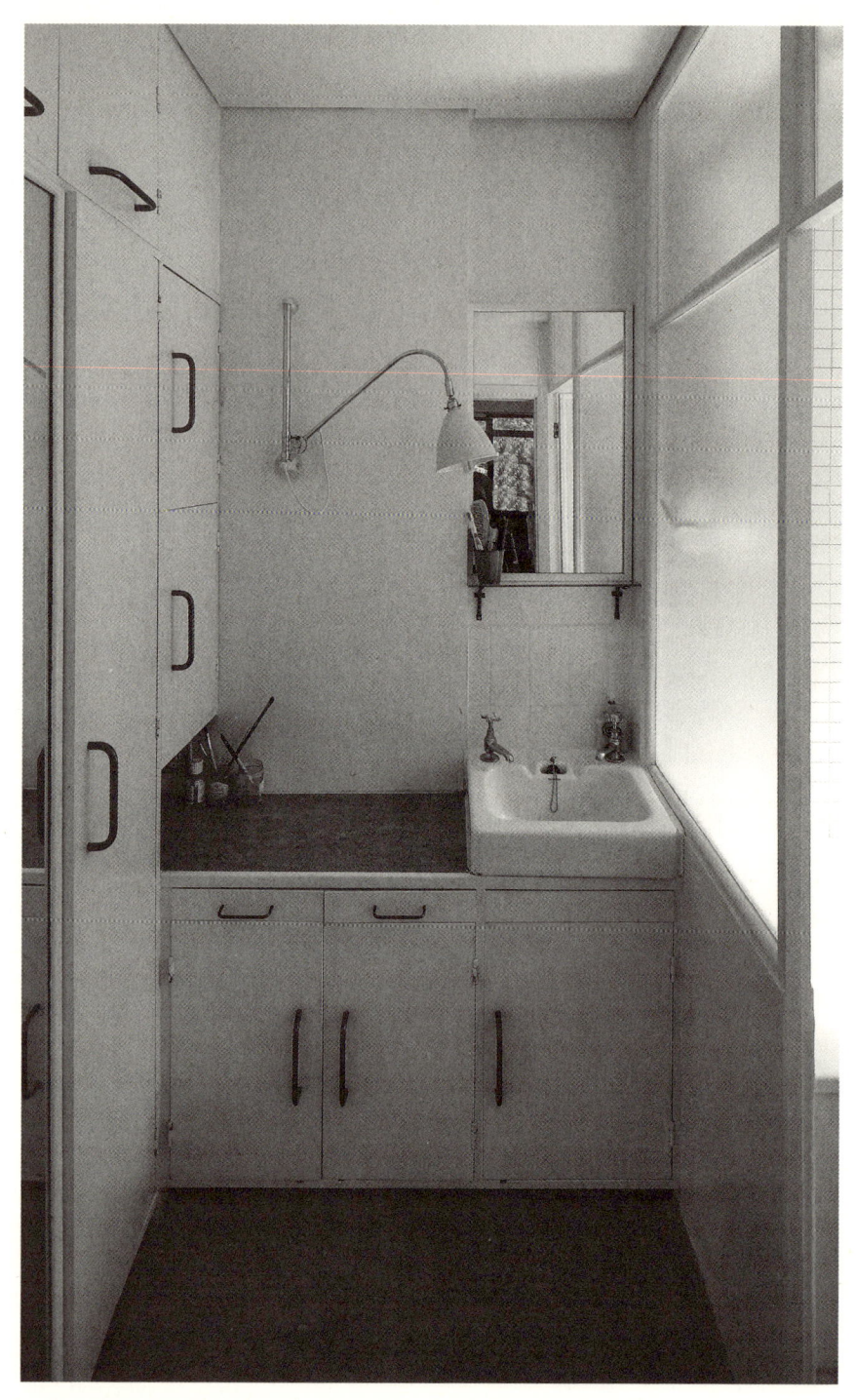

Interior, Isokon flats, Hampstead, London (Wells Coates, 1934)

or business person', the flats were ideal for refugees from Nazi Germany; early tenants included Walter Gropius, Marcel Breuer and László Moholy-Nagy, as well as Adrian Stokes and, of all people, Agatha Christie, who compared the block to 'a giant liner which *ought* to have had a couple of funnels, and then you went up the stairs and through the door of your flat and there were the trees tapping on the window'.[112] There was also the future television cook Philip Harbin, who prepared meals in the communal 'Isobar'. 'As a real-life manifesto of the modern movement,' John Summerson later wrote,

> the Isokon flats were a sensational success; and there is perhaps no other English building which so neatly interprets the ideals of CIAM and MARS. It is not quite architecture and not quite engineering but the work manifestly of an engineer-architect . . . If there are limitations to this heroically technological approach they become apparent if we compare Coates's work with Fry's. Fry's Kensal House is a humane and cheerful building. About Isokon flats there is not the flicker of a smile.[113]

Then there were the architects who came to Britain from Continental Europe. William Lescaze, a Swiss-American, who designed houses and boarding houses at the progressive Dartington Hall School in Devon; Ernö Goldfinger, born in Budapest, who came to London via Paris; and Berthold Lubetkin, a Russian born in Georgia. Lubetkin came to England in 1931 via Moscow, St Petersburg, Warsaw, Berlin and Paris, where he had practised and built. A charismatic, compelling and complex individual, this brilliant designer soon dominated Modernist architectural circles. John Summerson recalled that 'we were always impressed by foreigners (not by colonials). Especially by Lubetkin with his enormous ability & charm. . . . I at once had the impression that he thought all English architecture childish. At MARS meetings his eloquence was apt to dominate discussion.'[114] Mysterious and a myth-maker all his long life, Lubetkin maintained some sort of connection with the Soviet authorities; when he contributed articles to the *Architectural Review* in 1932, he was introduced by the editor as 'one of the most famous proletarian architects'.[115] J. M. Richards recalled that he was the first man he remembered seeing with a zip-fastener on his trousers.[116]

In 1932, Lubetkin joined with a group of six disaffected Modernist-minded students from the Architectural Association: Godfrey Samuel, Michael Dugdale, Valentine Harding, Anthony Chitty, Lindsay Drake and Francis Skinner. They formed a practice called Tecton, but it was always clear that the older and much more experienced Russian was *primus inter pares*. Tecton came to public attention not with buildings for human beings but with structures for less demanding users: animals. Through Solly Zuckerman, then Research Anatomist to the Zoological Society of London, Lubetkin and Tecton were commissioned to design a new Gorilla House in 1932. After rapid research, a circular reinforced-concrete structure was built on the Society's Regent's Park site. Other structures

Penguin Pool, London Zoo, Regent's Park, London (Berthold Lubetkin and Tecton, with Ove Arup and Felix Samuely, 1934)

followed: in London, at the Society's outpost in Whipsnade, and at Dudley Zoo in Staffordshire. Of these, the most celebrated was the Penguin Pool in London, built in 1933–34. It was an astonishing exercise in abstract, sculptural geometry, with interlocking curved ramps of thin reinforced concrete placed within a stretched oval enclosure – a solution that could not have been realised without the engineering genius of the Dane, Ove Arup, and the German refugee, Felix Samuely. For Henry-Russell Hitchcock, writing in the catalogue to the 1937 exhibition on *Modern Architecture in England*, 'It was that unique monument, the Penguin Pool by Lubetkin and Tecton . . . which first dramatically attracted the attention of the world to developments in England'.[117]

Buildings for humans followed, notably Highpoint, a block of middle-class flats on the top of Highgate Hill. These were intended as a manifesto for Modernism and an advertisement for the advantages of living in those high flats to which Modernists were ideologically committed. As Lubetkin's biographer remarked, 'Even before it was completed in 1935, Highpoint One had become the flagship

Interior, Flat 1, Highpoint One, Highgate, London (Berthold Lubetkin and Tecton, 1935)

building of the Modern Movement in England.'[118] The client was Sigmund Gestetner, the son of the Hungarian-born founder of the office equipment firm. The seven-storey block of flats on a Cross of Lorraine plan was built entirely of reinforced concrete, with Arup as consultant, and manifested the influence of Le Corbusier's 'Five Points of the New Architecture' in such aspects as the flat roof, the wide, horizontal windows and the upper six floors being raised up on pilotis. The projecting balconies, with their curvilinear cyma, or S-shape, profile, would become a cliché of British modernism after the Second World War. Although the advent of Highpoint provoked the formation of the Highgate Preservation Society to make sure nothing like it happened again, the building elicited a favourable critical response from sympathisers. Le Corbusier himself visited and admired it, while Hitchcock declared it to be 'one of the finest, if not absolutely the finest, middle-class housing projects in the world'.[119] Applying the same techniques to housing the working class, which Lubetkin, with his Marxist sympathies, hoped to do, would have to wait, although the London Borough of Finsbury would soon commission a Health Centre from Tecton.

Finally, there were the architects who arrived as refugees from Germany after Hitler became chancellor in 1933, the most famous being Erich Mendelsohn and Walter Gropius. As a Jew, Mendelsohn left almost immediately and was well received in England, particularly by Charles Reilly, for whom he was 'the most brilliant architect in Europe of the modern school, the one who seemed able to give an almost classical grace to a group of functional factory buildings'.[120] The RIBA successfully appealed for Mendelsohn to have his temporary residence permit extended and he announced his intention to apply for British citizenship. However, at a time of economic difficulty and in a climate of increasing xenophobia, there was feeling against foreign architects practising in Britain. Hence the compromise solution of partnerships with native architects – Gropius with Maxwell Fry, and Marcel Breuer with F. R. S. Yorke. Mendelsohn entered into partnership with the designer-turned-architect Serge Chermayeff, who, although he had been born in Grozny in Chechnya, was an Old Harrovian.

Mendelsohn & Chermayeff built comparatively little in England but demonstrated that, with a reasonable budget and sufficient attention to detail, modern architecture could be stylish, sophisticated and successful. Two of their buildings were private houses. One, Shrub's Wood near Chalfont St Giles for R. J. Nimmo, was a long, dynamic composition in a Picturesque landscape, its horizontality, generous interior spaces and the elegant, curvilinear staircase enclosed within a curved glazed wall, exhibited the character of Mendelsohn's earlier houses in Berlin. Mendelsohn & Chermayeff also designed what can arguably be claimed as the finest Modern Movement building in Britain erected before the Second World War: the De La Warr Pavilion at Bexhill-on-Sea in Sussex. The commission came through a competition held in 1933. The Mayor of Bexhill, the young 9th Earl De La Warr, was a Socialist and a supporter of Ramsay MacDonald's government. He was determined that the proposed pavilion, containing conference facilities and a restaurant, should be built by the Corporation and not handed to private developers; he also seems to have been determined to secure a modern design. At the recommendation of the RIBA, the assessor was Thomas Tait; the competition brief stated that 'No restrictions as to style of architecture will be imposed, but buildings must be simple, light in appearance and attractive, suitable for a holiday resort. Heavy stonework is not desirable. . . . Modern steel-framed or ferro-concrete construction may be adopted, but walls and roofs must be well insulated for heat and sound.'[121] The design by Mendelsohn & Chermayeff was placed first out of 230 entries. After economies had been made and a welded steel frame substituted for the intended concrete construction, the principal building containing an entertainments hall and a restaurant was completed in 1935, albeit leaving part of the original scheme unexecuted.

The pavilion was a composition of dramatic horizontals, with the long flat elevations broken by Mendelsohn's semi-circular projecting glazed staircase bays, while long open terraces on two floors faced

De La Warr Pavilion, Bexhill-on-Sea, Sussex (Mendelsohn & Chermayeff, 1935)

De La Warr Pavilion, Bexhill-on-Sea, Sussex (Mendelsohn & Chermayeff, 1935)

the sea. Nothing quite like it had been seen in Britain before and the architectural press was ecstatic. The *Architect and Building News* considered that its special character was owing to two qualities: 'One is the sense of "open-ness" of the building; one has the sense of walking within enclosed space rather than in a structure. The other is the exquisite finish of the design, so far as structural details are concerned.'[122] But Bexhill remained a conservative place, full of retired colonels and civil servants, and there were rumblings of discontent about the import of Modernism and the employment of 'alien' architects, the latter complaint stirred up by the British Union of Fascists in the *Architects' Journal*.

Despite his eminence, Gropius, the former director of the Bauhaus, was able to build little more in Britain than a few houses. Ambitious schemes for new buildings at colleges in Oxford and Cambridge came to nothing, and he left for the United States in 1937 to take up a teaching appointment at Harvard University. A last building, the village college for Henry Morris at Impington near Cambridge, was carried out after his departure by Gropius and Fry's assistant, Jack Howe. This was, however, a work of considerable significance. The composition, placed in a mature landscape, was loose, and the architectural elements undemonstrative, the most conspicuous being the hall with its tapering plan and sloping roof. The gently curved adult wing adopted the repeating English motif of the bay-window, but perhaps most important of all was the fact that the buildings were faced in brick, with no concrete visible. 'Can it have been the effect of English picturesque notions on the more rigid intellect of Gropius?' wondered Nikolaus Pevsner, for whom this was 'One of the best buildings of its date in England, if not the best'.[123]

By the late 1930s, the Modern Movement in England had begun to become more pragmatic, perhaps more English. Writing about architecture in Britain in 1939, Pevsner commented on a 'reversion to brick', which 'is a tendency undeniable and reasonable', and was certain that 'a British Modern Movement is possible, and in fact exists'.[124] John Gloag, on the other hand, who had at first been enthusiastic about the New Architecture, concluded during the Second World War that, 'So far no great English architect has understood and controlled and interpreted its possibilities, as Inigo Jones mastered and interpreted the Italianate architecture of the Renaissance. The modern movement does not yet speak English.'[125]

What is certain is that by the time the outbreak of war brought building to a halt, the leading modern architects had abandoned the fashion for plain smooth surfaces and flat roofs (the image of Continental modernity which Ernö Goldfinger dismissed as '"Kasbah" architecture – all the white stuff')[126] in favour of materials that had texture and colour, and weathered better in the English climate: brick, timber and even stone. In 1936, F. R. S. Yorke's partner made him promise he would never build another concrete house because of the difficulty of cutting openings into reinforced-concrete walls, and at the end of the decade both he and Mary Crowley (later Mary Medd), the first architect to be employed by Hertfordshire County Council, designed terraces and groups of houses in plain brick with monopitch

Impington Village College, Impington, Cambridgeshire (Gropius & Fry, with Jack Howe, 1937)

roofs. Goldfinger's own terrace on Willow Road in Hampstead was faced in brick, as was Oliver Hill's nearby Hill House. Walter Gropius even designed The Wood House in Kent with a cedar cladding over a timber frame – and a shallow monopitch roof.

Lionel Brett explained what had happened in his book *Houses*, published after the war, recalling how:

> The modern house arrived in a blaze of glory and after a brief summer of astonishing beauty faded like a flower in the frost. Luckily, these facts had become obvious before the 'thirties ended and steps were being taken to meet them. Concrete paints and stuccoes were devised to resist cracking and streakiness. Washable glazed wall-tiling of various sorts was successfully tried in London and other big towns. Above all, the advantage of materials such as brick and stone which become steadily more beautiful with age were re-discovered. A fair number of completely modern houses

were faced with brick, and it became a fashionable contrast to place walls of the roughest rubble alongside the new smooth white ones. Even the flat roof ceased to be compulsory.[127]

In other words, the Modernists were at last recognising the practical sense of the well-tried building conventions that, blinded by science and by fashion, they had sneered at when employed by the 'Traditionalist' architects they despised.

The new pragmatism of this 'British Modern Movement' was a direct response to the manifest failings of the pioneer buildings. Four-inch-thick concrete walls provided little insulation, allowed no space for the introduction of cables, pipes and other services, while the reinforcement, so near the surface, would begin to rust. If rendered brick had been used, the render soon cracked and crazed. Metal windows corroded, while large areas of glazing let in the cold. 'Ornament was banished (the word ceased to be used unless qualified by the epithet "superfluous"),' Brett recalled, 'and with it went the various projections, copings, cornices, string courses, etc., which had traditionally served to throw rainwater clear of the wall face and protect it from penetration.'[128] 'On a cold, damp November or February day, those ultra-modern houses looked and indeed were, anything but comfortable,' Gloag could write in 1944. 'After a few years of exposure to the English climate, they looked shoddy and woebegone, and were streaked with dirty smears where rain had dribbled down the walls.'[129] The bright, pristine machine-like modernity striven for by their creators was preserved only in the initial photographs, usually taken on a sunny day. Where those buildings survive today, it is noticeable how most of them have undergone expensive restorations by firms specialising in dealing with such structures, sometimes almost to the point of complete rebuilding.[130] Evelyn Waugh put it more brutally in 1938:

> In a few months our climate began to expose the imposture. The flat white walls that had looked as cheerful as a surgical sterilizing

plant became mottled with damp; our east winds howled through the steel frames of the windows. The triumphs of the New Architecture began to assume the melancholy air of a deserted exhibition, almost before the tubular furniture within had become bent and tarnished.[131]

Of all the aspects of the modernist aesthetic, the one most tenaciously maintained by its advocates was the flat roof. Even when this was reluctantly abandoned on practical grounds, it was only in favour of a gently sloping monopitch. The argument had little to do with practicality; the appeal of a flat roof was symbolic, even poetic, just as, to the opponents of modernism, 'a flat roof was the badge of bolshevism'.[132] 'Whatever the practical pros and cons of a flat roof,' Alan Powers concluded,

> there is a symbolic quality about it that eluded expression in the 1930s and is still seldom discussed today. To understand it, one needs to approach the subject through a thinker such as the French philosopher Gaston Bachelard, who interpreted houses as images of the individual psyche, with the implication that a flat roof allows a swifter passage upwards to a kind of transcendental state, which may also be interpreted as a sexual arousal. No other explanation seems quite to account for the fervour with which this particular aspect of building was contested by supporters and opponents alike.[133]

There was, however, much more to the change in modern architecture by the end of the decade than a reaction to the practical failings of flat-roofed concrete buildings. The more sophisticated architects had never believed in pure Functionalism and were interested in developing a modern architectural tradition as valid as the Classical. This was above all true of Lubetkin who, in 1937, insisted, 'If modern architecture is to make the progress of which it is capable, it should go without saying that every building fulfils the purpose for which it is intended; this should be the starting point, not the ultimate criterion.' The previous year he had argued that the modern architect:

> should abandon his theories of pure functionalism and approach architecture as an artist who, at the same time, has a fundamental mastery of the techniques of his art. It is essential that the modern architect be a master of modern techniques of building and of materials if his buildings are to be more acceptable and more efficient. But it is also essential for him to remember that the tradition of his profession is intimately connected with a special imagination which should make his buildings reflect contemporary aesthetics.[134]

The contemporary aesthetic that particularly enriched architecture and interiors was Surrealism, as can be seen in the work of Lubetkin and Goldfinger.

Lubetkin's approach was most clearly expressed in Highpoint Two, designed in 1936 (Plate 37). Owing to planning restrictions, it was smaller and yet more expensive in conception than Highpoint One. It was also very different in appearance. Instead of the earlier monolithic expression of concrete, Lubetkin adopted a symmetrical, carefully proportioned framed structure with an infill of materials that weathered better: brick, tile and glass blocks. The result was a more complex and texturally rich building, subtle and allusive with the prominent device of Greek caryatids, casts of those on the Erechtheum supplied by the British Museum, supporting the thin, curved concrete entrance canopy. This Classical reference both baffled and outraged. For while the *Architectural Review* considered that, 'in its careful attention to the dignity that richness of modelling and texture can produce and its interest in a less abstract architectural language', Highpoint Two was 'an important move forward from functionalism',[135] a politically active student at the Architectural Association, Anthony Cox, condemned the building in language reminiscent of political debate in Stalin's Soviet Union. 'Highpoint I stands on tiptoe and spreads its wings;

Highpoint II sits back on its haunches like Buddha,' he wrote in the short-lived student magazine *Focus*:

> The intellectual approach which has produced what we know as modern architecture is fundamentally a functionalist approach.... My contention is that the recent work of Tecton shows a deviation from this approach. It is more than a deviation of appearance; it implies a deviation of aim. . . . Is it really an 'important move forward from functionalism', from which development is possible; or is it a symptom of decline, an end in itself?[136]

Cox was in a minority, however, and Lubetkin's and Tecton's buildings – including Highpoint Two – were generally admired by those sympathetic to artistic progress in architecture. A particular critical success was the Finsbury Health Centre, which, especially in its use of tile and glass bricks, anticipated the modern aesthetic of the 1950s. But when, a few years earlier, two doctors wished to house a medical and sociological experiment in South London, they turned not to an architect but to an engineer who had established himself as one of the most radical designers in the country. The Pioneer Health Centre in Peckham by Sir Owen Williams, with its reinforced-concrete structure and extensive areas of glazing, was 'a modern building designed as a laboratory for the study of human biology'.[137]

Being an engineer, Williams might seem to present an anomaly in any discussion of the Modern Movement in Britain, yet he had designed a building which, in terms of structural innovation and the

The former Pioneer Health Centre, Peckham, London (Owen Williams, 1935)

Interior, Flat 56, Highpoint Two, Highgate, London (Berthold Lubetkin and Tecton, 1938)

expressive use of glass and reinforced concrete, made many of the celebrated creations of the architect members of the MARS Group seem minor. Williams had no time for the sociological pretensions of the New Architecture; he was a bloody-minded engineer who was only interested in getting things built, ideally in reinforced concrete. He had a profound understanding of structure and of the benefits of grid-line planning and of organised dimensional systems. But although he was always interested in economy, Williams succeeded in expressing the massive, fluid weightiness of concrete. The result was structures very different from the thin, planar aesthetic of the work of most Modern Movement architects. Yet Williams rejected the much-vaunted concept of 'structural expression': 'Modernism,' he announced in 1930, 'when it said "express the structure", was again trying a method of effectiveness and was then even more objectionable than the whole-hearted adoption of archaic forms. Why should the structure be expressed any more than any other part of the building – the drains for example? Why not leave it to express itself?'[138]

Williams was a phenomenon. Having been apprenticed to the Metropolitan Electric Tramway Company and acquired experience working for the Trussed Concrete Steel Company, he was knighted at the age of thirty-four for his work as consulting engineer at the 1924 British Empire Exhibition at Wembley. The various structures erected, including the stadium, and the famous Wembley lions, were all of reinforced concrete and were designed by the firm of Simpson & Ayrton. Williams continued to collaborate with Maxwell Ayrton on bridges for several road schemes. In Scotland the most notable were the Findhorn Bridge, between Perth and Inverness, and the peculiar concrete suspension bridge at Montrose. In England, Williams and Ayrton designed the elegant and carefully detailed Wansford Bridge, a structure of mass, rather than reinforced, concrete to carry the Great North Road over the River Nene.

By the end of the decade, Williams was tired of collaborating with architects and was convinced he could design and execute buildings by himself. His opportunity came in 1929 when he was appointed by Gordon Hotels Ltd to replace Wallis, Gilbert & Partners as designer of the new Dorchester Hotel. What followed became part of the mythology of modern architecture in Britain. To replace the Italianate magnificence of Dorchester House in Park Lane and to fulfil 'the requirements of a first class hotel' (defined as 'the maximum amount of light, sunshine and fresh air, the minimum amount of noise'),[139] Williams proposed a structure of reinforced concrete, to be constructed within a permanent external shuttering of terrazzo, or reconstituted marble and cement panels. The structure was remarkable, with the spine and wings containing bedrooms rising above a massive reinforced-concrete slab covering the ground and mezzanine floor public spaces – apparently making the Dorchester the safest building in London during the Blitz a decade later.

The client began to become anxious, however, especially as Williams wished to avoid any decoration either externally or in the public spaces, conceiving of the ballroom as a 'great whitewashed barn'.[140] As this was not the sort of thing that the expected wealthy patrons of the hotel might relish, Williams was asked if he would work with the well-known architect W. Curtis Green. Naturally he refused and, less than six months after he was appointed, resigned. As his then assistant, J. M. Richards, later recalled, 'He gave himself the pleasure of sending round in a taxi to Curtis Green's office, with his compliments, a load of unfinished drawings and half-completed calculations, knowing that neither Curtis Green nor any member of his staff would be able to make head or tail of them.' As the concrete structure had already reached ground-floor level and as time was tight, there was little Green could do other than re-style the exterior elevations with Deco detailing and metalwork, retaining the terrazzo panels, and design the interior spaces. To celebrate the opening of the resulting compromise, the hotel published *A Young Man Comes to London* ('An Original Short Story by Michael Arlen'), together with essays about the building and perspectives of Green's Classical interior. Of Williams's role in designing and planning the structure there was not a word – not even in C. H. Reilly's contribution, in which he wrote, 'No building could be more frank and functional in its main lines, that is to say more true to the modern stand-point than this upstanding mass of clean walling, exhibiting clearly every major aim of its structure.'[141]

Williams remained bitter about the Dorchester affair. Although it is hard to imagine an austere, unornamented concrete hotel being a commercial success, he had been insensitively treated. The pity is, perhaps, that he was not invited to work with his friend Oliver Bernard on the interiors. For Williams certainly had his limitations as a designer; his one realised venture outside the production of industrial or institutional buildings, a concrete synagogue in Dollis Hill, was scarcely an unqualified success. Other opportunities soon came his way, however.

In 1929 there was the commission for the *Daily Express* in Fleet Street (see above), in which his was the dominant role. Writing in the *Architectural Review*, Serge Chermayeff contrasted this sleek new building in glass and Vitrolite with the monumental Deco newspaper

The former *Daily Express* Building, Manchester (Owen Williams, 1939)

office recently constructed a little further up Fleet Street, arguing that, whereas 'The *Telegraph* flaunts innumerable petticoats nicely edged with familiar Paris lace', the *Express* is 'quietly elegant in a tight fitting dress of good cut which tells with frankness and without prudery of the well-made figure wearing it'. Hitchcock, by contrast, found it 'a colossal parody of contemporary American shop fronts'.[142] So pleased was the *Daily Express* with its new home that it commissioned Williams to design two more buildings for the paper, in Manchester and Glasgow, for which he acted as architect and engineer.

Williams's greatest achievement was a factory, the Packed Wet Goods Factory for the Boots Company, erected on a virgin site at Beeston, near Nottingham (Plate 33). The design consisted of a four-storey concrete flat slab structure on a rigid grid layout, interspersed by large open full-height atria top-lit by round glass prisms, the largest being 600 feet long. As David Cottam, Williams's biographer, has written, 'The most important aspect of this building is the complete subservience of almost every feature of its design to the efficiency of the structural layout and the dominance of

Boots, D10 ('Wets' Building), Beeston, Nottinghamshire (Owen Williams, 1932)

an uncompromising functionalist approach in even the smallest details.'[143] The completed building was nevertheless impressive and dramatic as an architectural composition, with the visible concrete piers with splayed tops supporting cantilevered glazed galleries. The principal, incomplete, elevation consisted of three long bands of industrial glazing, 365 feet long, raised above the ground floor and running continuously to and around canted corners.

Williams designed other structures at Beeston for Boots: a fire station and, more important, the 'Drys' building, completed in 1938. Running parallel with the 'Wets' building, this was originally intended to be similar in design, but in the event Williams adopted a different design. As the large open internal spaces combined with the glass curtain walls made the 'Wets' building expensive to heat, the later building has less glazing and no atria. In consequence, it might seem to lack the same visual impact. Pevsner, for instance, while considering the 'Wets' building 'a milestone in modern architecture', found 'the more recent part . . . less bold and less successful'.[144] Many architects may well have resented Williams muscling in on their profession, but there was no denying the scale and boldness of his Boots factory.

Boots, D6 ('Drys' Building), Beeston, Nottinghamshire (Owen Williams, 1938)

The editors of *Building* had the grace to recognise that no modern architect could have produced such a thing: 'it is difficult for a trained architect to be of the true functionalist faith – his aesthetic training and temperament make it almost impossible. And thus it is hardly surprising that Britain's most outstanding functionalist building has not been designed by an architect at all, but by an engineer.'[145]

While Williams was a conspicuous pioneer in Britain, several aspects of the Boots factory derived from American practice. Nor was he alone in using extensive areas of glazing – the contemporary Viyella Factory in the centre of Nottingham, by Frank Broadhead, also used wide bands of window from floor to ceiling. And then there were the Schocken department stores in Germany by Mendelsohn, the inspiration for the Peter Jones department store in London, with its continuous glass curtain wall curving elegantly from the King's Road into Sloane Square. Designed by William Crabtree in association with the firm's architects, Slater & Moberly, Charles Reilly was consultant. Reilly had been head of the Liverpool School when Crabtree was a student, and one of the projects he had set was the design of a department store in Oxford Street.

The Peter Jones store topped the 'Scoreboard', a poll of 1939 by the *Architects' Journal* to find the best modern buildings in Britain. Some three dozen 'well-known people in whose judgement of architecture they would have confidence' were asked by the editors to list 'the six recent British buildings which they considered of the greatest merit'.[146] The results may well reflect the fact that the artists, writers and others approached rarely strayed beyond West London; Williams only secured five votes for his buildings, but while the firm of Tecton secured the most votes – for the zoo buildings, for the Finsbury Health Centre and for both Highpoints – none of their buildings was the most popular. The three that were reflect a range of modernistic styles. Peter Jones was a worthy winner, but second came Battersea Power Station with its brick exterior given a 'jazz modern' treatment by Giles Gilbert Scott. The LPTB headquarters above St James's Park Station came third, a building by Charles Holden that might be characterised as American stripped-Classical.

Looking back after half a century, John Summerson considered that, 'the Modern Movement had made very little headway in Britain by 1939 and there were no more than perhaps a dozen buildings which might be expected to interest a sophisticated foreign critic'.[147] As Alan Powers, has written, 'At the end of the 1930s, there was a concern shared by conservatives, such as [Christopher] Hussey and Kenneth Clark, as much as by left-wing thinkers, as to whether Modernism could become popular and widespread without losing its integrity.' A possible solution to the dilemma lay in the house built for himself and his family by Serge Chermayeff in Sussex. Called Bentley Wood, this elegant building represented an important step in the naturalisation and the sophistication of the Modern Movement in Britain and secured much critical acclaim. Today, the story of its genesis and fate may seem a particularly poignant episode in the history of British architecture between the world wars. 'It may not be too far-fetched to suggest that what Bentley Wood stood for was

Bentley Wood, near Halland, Sussex (Serge Chermayeff, 1938)

precisely a modern form of Englishness, a fusion that reactionaries and revolutionaries alike had failed to predict.'[148] The house was proposed in 1936 and, after the customary arguments with the local authority, work began the following year.

The basic concept was a two-storey structural grid not of concrete but of timber; the side walls were also clad in timber. On the principal, south-facing elevation, the large windows on ground and first floors were set back behind the grid while the building itself stood on a terrace in a landscape designed in collaboration with Christopher Tunnard. On one side, the terrace and a flanking wall projected forwards to a platform where a sculpture, *Recumbent Figure* by Henry Moore, was placed. The completed house was much admired and much visited. Two decades later, the design still seemed to have a freshness and relevance while the other pioneering Modern Movement houses of the 1930s looked dated. In 1959 Summerson could write that, 'Among country houses easily the most memorable is Chermayeff's timber house for himself at Halland . . . whose beautifully sited hollow rectangles suppressed every vanity of "style" and merely touched the environment into conscience of form; it was the most aristocratic English building of the decade.'[149]

Chermayeff would not, however, enjoy living in his masterpiece for very long. As architectural difficulties grew with the threat of war, he was declared bankrupt in 1939 and soon afterwards decided to cross the Atlantic. Meanwhile, the Henry Moore ended up in the Tate Gallery and the house was sold, subsequent owners enlarging and mutilating it after the Second World War. Today, like so many other much-vaunted examples of the pioneering Movement in Britain, it is only possible to appreciate its designer's original intentions through the medium of contemporary photographs.

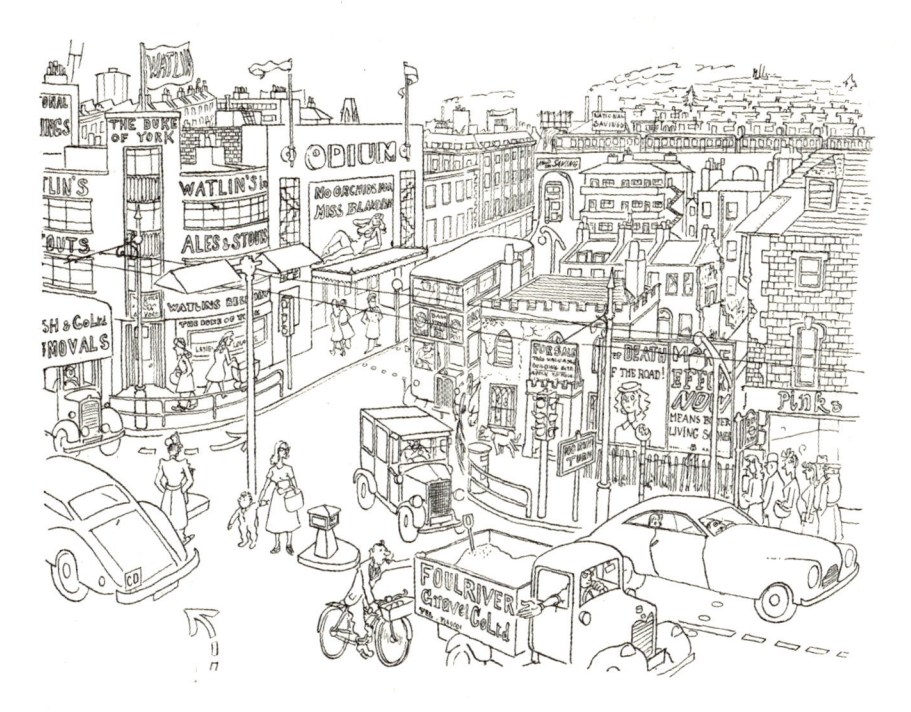

'Drayneflete 1949' (Osbert Lancaster, 1949)

ACKNOWLEDGEMENTS

In its author's absence, this book has been a team effort. My principal debt is to John East, who put his archive at our disposal and also undertook most of the original photography and photographic editing. For the Twentieth Century Society, its Director, Catherine Croft, and its former Chairman, Alan Powers, have been reliable sources of help and advice. Michael Hall of the *Burlington* magazine and John Goodall of *Country Life* have also been generous with advice and support. Some of the literary allusions were supplied by Gavin's friend Jan Piggott, formerly Head of English at, and historian of, Gavin's old school, Dulwich College. By a happy coincidence, one of Jan's former pupils, Nick de Somogyi, has been this book's diligent and at times inspired copy editor. Andrew Franklin, who has published books by both Gavin and myself in the past, commissioned this one, and it was seen through the press at Profile with care and enthusiasm by Nick Humphrey and Georgina Difford. I am further grateful to freelancers Rich Carr, for his meticulous text design; Lesley Hodgson, for her deft and resourceful picture research; and to our indexer, Hilary Bird.

PICTURE CREDITS

All the photography in this book is the work of John East (john.east@hotmail.com), with the exception of the following:

p. 127: Exterior and interior; The Queen's Dolls' House, Windsor Castle (Royal Collection Trust / © His Majesty King Charles III 2023. Photographer: David Cripps)

p. 145: Interior; Royal Horticultural Society, London (© Arcaid Images/Alamy Stock Photo)

p. 162: Quarry Hill Flats, Leeds (© Allan Cash Picture Library/Alamy Stock Photo)

p. 175: British Pavilion, Paris Exposition (© adoc-photos/Corbis via Getty Images)

p. 207: Regent Cinema, Brighton (© Pastpix/TopFoto)

p. 221: Firestone Factory, Greater London (© Fox Photos/Hulton Archive/Getty Images)

p. 226: 'Pseudish' (© Osbert Lancaster/Courtesy of Clare Hastings)

p. 227: 'Pont Street Dutch' (© Osbert Lancaster/Courtesy of Clare Hastings)

p. 242: The former Willans and Robinson Factory, Queensferry (© RIBA Collections)

p. 247: British Government Pavilion, British Empire Exhibition (© Chronicle/Alamy Stock Photo)

p. 275: 'Stockbrokers Tudor' (© Osbert Lancaster/Courtesy of Clare Hastings)

p. 277: 'By-Pass Variegated' (© Osbert Lancaster/Courtesy of Clare Hastings)

p. 290: Cock Rock, Devon (© RIBA Collections)

p. 295: Hammels, Oxfordshire (© Country Life/Future Publishing Ltd)

p. 298: Crowhurst Place, Surrey (© Country Life/Future Publishing Ltd)

p. 345: Leith House, City of London (© Architectural Press Archive/RIBA Collections)

p. 350: Interior; Gayfere House, London (© RIBA Collections)

p. 354: British Embassy, Washington DC (© TopFoto)

p. 356: Beech Grove Hall, RAF Manby, Lincolnshire (© Graham Buchan Innes)

p. 381: Norfolk House, London (Public Domain/British History Online)

p. 401: Interior; St Catherine's, London (© Look and Learn)

p. 402: Christian Science Church, London (© Alex Lentati/Evening Standard/Shutterstock)

p. 405: Society of the Sacred Mission, Nottinghamshire (© Newark Advertiser/Picture Nottingham)

p. 408: St Agnes, London (© Cadbury Research Library: Special Collections, University of Birmingham, Ref: Freeman/453)

p. 465: Broadcasting House, London (© RIBA Collections)

p. 480: New Ways, Northampton (© 78 Derngate Northampton Trust)

p. 517: Bentley Wood, Sussex (© Architectural Press Archive/RIBA Collections)

p. 519: 'Drayneflete 1949' (© Osbert Lancaster/Courtesy of Clare Hastings)

While every effort has been made to contact copyright-holders of images reproduced in this book, the author and publishers would be grateful for information where they have been unable to trace them, and would be glad to make amendments in further editions.

NOTES

Introduction

1. Pevsner (1970), p. 215.
2. Giles Gilbert Scott, 'Inaugural Address', *Journal of the Royal Institute of British Architects* (11 November 1933).
3. Pevsner (1970), p. 138.
4. Robertson and Yerbury (1931), p. 92.
5. Trevelyan (1946), p. 524.
6. A. Taylor (1965), p. 178.
7. Richards (1962), p. 15.
8. Summerson (1959), p. 11.
9. Lord Esher, 'Preface', *Recent English Architecture* (1947).
10. Clunn (1932), p. 112.
11. Illustrated in Abercrombie (1939).
12. Blomfield (1934), p. 82.
13. *Architectural Review*, Vol. LXXV (January 1934), p. 1.
14. Editorial, *Focus*, No. 1 (Summer 1938).
15. Summerson (1998), p. 196.
16. Muggeridge (1940), p. 1.
17. Betjeman (1986), pp. 20–21.
18. 'A Letter to Michael Sadleir' [July 1949], in Clark (1964), pp. xiii–xvii (pp. xiv–xv).
19. Richards (1940), p. 10.
20. Anthony Jackson (1970), p. 26.
21. Anderson (1934), pp. 1–2.
22. McGrath (1934), p. 19.
23. Weaver (1922), p. vii.
24. Christopher Hussey, 'St Christopher's Garrison Church, New Delhi', *Country Life*, Vol. LXIX (9 May 1931), p. 577.
25. Christopher Hussey, 'St Christopher's Garrison Church, New Delhi', *Country Life*, Vol. LXIX (9 May 1931), p. 577.
26. See Stamp (1976).

Chapter 1
Armistice

1. For the Cenotaph and the Peace Celebrations, see Homberger (1976); Mary Lutyens and R. A. Storey, 'To the Editor', *Times Literary Supplement*, 26 November 1976, p. 1486; and Skelton and Gliddon (2008).
2. Cannadine (2011), p 189. See also Stamp (1977) and Borg (1991).
3. Wellesley (1925), p. 166.
4. *Architectural Review*, Vol. XXXVII (May 1915), p. 104. The articles on 'Memorials of War' were: 'I. Ancient', ibid. (February 1915), pp. 26–30 (signed 'R.R.P.'); 'II. Renaissance', ibid. (March 1915), pp. 44–50 ('R.R.P.'); 'III. Napoleonic', ibid. (April 1915), pp. 62–71 ('A.E.R.' and 'R.R.P.'); 'IV. Modern British', ibid. (May 1915), pp. 95–104 ('A.E.R.' and 'R.R.P.'); 'V. Modern French', ibid., Vol. XXXVIII (July and August 1915), pp. 7–12 and 20–25 ('A.E.R.' & 'R.R.P.'); 'VI. Modern Italian', ibid. (October 1915), pp. 73–8 ('A.E.R.' and 'R.R.P.'); 'VII. American', ibid. (December 1915), pp. 106–13 ('A.E.R.' and 'R.R.P.'); and 'VIII. German', ibid., Vol. XL (November 1916), pp. 101–9 (unsigned, but probably by Richardson).
5. *The Architects' and Builders' Journal*, 8 November 1916, p. 210; Webb (1921), pp. 21 and 114.
6. Barker and Hyde (1982), p. 50. See also Beaufoy (1997) and Gilbert (2004).
7. Lethaby (1922), p. 65.

8. *Builder* (7 February 1919), p. 116, quoted in King (1998), p. 128.
9. Quoted in Connelly (2002), p. 113.
10. Chesterton (1936), p. 240.
11. See Inglis (1992).
12. Quoted in King (1998), p. 76.
13. Skelton and Gliddon (2008), pp. 49–57.
14. *Hertfordshire Mercury*, 28 January 1922.
15. Graves and Hodge (1941), pp. 19–20.
16. Hussey (1929).
17. Inglis (1992), p. 601.
18. For good examples of crosses and of other types of memorial, see Marriott (1924), pp. 201–3.
19. Moore (1999), p. 130.
20. Chesterton (1936), pp. 237–8.
21. Wellesley (1925), p. 169.
22. Blomfield (1932), p. 181.
23. For Jagger, see Baldry (1935), Compton (1985) and Compton (2004).
24. See D. Edwards (1999).
25. Graves and Hodge (1941), pp. 3–4.
26. Winter (1998), p. 85.
27. Kernot (1927), p. 4.
28. Baker (1944), p. 93.
29. Quoted in ibid., p. 97.
30. Nairn and Pevsner (1962), p. 144.
31. Hay (1931), p. 121. See also Weaver (1927) and Hamilton (1932).
32. Hay (1931), p. 7.
33. J. Lawton Wingate, PRSA, quoted in Hussey (1931).
34. *Architecture*, Vol. 5, No. 27 (August 1927), 'Scottish National War Memorial Souvenir Issue', p. 4.
35. Hamilton (1932), p. 7.
36. Hussey (1931), p. 91.
37. Symondson (1988), p. 22.
38. See Homberger (1976) and Crellin (2002).
39. Winter (1999), p. 54.
40. M. Lutyens (1991), p. 191.
41. Hussey (1950), p. 392. See also Amery and Richardson (1981), p. 149.
42. Winter (1998), p. 18.
43. For the story of the Unknown Warrior, see Blythe (1963), pp. 1–14.
44. Quoted in Hussey (1950), p. 375.
45. *Catholic Herald*, 19 November 1921, quoted in Gregory (1994), p. 199.
46. Ware (1937), p. 56.
47. Ibid., pp. 56–7.
48. Lutyens, 'Memorandum' (August 1917), Commonwealth War Graves Commission Archive, Maidenhead, Berkshire [CWGC/1/1/5/1].
49. See Ware (1937) and Longworth (1967).
50. Percy and Ridley (1985), pp. 351–2 (12 July 1917).
51. Lutyens, 'Memorandum' (August 1917).
52. Baker (1944), p. 88.
53. For Holden's intriguing relationship with the IWGC, see the accounts in Crellin (2002) and Karol (2007).
54. Commonwealth War Graves Commission, quoted in Stamp (1977), in which the careers of all the Assistant Architects are outlined. See also Skelton and Gliddon (2008).
55. Baker (1944), p. 90.
56. W. C. Von Berg to the author, 13 August 1977.
57. See Fuchs (2004).
58. See Dendooven (2001).
59. Blomfield (1932), p. 189.
60. Sassoon (1991), pp. 57–8.
61. *Berliner Tageblatt*, 16 September 1928, quoted in Blomfield (1932), p. 191.
62. Blomfield (1932), p. 189.
63. Quoted in Longworth (1967), p. 100.
64. Skelton and Gliddon (2008), p. 94.
65. See the *Journal of the Society for the Study of Architecture in Canada*, Vol. 33, No. 1 (2008), which is devoted to Allward and the Vimy memorial.
66. For the full story, which largely exonerates Lutyens, see Skelton and Gliddon (2008), pp.140–44. See also David Marr, *Sydney Morning Herald*, 26 April 1997.
67. For the problems encountered, and for a detailed analysis of the design, see Stamp (2006a).
68. Butler (1950), Vol. 3, p. 41.
69. Hay (1931), pp. 151–2.
70. Ibid., pp. 153–4.
71. Dyer (2009), p. 128.

Chapter 2
The Grand Manner

1. There was only a model in the Indian Pavilion: see Rohan (2002).
2. Robert Byron (1931), p. 2. Byron's articles on 'New Delhi' in *Country Life* were in Vols LXIX (6 June 1931), pp. 708–16; (13 June 1931), pp. 754–61; (20 June 1931), pp. 782–9; (27 June 1931), pp. 808–15; and LXX (4 July 1931), pp. 12–19. There is now an impressive literature on New Delhi: see in particular Hussey (1950); Irving (1981); Stamp (1981a); Grant Irving, Jane Ridley and Gavin Stamp in Hopkins and Stamp (2002); Nath (2002); and Sonne (2003).
3. [For details of this fraught relationship, often referred to here but not explained, see Irving (1981). RH.]
4. Byron (1931), pp. 18–19.
5. Ibid., p. 11.
6. 'A World Style in Architecture', *The Builder*, Vol. XCIII (1907), p. 306, quoted in Sonne (2003), p. 190.
7. Ford (1934), p. 76.
8. A. Edwards (1924), p. 105.
9. *Architectural Review*, Vol. LXII (December 1927), p. 223.
10. Marriott (1924), pp. 134–5.
11. Gloag (1931), pp. 152–3.
12. *Architect and Building News*, 19 March 1926, p. 223.
13. A. Edwards (1924), p. 68.
14. Ibid., pp. 115 and 113.
15. Ibid. p. 117.
16. Fellows (1985), p. 123.
17. *Architect and Building News*, Vol. CXXIII, 3 January 1930, pp. 14–19, quoted in Fellows (1985), p. 123.
18. Byron (1931), p. 30.
19. G. Scott (1924), p. 264.
20. Ibid., p. 203.
21. Ibid., pp. 239–45.
22. Ibid., p. 239.
23. Barman (1925b), pp. 281–2.
24. A. Edwards (1924), p. 94.
25. See Harvey (1925) and Barman (1925a).
26. Dircks (1923), p. 9.
27. Ibid., p. 1.
28. Hussey (1950), p. 522.
29. *Architectural Review*, Vol. LIV (October 1923), pp. 152–4.
30. *Architect and Building News*, Vol. CLXXVII (21 January 1944), p. 60.
31. Sir Edwin Lutyens, RA, 'Wren and his Tradition. The Teaching of Brick. Modern Foibles', *The Times*, 20 October 1932.
32. R. Lutyens (1970).
33. Summerson (1981), p. 52 (reprinted in Summerson (1990), p. 256).
34. Ramsey (1923).
35. G. Scott (1924), p. 204.
36. Pevsner (1979), p. 225.
37. Newman (2000), p. 440.
38. Reilly (1935b), p. 113.
39. Pevsner (1958), p. 413.
40. Pevsner (1953a).
41. Reilly (1935b), p. 115.
42. Reilly (1931d) (reprinted as Appendix B in Thomas (1963), p. 62).
43. Thomas (1963), p. 29.
44. Newman (1995), p. 589.
45. Reilly (1929), p. 393.
46. Summerson (1934), p. 424.
47. Reilly (1935b), p. 114.
48. Reilly (1930a), p. 384.
49. David Lloyd, in Pevsner and Lloyd (1967), p. 526.
50. Priestley (1934), pp. 9–13.
51. Goodhart-Rendel (1953), p. 243 (the 'Corinthian agony' being that of Edwin Cooper's Marylebone Town Hall, designed in 1914).
52. Marriott (1924), p. 122.
53. Ibid., p. 144.
54. Ibid., p. 143.
55. Ibid., pp. 141–2.
56. Ibid., p. 131.
57. Lancaster (1938), p. 64.
58. *Architectural Review*, Vol. LXXI (1932), p. 136.
59. Ibid.
60. Goodhart-Rendel (1953), p. 237.
61. Obituary, *Journal of the Royal Institute of British Architects*, Vol. XLIX (July 1942), p. 154.
62. Powers (1982), p. 17.

63. A. E. Richardson, 'Cooper, Sir (Thomas) Edwin', *Dictionary of National Biography* (1959).
64. Marriott (1924), p. 139.
65. Goodhart-Rendel (1953), p. 238.
66. A. Edwards (1928), pp. 91–2.
67. Goodhart-Rendel (1953), p. 236.
68. Byron (1932a), p. 27.
69. For Soane's interiors, see Steele and Yerbury (1930); for the rebuilding by Baker, assisted by the Arts and Crafts architect F. W. Troup, see Neil Jackson (1985); and for Scott's Soanian design for the telephone kiosk, see Stamp (1989).
70. Goodhart-Rendel (1953), p. 238.
71. M. Lutyens (1991), p. 211.
72. Goodhart-Rendel (1953), p. 234.
73. Reilly (1925), p. 288.
74. Ibid., p. 284.
75. M. Richardson (1987).
76. *Journal of the Royal Institute of British Architects* (11 March 1933), p. 365.
77. See Butler (1950).
78. [As remembered by Hal Kent, a contemporary member of Lutyens's office. Unidentified source. RH.]
79. Goodhart-Rendel (1953), p. 233.
80. [Unidentified source. RH.]
81. [Unidentified source. RH.]
82. 'Middleton Park, Oxfordshire', *Country Life* (5 and 12 July 1946), pp. 28–31 and 74–7.
83. Ibid.
84. Rohan (2002), pp. 119 and 128.
85. 'Daniel' [John Summerson], 'Architect Laureate', *Night and Day*, 28 October 1937, reprinted in Hawtree (1985), pp. 195–7.

Chapter 3
Swedish Grace

1. Goodhart-Rendel (1932), p. 594.
2. Reilly (1931b), p. 7.
3. *Architectural Review*, Vol. LVIII (July 1925), p. 3.
4. H. Robertson (1926), p. 175.
5. See the select bibliography of articles in Robertson and Yerbury (1989); and Yerbury (1987).
6. Rasmussen (1990), p. 19.
7. Brandon-Jones (1979), p. 97.
8. Easton (1924), p. 1.
9. H. Robertson (1926), p. 174.
10. H. Robertson (1962), p. 855.
11. Goodhart-Rendel (1922), p. 55.
12. A. Richardson (1928a), p. 401.
13. A. Richardson (1928b), p. 300.
14. Atkinson (1923), p. 4.
15. H. Robertson (1922), p. 46.
16. Yerbury (1928), p. 6.
17. Brandon-Jones (1979), p. 98.
18. Yerbury (1931), p. viii.
19. Jordan (1954), p. 237.
20. 'Buildings at Hilversum', *Architectural Association Journal*, Vol. L (1 June 1934), p. 17.
21. D. Walker (1989), pp. 34–5.
22. Yerbury (1928), p. 6.
23. Ahlberg (1925), p. v.
24. H. Robertson (1924), p. 25.
25. M. Robertson (1925), p. 124.
26. Gloag (1931), p. 183.
27. *Architectural Review*, Vol. LIV (December 1923), p. 201.
28. Williams-Ellis (1933), p. 55.
29. H. Robertson (1962), p. 956.
30. Anson (1960), pp. 337–8.
31. 'The Stockholm Exhibition, 1930: Gunnar Asplund, Architect', *Architect and Building News* (27 June and 4–11 July 1930), reprinted in Robertson and Yerbury (1989), p. 116.
32. James Bone, 'Foreword' to Yerbury (1935), quoted in Robertson and Yerbury (1989), p. 17.
33. Pevsner (1962), pp. 259–60.
34. *Architects' Journal* (25 May 1932).
35. See M. Richardson (1984).
36. Casson (1938), p. 48.
37. Fisker and Yerbury (1927), p. 5.
38. Pevsner (1939).
39. *Architectural Review*, Vols LII (1922) [Taut]; LIII (1923) [Mendelsohn]; LIV (1923) [Poelzig]; and LV (1924) [Gropius].
40. Newton (1927), p. 1.

41. Gloag (1931), p. 197.
42. Howard Robertson, 'The Hamburg "Chile Haus": Fritz Höger, Architect' (*Architect and Building News*, 8 November 1929), reprinted in Robertson and Yerbury (1989), p. 97.
43. Editorial, *Architectural Review*, Vol. LIX (January 1926), p. 2.
44. Goodhart-Rendel (1953), p. 263.
45. A. Edwards (1925), pp. 198–9.
46. *Architectural Review*, Vol. LVII (March 1925), pp. 61–4.
47. Pevsner, 1939, p. 2.
48. Pick *et al.* (1931), p. 16.
49. Shand (1930a), p. 24.
50. Ibid., pp. 20–21.
51. Gray (1996), p. 91.
52. Shand (1930a), p. 16.
53. Gray (1996), p. 80.
54. Bernard (1930), pp. 268 and 274.
55. Pick *et al.* (1931), pp. 10 and 5.
56. Richards (1940), pp. 87–8.
57. Bertram (1938), p. 55.
58. *Daily Telegraph*, 6 January 1928.
59. Fry (1932), p. 219, partially quoted in Hickman (1979), p. 158.
60. Beauman (1982), p. 110.
61. Pevsner and Wedgwood (1966), p. 415.
62. Ibid.
63. See Powers (1984).
64. Hopkins (2002).
65. See Campbell (2002).
66. Percy and Ridley (1985), p. 432 (3–4 October 1933).
67. Williams-Ellis and Summerson (1934), p. 30.
68. Richards (1940), pp. 75–6.
69. Carrington (1935), p. 6 ('Introduction').
70. H. Robertson (1962), p. 1120.
71. Williams-Ellis and Summerson (1934), p. 18.
72. H. Robertson (1928), quoted in Robertson and Yerbury (1989), p. 13.
73. H. Robertson (1926), p. 182.
74. Robertson and Yerbury (1928), p. 5.
75. Holt (1928), p. lvi.
76. Stratton (1928), p. 1.
77. Holt (1928).
78. Gloag (1931), p. 199.
79. *Architectural Association Journal*, Vol XLII (February 1926), p. 155.
80. Pevsner (1939), p. 16.
81. Quoted in Scarlett and Townley (1975), p. 60.
82. Pevsner (1939), p. 4.
83. Duncan (1933), p. 50.
84. Blake (1925a) p. 32, and Blake (1925b), p. 181.
85. Hastings (1925), p. 14.
86. *Architectural Association Journal*, Vol. XLII (February 1926), p.156.
87. Scarlett and Townley (1975), p. 61.
88. An unnamed French critic, quoted in Battersby (1969), p. 149.
89. Hastings (1925), p. 3.
90. Ibid., p. 34.
91. Blomfield (1934), p. 82.

Chapter 4
Brave New World

1. Burke (1934), p. 35.
2. Myerscough-Walker (1934), p. 239.
3. Graves and Hodge (1941), p. 2.
4. See Stamp and Greenberg (2002), p. 137.
5. See D. Sharp (1984).
6. Bradley and Pevsner (1997), p. 592.
7. Powers (1984), p. 56.
8. See Stamp (2004a).
9. Salmon (1922), p. 17. The article was unsigned, but the attribution to Salmon (then editor of the *Quarterly*) is given in O'Donnell (2003), p. 60.
10. 'Architectural Criticism from the "New Statesman"', *Architectural Association Journal*, Vol. XL (September 1924), p. 70.
11. Fry (1975), pp. 94–5.
12. Reilly (1930b), p. 526.
13. Ibid., p. 529.
14. Goodhart-Rendel (1953), p. 236.
15. Saint (1984), p. 35.
16. Ibid.
17. Reilly (1938), p. 227.
18. Ibid.
19. *Architectural Review*, Vol. LXI (January 1927), p. 16.
20. Fry (1975), p. 136.

21. *Devonshire House, Piccadilly* (London: Devonshire House Ltd, 1925), p. 31.
22. Lancaster (1939), p. 66.
23. Atkinson (1938).
24. Lancaster (1938), p. 70.
25. R. Lutyens (1930), pp. 185 and 183.
26. Bossom (1934), p. 9.
27. Ibid., p. 138.
28. A. Edwards (1924), pp. 16–17.
29. Ibid., pp. 19–25.
30. Williams-Ellis and Summerson (1934), p. 34.
31. Gloag (1931), p. 181.
32. A. Edwards (1924), p. 16.
33. See also Bettley (1987).
34. Simpson (1999), p. 63.
35. Shand (1929), p. 223.
36. See 'A City Tower of Healing', reproduced in Stamp (1982b), p. 118.
37. Reilly (1931a), pp. 396–7.
38. Shand (1929), p. 217.
39. Ibid., p. 223.
40. Saler (1999), p. 16 and *passim*.
41. Reilly (1931a), p. 399.
42. Butler (1926), p. 275.
43. A. Edwards (1929).
44. Goodhart-Rendel (1953), p. 263.
45. Saint (1984).
46. Hillier (1985), p. 13
47. Lancaster (1939), p. 72.
48. John Betjeman, 'Antiquarian Prejudice' (1937), reprinted in Betjeman (1960), pp. 54–72 (p. 67).
49. Benton and Benton (2003), p. 19.
50. Graves and Hodge (1941), p.127.
51. Quoted in ibid., p. 225.
52. Ibid., p. 124.
53. Shand (1930a), p. 17.
54. Ison (1982), p. 31.
55. Atkinson (1934), p. 86.
56. Ison (1982), p. 33.
57. Ibid., p. 36.
58. Gray (1996), p. 41.
59. Shand (1930a), p. 19.
60. Ibid., pp. 16 and 19n.; Gray (1996), p. 60.
61. Gray (1996), pp. 64–6.
62. Ibid., p. 70.
63. Goodesmith (1936), p. 39.
64. Shand (1930a), p. 18.
65. Gray (1996), p. 58.
66. Benton and Benton (2003), p. 27.
67. Gray (1996), p. 108.
68. Sidney L. Bernstein, in Cromie *et al.* (1936), p. 3.
69. Julian Leathart, 'Structure and Facing', in ibid., p. 13.
70. Ian Jack, 'Ghosts in the Stalls', *Guardian*, 26 June 2004.
71. Quoted in Wallis (1933), p. 310.
72. Ibid., p. 301.
73. Stamp (1986), p. 13; Yeomans and Cottam (2001), p. 14.
74. *Architectural Review*, Vol. LXXII (July 1932), p. 40. (The poem was by Michael Dugdale.)
75. Skinner (1997), p. 12.
76. Wallis (1933), p. 302.
77. Holme (1935), pp. 124–5; Skinner (1997), p. 232.
78. H. S. Goodhart-Rendel in Wallis (1933), p. 311; *Journal of the Royal Institute of British Architects* (11 March 1933), p. 368.
79. Holme (1935), p. 111.
80. Skinner (1997), p. 270.
81. Priestley (1934), p. 4.
82. *Architectural Review*, Vol. LXXII (July 1932), p. 40.
83. Williams-Ellis and Summerson (1934), p. 34.
84. *Architectural Association Journal*, Vol. XLII (April 1926), p. 203.
85. Ibid.
86. See R. Oliver (1983).
87. See *Cambridge University Library* (1934), p. 6; Brooke (1998).
88. Reilly (1935c), p. 75.
89. Lancaster (1959), p. 150.
90. Lancaster (1938), p. 66.
91. Hall (2002), p. 63.
92. Christopher Hussey, 'Ridgemead, Englefield Green', *Country Life*, Vol. LXXXVII (10 February and 17 February 1940); Stamp and Richardson (1983).
93. *Recent English Architecture* (1947), plate 55.
94. Christopher Hussey, 'Yaffle Hill, Dorset', *Country Life*, Vol. LXXIV (8 July 1933), pp. 14–19.

95. Williams-Ellis and Summerson (1934), p. 34.
96. Illustrated in Saint (1999), p. 142.
97. Ibid., p. 131.
98. See Bonham-Carter (1958).
99. Pevsner (1952).
100. Ibid. See also Emery (1970).
101. Mandler (1997), p. 254.
102. Worsley (2002), pp. 54, 32 and 43. See also Airs (2002).
103. Nevill (1925), p. 44.
104. Ibid., pp. 17–18.
105. Marks (1983), pp. 181–2.

Chapter 5
Tutankhamun

1. For the scandalous lack of protection afforded public spaces in London, see *London's Squares: How to Save Them* (London: The London Society, 1927).
2. *Architect and Building News* (9 November 1928), p. 600.
3. Graves and Hodge (1941), p. 114.
4. See Curl (1982), p. 197. See also Curl (1994).
5. Graves and Hodge (1941), p. 115.
6. Frayling (2003), p. 46.
7. Pevsner (1973), p. 359.
8. *Architect & Building News*, Vol. CXXXV (21 July 1933), p. 63.
9. Tait's initial design sketches are reproduced in *The Architectural Work of Sir John Burnet and Partners* (Geneva: Masters of Architecture, 1930). For Elcock & Sutcliffe, see S. Smith (2004), pp. 225–6.
10. H. Robertson (1932), p. 139.
11. Waugh (1978), p. 54.
12. Skinner (1997), pp. 121–2.
13. Ibid., p. 151.
14. *Illustrated London News*, 20 May 1933; quoted in Hitchmough (1992).
15. Morand (1928), p. v.
16. McDonald (1931), p. 118.
17. Byron (1928), p. 52.
18. Byron (1932a), p. 40. See also Knox (2003), pp. 268–9 and 273.
19. Byron (1932a), p. 42.
20. An idea suggested in *Seahorse: The Newsletter of the Friends of the Midland Hotel, Morecambe*, No. 9 (June 2003), p. 12.
21. Barnes (1925), p. 217.
22. See Stamp (2004c).
23. Lawrence (1924), p. 44.
24. Williams-Ellis and Williams-Ellis (1924), p. 82.
25. See Rohan (2002).
26. Byron (1931).
27. Stamp (2016).
28. Christopher Hussey, 'St Christopher's Garrison Church, New Delhi', *Country Life*, Vol. LXIX (9 May 1931), p. 577.
29. See Stamp (1976).
30. Quoted in Hussey (1950), pp. 492–3.
31. Shoosmith (1938), p. 204.
32. Christopher Hussey, 'A Crusaders' Castle of Today: Government House, Jerusalem', *Country Life* (31 October 1931), p. 486.
33. Fuchs and Herbert (2000), pp. 282 and 327.
34. Brooke (1998), p. 225.
35. 'Antiquarian Prejudice' (1937), reprinted in Betjeman (1960), p. 68.
36. W. Curtis Green, quoted in Joseph Emberton, 'Is Modern Architecture on the Right Track?', *The Listener*, 26 July 1933, p. 126.
37. See Harte and Stamp (1979) and Stamp (2000).
38. *The Architects' Journal*, 11 January 1934, p. 65.
39. Pevsner and Hubbard (1971), p. 86.
40. Reilly (1935c), p. 73. See also *The Story of the Mersey Tunnel* (1934).
41. Bossom (1934), pp. 18–19 and 15.
42. Byron (1932a), p. 28.
43. Ibid., p. 30.
44. Ibid., p. 27.
45. *Architect and Building News*, Vol. CXXXII, 18 November 1932, p. 198.
46. Mortimer (1933), pp. 17–18.
47. Illustrated in the *Architect and Building News*, 10 February 1933, pp. 190–91.
48. D. Walker (1989), p. 29.
49. Ibid., p. 35.

50. Tait's report (29 June 1934), quoted in ibid., p. 39.
51. On Saarinen's influence, see ibid., p. 53.
52. Ibid., p. 49.

Chapter 6
Merrie England

1. Clunn (1927), p. 128.
2. Stewart-Liberty (1924), p. 7.
3. *Architectural Review*, Vol. LV (May 1924), p. 180.
4. Bertram (1938), p. 61.
5. Richards (1962), p. 99.
6. E. Maxwell Fry, 'The Design of Dwellings', in Gloag (1934), plate 6.
7. Baillie Scott and Beresford (1933), p. 6.
8. Nash (1932), p. 37.
9. Gloag (1934), pp. 19–20.
10. Bertram (1935), p. 21.
11. John Gloag, 'The Suburban Scene', in Williams-Ellis (1938), p. 199.
12. Lancaster (1938), p. 60.
13. Lancaster (1939), p. 68.
14. Lancaster (1938), pp. 60.
15. Ibid., p. 62. See also Lancaster (1939), p. 70.
16. Lancaster (1938), p. 68.
17. Marjorie Noble, *Marc Noble: A Memoir* (London: Country Life, 1918), quoted in Aslet (1982), p. 156.
18. Bertram (1938), p. 58.
19. See Hobhouse (2002).
20. Mandler (1997), p. 232.
21. Leathart (1940), pp. 123–4.
22. G. Walker (2003), p. ix.
23. Stamp (1982a), p. 19.
24. Lancaster (1939), p. 70.
25. Rosemary Hill, 'Smocks', *London Review of Books*, 5 December 1991.
26. Cuffe (1931), p. 151.
27. Ibid.
28. Priestley (1934), p. 6.
29. Betjeman (1960), p. 54.
30. Waugh (1974), pp. 55–6.
31. Baldwin (1928), p. 9.
32. Mandler (1997), p. 241.
33. Ibid., p. 226. I am much indebted here to Mandler's incisive chapter on the 1920s: 'Land without Lords: The Nadir of the Country House'.
34. Nevill (1925), pp. 44–5.
35. Mandler (1997), p. 229.
36. Ibid., p. 226.
37. Barron (1929), p. 3.
38. Waugh (1962), pp. 137–44.
39. 'The Seaside Home of a Famous Humorist', *Arts and Decoration* (August 1939), pp. 16–18; Klein (1994), p. 83.
40. H. C. Bradshaw, in Abercrombie (1939), p. 104.
41. Smithells (1936), p. 159.
42. Baillie Scott and Beresford (1933), p. 5.
43. 'Sir Edwin Lutyens at the AA', *Architectural Association Journal*, Vol. XLVIII (August 1932), pp. 65–6.
44. As suggested by Gradidge (1979).
45. Powers (1989), p. 11.
46. *Country Life* (20 January 1938), quoted in Powers (2004), p. 69.
47. Campbell, lecture delivered c. 1943, quoted in Powers (1997), p. 25.
48. Powers (2004), p. 73.
49. *Recent English Architecture* (1947), plate 57.
50. Ibid., plate 53.
51. Abercrombie (1939), p. 53.
52. Phillips (1939), pp. 7 and 46–7.
53. *Architectural Review*, Vols. LX (July 1926), p. 24, and (for illustrations) LXIV (December 1928), p. 238. See also Rasmussen (1990), p. 16.
54. Blomfield (1934), p. 68.
55. *The Smaller House: Being Selected Examples of the Latest Practice in Modern English Domestic Architecture* (London: Architectural Press, 1924), p. 57.
56. Jekyll (1900), pp. 1–2.
57. Aslet (1982), p. 156.
58. Nairn and Pevsner (1962), p. 68.
59. Ibid., p. 334.
60. Aslet (1982), p. 174.
61. Ibid., p. 181.
62. R. Hill (2021), chapter 7. See also Wainwright (1989).
63. Barron (1929), p. 168.
64. Ibid., p. 50.
65. Ibid., p. 174.

66. Ibid., pp. 90–94. See also Fred Redwood, 'A Passion for Pastiche', *Sunday Telegraph Review*, 21 April 2002, p. 19.
67. Barron (1929), pp. 188 and 186.
68. *The Downland Post*, 1 June 1925; also see ibid., 1 June 1924.
69. Barron (1929), p. 182.
70. [See Joshua Hendren, 'Live in the Historic Sussex Mansion that Inspired the Classic Board Game Cluedo', *Tatler*, 16 July 2021. RH.]
71. Barron (1929), pp. 176–8.
72. Ibid., p. 180. Monk's Rest is in Hillside Road, Pond Cottage is in Pinner Hill: see Cherry and Pevsner (1991), p. 288.
73. Alan Jackson (1973), p. 244.
74. Osmond (2003), pp. 89–90.
75. Ibid., p. 99.
76. N. Taylor (1968), p. 160.
77. See G. Smith (1982), p. 4.
78. Illustrated in Oliver, Davis and Bentley (1981), p. 39.
79. Nairn (1966), p. 221.
80. Pevsner (1970), p. 138.
81. Richards (1940), p. 92.
82. *Magdalene College Cambridge, formerly Monks' Hostel 1428–1542–1928: Appeal for Funds for the Erection of a New Court* (Cambridge: Cambridge University Press, 1928).
83. Tomlinson (1933), p. 785.
84. Tyack (1997), pp. 305 and 300.
85. Baker (1944), p. 136.
86. Ibid.
87. *Architect and Building News*, Vol. CXXII (12 July 1929), p. 34.
88. Cromie *et al.* (1936), p. 24.
89. *Architecture Illustrated*, Vol II (September 1931), p. 90.
90. Bertram (1938), pp. 56–7.
91. A. Richardson (1935); Burke (1930).
92. B. Oliver (1947), p. 148.
93. Williams (1924), p. 204.
94. For the history of the pub and the campaign for 'improvement', see Brandwood, Davison and Slaughter (2004).
95. Quoted in ibid., p. 86.
96. C. R. Ashbee, 'Masters of the Art Workers Guild from the Beginning till AD 1934', unpublished typescript at the Art Workers' Guild, quoted in S. Oliver (2004), p. 332.
97. See S. Oliver (2004).
98. B. Oliver (1947), p. 131.
99. Brandwood, Davison and Slaughter (2004), pp. 50–51.
100. Quennell and Quennell (1935), pp. 79 and 82.
101. B. Oliver (1947), pp. 80–83.
102. Ibid., p. 86.
103. Priestley (1934), p. 77.
104. *Brighton Herald*, quoted in Atkinson, Matthews *et al.* (1990), p. 47.
105. *Brighton & Hove Herald*, 4 August 1934.
106. Bertram (1938), pp. 58–9.
107. J. B. Priestley, 'Houses', *Saturday Review*, 11 June 1927, quoted in Ward and Ward (1978), p. 47.
108. Leathart (1940), p. 124.
109. Rasmussen (1937), p. 304.
110. Oliver, Davis and Bentley (1981), p. 33.
111. Ibid., pp. 161 and 157. See also Stamp (1981b).
112. L. Scott (1934), p. 33.
113. Oliver, Davis and Bentley (1981), p. 202.
114. Waymark (2000).
115. Betham (1934), p. 203.
116. Allen (1934), p. 149.
117. *The Daily Mail Ideal Houses Book* (London: Associated Newspapers, 1927), p. 59.
118. Waymark (2000), pp. 37 and 47.
119. Green and Wolff (1933), pp. 137 and 165.
120. O. Green (1987), p. 89.
121. E. S. Turner, 'The Thought of Ruislip', review of Oliver Green, ed., *Metro-land: British Empire Exhibition Number*, *London Review of Books*, 2 December 2004.
122. Waymark (2000), p. 65.
123. Peter Way, 'Once it was all fields', *The Sunday Times Magazine*, 11 February 1968, p. 27. In fact, 'the fine Station Road, in Hayes' had already been illustrated in Boorman (1952).
124. H. C. Bradshaw, in Abercrombie (1939), p. 103.
125. Oliver, Davis and Bentley (1981), p. 117.
126. Stanley C. Ramsey, 'The Ready Built House', in Abercrombie (1939), p. 138.

127. Quennell and Quennell (1935), p. 31.
128. Alan Jackson (1973), pp. 151–6.
129. Rasmussen (1937), p. 270.
130. Stanley C. Ramsey, 'The Ready Built House', in Abercrombie (1939), p. 133.
131. Betjeman (1960), p. 55.
132. Lancaster (1938), p. 68.
133. Richards (1946), pp. 11–12 and 15. See also Jones (1947).
134. Richards (2013), p. 188.
135. Richards (1946), p. 15.
136. Oliver, Bentley and Davis (1981), p. 206. See also Stamp (2006b).

Chapter 7
New Georgians

1. Rasmussen (1937), p. 388.
2. Myerscough-Walker (1939), plate 13.
3. Phillips (1924), p. 9.
4. Reilly (1931b), p. 39.
5. Lancaster (1938), p. 64.
6. A. Edwards (1924), pp. 164–5.
7. M. Robertson (1924), p. 12. The author had been Deputy Chief Architect to the Ministry of Health Housing Department.
8. Ibid., p. 38.
9. Williams-Ellis (1928), pp. 123 and 173.
10. Goodhart-Rendel (1953), p. 243.
11. [John Summerson, unpublished typescript autobiography, chapter 4 (p. 3). RIBA Collections, Sir John Summerson Papers, Series 3: 'Papers relating to the preparation and publication of works by Summerson, ca. 1930–1990', SuJ/40/4 ('Biographical memoranda, including notes from Summerson's diaries, letters, illustrations and cuttings [for a proposed autobiography])'. RH.]
12. A. Richardson (1924), p. 206 (original emphasis).
13. L. Brett (1951), p. 20.
14. Wattjes (1927), plates 260–64.
15. *Recent English Architecture* (1947), plate 54.
16. Waugh (1984), p. 216.
17. Powers (2004), p. 94.
18. Ibid., p. 12.
19. Clifford Holliday, in Abercrombie (1939), p. 60 ('Vested interests, the high cost of land, the unhealthy state of most towns, and the absence of adequate town-planning schemes for urban areas make the building of [provincial] town houses almost an impossibility').
20. Turnor (1952), pp. 186–7.
21. 'Foreword by Mrs Wilfrid Ashley', *Architecture Illustrated* (August 1931), p. 36.
22. See Powers (2004), p. 41.
23. Christopher Hussey, 'Four Regency Houses', *Country Life*, Vol. LXIX (11 April 1931), pp. 450–56.
24. *Architectural Review*, Vol. LXXII (August 1932), plate III, pp. 52–3.
25. Lancaster (1939), p. 74.
26. Ibid.
27. Lancaster (1938), p. 64.
28. Richards (1940), p. 87.
29. Earle to the First Commissioner, 11 November 1925, quoted in Stamp and Greenberg (2002), p. 135.
30. Lutyens to Earle, 1926, quoted in ibid.
31. Charles Moore to the British Ambassador, 1927, quoted in ibid., p. 129.
32. Lansbury, response to 'Urgent Question' in House of Commons, 3 November 1930, quoted in ibid., p. 142.
33. Brooke to Sir Richard Allison, Chief Architect of Office of Works, copied to Lutyens, quoted in ibid., p. 139.
34. Lancaster (1938), p. 64.
35. Shand (1930b), p. 152.
36. *Recent English Architecture* (1947), plate 15.
37. Shand (1930b), p. 153.
38. Bertram (1938), p. 45.
39. Shand (1930b), p. 158.
40. For a full history of telephone kiosks, see Stamp (1989).
41. *Architect and Building News*, 10 April 1925, p. 280.
42. Judd (1936), p. 175.
43. Goodhart-Rendel (1953), p. 248.
44. *Architectural Review*, Vol. LX (September 1926), p. 101.
45. Reilly (1931b), p. 153.
46. Blomfield (1934), p. 168.
47. Gater (1937), p. 38.
48. Richards (1940), p. 86.

49. Pevsner (1939), p. 32.
50. Lancaster (1938), p. 72.
51. Reilly (1931c), p. 301.
52. *Architectural Review*, Vol. LXVI (July 1929), p. 7.
53. Hughes (1971), p. 46.
54. De Soissons (1988), p. 48.
55. Reiss (1927), p. 177.
56. *Architectural Review*, Vol. LXIII (April 1928), p. 144.
57. Reilly (1935c), p. 72.
58. Powers (2004), p. 64.
59. Turnor (1952), p. 198.
60. Rasmussen (1937), pp. 250–52.
61. Holliday, in Abercrombie (1939), p. 61.
62. Stamp (1982a), p. 20.
63. Byron (1937a), p. 24.
64. Goldring (1937), p. 71.
65. Clunn (1932), p. 112.
66. Drinkwater (1937), pp. 300–301.
67. Byron (1937a), p. 26.
68. Ibid., p. 12.
69. Chancellor (1908), p. 372.
70. Ibid., p. xiv.
71. Darwin (1925), p. 23.
72. Clunn (1927), p. 166.
73. Clunn (1932), p. 185.
74. Leslie (1937), p. 120.
75. Knox (2003), p. 383.
76. Byron (1938), p. 949.
77. Steele and Yerbury (1930).
78. Clunn (1932), p. 26.
79. N. Jackson (1985), pp. 51–74.
80. *Building News*, 28 July 1922, quoted in ibid., p. 57.
81. *The Times*, 25 July 1923, quoted in ibid., p. 61.
82. Ibid., p. 72.
83. Pevsner (1973), p. 182.
84. See Harte and North (1991).
85. *London's Squares: How to Save Them* (London: The London Society, 1927), p. 7.
86. See Stamp (2001), pp. 20–22.
87. Betjeman (1932), p. 125.
88. *The Times*, 16 July 1924.
89. Clunn (1932), p. 482.
90. See Webb (1921).
91. Several are illustrated and discussed in Keen (1930).
92. Clunn (1932), p. 116.
93. Byron (1937a), pp. 13–15.
94. A. Richardson (1933), p. 100.
95. Byron (1937a), p. 15; Byron (1938), p. 949.
96. See Lord Clonmore, 'A "Partner with the Enemy"' and 'What Public Opinion Says', *Architectural Review*, Vol. LXXIII (January 1933), pp. 9 and 11; Osbert Burdett, 'Carlton House Terrace: The Chance for the Defence', ibid. (February 1933), pp. 49 and 98 (and subsequent correspondence).
97. Knox (2003), pp. 263–5.
98. Goldring (1940), p. 50; *New Statesman and Nation*, 27 August 1932.
99. Goldring to William Palmer, secretary of the Society for the Protection of Ancient Buildings, 30 July 1937 [SPAB Archives].
100. For a detailed account of the foundation of the Georgian Group and its early history, see Stamp (2012). See also Hind (1986) and Knox (2003).
101. Byron (1937a), p. 24.
102. *Architect and Building News*, 17 January 1936, p. 89; for the mutilation of Nos. 120–22 Maida Vale, see Dorothy Warren Trotter's letter in *Country Life* (25 January 1936), p. 103, and 'Obituaries of Buildings: No. 45', *Architect and Building News* (3 January 1936), pp. 4–5.
103. Mrs Philip Trotter, 'Notes on Review of Robert Byron's pamphlet, "How We Celebrate the Coronation"', (n.d.), [SPAB Archives]; letter to *Kilburn Times* (3 September 1937).
104. See Sagar (1982), p. 227.
105. Georgian Group, minutes for 22 December 1937 and 2 March 1938, [Georgian Group Archives]; *Architectural Review*, Vol. LXXXIV (October 1938), p. 199.
106. Thomas (1963), p. 37.
107. See Stamp (2004b). [Sir Josiah, later Baron Stamp, was Gavin Stamp's great-uncle. RH.]
108. Ralph Parker, 'Shutters up in Portland Town', *Architectural Review*, Vol. LXXXIII (June 1938), an issue which also illustrated Oslo Court and Stockleigh Hall by Atkinson & Alexander; Stockleigh Hall in Prince Albert Road

was awarded the RIBA's London medal in 1937.
109. Transcript, 'Farewell Brunswick Square' (courtesy of the late Sir John Summerson). The debate was broadcast at 8.30 p.m. on 4 January 1938.
110. Byron to Summerson, 5 January 1938 (courtesy of the late Sir John Summerson).
111. Byron (1937b), p. 1009.
112. Byron (1937a), p. 8.
113. Editorial, *Architect and Building News* (17 January 1936), p. 89.
114. Goldring (1940), p. 44.
115. Sir James Richards to the author, 18 April 1982.
116. Quoted in Jencks (1977), p. 14.

Chapter 8
Modern Gothic

1. See K. Richardson (2002).
2. For a list, organised by architect, see Harwood and Foster (1998).
3. Maufe (1935), p. 295.
4. *Centenary Chronicle*, 10 July 1933, p. 42.
5. Goodhart-Rendel (1953), p. 249.
6. Maufe (1935), p. 294.
7. See Stamp (2002).
8. Marriott (1924), p. 99.
9. Goodhart-Rendel (1953), p. 248.
10. On Bodley, see Hall (2014).
11. Quoted in Comper (1947), p. 11.
12. Cachemaille-Day (1933), p. 828.
13. *Journal of the Royal Institute of British Architects* (26 May 1928), p. 472.
14. Symondson (1991).
15. Drummond (1934), p. 101.
16. Ibid., p. 116.
17. Maufe (1935), p. 307.
18. Pevsner (1960), p. 163.
19. Maufe (1935), p. 310.
20. Cachemaille-Day (1933), p. 836.
21. Cotton (1951), p. 14.
22. *The Architects' Journal*, 11 January 1934, p. 65.
23. *Architectural Review*, Vol. LXXIII (June 1933), p. 229.
24. Maufe (1935), p. 294.
25. Quoted in Symondson and Bucknall (2006), p. 170.
26. Ibid., pp. 166–8.
27. Hammond (1960), pp. 74–6.
28. Ibid., p. 4.
29. Ibid., p. 71.
30. Gill (1947), p. 414 (Eric Gill to Graham Carey, 1 January 1939).
31. Comper (1947), p. 30 (writing in 1939).
32. Cachemaille-Day (1933), pp. 826–7.
33. Rothery (1991), p. 164.
34. Drummond (1934), p. 127.
35. Ibid., p. 134.
36. *Architectural Review*, Vol. LXXIII (June 1933), p. 229.
37. Reilly (1935a), p. 164 (quoted in Ward (1998), p. 99).
38. Ibid.
39. Maufe (1935), p. 295.
40. Goodhart-Rendel (1953), p. 281.
41. Maufe (1935), p. 295.
42. Reilly (1935a), p. 163.
43. Maufe (1935), p. 308 (discussion after Maufe's lecture).
44. See Goodhart-Rendel (1918).
45. Goodhart-Rendel (1953), pp. 281–2.
46. Cachemaille-Day (1933), quoted in A. Hill (1991), p. 21.
47. Anson (1960), pp. 319–27.
48. Anson (1948), p. 42.
49. K. Richardson (2002), p. 26.
50. R. Lutyens (1970), p. 7.
51. Goodhart-Rendel (1953), p. 252.
52. Reilly (1931b), p. 148; the chapter on Scott had first been published in *Building* in 1929.

Chapter 9
The Shape of Things to Come

1. Weaver (1922), p. vii.
2. Etchells (1928), p. 156.
3. L. Brett (1951), pp. 20–22.
4. Summerson (1959), p. 11.
5. John Summerson [?], review of Hitchcock and Bauer (1937), *Journal of the Royal Institute of British Architects* (22 May 1937), p. 746.
6. Pevsner (1939), p. 35.
7. Lancaster (1938), p. 80.
8. Pevsner (1936), p. 206.

9. Richards (1940), p. 81.
10. Summerson to Ben Nicholson, 31 December 1940, quoted in Powers (2007), p. 63.
11. Gloag (1931), p. 210.
12. Leathart (1940), p. 169.
13. Lancaster (1938), p. 80.
14. Graves and Hodge (1941), p. 262.
15. Stillman and Cleary (1949), p. 17.
16. Powers (2005), p. 13.
17. *Architectural Review*, Vol. LXXII (November 1932), p. 198.
18. See J. Smith (2005).
19. McGrath (1934), p. 19.
20. Duncan (1933), p. vi.
21. 'Editorial', *Focus*, No. 4, (Summer 1939), p. 13. For 'The AA Affair, 1938', see Powers (1987), pp. 17–18.
22. Leathart (1940), p. 156.
23. Duncan (1933).
24. Yorke (1934), p. 6.
25. Pevsner (1936), pp. 206–7.
26. Casson (1938), p. v.
27. Wornum (1927), p. 237.
28. Oliver Hill, in Abercrombie (1939), p. 227.
29. Yorke (1934), p. 12.
30. H. Robertson (1932), pp. 125–7.
31. Pick, Holden and Edwards (1931), p. 3.
32. Ibid., p. 22.
33. H. Robertson (1932), p. 150.
34. Goodhart-Rendel (1953), p. 268.
35. Powers (2005), p. 124.
36. Goodhart-Rendel (1953), p. 267.
37. Alan Powers, 'Goodhart-Rendel: The Appropriateness of Style', in Stamp (1979), p. 46 (quoting John Summerson).
38. The advertisement was published (among elsewhere) in the *Architectural Review*, Vol. LXXV (November 1934), p. xxi.
39. Myerscough-Walker (1934), p. 253.
40. Leathart (1940), p. 152.
41. McGrath and Frost (1937), p. viii.
42. For such new materials, see Myerscough-Walker (1934), and Wright (1981).
43. Frost (1929), p. 272.
44. McGrath (1934), pp. 86–7.
45. Carey (1984), p. 99.
46. McGrath (1934), p. 87.
47. O'Donovan (1995), pp. 127–8.
48. The second prize was won by Paul Nash, the third by Vanessa Bell: see *Architectural Review*, Vol. LXVII (May 1930), p. 281; Vol. LXVIII (July 1930), p. 41; ibid. (November 1930), pp. 193 and 203; and ibid. (December, p. 242).
49. Byron (1932b), p. 47.
50. Hitchcock and Bauer (1937), p. 10.
51. *Daily Express*, 2 December 1936. See also Piggott (2004).
52. Duncan (1933), p. 62.
53. 'The Craftsman's Portfolio: Electric Signs', *Architectural Review*, Vol. LXX (July 1931), p. 27.
54. Burke (1934), pp. 228–30.
55. See Benton (1990).
56. Powers (2007), p. 35.
57. Joseph Emberton, 'Is Modern Architecture on the Right Track?', *The Listener*, 26 July 1933, p. 130.
58. Yorke (1934), p. 16.
59. Bertram (1938), pp. 65–6.
60. Le Corbusier (1927), p. xiv (quoting the 'Hospital' number of the *Architects' Journal*, 24 June 1925).
61. Ibid., pp. 4, 6 and 227.
62. Gloag (1931), pp. 200–201 and 186–7.
63. H. S. Goodhart-Rendel, in Anderson (1934), pp. 36–8.
64. Blomfield (1934), pp. 72–3.
65. Aldous Huxley, 'Notes on Decoration', *The Studio* (c. 1930), quoted in Powers (2007), p. 45.
66. Le Corbusier (1927), p. 92.
67. Waugh (1984), p. 216.
68. Le Corbusier (1927), p. 107.
69. McGrath (1934), pp. 87–8.
70. Le Corbusier (1935), p. 6.
71. *Airports and Airways* (London: RIBA, 1937), p. 6.
72. See Bingham (2004).
73. For Speke, see Smith and Toulier (2000).
74. Graham Dawbarn, 'Service Buildings', in Drew (1945).
75. Yorke (1934), p. 16.
76. Goodhart-Rendel (1953), p. 267.
77. Ibid., p. 268.
78. *Architectural Review*, Vol. LXXVII (January 1935), p. 11.

79. Pevsner (1939), pp. 20–21.
80. Ibid., p. 31.
81. Ibid., p. 23.
82. Ibid, p. 29.
83. Pevsner (1953b), p. 118.
84. B. Oliver (1947), p. 133.
85. Leathart (1940), p. 193; Pevsner (1939), pp. 35–6.
86. Richards (1940), p. 89.
87. Bertram (1938), p. 64.
88. For Mackintosh and Bassett-Lowke, see Crawford (1994) and Stamp (1996). See also Fuller (1984) and Bassett-Lowke (1999).
89. Yorke (1937), p. 14.
90. Abercrombie (1939), p. xi.
91. *The Architects' Journal*, 14 March 1928, p. 376.
92. The house had already been published (by 'Silhouette': 'New Ways', *Architectural Review*, October 1926, pp. 175–9).
93. Waugh (1962), pp. 142 and 146.
94. Summerson (1959), p. 12.
95. *Architectural Review*, Vol. LXXIV (September 1933), p. 94.
96. Quoted in Guise and Brook (2008), p. 16.
97. Powers (2005), p. 104.
98. The title and theme of Peter (2007).
99. Fry (1970), p. 596.
100. Powers (2005), p. 115.
101. See Denby (1938) and Darling (2007).
102. Fry (1975), pp. 143–4.
103. Summerson (1959), p. 12.
104. Quoted in Sharp and Rendel (2008), p. 46.
105. Quoted in ibid., p. 53.
106. Quoted in Anthony Jackson (1970), p. 27.
107. *Country Life*, Vol. LX (19 September 1931), p. 308.
108. [*An Ultra Modern House* (1931), now available on the BFI website: player.bfi.org.uk/free/film/watch-ultra-modern-house-1931-online. RH.]
109. Summerson (1993), p. 305.
110. Quoted in D. Sharp (1994), p. 55.
111. McGrath (1934), p. 96.
112. Quoted in Cantacuzino (1978), p. 62.
113. Summerson (1989), pp. 241–2.
114. Summerson to the author, 8 August 1979.
115. *Architectural Review*, Vol. LXXI (May 1932), p. 173.
116. Richards (2013), p. 131.
117. Hitchcock and Bauer (1937), p. 25.
118. Allan (1992), p. 256.
119. Hitchcock and Bauer (1937), p. 25.
120. Reilly (1938), p. 292.
121. Quoted in Brook (1987), p. 25.
122. *Architect and Builder's News* (20 December 1935), p. 343, almost certainly written by John Summerson, and quoted in Powers (2001), p. 77.
123. Pevsner (1970), pp. 412–13.
124. Pevsner (1939), pp. 23 and 33.
125. Gloag (1944), p. 163.
126. Stamp (1982a), p. 19.
127. L. Brett (1947), p. 37.
128. Ibid., p. 36.
129. Gloag (1944), p. 162.
130. See the commentaries in Powers (2005).
131. Waugh (1984), p. 216.
132. L. Brett (1947), p. 15.
133. Powers (2005), p. 25.
134. *American Architect and Architecture* (February 1937 and December 1936), quoted in Allan (1992), p. 139.
135. *Architectural Review*, Vol. LXXXIV (October 1938), p. 166.
136. 'Highpoint Two, North Hill, Highgate', *Focus II* (1938), pp. 76–9.
137. Pearse and Crocker (1943), p. 68.
138. 'How to Achieve Beauty', *Aberdeen Press*, 12 February 1930, quoted by David Cottam in Stamp (1986), p. 163.
139. Francis Towle, 'A Brief History of a New Enterprise', in Arlen (1931), p. 29.
140. Stamp (1986), p. 54.
141. C. H. Reilly, 'An Architect's Problem – How it was Solved', in Arlen (1931), pp. 36–7.
142. *Architectural Review*, Vol. LXXII (July 1932), p. 2; Hitchcock and Bauer (1937), p. 29.
143. Stamp (1986), p. 72.
144. Pevsner (1979), p. 70.
145. *Building* (September 1932), p. 392, quoted by Cottam in Stamp (1986), p. 82.
146. *Architects' Journal*, 25 May, 1938, p. 851.
147. Summerson (1989), p. 243.
148. Powers (2001), p. 139.
149. Summerson (1959), p. 17.

BIBLIOGRAPHY

Abercrombie, Patrick, ed., *The Book of the Modern House: A Panoramic Survey of Contemporary Domestic Design* (London: Waverley, 1939).

Ahlberg, Hakon, *Swedish Architecture of the Twentieth Century* (London: Ernest Benn, 1925).

Airs, Malcolm, ed., *The Twentieth Century Great House* (Oxford: University of Oxford Department for Continuing Education, 2002).

Allan, John, *Berthold Lubetkin: Architecture and the Tradition of Progress* (London: RIBA, 1992).

Allen, Gordon, 'Building to Sell', in Betham (1934), pp. 137–53.

Amery, Colin, and Margaret Richardson, eds, *Lutyens: The Work of the English Architect Sir Edwin Lutyens (1869–1944)* (London: Arts Council of Great Britain, 1981).

Anderson, M. L., ed., *International Architecture, 1924–1934: Catalogue to the Centenary Exhibition of the Royal Institute of British Architects* (London: RIBA, 1934).

Anson, Peter F., *Churches: Their Plan and Furnishing* (Milwaukee: Bruce, 1948).

———, *Fashions in Church Furnishings, 1840–1940* (London: Faith Press, 1960).

Arlen, Michael, *A Young Man Comes to London: An Original Short Story* (London: Dorchester Hotel, 1931).

Aslet, Clive, *The Last Country Houses* (New Haven: Yale Univeristy Press, 1982).

Atkinson, Clive, David Matthews, Andrew Savile, Robert Tunna and Tim Weighill, *A Guide to the Buildings of Brighton* (Macclesfield: McMillan Martin, 1990).

Atkinson, Robert, 'The Excursion to Holland', *Architectural Association Journal*, Vol. XXXIX (June 1923).

———, 'Design in Public Buildings', in Gloag (1934), pp. 83–94.

———, 'Shutters up in Portland Town', *Architectural Review*, Vol. LXXXIII (June 1938), pp. 287–94.

Baillie Scott, M. H., and A. Edgar Beresford, *Houses and Gardens* (London: Architecture Illustrated, 1933).

Baker, Herbert, *Architecture and Personalities* (London: Country Life, 1944).

Baldry, A. L., et al., *The Charles Sargeant Jagger Memorial Exhibition, 1935: War and Peace Sculpture* (London: Royal Society of Painters in Water Colours, 1935).

Baldwin, Stanley, *The Preservation of Ancient Cottages: An Appeal by the Rt. Hon. Stanley Baldwin, MP* (London: Royal Society of Arts, 1928).

Barker, Felix, and Ralph Hyde, *London as it Might Have Been* (London: John Murray, 1982).

Barman, Christian, [1925a] *The Danger to St Paul's* (London, 1925).

———, [1925b] 'The Portrait of Architecture', *Architecture: The Journal of the Society of Architects*, Vol. III (April 1925).

Barnes, Harry, 'The British Empire Exhibition, Wembley', *Architectural Review*, Vol. LV (June 1924).

Barron, P. A., *The House Desirable: A Handbook for Those Who Wish to Acquire Homes that Charm* (London: Methuen, 1929).

Bassett-Lowke, Janet, *Wenman Joseph Bassett-Lowke: A Memoir of his Life and Achievements, 1877–1953* (Chester: Rail Romances, 1999).

Battersby, Martin, *The Decorative Twenties* (London: Studio Vista, 1969).

Beaufoy, Helena, '"Order out of Chaos": The London Society and the Planning of London 1912–1920', *Planning Perspectives*, Vol. XII (1997), pp. 135–64.

Beauman, Sally, *The Royal Shakespeare Company: A History of Ten Decades* (Oxford: Oxford University Press, 1982).

Benton, Charlotte, and Tim Benton, 'The Style and the Age', in Benton, Benton and Wood (2003), pp. 12–27.

Benton, Charlotte, Tim Benton and Ghislaine Wood, eds, *Art Deco 1910–1939* (London: V&A, 2003).

Benton, Tim, 'The Myth of Function', in Paul Greenhalgh, ed., *Modernism in Design* (London: Reaktion, 1990), pp. 41–52.

Bernard, Oliver P., 'United Arts of Europe. A Visit to Berlin', *Building* (April 1930).

Bertram, Anthony, *The House: A Machine for Living In: A Summary of the Art and Science of Homemaking Considered Functionally* (London: A. & C. Black, 1935).

———, *Design* (Harmondsworth: Penguin, 1938).

Betham, Ernest, ed., *House Building 1934–1936* (London: Federated Employers' Press, 1934).

Betjeman, John, 'The Truth about Waterloo Bridge', *Architectural Review*, Vol. LXXI (April 1932).

———, *First and Last Loves* (1952; London: Grey Arrow, 1960).

———, *Ghastly Good Taste; or, a Depressing Story of the Rise and Fall of English Architecture* (1933; London: Century Hutchinson, 1986).

Bettley, James, *Lush and Luxurious: The Life and Work of Philip Tilden, 1887–1956* (London: RIBA, 1987).

Bingham, Neil, 'Arrivals and Departures: Civil Airport Architecture in Britain during the Interwar Period', in Julian Holder and Steven Parissien, eds, *The Architecture of British Transport in the Twentieth Century* (London: Yale University Press, 2004).

Blake, Vernon, [1925a] 'Modern Decorative Art', *Architectural Review*, Vol. LVIII (July 1925)

———, [1925b] 'Modern Decorative Art – II', *Architectural Review*, Vol. LVIII (November 1925).

Blomfield, Sir Reginald, *Memoirs of an Architect* (London: Macmillan and Co., 1932).

———, *Modernismus* (London: Macmillan and Co., 1934).

Blythe, Ronald, *The Age of Illusion: England in the Twenties and Thirties, 1919–1940* (London: Hamish Hamilton, 1963).

Bonham-Carter, Victor, *Dartington Hall: The History of an Experiment* (Ithaca, New York: Cornell University Press, 1958).
Boorman, H. R. Pratt, *Kentish Pride* (Maidstone: Kent Messenger, 1952).
Borg, Alan, *War Memorials: From Antiquity to the Present* (London: Leo Cooper, 1991).
Bossom, Alfred C., *Building to the Skies: The Romance of the Skyscraper* (London: Studio, 1934).
———, *Bossom Family Christmas Cards 1915 to 1947: With a Word About the Events that Inspired Them* (London: Fanfare Press, 1948).
Bradley, Simon, and Nikolaus Pevsner, *The Buildings of England: London 1: The City of London* (London: Yale University Press, 1997).
Brandon-Jones, John, 'An Interview with John Brandon-Jones: "Bliss Was it in That Dawn to Be Alive"', in Stamp (1979).
Brandwood, Geoff, Andrew Davison and Michael Slaughter, *Licensed to Sell: The History and Heritage of the Public House* (London: English Heritage, 2004).
Brett, C. E. B., *Court Houses and Market Houses of the Province of Ulster* (Belfast: Ulster Architectural Heritage Society, 1973).
Brett, Lionel, *The Things We See: No. 2: Houses* (West Drayton: Penguin, 1947).
———, 'Ends and Beginnings', in *One Hundred Years of British Architecture 1851–1951* (London: RIBA, 1951).
Brook, Jeremy, 'The Story of the De La Warr Pavilion', in *Erich Mendelsohn 1887–1953: A Touring Exhibition organised by Modern British Architecture 1987* (London: Modern British Architecture, 1987).
Brooke, Christopher, 'The University Library and its Buildings', in Peter Fox, ed., *Cambridge University Library: The Great Collections* (Cambridge: Cambridge University Press, 1998).
Buck, Gordon, *A Pictorial Survey of Railway Stations* (Oxford: OPC Railprint, 1992).
Burke, Thomas, *The English Inn* (London: Longmans & Green, 1930).
———, *London in My Time* (London: Rich and Cowan, 1934).
Butler, A. S. G., *The Substance of Architecture* (London: Constable, 1926).
———, *The Architecture of Sir Edwin Lutyens*, 3 vols (London: Country Life, 1950).
Byron, Robert, 'The Psychology of Eastern Monasticism: Its Relation to the Twentieth Century', *Architectural Review*, Vol. LXIV (August 1928).
———, 'New Delhi', *Architectural Review*, Vol. LXIX (January 1931).
———, [1932a] *The Appreciation of Architecture* (London: Wishart and Co., 1932).
———, [1932b] 'Broadcasting House', *Architectural Review*, Vol. LXXII (August 1932).
———, [1937a] *How We Celebrate the Coronation* (London: Architectural Press, 1937).
———, [1937b] 'The Destruction of Georgian London', *New Statesman and Nation* (11 December 1937).
———, 'The Secrets of Abingdon Street', *New Statesman and Nation* (4 June 1938).
———, *The Road to Oxiana* (1937; Harmondsworth: Penguin, 1992).
Cachemaille-Day, N. F., 'Ecclesiastical Architecture in the Present Age', *Journal of the Royal Institute of British Architects* (14 October 1933).
Cambridge University Library 1400–1934: with a description of the New Building Opened by His Majesty the King (Cambridge: Cambridge University Press, 1934).
Campbell, Louise, '"A Curious Heritage": Humanism, Modernism and Rome Scholars in Architecture during the 1920s and 1930s', in Hopkins and Stamp (2002).

Cannadine, David, 'War and Death, Grief and Mourning in Modern Britain', in Joachim Whaley, ed., *Mirrors of Mortality: Studies in the Social History of Death* (1981; Abingdon: Routledge, 2011).

Cantacuzino, Sherban, *Wells Coates: A Monograph* (London: Gordon Fraser, 1978).

Carey, Hugh, *Mansfield Forbes and his Cambridge* (Cambridge: Cambridge University Press, 1984).

Carrington, Noel, ed., *Portmeirion Still Further Explained: Essays by Several Hands* (Birmingham: Kynoch Press, 1935).

Casson, Hugh, *New Sights of London: The Handy Guide to Contemporary Architecture* (London: London Transport, 1938).

Chancellor, E. Beresford, *The Private Palaces of London, Past and Present* (London: Kegan Paul, Trench, Trübner, 1908).

Cherry, Bridget, and Nikolaus Pevsner, *The Buildings of England: London 3: North West* (London: Penguin, 1991).

Chesterton, G. K., *Autobiography* (London: Hutchinson, 1936).

Clark, Kenneth, *The Gothic Revival: An Essay in the History of Taste*, second edition (1962; Harmondsworth: Pelican, 1964).

Clunn, Harold P., *London Rebuilt 1897–1927: An Attempt to Depict the Principal Changes which Have Taken Place, with some Suggestions for the Further Improvement of the Metropolis* (London: John Murray, 1927).

———, *The Face of London: The Record of a Century's Changes and Developments* (London: Simpkin Marshall Ltd, 1932)

Comper, J. N., *Of the Atmosphere of a Church* (London: Sheldon Press, 1947).

Compton, Ann, ed., *Charles Sargeant Jagger: War and Peace Sculpture* (London: Imperial War Museum, 1985).

———, *The Sculpture of Charles Sargeant Jagger* (London: Henry Moore Foundation in association with Lund Humphries, 2004).

Connelly, Mark, *The Great War, Memory and Ritual Commemoration in the City and East London, 1916–1939* (Woodbridge: Royal Historical Society, 2002).

Cotton, Vere E., *Liverpool Cathedral: The Official Handbook of the Cathedral Committee*, eleventh edition (Liverpool: Littlebury, 1951).

Crawford, Alan, 'Lost and Found: Architectural Projects after Glasgow', in Pamela Robertson, ed., *C. R. Mackintosh: The Chelsea Years 1915–1923* (Glasgow: Hunterian Art Gallery, 1994).

Crellin, David, '"Some Corner of a Foreign Field": Lutyens, Empire and the Sites of Remembrance', in Hopkins and Stamp (2002).

Cromie, Robert, Sidney L. Bernstein et al., *Modern Cinemas* (London: Architectural Press, 1936).

Cuffe, Lionel, 'William Morris', *Architectural Review*, Vol. LXIX (May 1931).

Curl, James Stevens, *The Egyptian Revival: An Introductory Study of a Recurring Theme in the History of Taste* (London: George Allen and Unwin, 1982).

———, *Egyptomania: The Egyptian Revival; A Recurring Theme in the History of Taste* (Manchester: Manchester University Press, 1994).

Dannatt, Trevor, ed., *Architects' Yearbook Nine* (London: Elek Books, 1960).

BIBLIOGRAPHY

Darling, Elizabeth, 'Kensal House: The Housing Consultant and the Housed', *Twentieth Century Architecture*, No. 8 [*British Modern: Architecture and Design in the 1930s*] (2007).

Darwin, Bernard, 'The New Devonshire House', in *Devonshire House, Piccadilly* (London: Devonshire House Ltd, 1925).

Denby, Elizabeth, 'Kensal House: An Urban Village', in *Flats: Municipal and Private Enterprise* (London: Ascot Gas Water Heaters Ltd, 1938).

Dendooven, Dominiek, *Menin Gate and Last Post: Ypres as Holy Ground* (Koksijde: De Klaproos, 2001).

Dircks, Rudolf, ed., *Sir Christopher Wren A.D. 1632–1723: Bicentenary Memorial Volume published under the auspices of the Royal Institute of British Architects* (London: Hodder & Stoughton, 1923).

Drew, Jane B., ed., *Architects' Year Book* (London: Paul Elek, 1945).

Drinkwater, John, *Robinson of England* (London: Methuen, 1937).

Drummond, Andrew Landale, *The Church Architecture of Protestantism: An Historical and Constructive Study* (Edinburgh: T. & T. Clark, 1934).

Duncan, R. A., *The Architecture of a New Era: Revolution in the World of Appearance* (London: Denis Archer, 1933).

Dyer, Geoff, *The Missing of the Somme* (1994; London: Phoenix, 2009).

Easton, John Murray, 'The Stadhus at Stockholm', *Architectural Review*, Vol. LV (January 1924).

Edwards, A. Trystan, *Good and Bad Manners in Architecture* (London: Philip Allan & Co., 1924).

———, 'What the Building Said', *Architecture: The Journal of the Society of Architects*, Vol. III (February 1925).

———, 'High Words in Piccadilly, or *What* Barclay's Bank *said to* The Westminster Bank', *Architectural Review*, Vol. LXIII (March 1928), pp. 88–92.

———, 'The Moor of Argyle Street', *Architectural Review*, Vol. LXV (1929).

Edwards, Deborah, *'This Vital Flesh': The Sculpture of Rayner Hoff and his School* (Sydney: Art Gallery of New South Wales, 1999).

Emery, Anthony, *Dartington Hall* (Oxford: Clarendon Press, 1970).

Etchells, Frederick, 'Le Corbusier: A Pioneer of Modern European Architecture', *The Studio*, Vol. XCVI (September 1928).

Fellows, Richard A., *Sir Reginald Blomfield: An Edwardian Architect* (London: A. Zwemmer, 1985).

Fisker, Kay, and F. R. Yerbury, eds, *Modern Danish Architecture* (London: Ernest Benn, 1927).

Ford, Ford Madox, *It Was the Nightingale* (London: William Heinemann Ltd, 1934).

Frayling, Christopher, 'Egyptomania', in Benton, Benton and Wood (2003).

Frost, A. C., 'Finella: A House for Mansfield D. Forbes, Esq.', *Architectural Review*, Vol. LXVI (December 1929).

Fry, E. Maxwell, 'Shakespeare's Stratford – and Ours', *Architectural Review*, Vol. LXXI (June 1932).

———, 'Historic Pioneers: Architects and Clients', *Architects' Journal* (11 March 1970).

———, *Autobiographical Sketches* (London: Elek, 1975).

Fuchs, Ron, 'Sites of Memory in the Holy Land: The Design of the British War Cemeteries in Mandate Palestine', *Journal of Historical Geography*, Vol. XXX, No. 4 (October 2004), pp. 643–64.

Fuchs, Ron, and Gilbert Herbert, 'Representing Mandatory Palestine: Austen St Barbe Harrison and the Representational Buildings of the British Mandate in Palestine, 1922–37', *Architectural History*, Vol. XLIII (2000), pp. 281–333.

Fuller, Roland, *The Bassett-Lowke Story* (London: New Cavendish Books, 1984).

Fussell, Paul, *The Great War and Modern Memory* (London: Oxford University Press, 1975).

Gater, G. H., ed., *London Housing* (London: London County Council, 1937).

Gilbert, David, '*London of the Future*: The Metropolis Reimagined after the Great War', *Journal of British Studies*, Vol. 43 (January 2004), pp. 91–119.

Gill, Eric, *Letters of Eric Gill*, ed. Walter Shewring (London: Jonathan Cape, 1947).

Gloag, John, *Men and Buildings* (London: Country Life, 1931).

———, ed., *Design in Modern Life* (London: George Allen & Unwin, 1934).

———, *The Englishman's Castle: A History of Houses, Large and Small, in Town and Country, from A.D. 100 to the Present Day* (London: Eyre & Spottiswoode, 1944).

Goldring, Douglas, *Pot Luck in England* (London: Chapman & Hall, 1936).

———, 'The Georgian Group', *Architectural Review*, Vol. LXXXII (August 1937).

———, *Facing the Odds* (London: Cassell, 1940).

Goodesmith, Walter, 'I: Design at Home', *Modern Cinemas* (London: Architects' Journal, London 1936).

Goodhart-Rendel, H. S., 'The Churches of Brighton and Hove', *Architectural Review*, Vol. XLIV (1918), pp. 23–9, 59–63, and 75–9.

———, 'English Students and Dutch Reviewers', *Architectural Association Journal*, Vol. XXXVIII (August 1922).

———, 'First Impressions', *Architects' Journal*, Vol. LXXV (4 May 1932).

———, *English Architecture since the Regency* (London: Constable, 1953).

Gradidge, Roderick, 'The Architecture of Oliver Hill', *Architectural Design*, Vol. XL (1979), pp. 30–41.

Graves, Robert, and Alan Hodge, *The Long Week-End: A Social History of Great Britain 1918–1939* (1940; New York: Macmillan, 1941).

Gray, Richard, *Cinemas in Britain: One Hundred Years of Cinema Architecture* (London: Lund Humphries, 1996).

Green, Frank, and Dr Sidney Wolff, *London and Suburbs, Old and New: Useful Knowledge for Health and Home* (London: Souvenir Magazines, 1933).

Green, Oliver, ed., *Metro-land: 1932 Facsimile Edition* (Harpenden: Oldcastle Books, 1987).

Gregory, Adrian, *The Silence of Memory: Armistice Day 1919–1946* (Oxford–Providence: Berg, 1994).

Guise, Barry, and Pam Brook, *The Midland Hotel: Morecambe's White Hope* (Lancaster: Palatine Books, 2008).

Hall, Michael, '*Country Life* and New Country Houses Between the Wars', in Airs (2002).

———, *George Frederick Bodley and the Later Gothic Revival in Britain and America* (New Haven: Yale University Press, 2014).

Hamilton, General Sir Ian, 'Introduction', *The Scottish National War Memorial* (Edinburgh: Grant and Murray 1932).

Hammond, Peter, *Liturgy and Architecture* (London: Barrie and Rockliff, 1960).

Harcourt-Smith, *The Last of Uptake; or, The Estranged Sisters*, illustrated by Rex Whistler (London: Batsford, 1942).

Harte, Glynn Boyd, and Gavin Stamp, *Temples of Power* (Burford: Cygnet, 1979).

Harte, Negley, and John North, *The World of UCL: 1828–1990* (London: University College London, 1991).

Harvey, William, *The Preservation of St Paul's Cathedral and Other Famous Buildings: A Textbook on the New Science of Conservation, including an Analysis of Movements in Historical Structures Prior to their Fall* (London: Architectural Press, 1925).

Harwood, Elain, and Andrew Foster, 'Places of Christian Worship 1914–1990: A Selection of Christian Places of Worship', *Twentieth Century Architecture*, No. 3 (1998), pp. 104–28.

Hastings, H. de C., 'A General Review', *Architectural Review*, Vol. LVIII (July 1925).

Hawkins, Jennifer, and Marianne Hollis, eds, *Thirties: British Art and Design before the War* (London: Arts Council of Great Britain, 1979).

Hawtree, Christopher, ed., *Night and Day* (London: Chatto & Windus, 1985).

Hay, Ian [Major John H. Beith], *Their Name Liveth: The Book of the Scottish National War Memorial* (London: John Lane, 1931).

Hebert, A. G., *Liturgy and Society: The Function of the Church in the Modern World* (London: Faber, 1935).

Hickman, Douglas, *A Shell Guide: Warwickshire* (London: Faber, 1979).

Hill, Anthony, 'N.F. Cachemaille-Day: A Search for Something More', *Thirties Society Journal*, No. 7 (1991), pp. 20–27.

Hill, Rosemary, *Time's Witness: History in the Age of Romanticism* (London: Allen Lane, 2021).

Hillier, Bevis, *Art Deco of the 20s and 30s* (1968; New York: Schocken, 1985).

Hind, Charles, 'Sound and Fury: The Early Days of the Georgian Group', *The Georgian Group: Report and Journal* (1986), pp. 45–54.

Hines, Colin, *Art Deco London* (London: Park House, 2003).

Hitchcock, Henry-Russell, junior, and Catherine K. Bauer, *Modern Architecture in England* (New York: Museum of Modern Art, 1937).

Hitchmough, Wendy, *Hoover Factory: Wallis, Gilbert and Partners* (London: Phaidon, 1992).

Hobhouse, Hermione, '"An Architect Animated by the Spirit of his Subject": Lutyens's Exhibition Buildings', in Hopkins and Stamp (2002).

Holme, C. G., ed., *Industrial Architecture* (London: The Studio, 1935).

Holt, Gordon H. G., 'The Merit of Le Corbusier', *Architectural Review*, Vol. LXIII (March 1928).

Homberger, Eric, 'The Story of the Cenotaph', *Times Literary Supplement*, 12 November 1976, pp. 1429–30.

Hopkins, Andrew, 'Lutyens's Plans for the British School at Rome', in Hopkins and Stamp (2002), pp. 69–86.

——, 'The Source for Lutyens's Memorial to the Missing of the Somme', *Burlington Magazine*, Vol. CLXIV (August 2022), pp. 516–21.

Hopkins, Andrew, and Gavin Stamp, eds, *Lutyens Abroad: The Work of Sir Edwin Lutyens Outside the British Isles* (London: British School at Rome at the British Academy, 2002).

Hughes, Michael, ed., *The Letters of Lewis Mumford and Frederick J. Osborn: A Transatlantic Dialogue, 1938–70* (Bath: Adams and Dart, 1971).

Hurst, Sidney C., *The Silent Cities: An Illustrated Guide to the War Cemeteries and Memorials to the 'Missing' in France and Flanders: 1914–1918* (London: Methuen, 1929).
Hussey, Christopher, *Tait McKenzie: A Sculptor of Youth* (London: Country Life, 1929).
———, *The Work of Sir Robert Lorimer, KBE, ARA, RSA* (London: Country Life, 1931).
———, *The Life of Sir Edwin Lutyens* (London: Country Life, 1950).
Ind, Rosemary, *Emberton* (London: Scolar Press, 1983).
Inglis, K. S., 'The Homecoming: The War Memorial Movement in Cambridge, England', *Journal of Contemporary History*, Vol. XXVII, (October 1992), pp. 583–606.
Irving, Robert Grant, *Indian Summer: Lutyens, Baker and Imperial Delhi* (New Haven: Yale University Press, 1981).
Ison, Walter, 'The Regent, Brighton: "Europe's Wonder House of Entertainment"', *The Journal of the Decorative Arts Society 1890–1940*, No. 6 (1982), pp. 31–6.
Jackson, Alan A., *Semi-Detached London: Suburban Development, Life and Transport, 1900–39* (London: George Allen & Unwin, 1973).
Jackson, Anthony, *The Politics of Architecture: A History of Modern Architecture in Britain* (London: Architectural Press, 1970).
Jackson, Neil *F. W. Troup, Architect: 1859–1941* (London: Building Centre Trust, 1985).
Jekyll, Gertrude, *Home and Garden: Notes and Thoughts, Practical and Critical, of a Worker in Both* (London: Longmans, Green, 1900).
Jencks, Charles, *The Language of Post-Modern Architecture* (New York: Rizzoli, 1977).
Jones, Barbara, 'The Pattern of Suburbia', in A. G. Weidenfeld, ed., *The Changing Nation* (London: Contact Publications, London 1947), pp. 9–14.
Jordan, R. Furneaux, 'Dudok and the Repercussions of his European Influence', *Architectural Review*, Vol. CXV (April 1954).
Judd, F. J., 'Kiosks', *Post Office Electrical Engineers' Journal*, Vol. XXIX (October 1936), pp. 174–7.
Karol, Eitan, *Charles Holden, Architect* (Donington: Shaun Tyas, 2007).
Keen, Arthur, *Charing Cross Bridge* (London: Ernest Benn, 1930).
Kernot, C. F., *British Public Schools War Memorials* (London: Roberts and Newton, 1927).
King, Alex, *Memorials of the Great War in Britain: The Symbolism and Politics of Remembrance* (New York: Berg, 1998).
Klein, Richard, *Le Touquet Paris-Plage: La Côte d'Opale des années Trente* (Paris: Institut Français d'Architecture/ Éditions Norma, 1994).
Knox, James, *Robert Byron: A Biography* (London: John Murray, 2003).
Lancaster, Osbert, *Pillar to Post: The Pocket Lamp of Architecture* (London: John Murray, 1938).
———, *Homes Sweet Homes* (London: John Murray, 1939).
———, *Here, Of All Places: The Pocket Lamp of Architecture* (London: John Murray, 1959).
———, *Scene Changes* (London: John Murray, 1978).
Lawrence, G. C., ed., *The British Empire Exhibition 1924: Official Guide* (London: Fleetway Press, 1924).
Le Corbusier, *Towards a New Architecture*, trans. Frederick Etchells (London: John Rodker, 1927).
———, *The City of To-morrow and its Planning*, trans. Frederick Etchells (London: John Rodker, 1929).

BIBLIOGRAPHY

———, *Aircraft* (London: The Studio, 1935).
Leathart, Julian, *Style in Architecture* (London: Thomas Nelson, 1940).
Leslie, Shane, *Men Were Different: Studies in Late Victorian Biography* (London: Michael Joseph, 1937).
Lethaby, W. R., 'Memorials of the Fallen: Service or Sacrifice?', in Lethaby, *Form in Civilization: Collected Papers on Art and Labour* (London: Oxford University Press, 1922), pp. 56–65.
Longworth, Philip, *The Unending Vigil: A History of the Commonwealth War Graves Commission, 1917–1967* (London: Constable, 1967).
Lubetkin, Berthold, 'Lubetkin: The Untold Story', *World Architecture*, No. 24 (1993).
Lutyens, Mary, *Edwin Lutyens by his Daughter* (1980; London: Black Swan, 1991).
Lutyens, Robert 'The Grosvenor Estate (Or for that Matter, Any Other)', *Architectural Review*, Vol. LXVII (April 1930).
———, *Notes on Sir Edwin Lutyens: Two Sets of Notes for a Lecture to the Art Workers Guild, June 18th 1969* (London: Art Workers' Guild, 1970).
McDonald, John R. H., *Modern Housing: A Review of Present Housing Requirements in Great Britain* (Glasgow: Carson and Nicol, 1931).
McGrath, Raymond, *Twentieth Century Houses* (London: Faber and Faber, 1934).
McGrath, Raymond, and A. C. Frost, *Glass in Architecture and Decoration* (London: Architectural Press, 1937).
Mandler, Peter, *The Fall and Rise of the Stately Home* (New Haven and London: Yale University Press, 1997).
Marks, Richard, *Burrell: A Portrait of a Collector, Sir William Burrell, 1861–1958* (Glasgow: Richard Drew, 1983).
Marriott, Charles, *Modern English Architecture* (London: Chapman and Hall, 1924).
Maufe, Edward, 'Modern Church Architecture' (lecture delivered 17 December 1934), *Journal of the Royal Institute of British Architects*, Vol. XLII (12 January 1935).
Mebes, Paul, *Um 1800: Architektur und Handwerk in Letzen Jahrhundert ihrer Traditionellen Entwicklung* (Munich: F. Bruckmann, 1908).
Moore, Jerrold Northrop, *F. L. Griggs (1876–1938): The Architect of Dreams* (Oxford: Clarendon Press, 1999).
Morand, Dexter, *The Monumental and Commercial Architecture of Great Britain of the Present Day*, 2 vols (London: John Tiranti & Co., 1928–30).
Mortimer, Raymond, 'Shell-Mex House', *Architectural Review*, Vol. LXXIII (January 1933).
Muggeridge, Malcolm, *The Thirties: 1930–1940 in Great Britain* (London: Hamish Hamilton, 1940).
Murphy, N. T. P., *In Search of Blandings* (London: Martin Secker & Warburg, 1986).
Myerscough-Walker, R., 'The Truth, The Whole Truth, and Nothing But the Truth', in Betham (1934).
———, *Choosing a Modern House* (London: Studio, 1939).
Nairn, Ian, *Nairn's London* (Harmondsworth: Penguin, 1966).
Nairn, Ian, and Nikolaus Pevsner, *The Buildings of England: Surrey* (Harmondsworth: Penguin, 1962).
Nash, Paul, *Room and Book* (London: Soncino Press, 1932).
Nath, Aman, *Dome over India: Rashtrapati Bhavan* (Delhi: India Book House, 2002).

Nevill, Ralph, *English Country House Life* (London: Methuen, 1925).
Newman, John, *The Buildings of Wales: Glamorgan* (London: Penguin, 1995).
———, *The Buildings of Wales: Gwent/Monmouthshire* (London: Yale University Press, 2000).
Newton, W. G., 'Ourselves and Europe', *Architectural Review*, Vol. LXI (January 1927).
O'Donnell, Raymond, *The Life and Work of James Salmon, Architect, 1873–1924* (Edinburgh: Rutland Press, 2003).
O'Donovan, Donal, *God's Architect: A Life of Raymond McGrath* (Bray: Kilbride Books, 1995).
Oliver, Basil, *The Modern Public House* (London, 1934).
———, *The Renaissance of the English Public House* (London: Faber, 1947).
Oliver, Paul, Ian Davis and Ian Bentley, *Dunroamin: The Suburban Semi and its Enemies* (London: Pimlico, 1981).
Oliver, Richard, *Bertram Grosvenor Goodhue* (New York: Architectural History Foundation, 1983).
Oliver, Stephen, 'Basil Oliver and the End of the Arts and Crafts Movement', *Architectural History* Vol. XLVII (2004), pp. 329–60.
Osmond, Sam, *Harold Falkner: More than an Arts and Crafts Architect* (Chichester: Phillimore, 2003).
Östberg, Ragnar, *The Stockholm Town Hall* (Stockholm: P. A. Norstedt och Söner, 1929).
Pearse, Innes H., and Lucy H. Crocker, *The Peckham Experiment: A Study in The Living Structure of Society* (London: George Allen and Unwin, London, 1943).
Percy, Clayre, and Jane Ridley, eds, *The Letters of Edwin Lutyens to his wife Lady Emily* (London: Collins, 1985).
Peter, Bruce, *Form Follows Fun: Modernism and Modernity in British Pleasure Architecture 1925–1940* (London: Routledge, 2007).
Pevsner, Nikolaus, *Pioneers of the Modern Movement: From William Morris to Walter Gropius* (London: Faber and Faber, 1936).
———, 'The Modern Movement' ('on British architecture 1924–1939'), unpublished typescript for a cancelled edition of the *Architectural Review* [Special Collections, Getty Center for the History of Art and the Humanities, Los Angeles; partially published in *Twentieth Century Architecture 8, British Modern: Architecture and Design in the 1930s* (London: Twentieth Century Society, 2007)] (1939).
———, *The Buildings of England: South Devon* (Harmondsworth: Penguin, 1952).
———, [1953a] *The Buildings of England: Derbyshire* (Harmondsworth: Penguin, 1953).
———, [1953b] *The Buildings of England: Hertfordshire* (Harmondsworth, Penguin, 1953).
———, *The Buildings of England: North Somerset and Bristol* (Harmondsworth: Penguin, 1958).
———, *The Buildings of England: Buckinghamshire* (Harmondsworth: Penguin, 1960).
———, *The Buildings of England: North-East Norfolk and Norwich* (Harmondsworth: Penguin, 1962).
———, *The Buildings of England: Cambridgeshire*, (1954; second edition, Harmondsworth: Penguin, 1970).
———, *The Buildings of England: London: Volume One: The Cities of London and Westminster*, third edition, rev. ed. Bridget Cherry (Harmondsworth: Penguin, 1973).

———, *The Buildings of England: Nottinghamshire*, second edition, rev. ed. Elizabeth Williamson (London: Penguin, 1979).

Pevsner, Nikolaus, and Edward Hubbard, *The Buildings of England: Cheshire* (Harmondsworth: Penguin, 1971).

Pevsner, Nikolaus, and David Lloyd, *The Buildings of England: Hampshire and the Isle of Wight* (Harmondsworth: Penguin, 1967).

Pevsner, Nikolaus, and Alexandra Wedgwood, *The Buildings of England: Warwickshire* (Harmondsworth: Penguin, 1966).

Phillips, R. Randal, *Small Family Houses* (London: Country Life, 1924).

———, *Houses for Moderate Means*, second edition (London: Country Life, 1939).

Pick, Frank, Charles Holden and W. P. N. Edwards, *A Note on Contemporary Architecture in Northern Europe, written as a result of a tour of Holland, Germany, Denmark and Sweden . . . 20 June–7 July 1930* (London: London Transport, 1931).

Piggott, J. R., *Palace of the People: The Crystal Palace at Sydenham 1854–1936* (London: Hurst & Co., 2004).

Powers, Alan, 'Corinthian Epics: The Architecture of Sir Edwin Cooper', *Thirties Society Journal*, No. 2 (1982), pp. 13–18.

———, 'Edwardian Architectural Education: A Study of Three Schools', *AA Files*, No. 5 (1984), pp. 48–59.

———, ed., *H. S. Goodhart-Rendel 1887–1959* (London: Architectural Association, 1987).

———, *Oliver Hill: Architect and Lover of Life, 1887–1968* (London: Mouton Publications, 1989).

———, ed., *John Campbell: Rediscovery of an Arts and Crafts Architect* (London: The Prince of Wales's Institute of Architecture, 1997).

———, *Serge Chermayeff: Designer, Architect, Teacher* (London: RIBA, 2001).

———, *The Twentieth Century House in Britain: From the Archives of 'Country Life'* (London: Aurum Press, 2004).

———, *Modern: The Modern Movement in Britain* (London: Merrell, 2005).

———, *Britain: Modern Architectures in History* (London: Reaktion, 2007).

Priestley, J. B., *English Journey: Being a Rambling but Truthful Account of What One Man Saw and Heard and Felt and Thought During a Journey through England During the Auutumn of the Year 1933* (London: Harper & Brothers, 1934).

Quennell, Marjorie, and C. H. B. Quennell, *The Good New Days* (London: Batsford, 1935).

Ramsey, Stanley C., 'Wren's Influence on Modern Design', *Architects' Journal*, Vol. LVII (1923).

Rasmussen, Steen Eiler, *London: The Unique City* [first published as *London* (Copenhagen: Nordisk Verlag, 1934)] (London: Jonathan Cape, 1937).

———, 'First Impressions of London: or, Sir Edwin in Wonderland' [edited and translated by Andrew Saint from *Wasmuths Monatshefte für Baukunst*, Vol. XII (1928), pp. 304–13], *AA Files*, No. 20 (Autumn 1990), pp. 16–21.

Recent English Architecture 1920–1940: Selected by the Architecture Club (London: Country Life, 1947).

Reilly, C. H., 'Britannic House, Finsbury Circus', *Architecture: The Journal of the Society of Architects*, Vol. III (April 1925).

———, 'Eminent Living Architects and Their Work: E. Vincent Harris', *Building* (September 1929).
———, [1930a] 'Some Younger Architects of Today: E. Berry Webber', *Building* (September 1930).
———, [1930b] 'Some Younger Architects of Today: Herbert J. Rowse', *Building* (December 1930).
———, [1931a] 'Representative Architects of Today: Charles Holden', *Building* (September 1931).
———, [1931b] *Representative British Architects of the Present Day* (London: B. T. Batsford, 1931).
———, [1931c] 'Some Younger Architects of Today: Grey Wornum', *Building* (July 1931).
———, [1931d] 'Some Younger Architects of Today: Percy Thomas', *Building* (February 1931)
———, [1935a] 'Some Recent Churches', *Architectural Review*, Vol. LXXVII (April 1935).
———, [1935b] 'The Town Hall Problem', *Architectural Review*, Vol. LXXVII (March 1935).
———, [1935c] 'The Year's Work', *Architects' Journal* (10 January 1935).
———, *Scaffolding in the Sky. A Semi-Architectural Autobiography* (London: Routledge, 1938).
Reiss, R. L., 'The Significance of Welwyn Garden City', *Architectural Review*, Vol. LXI (May 1927).
Richards, J. M., *An Introduction to Modern Architecture* (Harmondsworth: Penguin, 1940).
———, *The Castles on the Ground* (London: Architectural Press, 1946).
———, *Memoirs of an Unjust Fella* (1970; London: Faber, 2013).
Richardson, A. E., *Monumental Classic Architecture in Great Britain and Ireland during the Eighteenth and Nineteenth Centuries* (London: B. T. Batsford, 1914).
———, 'The Renewal of Vitality in Building', *Architectural Association Journal*, Vol. XL (February 1924).
———, [1928a] 'The Training of Architects', *Architectural Association Journal*, Vol. XLIV (March 1928).
———, [1928b] 'The Way We Are Going', *Building* (July 1928).
———, *Georgian England: A Survey of Social Life, Trades, Industries and Art from 1700 to 1820* (London: B. T. Batsford, 1931).
———, 'Must the Adelphi Go?', *Architectural Review*, Vol. LXXIII (March 1933).
———, *The Old Inns of England* second edition (London: Batsford, 1935).
Richardson, A. E., and C. Lovett Gill, *London Houses from 1660 to 1820: A Consideration of their Architecture and Detail* (London: B. T. Batsford, 1911).
Richardson, Kenneth, *The 'Twenty-Five' Churches of the Southwark Diocese: An Inter-War Campaign of Church-Building* (London: Ecclesiological Society, 2002).
Richardson, Margaret, *66 Portland Place: The London Headquarters of the Royal Institute of British Architects* (London: RIBA, 1984).
———, 'A Lutyens Skyscraper', *Thirties Society Journal*, No. 6 (1987), pp. 3–7.
Robertson, Howard 'Modern Dutch Architecture', *Architectural Review*, Vol. LI–LII (1922).
———, 'Modern Sweden', *Architectural Review*, Vol. LVI (July 1924).
———, *Architecture Explained* (London: Ernest Benn Ltd, 1926).
———, 'The Rue Mallet-Stevens, Paris', *Architect and Building News* (20 January 1928).
———, *Modern Architectural Design* (London: Architectural Press, 1932).

———, 'Obbligato to Architecture: Part 4', *The Builder* (April 1962); 'Part 6' (May 1962); 'Part 9' (June 1962).

Robertson, Howard, and F. R. Yerbury, *Examples of Modern French Architecture* (London: Ernest Benn, 1928).

———, 'Poverty and Promise: Examples of Dutch Detail', *The Architect & Building News*, 23 October 1931.

———, *Travels in Modern Architecture 1925–1930* (London: Architectural Association, 1989).

Robertson, Manning, *Everyday Architecture. A Sequence of Essays Addressed to the Public* (London: T. Fisher Unwin, 1924).

———, 'The Excursion to Stockholm', *Architectural Association Journal*, Vol. XLI (December 1925).

Rohan, Timothy M., 'Lutyens, the Miniature and the Gigantic', in Hopkins and Stamp (2002).

Rothery, Sean, *Ireland and the New Architecture, 1900–1940* (Dublin: Lilliput, 1991).

Roulin, Dom E., *Modern Church Architecture*, trans. C. Cornelia Craigie and John A. Southwell (London: B. Herder, 1947).

Sagar, Keith, *The Life of D. H. Lawrence* (London: Methuen, 1982).

Saint, Andrew, 'Americans in London: Raymond Hood and the National Radiator Building', *AA Files*, No. 7 (September 1984), pp. 30–43.

———, 'Wright and Great Britain', in Anthony Alofsin, ed., *Frank Lloyd Wright: Europe and Beyond* (Berkeley: University of California Press, 1999), pp. 121–46.

———, *Architect and Engineer: A Study in Sibling Rivalry* (London: Yale University Press, 2007).

Saler, Michael T., *The Avant-Garde in Interwar England: Medieval Modernism and the London Underground* (New York: Oxford University Press, 1999).

Salmon, James, 'American Architecture', *The Quarterly Illustrated of the Incorporation of Architects in Scotland*, No. 2 (Summer 1922).

Sassoon, Siegfried, *Selected Poems* (1968; London: Faber, 1991).

Scarlett, Frank, and Marjorie Townley, *Arts Décoratifs 1925: A Personal Recollection of the Paris Exhibition* (London: Academy Editions, 1975).

Scott, Geoffrey, *The Architecture of Humanism: A Study in the History of Taste*, second edition (London: Constable, 1924).

Scott, Sir Leslie, 'Preservation of the Countryside', in Betham (1934).

Shand, P. Morton, 'Underground', *Architectural Review*, Vol. LXVI (November 1929).

———, [1930a] *The Architecture of Pleasure: Modern Theatres and Cinemas* (London: B. T. Batsford, 1930).

———, [1930b] 'The Post-War Post Office: Recent Tendencies in Post Office and Telephone Exchange Design', *Architectural Review*, Vol. LXVIII (October 1930).

Sharp, Dennis, ed., *Alfred C. Bossom's American Architecture, 1903–1926* (London: Book Art, 1984).

———, ed., *Connell, Ward and Lucas: Modern Movement Architects in England 1929–1939* (London: Book Art, 1994).

Sharp, Dennis, and Sally Rendel, *Connell, Ward and Lucas: Modern Movement Architects in England 1929–1939* (London: Frances Lincoln, 2008).

Sharp, Thomas, *Town and Countryside: Some Aspects of Urban and Rural Development* (London: Oxford University Press, 1932).
Shoosmith, A. G., 'Present Day Architecture in India', *The Nineteenth Century and After*, Vol. CXX (1938).
Simpson, Richard, 'Classicism and Modernity: The University of London's Senate House', *Bulletin of the Institute of Classical Studies*, Vol. XLIII (1999), pp. 41–95.
Skelton, Tim, and Gerald Gliddon, *Lutyens and the Great War* (London: Frances Lincoln, 2008).
Skinner, Joan S., *Form and Fancy: Factories and Factory Buildings by Wallis, Gilbert & Partners, 1916–1939* (Liverpool: Liverpool University Press, 1997).
Smith, Graham Paul, *Ernest George Trobridge, 1884–1942: Architect Extraordinary* (Oxford: Oxford Polytechnic, 1982).
Smith, Janet, *Liquid Assets: The Lidos and Open Air Swimming Pools of Britain* (London: English Heritage, 2005).
Smith, Paul, and Bernard Toulier, eds, *Berlin Tempelhof, Liverpool Speke, Paris Le Bourget: Airport Architecture of the Thirties* (Paris: Éditions du Patrimoine, 2000).
Smith, Simon, *Ralph Maynard Smith: A Haunted Man: Painter, Writer, Architect (1904–1964): His Life and Work*, 'with a Commentary by Gavin Stamp' (London: Wolseley Fine Arts, 2004).
Smithells, Roger, ed., *Modern Small Country Houses* (London: Country Life, 1936).
Soissons, Maurice de, *Welwyn Garden City: A Town Designed for Healthy Living* (Cambridge: Publications for Companies, 1988).
Sonne, Wolfgang, *Representing the State: Capital City Planning in the Early Twentieth Century* (London: Prestel, 2003).
Stamp, Gavin, 'Indian Summer', *Architectural Review*, Vol. CLIX (June 1976), pp. 365–72.
———, *Silent Cities: An Exhibition of the Memorial and Cemetery Architecture of the Great War* (London: RIBA, 1977).
———, ed., *Britain in the Thirties* [*Architectural Design*, Vol. XLIX, Nos. 10–11] (1979).
———, [1981a] 'India: End of the Classical Tradition', *Lotus International*, Vol. XXXIV, No. 1 (1981).
———, [1981b] 'Through Eden Park to Arcady', *Event* (4–10 March 1981), pp. 16–18.
———, [1982a] 'Conversation with Ernö Goldfinger', *Thirties Society Journal*, No. 2 (1982), pp. 19–24.
———, [1982b] *The Great Perspectivists* (London: Trefoil Books, 1982).
———, ed., *Sir Owen Williams 1890–1969* (London: Architectural Association, 1986).
———, *Telephone Boxes* (London: Chatto & Windus, 1989).
———, 'The London Years' in Wendy Kaplan, ed., *Charles Rennie Mackintosh* (New York: Abbeville Press, 1996).
———, 'Giles Gilbert Scott and Bankside Power Station', in Rowan Moore and Raymund Ryan, *Building Tate Modern: Transforming Giles Gilbert Scott* (London: Tate Gallery, 2000).
———, 'The South Bank Site', in Elain Harwood and Alan Powers, eds, *Twentieth Century Architecture 5: Festival of Britain* (London: Twentieth Century Society, 2001).
———, *An Architect of Promise: George Gilbert Scott Junior (1839–1897) and the Late Gothic Revival* (Donington: Shaun Tyas, 2002).

———, 'Lost C20 Buildings: Ramsgate Aerodrome', *The Twentieth Century Society Newsletter* (Spring 2003), pp. 8–9.

———, [2004a] 'An Architect of the *Entente Cordiale*: Eugène Bourdon (1870–1916): Glasgow and Versailles', in *Architectural Heritage: The Journal of the Architectural Heritage Society of Scotland*, Vol. XV, Issue 1 (November 2004), pp. 80–116.

———, [2004b] 'Early Twentieth-Century Stations', in Julian Holder and Steven Parissien, eds, *The Architecture of British Transport in the Twentieth Century* (London: Yale University Press, 2004).

———, [2004c] '"How is it that there is no Modern Style of Architecture?": "Greek" Thomson versus Gilbert Scott', in Mari Hvattum and Christian Hermansen, eds, *Tracing Modernity: Manifestations of the Modern in Architecture and the City* (London and New York: Routledge, 2004), pp. 103–23.

———, [2006a] *The Memorial to the Missing of the Somme* (London: Profile, 2006).

———, [2006b] 'Neo-Tudor and its Enemies', *Architectural History*, Vol. XLIX (2006), pp. 1–33.

———, 'How We Celebrated the Coronation: The Foundation and Early Years of the Georgian Group', *Georgian Group Journal*, Vol. XX (2012), pp. 1–21.

———, 'The Tragedy and Triumph of a British Architect in New Delhi', *Apollo: The International Art Magazine*, 31 May 2016.

Stamp, Gavin, and Allan Greenberg, '"Modern Architecture as a Very Complex Art": The Design and Construction of Lutyens's British Embassy in Washington DC', in Hopkins and Stamp (2002).

Stamp, Gavin, and Margaret Richardson, 'Lutyens in Spain', *AA Files*, No. 3 (January 1983), pp. 51–9.

Steele, H. Rooksby, and F. R. Yerbury, *The Old Bank of England, London* (London: Ernest Benn, 1930).

Stewart-Liberty, Ivor, *Liberty's Tudor Shop, Great Marlborough Street, Regent Street, London* (London: Liberty's, 1924).

Stillman, C. G., and R. Castle Cleary *The Modern School* (London: Architectural Press, 1949).

The Story of the Mersey Tunnel: Officially named Queensway (Liverpool: Charles Birchill & Sons, 1934).

Stratton, P. M., 'The Line from France', *Architectural Review*, Vol. LXIV (July 1928).

Summerson, John, 'Recent Work of Mr E. Vincent Harris', *Country Life*, Vol. LXXV (28 April 1934).

———, *John Nash: Architect to King George IV* (London: George Allen & Unwin, 1935).

———, 'Introduction' to Trevor Dannatt, *Modern Architecture in Britain* (London: Batsford, 1959), pp. 11–28.

———, 'Arches of Triumph: The Design for Liverpool Cathedral', in Amery and Richardson (1981), pp. 44–52.

———, 'Architecture' in Boris Ford, ed., *The Cambridge Guide to the Arts in Britain: Volume 8: The Edwardian Age and Inter-War Years* (Cambridge: Cambridge University Press, 1989).

———, *The Unromantic Castle* (London: Thames and Hudson, 1990).

———, 'The MARS Group and the Thirties', in John Bold and Edward Chaney, eds, *English Architecture Public and Private: Essays for Kerry Downes* (London: Hambledon, 1993), pp. 303–10.

———, 'The Mischievous Analogy' [Lecture to the Architectural Association, 1941], in Summerson, *Heavenly Mansions, and Other Essays on Architecture* (London: W. W. Norton & Company, 1998), pp. 195–218.

Symondson, Anthony, *The Life and Work of Sir Ninian Comper 1864–1960* (London: Royal Institute of British Architects, 1988).

———, 'John Betjeman and the Cult of J. N. Comper', *Thirties Society Journal*, No. 7 (1991), pp. 2–13.

Symondson, Anthony, and Stephen Arthur Bucknall, *Sir Ninian Comper: An Introduction to his Life and Work* (Reading: Spire Books; London: Ecclesiological Society, 2006).

Taylor, A. J. P., *English History 1914–1945* (Oxford: Clarendon Press, 1965).

Taylor, Nicholas, 'The Private World of Dippenhall', *Architectural Review*, Vol. CXLII (February 1968).

Thomas, Sir Percy, *Pupil to President: Memoirs of an Architect* (Leigh-on-Sea: F. Lewis, 1963).

Tomlinson, Harold, 'Buildings at Cambridge', *Architects' Journal*, 15 June 1933.

Trevelyan, G. M., *English Social History. A Survey of Six Centuries: Chaucer to Queen Victoria*, second edition (London: Longmans, Green and Co., 1946).

Turnor, Reginald, *The Smaller English House 1500–1939* (London: Batsford, 1952).

Tyack, Geoffrey, 'Baker and Lutyens in Oxford: The Building of Rhodes House and Campion Hall', *Oxoniensia*, Vol. LXII (1997), pp. 287–308.

Wainwright, Clive, *The Romantic Interior: The British Collector at Home, 1750–1850* (London and New Haven: Yale University Press, 1989).

Walker, David M., *St Andrew's House: An Edinburgh Controversy 1912–1939* (Edinburgh: Historic Buildings and Monuments, 1989).

Walker, Greg, *The Private Life of Henry VIII* (London: I. B. Tauris, 2003).

Wallis, Thomas, 'Factories', *Journal of the Royal Institute of British Architects*, series 3, Vol. XL (25 February 1933), pp. 301–12.

Ward, Fiona, 'Merseyside Churches in a Modern Idiom: Francis Xavier Velarde and Bernard Miller', in *Twentieth Century Architecture*, No. 3 (1998), pp. 94–102.

Ward, Mary, and Neville Ward, *Home in the Twenties and Thirties* (London: Ian Allan, 1978).

Ware, Fabian, *The Immortal Heritage: An Account of the Work and Policy of the Imperial War Graves Commission During Twenty Years, 1917–1937* (Cambridge: Cambridge University Press, 1937).

Wattjes, J. G., *Moderne Architectuur in Noowegen, Zweden, Finland, Denemarken, Duitschland, Tjechoslowakije, Oostenrijk, Zwitserland, Frankrijk, België, Engeland en Ver. Staten v. Amerika* (Amsterdam: Kosmos, 1927).

Waugh, Evelyn, *Decline and Fall* (1928; London: Chapman & Hall, 1962).

———, *Labels: A Mediterranean Journal* (1930; London: Gerald Duckworth & Co., 1974).

———, *Scoop* (1938; London: Eyre Methuen, 1978).

———, 'A Call to the Orders' [*Country Life*, Supplement, 26 February 1938], in *The Essays, Articles and Reviews of Evelyn Waugh*, ed. Donat Gallagher (London: Methuen 1984), pp. 215–18.

Waymark, Peter, *A History of Petts Wood: Millennium Edition* (1979; Petts Wood: Petts Wood Residents' Association, 2000).
Weaver, Lawrence, *Small Country Houses of To-Day: Volume Two* (London: Country Life, 1922).
———, *The Scottish National War Memorial: The Castle, Edinburgh. A Record and Appreciation* (London: Country Life, 1927).
Webb, Aston, ed., *London of the Future: By the London Society* (London: E. P. Dutton 1921).
Wellesley, Lord Gerald, 'War Memorials', *Architecture: The Journal of the Society of Architects*, Vol III (February 1925).
Williams, Ernest Edwin, *The New Public-House* (London: Chapman & Hall, 1924).
Williams-Ellis, Clough, *England and the Octopus* (London: Geoffrey Bles, 1928).
———, *Lawrence Weaver: A Memoir* (London: Geoffrey Bles, 1933).
———, ed., *Britain and the Beast* (London: Readers' Union, 1938).
Williams-Ellis, Clough, and John Summerson, *Architecture Here and Now* (London: Thomas Nelson and Sons, 1934).
Williams-Ellis, Clough, and Amabel Williams-Ellis, *The Pleasures of Architecture* (London: Jonathan Cape, 1924).
Winter, Jay, *Sites of Memory, Sites of Mourning: The Great War in European Cultural History* (Cambridge: Cambridge University Press, 1998).
———, 'Forms of Kinship and Remembrance in the Aftermath of the Great War', in Winter and Emmanuel Sivan, eds, *War and Remembrance in the Twentieth Century* (Cambridge: Cambridge University Press, 1999), pp. 40–60.
Wornum, G. G., 'Modern Decoration', *Architectural Association Journal*, Vol. XLIII (June 1927).
Worsley, Giles, *England's Lost Houses: From the Archives of 'Country Life'* (London: Aurum Press, 2002).
Wright, Russell, *Signs of the Times: A Guide to the Materials of Modernism, 1927–1933* (London: Building Centre, 1981).
Yeomans, David, and David Cottam, *Owen Williams: The Engineer's Contribution to Contemporary Architecture* (London: Thomas Telford, 2001).
Yerbury, F. R., *Georgian Details of Domestic Architecture* (London: Ernest Benn, 1926).
———, *Modern European Buildings* (London: Victor Gollancz, 1928).
———, *Modern Dutch Buildings* (London: Ernest Benn, 1931).
———, *One Hundred Photographs* (London: Jordan-Gaskell, 1935).
———, *Frank Yerbury, Itinerant Cameraman: Architectural Photographs 1920–35* (London: Architectural Association, 1987).
Yorke, F. R. S., *The Modern House* (London: Architectural Press, 1934).
———, *The Modern House in England* (London: Architectural Press, 1937).
Yorke, F. R. S., and Frederick Gibberd, *The Modern Flat* (London: Architectural Press, 1937).
Yorke, F. R. S., and Colin Penn, *A Key to Modern Architecture* (London: Blackie and Son, 1939).

INDEX

Page numbers in *italic* refer to the illustrations

Abercrombie, Patrick 287, 345–6, 481–2
Aberdeen Art Gallery 51
Abingdon Street, London 395–7
Accrington 99
Adam, Robert 125, 192, 208, 380, 388
Adams, Holden & Pearson 18, 448
Addenbrooke's Hospital, Cambridge 45
Adelaide House, London 157–8, 243, *244*, 246, 267
The Adelphi, London 388, 390
Adelphi Hotel, Liverpool 185, *186*
Adshead, Stanley 23, 86, 87, 341, 344, 367
Africa House, London 107, *108*
Agecroft Hall, Manchester 232
Ahlberg, Hakon 141
Aish, Clifford 210
Albert Memorial, London 2
Albi Cathedral 56, 155, 409, 439
All Hallows, Twickenham 397–8, *397*, 399, 400
All India Arch, New Delhi 72
Allen, Gordon 329–30
Allenby, General Edmund 252n.
Allison, Sir Richard 267, 357
Allward, Walter S. 73
Amersham, Bucks 490–2
Amery, Colin 2
Amsterdam School 134, 236
Anderson, Alexander 394
Angell, T. G. 293–4, *293*

Anglo-Catholic Society of SS. Peter and Paul (SSPP) 440, 441
Anglo-Iranian Oil Company 121–2
Anglo-Properties 119
Anson, Peter 145–6, 440–1
Antoniuskirche, Basel 427
Anzac Memorial, Sydney 53
Architect and Building News 88, 131, 233–4, 263, 314–16, 503
The Architects' Journal 18–19, 312, 343, 468, 503, 516–17
Architectural Association (AA) 24, 41, 131, 132–4, 136–7, 175–6, 181, 224, 341, 453, 498, 508–9
Architectural Review 6, 7, 23, 24, 36, 43, 80, 86, 112, 131, 141, 147, 151, 153, 166, 174, 189, 191, 202, 219, 245–6, 248, 263, 272, 273, 280, 296, 357, 361–2, 368–9, 386, 389, 391, 412, 452, 463, 464, 466, 476, 482, 486, 498, 508, 512–13
Architecture 59
Architecture Club 17–18, 106n., 141, 229, 258, 291, 347, 358, 389
Armitage, Joseph 111, 321
Arnos Grove Station, London 18, 201n.; Plate 6
Arras, France 71
Art Deco 16–18, 21, 144, 173, 199, 201–5, 254, 262, 474, 479

church architecture 168, 429
cinemas 205, 212, 236
commercial buildings 220, 235, 240, 459–60
and Egyptian style 238–40, 265
interiors 180, 237, 238, 256, 350–1, 416, 467
Art Nouveau 17, 171, 201, 275, 276–7, 336, 409, 481
Art Workers' Guild 280, 320
Artillery Memorial, Hyde Park Corner, London *vi*, 52–3 and n.
Arts and Crafts movement 23, 44–5, 55, 59, 72, 106, 117, 131–2, 142, 285, 429, 468, 469
Holden and 198
houses 21, 31, 287–90, 293, 297, 336, 340, 451
and neo-Tudor architecture 280–4
and pub design 318–20
Arup, Ove *498*, 499–500
Arup Associates 58n.
Ashbee, C. R. 50, 320
Ashcombe Tower, Devon 291
Ashford, Middlesex 403
Ashley, Henry Victor *237*; Plate 17
Ashley, Mr and Mrs Wilfrid 350
Ashmole, Bernard 490, *491*, *493*
Aslet, Clive 277, 299, 300
Asplund, Gunnar 146–7, 149, *150*, 164, 208, 483

Asquith, H. H. 232
Associated British Cinemas 213
Astley Hall, Chorley 46
Astoria Cinema, Brixton, London 210
Atkinson, Frank 185, *186*
Atkinson, Robert 15, 22, 87, 134, 147, 150, 180, 191, 207–8, *207*, 212, 238, 341, *341*, 378, 394, 397–8, 400, *401*, 467; Plate 19
Atkinson & Alexander 447, 477
Australia 73–4, *73*
Ayrton, Maxwell 249, 351, 511
Ayscoughfee Hall, Spalding 47
Bachelard, Gaston 507
Baggage Hall, Tilbury, London 114
Bailiffscourt, Climping 299–300, *299*
Baillie Scott, M. H. 273–4, 287–8, 290, 336, 481–2
Baines, Sir Frank 62, 119–20, 235
Baker, Sir Herbert 68, 182, 226, 395, 397
  Bank of England 120, 382–4, *383*
  churches 402, *402*
  New Delhi 23, 81, *81*, 249
  university buildings 312–14, *313*
  war memorials 44n., 47–8, 54–6, *55*, 65, 67, 70–1, 72, 73
Bakst, Leon 175, 208, 236
Baldwin, Stanley 283–4, 330
Ballets Russes 175, 202–3, 236
Bank of England, London 120, 382–4, *383*
Bank of Scotland, Glasgow 262
Bankside Power Station, London 256
Barclays Bank 117, 119, 397
Barker, Able Seaman Fred 61n.
Barleys, Offham 346–7, *347*
Barman, Christian 90 and n.
Barnes, Harry 248
Baroque style 95, 144, 145, 167, 169, 212, 225, 440
Barr, Ewen 210
Barron, P. A. 285, 300–4, 325
Bartlett School 344
Bartning, Otto 155, 424–6, *425*

Basildon Park, Berkshire 231–2
Bassett-Lowke, Wenman 154, 479–81
Bateman, C. E. 318
Bateman & Bateman 323–4, *323*, 334
Bath 403–4, *403*, 414
Battersby, Martin 201
Battersea Power Station, London 2, *2*, 4, 19, 254–6, *255*, 416, 516; Plate 21
Battle of the Styles 12
Baudot, Anatole de 421
Bauhaus 25, 166, 202, 503
Bayes, Gilbert 109, *138*
Baylin's Farm, Beaconsfield *292*, 293; Plate 24
BBC (British Broadcasting Corporation) 36, 394, 446
BBC building, London 351, 391n., 463–5, *464–5*, 494
Beach House, Worthing 351
Beaconsfield War Memorial 45, *46*, 50–1
Beaton, Cecil 29
Beaux-Arts style 13, 22, 30, 89, 116, 170, 171, 180, 181–2, 270, 453
Bedford Square, London 394
Beech Grove Hall, RAF Manby 356, *356*
Behrens, Peter 30–1, 154, 479–82, *480*
Beit, Sir Otto 47
Belcher, John 111
Belfast 95–6 and n.
Belgium 50, 64, 67–9, 72
Bellahouston Park, Glasgow 173
Bellot, Paul 424
Benois, Alexandre 208
Benson, A. C. 311–12
Bentley, Ian 327–9
Bentley, John Francis 90n., 402–3
Bentley Wood, Sussex 517–18, *517*
Benton, Charlotte and Tim 203, 212, 236n.
Beresford, A. Edgar 287–8
Berkeley Arms, Cranford, Middlesex 322; Plate 27
Berkhamsted 212, *213*, *384*, 385
Berlage, H. P. 134–5, *135*, 243

Berlin 3, 155, 159, 160–1, 264, 374, 426, 427
Bernal, J. D. 19
Bernard, Oliver P. 160–1, 467, 512
Bernini, Gian Lorenzo 249
Bernstein, Sidney 160, 215–16
Bertram, Anthony 164, 274–5, 277, 317, 325, 358, 468, 479
Betjeman, John 4, 6, 19, 28, 29, 36n., 203, 254, 282, 337, 386, 390, 402, 409, 412, 466
Bexhill-on-Sea 36, 501–3
Biddulph-Pinchard, C. H. 296, *296*, 297
Biedermeier architecture 343
Birchens Spring, Beaconsfield 290, *291*
Birmingham 51, 322–4, 332
Birmingham Airport 474
Birmingham Civic Society 359
Bishop's Stortford 54
Bjerke, Arvid 143–4
Black Horse, Northfield, Birmingham 323–4, *323*
Blackburn 157, 256
Blackpool Pleasure Beach 486–8, *487*
Blake, Vernon 157–8, 174
Blériot, Louis 27
Blomfield, Arthur 219
Blomfield, Sir Reginald 22–3, 44, 90, 161, 362, 386, 470–1, 494
  Carlton House Terrace 22, 389
  on cosmopolitanism 176, 297
  neo-Georgian architecture 340
  Modernismus 22
  Quadrant, Regent Street 85–8, *86*
  war memorials 52 and n., 65, 67–70, *71*, 387
Bloomfield, Edward *473*, 474
Board of Trade, London 102 and n.
Bodley, G. F. 407–8, 411
Bodley & Garner 314
Boer War (1899–1903) 43
Böhm, Dominikus 57, 155–7, 426, *426*, 427–9
Bolton, A. T. 383
Bone, Muirhead 197
Boot, Henry & Sons 334
Booth, Charles 409

INDEX 557

Boots Company factory, Beeston, Nottinghamshire 513–16, *514–15*; Plate 33
Bossom, Alfred 180, 193, 195, 259, 283n., 298
Bourdon, Eugène 182, 183
Bracken House, London 98n.
Braddell, Darcy 228, 309, 346–7, *347*, 349
Braddock, Thomas 215
Bradley Lodge, Stratford-upon-Avon 297–8
Bradshaw, Gass & Hope 98–9, *99*
Bradshaw, Harold Chalton 71–2, 167, 287, 335
Brandon-Jones, John 106, 136
Brangwyn, Frank 101, 115
Brasilia 94, 442
Brett, C. E. B. 96n.
Brett, Lionel 17, 344–5, 505–6
Brettingham, Matthew 381, *381*
Breuer, Marcel 16, 31, 130, 497, 500
Brewer, Cecil 41, 110–11, *110*
Briggs, Wolstenholme & Thornely 96
Brighton 207–8, *207*, 212, 324–5
Bristol 98, 99
Britannic House, London 121–2, 157, 194
British Berberg Ltd 220
British Embassy, Washington DC 179–80, 353–5, *354*
British Empire 5, 39, 41, 74, 249–50, 449
British Empire Exhibition, Wembley (1924) 34, 79, 126, 128, 143–4, 219, 247–9, *247*, 511
British Expeditionary Force 43
British Medical Association 198
British Museum, London 52, 68, 108, 240, 243, 375, 508
British School at Rome 167
British Sound Archive 4
British Telecom 360
British Union of Fascists 36, 503
Broadcasting House, London 351, 391n., 433, 463–5, *464–5*, 494
Broadhead, Frank 516

55 Broadway, London 195–8, *198*
Broderick, Cuthbert 95
Brooke, Frederick H. 355
Brooke, Rupert 321
Brooklyn Cottage, Salfords *305*
Bruce, Mrs Victor 472–3
Brunswick Square, London 385, 394–5
45 Buck Lane, Kingsbury, Middlesex *308*
Buckland & Haywood 95
Bucknell, L. H. 385
Budden, Lionel 52
The Builder 84
Bulloch, Archibald *355–6*, 356, 358
Burges, William 407, 441
Burke, Thomas 177–8, 318, 466
Burles House, Dippenhall *306*, 307
Burne-Jones, Edward 283
Burnet, Sir John 51–2, 68, 72, 108, 109, 180, *181*, 183, 220n., 317, 359
Burnet, Sir John & Partners 157–8, 238, 240
Burnet, Tait & Lorne *137–8*, 138, 243, *244*, 265–70, *269*, 476, *476*, 486
Burnett, P. V. 381
Burnham, Daniel H. 109
Burns, John 44, 387
Burrell, Sir William 232
Bury St Edmunds Cathedral 443–4
Busbridge, Surrey 47n.
Bush House, London 107, *109*, 183, 187–8, 194
Butler, A. S. G. 77, 122, 198–9
Butterfield, William 14, 407, 409, 440
Buttes, Polygon Wood, Belgium 72
Byrne, Barry 424
Byron, Robert 6, 23, 37, 80–3, 88, 120, 245–7, 249, 259–61, 269–70, 375, 377–8, 382, 388, 389, 391–2, 394–8, 464–5
Cachemaille-Day, N. F. 155, *155*, 171, 400, 408–9, 414, 418, 420–1, *420*, 438, *438–9*; Plate 7
Cambrai, France 72

Cambridge 12–13, 48, 339–40, 495
Cambridge Guildhall 12, 106, 353
Cambridge University 9, 10, 14, 57–8, 311, 360–1, 371, 503
Cambridge University Library 11–12, 13, 19, 57, 225, 253, 259; Plate 2
Cambridgeshire War Memorial 45, 48–50, *49*
Campbell, John A. 289–91
Campion Hall, Oxford 312
Canada 73
Canova, Antonio 386
Cape Dutch architecture 226, 228
Caplin, A. 302, *303*; Plate 28
Capstick, George T. 257
Cardiff 61
Carlisle 319–20, *319*, 322
Carlton cinemas 236
Carlton House Terrace, London 22, 389
Carreras Cigarette Factory, London 233–4, *235*, 236, 240, 242–3, 385; Plate 16
Carrère & Hastings 185, 189, 245
Carter, Howard 234, 235–6
Cascading Fountain, New Delhi *80*
Cashmore, F. Milton 262–3, *263*
Casson, Hugh 151, 455
Cathedral Church of the Holy Spirit, Guildford 433, *433*
Cathedral Church of the Redemption, New Delhi *82*
Catholic Herald 64
Cenotaph, Whitehall, London 8, 39–41, *40*, 59–60, 62–4
Chamberlain, Neville 29
Chambers, Sir Theodore 366
Chambers, Sir William 90 and n.
Chancellor, E. Beresford 378–9
Chapel Point, Mevagissey 291
Charing Cross Station, London 44, 385–6, 387
Charles, Ethel 9
Charterhouse School, Godalming 56–7, *56*, 413–14
Chatham 72
Cheadle, J. O. *46*

INDEX

Checkley, George 167, 495
Chelsea Hospital, London 95, 343, 354
Chermayeff, Serge 464, *465*, 501–3, *502–3*, 512–13, 517–18, *517*
Cherrill, Virginia 126
Chester House, Clarendon Place, London 361–2, *362*
Chesterfield House, London 380–1
Chesterfield Town Hall 98–9, *99*
Chesterton, G. K. 45, 50
Chesterton, Maurice 165 and n.
Chetwode, Penelope 36 and n., 250
Chicago 177, 180, 181, 182, 185–6, 188, 198, 259
Chilehaus, Hamburg 154–5, *154*
Chiltington Common, Pulborough 302
Chipping Camden, Gloucestershire 50
Chitty, Anthony 498
Christian Science Church, Westminster, London 402, *402*
Church of England 8, 64, 378, 399–400, 411
Church of the Epiphany, Gipton, Leeds 409, 438, *438*
Church of the First Martyrs, Bradford 418–19
Church of the Good Shepherd, Carshalton 441
Church of the Holy Cross, Greenford, Middlesex 317, 399, *437*, 438
Church of the Holy Rude, Stirling 59
Church of Our Lady and St Alphege, Bath 403–4, *403*
Church Rate Corner, Cambridge 287, *288*
CIAM (Congrès Internationaux d'Architecture Moderne) 492, 497
City of London 111
City of London churches 9–10, 91, 378, 399
Clare College, Cambridge 10, 57–8 and n., *57*, 360–1, *361*, 462

Claridge's ballroom, London 203
Clark, Sir Kenneth 19, 29, 390, 517
Clarke, Sidney 333
Clarke Hall, Denis 451
Classicism 19–20, 22–3, 30, 34, 42, 132
  in Cambridge 12, 13
  church architecture 440, 441
  civic buildings 98–102, 104–8
  commercial buildings 110–20, 122, 124
  New Delhi 83–4
  Scandinavian architecture 146, 152
  war memorials 51–3, 57, 59, 63, 67, 68, 72, 74
  see also Georgian architecture; neo-Georgian architecture
Clavering, Cecil 213
Clifton College 54
Clunn, Harold P. 20, 271, 377, 380, 382 and n., 386–7, 454
Coates, Wells 14, 16, 30, 464, *465*, 495–7 and n., *495–6*
Cock Rock, Croyde 289, *290*
Cockerell, C. R. 13, 95
Cockrill, R. S. *316*
Coia, Jack 168, *169*, 431; Plate 8
Colchester Public Library 353
Coles, George 213–15, *215*, 236
Coleton Fishacre, Devon 291
Collins, M. E. and H. O. 233, *235*; Plate 16
Cologne 30, 33, 157, 425, 426, 427
Comben & Wakeling 331
Comet Inn, Hatfield 322, 447, 477–9 and n., *478*
Commercial Bank of Scotland, Glasgow 182
Comper, J. Ninian 61, *61*, 400, 411–13, *412*, 416–18, *417*, 420, 441; Plate 30
Connell, Amyas 30, 167, 490–2, 494
Connell, Ward & Lucas 97–8, 492n., 494; Plate 36
Cooper Sir Edwin 112–15, *113*, *115*
Copenhagen 152, 343, 424
Copnall, Edward Bainbridge 149

Coram's Fields, London 385, 394
Corbett, Harvey 194
Corbett Place, Hampshire 347
Cork 424
Corpus Christi Church, Aachen 427, *427*
Cottam, David 513–15
Council for the Preservation of Rural England 284, 328
Country Life 6, 21, 23, 34, 80, 91, 277, 294, 340, 348, 351, 389, 445, 492
County Hall, London 84, *85*
Cour House, Kintyre 21, 289; Plate 23
Courtauld, Stephen and Virginia 205
Courtauld's 181
Covent Garden market, London 384, 385
Cowles-Voysey, Charles 105–6, 353
Cowlishaw, W. H. 72
Cox, Anthony 508–9
Crabtree, William *17*, 19, 516
Cram, Ralph Adams 413
Crane, C. Howard 188
Cranwell, Lincolnshire 356
Crawford's Advertising 483
Crawley, George Abraham 298, *298*, 302
Creswell, H. B. *242*, 243n.
Cret, Paul 182
Crittall Works 482
Crowhurst Place, Lingfield 298–9, *298*
Crowley, Mary 504
Crown Commission 84–5
Croydon Airport 473–4
Crystal Palace, London 465–6
Cubism 171, 203, 236
Cuffe, Lionel 280, 281
Culliford, Leonard 7, 332; Plate 26
Culpin, E. G. 396
Culpin & Son 141, *141*
Culverhouse, P. A. 475
Cumberland Inn, Carlisle 319, *319*
Cunard Line 185, 471
Curl, James Stevens 235
Currey & Thompson 405–6, *405–6*
Curry, William 230

INDEX

Curzon Cinema, Mayfair, London 138
Daily Express building, London 14, 203–4, 238, *239*, 461, 467, 512–13; Plate 19
Daily Express building, Manchester 513, *513*
Daily Mail 304–5, 320, 330, 482
Daily Telegraph building, London 238, 513
Dalgleish & Pullen *471*, 472
Dalrymple-Hay, H. 386
Danish architecture 151–2
D'Arcy, Martin 312
Dartington Hall, Devon 230–1, *231*, 497
Davenport, John & Sons 323
Davies, W. G. 265
Davis, Arthur J. 23, 116, *116*
Davis, Ian 327–9
Dawbarn, Graham 474
Dawber, Sir Guy 23, 346, 347
Daylight Inn, Petts Wood 333, *335*
De La Warr Pavilion, Bexhill-on-Sea 36, 501–3, *502–3*
De Stijl 139, 173, 268, 491
Deane, Humphrey 228, 309, 346–7, *347*, 349
Delano & Aldrich 230
Delhi *see* New Delhi
Dellit, C. Bruce 53
Delville Wood, Somme 73
DeMille, Cecil B. 242
Denby, Elizabeth 489, *490*
Derry and Toms, London 188
Derwent, Lord 390, 391
Deutsch, Oscar 159, 213, 215
Devonshire House, Piccadilly, London 189–91, *190*, 245, 379
Diaghilev, Sergei 175, 236
Dick, R. Burns 266
Dick, Sir William Reid 52, 69, 269, 395, 396
Dickinson, Sir Arthur Lowes 494
Dinkel, E. M. 321
Dixon-Spain, J. E. 441
Doiran, Lake 72
Dollis Hill synagogue, London 424

Doman, C. L. J. 112, 114–15
Dorchester Hotel, London 23, *260*, 261, 380, 511–12
Dowson, Philip 58n.
Drage's (Everyman House), London 201
Drake, Lindsay 498
Dreamland, Margate 159
Drinkwater, George C. 310–11, *311*
Drinkwater, John 377
Drobecq, Pierre 286
Drum Inn, Cockington, Devon 321, *321*
Drummond, Andrew 413, 424, 425–6, 432
Duchy of Cornwall Estate, Kennington 340–1, 344, 367
Dudok, Willem Marinus 135–41, *139*, 168, 250
Dugdale, Michael 223, 498
Duncan, R. A. 173–4, 453, 454, 466, 482
Dunn, H. H. 353, 451n., *452*
Dutch architecture 131–41, 269, 289
Dutch Expressionism 17, 34–6, 134, 289, 309, 431
Dyer, Geoff 52n., 78
Dykes Bower, Stephen 405, 444
Earle, Sir Lionel 353
Earl's Court Exhibition Building, London 188
Early Christian architecture 18, 20, 168, 401, 402, 440
East Dulwich Estate, London 363–4, *363*
Easton, John Murray 131, 370–1, *371*
Easton & Robertson 106, 131, 144, *145*, 174–5
Ecclesiastical Commissioners 396
École des Beaux-Arts, Paris 30, 89, 116, 170, 171, 181–2, 270, 367
Eden, F. C. 400, 405
Edinburgh 58–60, 77, 266–70, *269*, 360n., 413
Edward, Prince of Wales (Edward VIII) 27, 296, 341
Edwards, A. Trystan 85, 87–8, 90 and n., 117–19, 157, 193, 199, 220n., 342, 357, 390

Edwards, W. P. N. 158, 163–4, 458–9
Egyptian style 17, 77, 157, 233–48, 265, 270
Elcock & Sutcliffe 238
Elgar, Sir Edward 166
Ellens, Rudgwick 300–1, *300*
Ellesmere, Earl of 388
Elmes, James 95
Elmhirst, Leonard and Dorothy 230
Elsom, C. G. 369
Eltham 408, 409
Eltham Palace, London *204–5*, 205
Ely Cathedral 48, 421
Emberton, Joseph 243, 245, 468, 486–8, *487*
Empire Cinema, Leicester Square, London 206
Empire State Building, New York 189, 215
Engelbrekt Church, Stockholm 429
English Folk Dance Society 281
Episcopal Church of Scotland 412
Eprile, Cecil 381
Epstein, Jacob 19, 197–8
Erich, Raymond 348
Ericson, Sigfrid 144
Esher, Lord 390
Étaples, France 67
Etchells, Frederick 25, 34, 172, 177, 386, 390, 445, 468, 483
Euston Arch, London 393
Ewhurst, Surrey 227
Exeter University 104
Exposition des Arts Décoratifs, Paris (1925) 16, 30, 172–6, *175*
Expressionism 73, 145, 409, 411, 424, 441
see also Dutch Expressionism; German Expressionism
Fahrenkamp, Emil 264
Fairweather, John 209
Falkland Palace 59
Falkner, Harold *306*, 307
Farnham, Surrey 307
Farquhar, Gordon 267
Fascism 168, 431
Faubourg d'Amiens Cemetery, France 71
Fields, Gracie 228

INDEX

Findhorn Bridge, Scotland 511
Finella, Cambridge 462–3, 494; Plate 32
Finsbury Health Centre 509, 516
Firestone Factory, Great West Road, London 16, 220, *221*, 223, 240
First World War *see* Great War
Fisher Building, Queens' College, Oxford 310–11, *311*
Fisker, Kay 152
Fitzwilliam Museum, Cambridge 13
Focus 24
Forbes, Mansfield 462, 463, 494; Plate 32
Forbes & Tate 292, 293; Plate 24
Forceville, France 67
Ford, Ford Madox 85
Forrest, G. Topham *170*, 363
Forsyth, W. A. 407
Foundling Hospital, Bloomsbury, London 384–5
Foundling Hospital School, Berkhamsted *384*, 385
France 67–8, 71–2, 74–8, 170–6
Frayling, Christopher 235–6, 327n.
Freemasons' Hall, London 236–8, *237*; Plate 17
Freud, Sigmund 130
Friends House, St Pancras, London 353
Frinton-on-Sea 21, 484
66 Frognal, Hampstead 494 and n.; Plate 36
20 Frognal Way, Hampstead 228, *229*
Frost, A. C. 25, 462–3
Fry, E. Maxwell 16, 31, 124, 165, 185, 189–90, 273, 386, 475n., 488–90, *490*, 492–3, 497, 500; Plate 35
Functionalism 147, 289, 310, 448, 450n., 467, 507–8
Fussell, Paul 63
Gallannaugh, Bertram 467n.
Gallipoli 72
Garden City movement 31
Garner 408
Gaumont-British 212–13
Gaumont Cinema, Salisbury 316–17

Gaumont Cinema, Holloway, London 188
Gaumont State Cinema, Kilburn, London 213–15
Gayfere House, London 350–1, *350*
General Post Office 32, 357–60
General Strike (1926) 8, 27
George V, King 20, 114, 304, 340, 357, 372, 389, 395–6, 414
George VI, King 357, 391n.
George, Bernard 188
George, Henry 229
Georgian architecture 9, 20, 30, 375–98, 440; *see also* neo-Georgian architecture
Georgian Group 9, 20, 376, 381–2, 389–98
German architecture 19, 30, 32, 34, 42, 84, 130, 132–3, 147, 153–61, 165, 170–1, 424–7
German Expressionism 17, 18, 36, 57, 154–5, 250, 426
Gestetner, Sigmund 500
Gibb, Sir Alexander & Partners 254
Gibberd, Frederick 94, 442, 488
Gibbons, J. Harold 400, 405, 411
Gibbs, Philip 46–7
Gibson, John 111
Gilbert, Walter 237n.
Gill, C. Lovett 111, 340
Gill, Eric 12, 19, 197–8, 280, 419, *419*, 433, 437, *485*, 486
Gill, Macdonald Plate 24
Gillespie, Kidd & Coia 168, *169*; Plate 8
Gillick, Ernest 52, 112
Glasgow 3, 51–2, *169*, 182–5, 209, 262, 467
Glasgow Empire Exhibition (1938) 173, 431
Glasgow School of Architecture 2, 181, 182, 183
Gledstone Hall, Yorkshire 125, *125*, 126
Gloag, John 87, 143, 154, 172, 194, 274–5, 449, 455, 469, 482, 504
Godfrey, Walter 298, *298*
Godmersham Park, Kent 348, *349*
Golders Green, London 414

Goldfinger, Ernö 4, 9, 14, 30, 130, 278–9, 374–5, *375*, 497, 504–5, 508
Goldring, Douglas 376, 388, 389–91, 398
Goldsborough, Francis 323–4
Goldsmith, G. H. 68
Gonville and Caius College, Cambridge 371
Goodesmith, Walter 210
Goodhart-Rendel, Harry S. 15, 24, 90n., 132–3, 199, 224, 351, 390, 453
 on Bank of England 121
 church architecture 404, 432, 435–7, *436*, 441, 442–3
 on civic buildings 106
 on commercial buildings 112–13, 117, 120–2, 187
 on Functionalism 469–70
 on Gothic Revival 407, 410
 Hay's Wharf, London 459–61, *460*
 on government buildings 343
 on RIBA Headquarters 129
 on streamlining 475–6
 on university buildings 361
 on Wren 91–2
Goodhue, Bertram Grosvenor 104, 224–5, 267, 269, 413
Gordon & Viner 314
Gordon Hotels Ltd 511–12
Gotch & Saunders 122
Gothenburg Exhibition (1923) 143–4
Gothic Revival 11, 12, 13, 20, 28, 29, 57, 85, 93, 111, 164, 406–19, 435–8, 440–4
Gracht, Ides van der 230
Gradige, Roderick 356n.
Gramophone Co. building, Hayes 219
Granada cinemas 215, *217*; Plate 12
Grant, T. F. W. 441
Graves, Robert 48, 53, 178, 205–6, 234, 236, 450
Gray, Richard 159, 208, 210, 212
Great Dixter, Northiam 294–5
Great House, Dedham 348
Great Swifts, Cranbrook 348
Great Thrift, Petts Wood *334*
Great War 6, 9, 23, 27, 28, 33–4, 39–78, 130, 178, 319, 453–4

INDEX

Great West Road factories, London 16, 218, 220–2, 223, 242, 270, 411
Great Western Railway 52, 475
Green, G. K. 303, *303*; Plate 28
Green, William Curtis 23, 116–17, *118*, 119, 254, 261, 346, 380, 512
Green's Playhouse, Glasgow 209
Greenwich Town Hall, London 141, *141*
Gresley, Nigel 475
Gretna Tavern, Carlisle 319
Gribloch House, Kippen, Stirlingshire 372–3, *373*
Griffith, D. W. 242
Griggs, F. L. 50, 299
Gropius, Walter 16, 31, 33, 130, 166, 203, 446, 451, 455, 488, 497, 500, 503–5, *505*
Grosvenor Estate, London 192
Grundtvig's Church, Copenhagen 152, 424
Guaranty Trust Building, New York 182
Guatemala 259
Guild of Handicrafts 50
Guildford 433, *433*
Guinness brewery, Park Royal, London 254
Gunn, Richard W. M. 182, *183*
Gunnersbury Avenue Estate, Ealing 332
Gunton & Gunton 381
Haig, Douglas 43, 76
Haileybury School 54
Hall, Edwin T. & E. Stanley 271, *273*
Hall, Stanley 370–1
Hall of Memory, Birmingham 51
Halliday, J. Theo 254; Plate 21
Halnaker, near Chichester 288
Hamburg 154–5, *154*
Hamilton, General Sir Ian 59–60
Hamlyn, W. H. 475
Hammels, Boars Hill, Oxfordshire 294, *295*
Hammond, Peter 418–19, 420
Hamp, Stanley 388
Hampstead, London 8, 228, *229*, 374, 494
Hampstead Golf Club House 317

Hampstead Preservation Society 374
Hampton Court 90, 122
Hanger Hill Garden Estate, Ealing 310, *310*
Harcourt-Smith, Simon 349
Hardiman, Alfred 147, *148*
Harding, Valentine 498
Hardwick, P. C. 56, 393
Harrington, Denis 229
Harris, E. Vincent 22, 95, 98 and n., 101–4, *103*, 113–14, 180
Harrison, Austen St Barbe 251–2
Harrow School 54
Hastings, Hubert de Cronin 130, 174, 175–6, 412
Hastings, Thomas 189–90, *190*, 379
Hawksmoor, Nicholas 9–10, 90 and n., 378
Hay, Ian 58, 77–8
Hayes 216, 219, 334–5
Hay's Wharf, London 459–61, *460*
Hayward Gallery, London 2, 338
Heal & Son, London 110–11, *110*
Hearst, William Randolph 232
Hebert, Fr Gabriel 421–2
Helme & Corbett 107, *109*
Henderson, A. Graham 183
Henekey's, High Holborn, London 324
Hening, Robert 230, *231*
Hennell, C. Murray 368
Hepworth, Philip D. 98, 167, 220n., 227, 346
Herkomer, Sir Hubert von 187
High Commissioner's Residence, Jerusalem 251–2
High and Over, Amersham 490–2, *491*, *493*
High Cross Hill House, Dartington 230, *231*
Highgate Preservation Society 8, 500
Highpoint One, Highgate 8, 499–500, *499*, 508, 516; Plate 37
Highpoint Two, Highgate 508–9, *510*, 516; Plate 37

Hill, Oliver 7–8, 15, 21–2, 25, 167, 227, 247, 278–9 and n., 289, *290*, 349–50, *350*, 456–7, 472, 477, 483–6, *484–5*, 505; Plates 14, 23, 34
Hill, Rosemary 280
Hillier, Bevis 201–2
Hilversum 138–9, *139*, 164
Hislop, Ian 2
Hitchcock, Henry-Russell 447, 465–6, 492, 499, 500, *513*
Hitler, Adolf 32, 500
Hobbs, Major General Sir Talbot 74
Hodge, Alan 48, 178, 205–6, 234, 236, 450
Hodnett, Edwin 45
Hoff, Rayner 53
Högalid Church, Stockholm 145, 422–4, *423*, 431
Höger, Fritz 154–5, *154*, 426, 427, 429
Holabird and Roche 181
Holden, Charles 14, 18, 19, 22, 67, 68, 72, 150, 163–4, 180, 195–8, *196*, *198*, 201n., 261–2, 270, 273, 458, 467, 516–17; Plate 6
Holden & Pearson Plate 6
Holford, R. S. 380
Holford, William 167
Holland House, London 134–5, *135*, 243
Holliday, A. Clifford 374, 405
Holt, Alfred & Co. 186
Holthanger, Wentworth 21, 483
Holzmeister, Clemens 252
Honeyman & Keppie 183
Hood, Raymond 188, 198–200, *200*, 267, 269, 271; Plate 10
Hoover Factory, Perivale ii, 222–3, *222*, 240–2, *241*; Plate 15
Hope, Thomas 351
Hopkins, Andrew 76n.
Horder, P. Morley 168
Hornsey Town Hall, London 139, *140*, 141
Hotel Ozonia, Canvey Island 309
Hounslow, London 437
House Building 1934–1936 329–30
Howard, Ebenezer 229, 283, 366, 367

Howe, George 230
Howe, Jack 504
Howitt, T. Cecil 96–7, *97*
Hoylake, Wirral 52
Hubbard, R. Pearce 167
Hudson, Edward 91, 288
Hudson, W. H. 198
Hughes, Hugh 21, 488
Hull 88
Hungerford Bridge, London 44 and n., 386, 387
Hurst, Sidney C. 68n.
Hussey, Christopher 41n., 48, 60, 63 and n., 115, 126, 169, 229, 250, 252, 278n., 290, 351, 390, 492, 517
Hutchinson, Major Kenneth 297–8
Huxley, Aldous 6, 27, 471
Huxley, Julian 19
Hyslop, Geddes 348
Hyver Hill, Barnet 229
Ideal Home exhibitions 304–5, 309, 330–1, 482
Ilford 45
Illustrated London News 242
Imperial Chemical Industries 119
Imperial War Graves Commission (IWGC) 8, 50, 52, 62, 64–9, 73, 262
Impington Village College 451 and n., 503–4, *505*
Imrie, G. Blair 293–4, *293*
India 3, 23, 36–7, 72, 79–84, 249–50, 252
India Buildings, Liverpool 186–7, *186*; Plate 11
India Gate, New Delhi *83*
Industrial Revolution 32
Inglis, Ken 50
Institute of Hygiene and Tropical Medicine, London 168
'International Architecture: 1924–33', London (1934) 32–3
International style 5, 168, 447
Ionides, Basil 203
Iraq 68–9
Irish National War Memorial, Dublin 61, *62*
Isokon Flats, Hampstead 495–7, *495–6*
Ison, Walter 208

Italian architecture 30, 32, 89, 167–70, 208, 210
Jack, Ian 217–18
Jackson, Sir Thomas Graham 235
Jacobsen, Theodore 384
Jacques, Richard 125
Jagger, Charles Sargeant *vi*, 52–3, 72, 119, 405
James, C. H. 147–8, *149*, 368, *368*
James, Edward 393
Jarrow March (1936) 8
Jeeves, Gordon 200–1
Jekyll, Gertrude 41n., 47, 67, 297
Jekyll, Sir Herbert and Lady 47n.
Jellicoe, Sir Geoffrey 165n.
Jenkins, Albert D. 474
Jenkinson, Charles 161
Jensen-Klint, P. V. 151–2, 424
Jersey, Earl of 125–6
Jerusalem 68, 243n., 251–2 and n., 405
Joass, J. J. 117
John Keble Church, Mill Hill 418, 419–20
Johnson, Amy 310
Johnson, Philip 447
Joldwynds, Surrey 484
Jones, H. C. & Co. 276
Jones, Inigo 42, 90n., 216, 504
Jones, Sydney R. 293
Jordan, Robert Furneaux 137
Journal of the Royal Institute of British Architects 41
Jugendstil 17
Juta, Jan 150, *151*
Kahn brothers 219, 220
Kampmann, Hack 152, *152*, 343
Karl-Marx-Hof, Vienna 161
Kaufmann, Oskar 160
Kay, Joseph 395
Keay, Lancelot *162–3*, 163
Keble College, Oxford 29
Kempton Park Waterworks, Sunbury-on-Thames 264–5, *264*
Kennedy, T. Warnett 168, 431
Kennington, Eric 165, 169, 478
Kensal House, Ladbroke Grove, London 489–90, *490*, 497
The Kensington Cinema, London 212

Kensington Library, London 98n.
Kent, Eugene 369
Kent, William 379
Kenyon, Arthur W. 155–7, *156*, 368, *368*, 369–70, 427, *428*
Kenyon, Sir Frederick 65, 71
Kernot, C. F. 54
King, W. J. 209–10
King and Queen Hotel, Brighton 324–5
King's Arms, Amersham, Bucks 318
The King's House, Burhill 372, *372*
Kingsbury, Middlesex 309
Kingston House, Bradford-on-Avon 278
Kingsway, London 107–9, *108*
Kipling, Rudyard 56, 64, 283
Kitson, Sydney 272
Klerk, Michel de 134
Knoblock, Edward 351
Knott, Ralph 84, *85*, 96
Kodak House, London 107–9, 180, *181*
Komisarjevsky, Theodore Plate 12
Korda, Alexander 278
Kropholler, A. J. 134
Lady Margaret Hall, Oxford 361, 414, *415*
Laing, J. 329
Lalique, René 203
Lamb, Thomas W. 206
Lambeth Bridge, London 70n., 119–20
Lancaster, Osbert 4, 7, *10*, 18, 29, 111, 191–2, 201, 202–3, 225–8, *226–7*, 275–7, *275*, *277*, 279–80, 286n., 337, 341, 351–2, 355, 364, 405, 440, 447, 450 and n., *519*
Lanchester, H. V. 23, 90n., 150
Lander, Felix 420
Landfall, Poole, Dorset 472, 484
Langtry-Langton, J. H. 419
Lansbury, George 354
Lansdowne House, London 379–80
L'Anson, Edward 111
Larkhall Estate, Lambeth 364–6, *365*
Laughton, Charles 19
Lawn Road Flats, Hampstead 16

INDEX

Lay, C. H. 228, *229*
Le Corbusier 7, 8, 21, 25, 34, 171–2, 177, 185 and n., 203, 229, 348, 447, 468–73, 474, 483, 500
Le Tréport, France 67
League of Nations 27
Leathart, Julian 159, 210, 216, 227, 278, 326, 449–50, 454, 461–2, 478
Leathart & Granger 212
Leeds 3, 88, 95, 103, 161, *162*
Leith, Gordon 68
Leith House, Gresham Street, London 344, *345*
Lerewentz, Sigurd 147
Lescaze, William 230, *231*, 497
Leslie, Shane 380
Letchworth Garden City 72, 136, 366–7
Lethaby, W. R. 44–5, 50, 386, 468
Lewis, E. Wamsley 160, *160*, 208; Plate 18
Liberty & Co. 271–2, *273*, 324
Lidbetter, Hubert 353
The Lido, Golders Green, London 209–10
Lipscombe, Guy 209–10
Little Garth, Syresham, Northamptonshire 297
Liturgical Movement 416, 418, 421–2, 427
Liverpool 3, 52, *162–3*, 163, 185–7, *186*, *188*, 332, 404
Liverpool Anglican Cathedral 20, 57, 93, 224, 246, 253, 314, 409, 413, 414–16, 442–4, *443–4*; Plate 38
Liverpool Metropolitan Roman Catholic Cathedral 23, 76, 93–4, *93*, 441–2, *442*
Liverpool School of Architecture 95, 181, 182, 185, 256, 340, 341, 429, 488–9, 495, 516
Livett, R. A. H. 161, *162*
Lloyd George, David 39, 44, 62
Lloyd's of London 114–15, *115*
Lloyd's Bank, Cornhill, London 124
London Building Act (1894) 119

London County Council (LCC) 84, 122, 180, 193, 338n., 363–4, *363*, 366, 381, 384–8, 391, 396, 400, 494
London Life Building 116
London, Midland & Scottish Railway (LMS) 393, 475, 486
London Passenger Transport Board (LPTB) 19, 32, 163–4, 305, 332–3, 516–17
London Power Company 254
London Society 44, 378, 385
London Underground 8, 14, 22, 31, 67, 72, 163–4, 261–2, 273, 458, 467
London University 18, 195, *196*, 201n., 384
London Zoo 7–8, 16, 498–9, *498*
Londoners' League 390, 392, 394
Loos, Adolf 374
Lorimer, Sir Robert 54, 58–60, 68, 72, 359, 412–13; Plate 3
Lorne, Francis 267
Louvencourt, France 67
Louverval, Cambrai 72
Lovat Fraser 208
Lubetkin, Berthold 4, 7–8, 14, 16, 18, 30, 130, 495n., 497–500, *498–9*, 507–9, *510*; Plate 37
Lucas, Colin 494
Lucas, William 74 and n.
Luckhardt, Gebrüder 374
Luton 253, *253*, 414
Lutyens, Sir Edwin 2, 5, 14, 23, 34, 43, 47n., 52, 65–6, 98, 167, 198, 278, 314, 318, 320, 347, 386, 387, 392
 church architecture 93–4, *93*, 441–2, *442*
 commercial buildings 3, 120–4, *123*, 157, 194–5, *195*
 country houses 125–6, *125*, 280, 288–9, 294–5, 297; Plates 5, 22
 and the Georgian Group 390
 government buildings 179, 353–5, *354*
 influence of 21, 37, 350
 neo-Georgian architecture 340
 New Delhi 36, 76, 80–1, *80*, *82–3*, 88, 91, 128, 249, 250; Plate 4
 pubs 321, *321*

 Queen's Dolls' House 126–8, *127*
 university buildings 13, 311–12
 war memorials 6, 39–41, *40*, 47, 51, 53n., 60–8, *62*, 71–8, *73*, *75*, 94, 103
 Wren's influence 90, 92–3
Lutyens, Robert 125–6, 192, 228, *392*, 393; Plate 5
Macartney, Sir Mervyn 91n.
Macedonia 72
McGrath, Raymond 21, 25, 30, 33, *151*, 453, 462–5, *465*, 472–3, 494; Plate 32
Machine Gun Corps Memorial, London 53
McKenna, Reginald 122, 288
McKenzie, Robert Tait 48, *49*
McKim, Mead & White 90n., 184–5, 224
Mackintosh, Charles Rennie 132, 182, 183, 224, 320, 336, 479–82
McLaren, Barbara 47
McLaren, Francis 47 and n.
McLean, William 252n.
McMorran, Donald 330
Macrae, Ebenezer J. 360n.
Magdalen College, Oxford 314
Magdalene College, Cambridge 13, 311–12
Magnoni, Carlo 50n.
Mainz-Bischofsheim 426
Mallet-Stevens, Robert 171, 173
Manchester 3, 171, 194–5, *195*, 332, 467
Manchester Central Library 102, *103*
Manchester Town Hall 102–3
Mandler, Peter 231, 277, 283–4, 285
Mannerism 84, 117, 167
Maple & Co. 331
Margate 159, 189
Marine Court, St Leonard's-on-Sea *471*, 472
Marks & Spencer 201, 393, *393*
Marlborough, Consuelo, Duchess of 298
Marlborough School 54
Marriott, Charles 19, 86–7, 106–10, 117, 407

MARS (Modern Architectural Research Group) 97–8, 492–7, 510
Marshall, Charles Beresford 20, 372, *372*
Marshall Mackenzie & Son 51
Martins Bank, Liverpool 186–7, *188*
Martin-Smith, D.F. 418
Mary, Queen 126–8
Marylands, Ewhurst 227; Plate 14
Marylebone Town Hall, London 114
Masey, Cecil 210, *211*, 216, *217*; Plate 12
Masonic Hospital, Ravenscourt Park, London 267
Masonic Temple, London 245 and n.
'Match House', Stockholm 146, *146*
Mather, Andrew 201, 213, *214*, 215
Matthew, John F. 58
Maufe, Edward 228–9, 371, 400, 406–7, 413, 416, 432–5, *433–4*; Plate 20
Mauger, Paul 369
Mayan architecture 236, 245, 254–9, 262, 269
Meads, Dippenhall *306*, 307
Mears, Joseph 212
Mebes, Paul 343
Mecklenburgh Square, London 385, 394–5
Medd, Henry *82*
Melnikov, Konstantin 172–3
Memorial to the Missing of the Somme 6, 71, 74–8, *75*, 94
Mendelsohn, Eric 16, 19, 130, 159, 161, 252, 446, 466, 500–3, *502–3*, 516
Mendelsohn & Chermayeff 31, 36, 393, 501–3, *502–3*
Menin Gate, Ypres 69–70, *71*
Mercantile Marine Memorial, London 72
Mercat Building, Glasgow 183
Merrick, Jay 237n.
Mersey Tunnel 18, 256–8, *257*
Merv, Turkmenistan 246–7
Messel, Oliver 395
Metroland 274, 332–3
Metropolitan Railway 332–3

Metropolitan Water Board 265, 370–1
Mewès & Davis 116
Middleton Park, Oxfordshire 125–6; Plate 5
Midland Bank 3, 122–4, *123*, 194–5, *195*
Midland Hotel, Morecambe 7–8, 21, 247, 484–6, *484–5*; Plate 34
Mies van der Rohe, Ludwig 477
Miller, Bernard 400, 404, 427–9, *428*
Miller, James 182, 262
Milles, Carl 146
Milne, Oswald P. 203, 291, 346
Ministry of Housing and Local Government 16
Ministry of Pensions, Acton 152, *153*, 342–3
Ministry of Works 32
Miramonte, Kingston 489
Mitchell, Reginald 475
Mitchells & Butlers 323
Mitford, Nancy 396
Mond, Sir Alfred 62
Mond Workshop and Laboratory, Cambridge 488
Monk's Rest, Pinner, Middlesex 305 and n.
Montague Burton 201
Montrose Bridge, Scotland 511
Moore, Henry 19, 197–8, 391n., *517*, 518
Moore, Leslie 410, *410*
Moore, Temple 407, 410, *410*, 411
Morand, Dexter 244–5 and n.
Morecambe 7–8, 21, 247, 484–6
Morris, Henry 353, 451n., 503–4
Morris, William 132, 142, 230n., 280, 283, 376, 481
Morrison, Herbert 387
Mortimer, Raymond 263–4
Moser, Karl 427
Mosley, Oswald 27
Mott, Hay & Anderson 266, *266*
Mount Royal, Marble Arch, London 475–6, *476*
Muggeridge, Charles 210
Mumford, Lewis 367

Munich Agreement (1938) 28, 29
Munstead Wood, Godalming 297; Plate 22
Murrell & Piggott *316*
Museum of Modern Art, New York 446, 465
Musman, E. B. 318, 322, 447, 477–9, *478*; Plate 27
Mussolini, Benito 32, 168, 357
Muzio, Giovanni 167, 220n.
Myer, Lt-Col G. Val 463–4, *464*
Myerscough-Walker, Raymond 178, 329, 339–40, 461, 488
Myllet Arms, Perivale 322
Nairn, Ian 57, 298–9, 309
Nash, John 14, 22, 85, 87, 90, 271, 336, 349, 377, 378, 389, 463, 494n.
Nash, Paul 274
National Museum of Wales, Cardiff 84, *84*
National Provincial Bank, London 112–13, *113*
National Radiator Building (Ideal House), London 188, 199–200, *200*; Plate 10
National Romanticism 141
National Trust 283 and n.
Nazi Germany 6, 16, 28, 31, 398, 497
Nebraska State Capitol 4, 104, 224–5, 269
neo-Georgian architecture 20–1, 32, 57, 125, 328, 339–75, 451
see also Georgian architecture
neo-Romanesque architecture 20, 168, 401–6, 422
neo-Tudor architecture 13, 21, 31, 125, 201, 217, 271–338, 479
Neu-Ulm, Germany 57, 426
Neuve-Chapelle, France 72
Nevill, Ralph 232, 284
New Bodleian Library, Oxford 14, 314
New Delhi 23, 36, 72, 76, 79–84, *80–3*, 91, 128, 249, 250, 252, 440; Plate 4
New Farm, Haslemere 494
New Kinema, Oxted *316*, 317
New St Pancras Church, London 385

INDEX

New Ship Inn, Brighton 325
New Statesman and Nation
   184–5, 382, 389
New Victoria Cinema, London
   236
New Victoria Theatre, London
   160, *160*; Plate 18
New Ways, Wellingborough
   Road, Northampton
   479–82, *480*
New York 177, 180, 182, 185–6,
   199, 246, 259, 267
New York Capitol 206
New Zealand 72
Newcastle-upon-Tyne 99, 266,
   266
Newman, F. Winton *237*;
   Plate 17
Newport Civic Centre 97–8
Newton, Sir Ernest 54, 85, 340
Newton, W. G. 54, 189
Nicholson, Sir Charles 400,
   411, 441
Nicolson, Christopher 393
Niemeyer, Oscar 442
Norfolk House, St James's
   Square, London 381–2,
   381
Norman & Dawbarn 474
Northampton 31, 452
Northern Ireland 95–6
Northfleet 413
Norwich City Hall 36, 97,
   147–8, *148–9*, 269
Notre-Dame du Raincy 56–7,
   171, 422, *422*
Nottingham Guildhall 96–7,
   97, 98
'Novecento' style 167
Noyelles-sur-Mer, France 68
Nun's Head pub, Nunhead
   279, *279*
Nye, David 212, *213*
Oakham School 54
Oban 414
Odeon cinemas 159, 201, 213,
   214, 215, *215*
Office of Works 119, *153*, 219,
   235, 266–7, 281, 342–3,
   353, 355–7
'Old English' style 280
Old Surrey Hall, Surrey 298–9,
   300, 302
Oliver, Basil 320–1, 324, 478
Oliver, Paul 327–9, 338

Olympia Exhibition building,
   London 486
O'Rorke, Brian 291
Osborn, Frederick 367
Ossulston Estate, Somers
   Town, London *170*
Östberg, Ragnar 142 and n.,
   143, 168, 208, 427
Oxford University 14, 29, 251,
   310–14, 361, 503
Oxted, Surrey 302
Paddington Station, London 52
Paget, Paul 348
Paisley, Scotland 54
Palestine 68, 251–2
Palestine Archaeological
   Museum, Jerusalem 251
Palladian architecture 209,
   285, 358
Palladio, Andrea 89
Palumbo, Rudolph 381–2
Pantheon, Oxford Street,
   London 201, 392–3, *392*
Paris 16, 30, 39, 42, 75, 89, 171,
   172–4, 184
Paris Exposition (1900) 278
Paris Exposition (1925) 130,
   199, 201, 203, 236
Paris Exposition (1937) 21
Park Lane Hotel, London
   179–80
Parliament 64, 180, 354, 378,
   387–9, 494
Passchendaele 67, 70–1
Paxton, Joseph 465
Peach, C. Stanley 243n.
Pearson, Lionel *vi*, 52–3
Peers, Sir Charles 281
Pegram, Alfred Bertram 61n., *61*
Penguin Pool, London Zoo
   498, 499
Percy Lodge, East Sheen 341,
   341
Perret, Auguste 56–7, 171, 421,
   422, *422*
Perret, Gustave *422*
Persia 246
Peruzzi, B. T. 116
Peter Jones, Sloane Square,
   London 16, *17*, 19, 461, 516
Peterhouse, Cambridge 13
Petts Wood, Orpington 329,
   331–3; Plate 26
Pevsner, Nikolaus 4–5, 6, 132,
   223, 237, 257, 384, 455, 515

Buildings of England 12, 299
on church architecture 414
on civic and government
   buildings 97–9, 102n., 148,
   152
on commercial buildings 158
on domestic architecture 230,
   298–9
and listed buildings 16, 459
on the Modern Movement
   173, 364, 447–8, 477–9,
   481, 504
on Shakespeare Memorial
   Theatre 166
on university buildings 13,
   310–11
Philadelphia Museum of Art
   231
Phillips, Amyas 299–300, *299*
Phillips, R. Randal 42–3, 294,
   340
Piacentini, Marcello 168, 220n.,
   431
Piccadilly Theatre, London 209
Pick, Frank 19, 32, 163, 198,
   458
Picturesque 169, *170*
Pierce, S. Rowland 147–8, *149*
Pilkington Brothers 461
Piloti (*Private Life* column)
   1, 2, 7
Pioneer Health Centre, Peck-
   ham 452, 489, 509–10, *509*
Piper, John 337
Pite, Beresford 197, 410
Plaza Cinema, Regent Street,
   London 208–9
Pleydell-Bouverie, David 474
Plumpton Place, Sussex 288–9
Plymouth 72
Poelzig, Hans 160, 222n.
Police Headquarters, Copenha-
   gen 152, *152*, 343
Pond Cottage, Pinner, Middle-
   sex *304*, 305
Poole, Dorset 228–9
Porri, Arthur G. 233, *235*;
   Plate 16
Port of London Authority 114
Port Tewfik, Egypt 72
Portmeirion, North Wales 22,
   169–70; Plate 9
Portsmouth 72, 411, 416
Post Offices 353, *355*, 357–8
Potters Bar Estate 331

Powers, Alan 181–2, 290, 348, 373, 451, 459–60, 461, 467, 488, 507, 517
Pozières British Cemetery 72
Pretoria 73
Priestley, J. B. 105, 223, 281, 324, 326
Prior, E. S. 429
Pritchard, Jack 495 and n.
Private Eye 1, 2, 4
Prospect Inn, Isle of Thanet 21
Provincial Cinematograph Theatres 207, 212
Pugin, A. W. N. 5, 275, 316–17, 325, 335
Pullman Court, Streatham 488
Punitzer, Martin 159
Quarr Abbey, Isle of Wight 424
Quarry Hill Flats, Leeds 161, *162*
Queen Anne style 13, 363–4
Queens College, Cambridge 13
Queens' College, Oxford 310–11, *311*
Queen's Dolls' House 126–8, *127*
Queensferry *242*, 243
Quennell, Marjorie and C. H. B. 27, 322 and n., 336
Radley School 54
Ramsey, Stanley C. 23, 87, 90n., 94–5, 337, 341, 344, 367
Ramsgate 189, 474
Rasmussen, Steen Eiler 131, 296, 326, 337, 339, 374
Ratton Wood, Sussex 346
Ravilious, Eric *484*, 486
Read, Herbert 398
Recent English Architecture 1920–1940 17–18, 106n., 141, 258, 291, 347
Rectory Gardens, Edgware 338
Red Lion, Grantchester 321
Red Lion, King's Heath, Birmingham 318
Redfern, Harry 312, 319–20, *319*, 322
Rees, Noel *334*
Rees, Verner O. 168
Regal Cinema, Marble Arch, London 210
Regency architecture 21, 23, 85, 87, 340, 348
Regency furniture 351–2

Regent Cinema, Brighton 22, 207–8, *207*, 212
Regent Street, London 70n., 84–8, *86*, 377, 378
Reid Memorial Church, Edinburgh 413
Reilly, Charles H. 90n., 98, 104n., 180, 258, 370, 500, 512
 on American Classicism 184–5
 on Battersea Power Station 256, 416
 on church architecture 402, 416, 429, 431, 435, 444
 on civic architecture 99–102, 103, 105
 on commercial buildings 121, 124, 186–7, 218
 Devonshire House, London 188–9, *190*
 on domestic architecture 362, 366
 on Holden 197, 198
 pupils 95, 124, 182, 185–6, 256, 340–1, 404, 429, 488–9, 516
 Representative British Architects of Today 22–4, 84, 130
 on university buildings 225
Reiss, R. L. 368–9
Reith, Sir John 463
Renaissance 13, 42, 89, 130, 184, 185, 208, 504
Rendel, Palmer & Tritton 387
Rennie, John 20, 377, 385–6, 388
Reviere, Raymond Britton 215
Rex cinemas 212, *213*, 216
Rhodes House, Oxford 312–14, *313*
Richards, J. M. 15, 164, 168, 273, 311, 337–8, 352, 364, 389, 398, 448, 479, 498, 512
Richardson, Sir Albert 42–3, 98n., 111, 112, 114, 133, 317–18, 340, 343–4, *345*, 351, 388, 390, 392, 393 and n., 399, 437–8, *437*, 457
Richardson, H. H. 187
Richmond Girls' High School, Yorkshire 54
Rickards, Edwin 41
Ridgemead, Englefield Green 228

Ritz Cinema, Farnworth 217–18
Ritz Hotel, London 117
Roberts, Keith 213
Robertson, Howard Morley 13, 25, 87, 130–2, 134, 142, 147, 154, 170–3, 238, 301n., 370–1, 458, 459
Robertson, Manning 142, 342–3
Rochdale 51
Rockefeller, John D. 225
Rogers, Richard 115
Rohan, Timothy 128
Roman Catholic Church 50, 93–4, 155, 168, 403, 405–7, 416, 418–19, 421–2, 426, 429–31, 440
Rome 76n., 93, 114, 116, 167, 208, 245
Rotha, Paul 206
Rothermere, Lord 385
Roux-Spitz, Michel 171
Rowse, Herbert J. 18, 25, 185–6, *186*, 256–9, *257*; Plate 11
Roxy-Palast, Berlin 159
Royal Academy 94, 197, 359, 386, 441
Royal Air Force 71, 356
Royal Air Force Memorial, London 52
Royal College of Art, London 98n.
Royal Commission on Historical Monuments 376
Royal Corinthian Yacht Club, Burnham-on-Crouch 486
Royal Fine Art Commission 72, 354, 359, 386
Royal Flying Corps 71
Royal Horticultural Hall, London 144, *145*, 370, 452
Royal Hospital School, Holbrook 95
Royal Institute of British Architects (RIBA) 9, 11, 12, 31, 41, 91, 193, 207, 220, 229, 359, 387, 500
 competitions 101
 exhibitions 32–3, 473
 Headquarters *26*, 129, 143, 149–51, *151*
 medals and prizes 111, 117, 138, 141, 142, 145, 147, 167, 208, 281, 362

INDEX

Presidential Address 445–6
Royal Insurance Company 117
Royal Mail Steam Packet
  Company 114
Royal Masonic Hospital,
  Ravenscourt Park 137–8,
  137–8
Royal Society of Arts 283 and
  n., 388
Rudderbar, Hanworth, London
  472–3
Rundkirche, Essen 425, *425*
Ruskin, John 29, 85, 134, 198,
  280, 409
Rutherford, Sir Ernest 12, 488
Saarinen, Eliel 269
Sackville, Lady 62n.
Saint, Andrew 187, 188,
  199–200, 229, 467n.
St Agnes, Kennington 407 and
  n., *408*
St Alban's, North Harrow
  155–7, *156*, 427, *428*
St Alphage's, Hendon 441
St Andrew's, Luton 253, *253*,
  435
St Andrew's, Marylebone 407
St Andrew's Gardens,
  Liverpool *162–3*, 163
St Andrew's House, Edinburgh
  266–70, *269*
St Andrew's Scottish war
  memorial church, Jerusalem
  405
St Anne's, Dennistoun 168
St Anne's Hill, Surrey 494
St Augustine's, Queen's Gate,
  London 440
St Augustine's, Pendlebury 408
St Catherine's, Hammersmith
  378, 400–2, *401*
St Christopher's, Liverpool 404,
  427–9, *428*
St Christopher's, Withington
  429
St Columba's, Anfield 404
St Columba's, Maryhill 431
St Columba's Catholic Church,
  Glasgow *169*
St Columbkille's, Rutherglen
  168, 431
St Cyprian's, Clarence Gate,
  London 412
St Faith's, Lee-on-the-Solent
  428, 429

St Francis's, Bournemouth 405
St Francis's, High Wycombe
  414
St Francis's, Isleworth 411
St Gabriel's, Blackburn 157,
  256, 416, 429, 431
St George's, Wash Common
  405
St George's Hall, Liverpool 102
St John's College, Cambridge
  371
St John's Renfield Church,
  Glasgow 413
St Kamillus Church and Asthma
  Hospital, Mönchengladbach *426*
St Katherine Coleman, London
  378, 400
St Margaret's House, London
  111
St Martin's Garrison Church,
  New Delhi 36–7, 250–1;
  Plate 1
St Mary, Kenton, London 411
St Mary the Virgin, Wellingborough 411, *412*; Plate 30
St Mary's, Bourne Street,
  London 441
St Matthew's Roman Catholic
  Church, Liverpool 404;
  Plate 29
St Michael and All Angels,
  Wythenshawe 171, 418,
  420–1, *420*
St Michael's Court, Cambridge
  106, *371*
St Monica's, Bootle 429–31,
  430; Plate 31
St Nicholas's, Burnage 409,
  438, *439*
St Paul's Cathedral, London 91
  and n., 92, 94, 116, 386
St Peter in Chains, Ardrossan
  168, *169*, 431; Plate 8
St Peter's, Gorleston-on-Sea
  419, *419*
St Philip's, Cosham, Portsmouth 416–18, *417*
St Saviour's Church, Eltham
  155, *155*, 439; Plate 7
St Silas's, Kentish Town 411
St Stephen Walbrook, London
  91–2
St Thomas the Apostle,
  Hanwell 433–5, *434*

St Wilfrid's, Brighton 435–7
  and n., *436*
St Wilfrid's, Halton, Leeds 429
St Wilfrid's, Harrogate 410, *410*
Saler, Michael T. 198
Salmon, James 183–4 and n.
Salvation Army 314–15
Samara'a, Iraq 247
Samuel, Godfrey 498
Samuely, Felix *498*, 499
Sarel, Walter 348
Sassoon, Siegfried 69–70
Sassoon House, Peckham 489
Savage, Rupert 245 and n.
Savoy Hotel, London 179
Savoy Theatre, London 203
Sawston Village College 353,
  451 and n., *452*
Scarlett, Frank 175
Scarlett & Ashworth 88
Scheffauer, Hermann George
  153
Schinkel, Karl Friedrich 111
Schocken stores, Germany 19,
  516
Schwarz, Rudolf 426–7, *427*
Scott, A. T. 182
Scott, Adrian Gilbert 360n.,
  362, 442
Scott, Chesterton and Shepherd Plate 13
Scott, Elisabeth 9, 36, 164–6
  and n.; Plate 13
Scott, Geoffrey 19–20, 88–90,
  96, 185
Scott, George Gilbert 2, 20,
  407, *408*
Scott, Sir Gilbert 2, 29, 248
Scott, Sir Giles Gilbert 23, 29,
  36, 74n., 137, 150, 180, 186,
  203, 224, 351, 372, 386, 406
  Battersea Power Station 2,
    2, 19, 254–6, *255*, 516;
    Plate 21
  church architecture 20–1, 93,
    253, *253*, 400, 403–4, *403*,
    406–7, 409–10, 413–16,
    415, 435, 442–4, *443–4*;
    Plate 38
  houses 451
  memorial to George V 395–6
  neo-Georgian architecture
    360–2, *361–2*
  neo-Tudor buildings 314–16,
    315

on planning 32–3
telephone boxes 358–60, *359*
university buildings 10, 11–12, 14, 19, 225, 259, 462; Plate 2
war memorials 56–8, *56–7*
Waterloo Bridge 266, 387
Scott, J. R. 51, 475 and n.
Scott, Sir Leslie 328
Scottish Legal Assurance Society, Glasgow 182–3
Scottish National War Memorial, Edinburgh 58–60, *59*, 77, 413; Plate 3
Scruby, Basil *7*, 333; Plate 26
Second World War 24, 398, 401, 446, 504
Sedding, J. D. 408
Seely, John 348
Seely & Paget *204–5*, 205, 427–9, *428*
Selfridges, London 109, 187–8, 194
Senate House, London University 195, *196*, 201n.
Shadbolt, Blunden 8, 303–7, *304–5*
Shakespeare Memorial Theatre, Stratford-upon-Avon 9, 34–5, *35*, 164–6, *166*, 199, 278; Plate 13
Shand, P. Morton 158–9, 160, 195–7, 206, 209–10, 212, 357, 358, 481
Sharp, Cecil 281
Sharp, Thomas 32
Shaw, Richard Norman 85–6, 132, 275, 277, 280, 318, 325, 335, 336, 363–4, 407
Shearman, E. C. 411, 424
Sheffield Education Department office 265
Sheffield Memorial Halls 102
Shell-Mex House, London 262–4, *263*
Shepherd, J. C. 165n.
Shepherd's Bush Pavilion Cinema, London 208, *209*, 245
Sheppard, John M. *384*, 385
Shipley, Sir Arthur 48–50
Shoosmith, Arthur G. 4, 25, 37, 250–3, 439–40; Plate 1
Shoosmith, Marjorie 4
Shreve & Lamb 189

Shrubs' Wood, Chalfont St Giles 501
Silver End, Essex 482
Simon, F. W. 185
Simpson, Sir John 249, 251
Simpson & Ayrton *247*, 511
Sisson, Marshall 21, 167, 353, 488
Sitwell, Sacheverell 6
Skinner, Francis 498
Skinner, Joan 222, 240
Slater & Moberly 516
Sledmere, Yorkshire 50n.
Sleigh, Alison 165n.
The Slip, Bosham 293–4, *293*
Small Downs House, Sandwich 296, *296*
Smith, Arnold Dunbar 110–11, *110*
Smith, Douglas H. *310*
Smith & Brewer 84, *84*, 457
Smugglers' Way, New Forest 8, 303–4
Soane, Sir John 111, 120, 348, 359–60, 382–4, *383*
Society of Friends 385
Society of Jesus 312
Society for the Protection of Ancient Buildings (SPAB) 20, 230n., 280, 283, 376, 383–4, 386, 388, 390–2
Society of the Sacred Mission, Kelham 405–6 and n., *405–6*
Soissons, Louis de 364–70, *365*, *368–9*
Somerford, Thomas 210
Somme, Battle of (1916) 74–8, 182
South Africa 73, 226, 228, 314
South Africa House, London 382, 389
Southampton 51, 62
Southampton Civic Centre 104–5, *104*, 224–5
Southern Railway 189, 216, 333, 334, 387, 475
Southport, Merseyside 51
Spain 210
Spanish City Cinema, Northfields, London 210, *211*, 226
Spanish Colonial architecture 18, 225–9, 405

Speke Airport, Liverpool *473*, 474
Spence, Basil 372–3, *373*
Squire, J. C. 389
Stahlkirche, Cologne 424–5
Stamp, Sir Josiah 393
Star and Garter Home, Richmond 114
Station Square, Petts Wood 333, *333*
Steiner, Rudolf 309
Stevens, Alfred 380
Stevenson, W. L. Plate 31
Stewart-Liberty, Ivor 272
Stilgoe, Henry E. *264*, 265
Stockbrokers' Tudor 275–7, *275*, 279–80, 286, 293–4, 333
Stockgrove Park House, Leighton Buzzard 346, *346*
Stockholm 30, 145–7, *148*, 422–4, *423*, 429, 435
Stockholm City Library 146–7, 149, *150*, 164
Stockholm Concert Hall 146, 147, *148*
Stockholm Exhibition (1930) 147, 483
Stockholm Town Hall 97, 131, 139, 142–3, *143*, 148, 150, 246, 409, 427, 431, 447
Stockport, Manchester 51
Stone, Edward A. 210
Stone, H. 369
Stopes, Marie 191 and n.
Stormont Parliament Building, Belfast 95–6 and n., *96*, 98
Storrs, Sir Ronald 252n.
Strand Palace Hotel, London 467
Strange, Clifford 138
Stratford-upon-Avon 9, 34–5, 164–6, 199, 278
Strathcona, Lord 107n.
Stratton, P. M. 172
Streatfeild & Atwell 54
Street, George Edmund 407, 409
Suez Canal 72
Sullivan, Leo Sylvester 180–1
Sullivan, Louis 182, 224
Summerson, John 4, 15–16, 24, 87, 94, 102, 128, 167–8, 170–1, 194, 223–4, 229,

INDEX

344, 390, 394–5, 407n., 446–8, 483, 490, 492–3, 497, 517, 518
Summit House, Red Lion Square, London 243–5
Sun House, Hampstead 16, 489; Plate 35
Surbiton *276*
Surrealism 508
Sutton Scarsdale, Derbyshire 231
Swales, Francis 109
Swansea Guildhall 4, 99–101, *100–1*, 104 and n., 224–5
Sweden 17, 30, 106, 129, 131, 141–7, 170–1, 422–4
Swedish Exhibition, London (1931) 147
Swedish Institute of Architects 149–50
Swedish Match Company 146, *146*
Swinbrook House, Oxfordshire 347
Switzerland 130, 416, 427
Sydney Harbour Bridge 265–6
Sykes, Sir Mark 50n.
Symondson, Anthony 418
Tait, Thomas S. 25, 52, 124, 135n., 138, 157, 173, 180, 220n., 238, 243, 267–70, 431, 482 and n., 501
Talbot Rice, David 19
Tanner, Messrs 180
Tapper, Sir Walter 23, 410–11
Tatton, Reginald 46
Taut, Bruno 153, 161
Taylor, A. J. P. 14, 15
Taylor, Nicholas 307
Taylor, Sir Robert 120, 382
Tecton 18, 498–500, *499*, 509, *510*, 516; Plate 37
Telephone Building, New York 177
Templewood, Norfolk 348
Tengbom, Ivar 145–7, *146*, *148*, 208, 422–4, *423*, 435
Tewin, Hertfordshire 47–8
Thames House, London 119, 129
Thiepval, France 74–8, *75*, 94
Thirties: British Art and Design Before the War, London (1979) 338 and n.
Thirties Society 14, 58n., 115, 435n.

see also Twentieth Century Society
Thomas, Sir Alfred Brumwell 95
Thomas, Percy 99–101, *100–1*, 104n., 393 and n., 473
Thompson, Edmund C. 257
Thomson, Alexander 248
Thomson, James Taylor 413
Thomson, Leslie G. 413
Thornely, Arnold 96, *96*
Thorp, John B. *93*, 94, 441
Tibbenham Tudor House, Northgate, Middlesex 330–1, *331*
Tilden, Philip 109, 149, 194
Tiles and Potteries Ltd 302
The Times 44n., 86, 282, 389
Titsey Estate, New Oxted 302
Tomlinson, Harold 340
Tournon, Paul 422
Town and Country Planning Act (1932) 32, 389
Town Planning Institute 359
Townley, Marjorie 175
Travers, Martin 440
Treasury 353, 355
Trehearne & Norman 107, *108*
Trent, Newbury 45
Trent, William E. *160*, 212, 316–17; Plate 18
Trevelyan, G. M. 14
Trobridge, Ernest 307–9, *308*
Trotter, Dorothy Warren 351, 390, 391–2 and n.
Trotter, Philip 390, 391n.
Troup, F. W. 382–4 and n.
Truelove, J. R. 68, 71
Trussed Concrete Steel Company 218–19, 511
Tudor Building Co. 332
Tudor Close, Rottingdean 302–3, *303*; Plate 28
Tudor House, London 271–2, *273*, 324
Tudor style *see* neo-Tudor architecture
Tunnard, Christopher 518
Turnor, Reginald 373
Tutankhamun, Pharaoh 17, 200, 234–6
Twentieth Century Society 3–4, 10, 97
see also Thirties Society
Twickenham Factory 227

Tyack, Geoffrey 312
Tyne Bridge 266, *266*
Tyne Cot Cemetery, Belgium 70–1
Tyson Smith, Herbert 52, *430*
UFA Universum Kino, Berlin 159
Underground Group 195–8, 201n.
Union Bank of Scotland, Glasgow 182, *183*
United States of America 177–200, 203, 205–10, 218–20, 223–5, 229–32, 245–6, 256–7
Universal Housing Co. 331
Uppingham School 54
Uren, Reginald 30, 139, *140*, 217
Valewood Farm, Haslemere 278n.
Vanbrugh, Sir John 90 and n.
Vardy, John 395, 397
Velarde, Francis Xavier 157, 256, 400, 404, 429–31, *430*; Plates 29, 31
Verity, Frank 208–9, *209*, 245
Vernon Court, London 309–10
Vernon House, Trafalgar Square, London 349–50
Viceroy's House, New Delhi 76, 80–1, *82*, 91, 128, 250; Plate 4
Vienna 161
Villers-Bretonneux Cemetery, Amiens 73–4, *73*
Vimy Ridge, France 73
Viollet-le-Duc, Eugène Emmanuel 461
Vitruvius 89
Von Berg, Wilfred 68
Voorhees, Gmelin & Walker 177
Vorkink & Wormser 289
Voysey, C. F. A. 105–6, 132, 277, 280, 336, 481–2
Vulliamy, Lewis 380
Vyella Factory, Nottingham 516
Waggoners' Memorial, Sledmere 50n.
Wahlman, Lars Israel 429
Wahlman, Westman and Lallerstedt 145
Walcot, William 44n., 115, 179, 245, 387

INDEX

Waldorf Astoria Hotel, New York 231–2
Walford, Geoffrey 494
Walker, David 138, 184n., 267
Walker, Ralph 177
Wall Street Crash (1929) 27
Wallis, Gilbert & Partners *ii*, 218–23, *221–2*, 240–2, *241*, 511; Plate 15
Wallis, Thomas 218–20
Walton, George 320, 481
Wansford Bridge 511
Ward, Basil 30, 167, 494
Wardman, Harry 179–80, 354–5
Ware, Fabian 64, 65, 72, 73
Ware, Isaac 380
Warren, Edward 69 and n.
Washington DC 179–80, 353–5
Waterhouse, Alfred 13, 14, 103, 134
Waterhouse, Paul 91
Waterloo Bridge, London 20, 21, 266, 377, 385–8
Waterloo Station, London 51
Watford Town Hall 106 and n.
Wattjes, J. G. 346
Waugh, Evelyn 6–7, 29, 238, 282, 285–6, 348, 445, 472, 482–3, 506–7
Weaver, Lawrence 34, 60n., 143–4, 174–5, 287, 445
Webb, Sir Aston 44, 85, 91, 301, 387
Webb, Maurice 132, *300*, 301 and n.
Webb, Philip 364
Webber, E. Berry 104–5 and n., *104*
Weedon, Harry *214*, 215
Weimar Republic 158, 424–5, 450
Weir, William 230
Wellesley, Lord Gerald 42, 51, 351, 393
Wells, A. Randall 107n., 429
Wells, H. G. 27, 455
Wells, Reginald F. 301–2
Welsh, Herbert 420
Welsh National War Memorial, Cardiff 61, *61*

Welwyn Garden City 136, 283, 366–70, *368–9*
Wembley Town Hall, London 138
West, J. G. 96n., 343, 356
West, Rebecca 19
West Wycombe, Bucks 283 and n.
Westminster Abbey, London 64
Westminster Bank, 116–19, *116*; Plate 25
Westminster Cathedral, London 90n., 402–3, 421
Westwood, P. J. 243, 245
Wheeler, C. A. 188
Whinney, T. B. 122
Whistler, Rex 348–9
White, James 384
White Rock Pavilion, Hastings 106
Whitehall Palace, London 95
Whitelands College, Putney 361
Wilbraham House, London 350
Willans and Robinson Factory, Queensferry *242*, 243
William Booth Memorial College, Denmark Hill 314–16, *315*
Williams, Algernon Bentley Plate 25
Williams, Alice Meredith 54, 58
Williams, Leopold J. 302; Plate 25
Williams, Sir Owen 23, 219, 238, *239*, 249, 261, 380, 424, 452, 467, 489, 509–16, *509*, *513–15*; Plate 33
Williams-Ellis, Amabel 249
Williams-Ellis, Clough 22, 31–2, 54, 144, 167–8, 169–71, 194, 223–4, 229, 249, 293, 343, 390; Plate 9
1–3 Willow Road, Hampstead 374, *375*
Wilson, Henry 173
Wilson, Woodrow 178
Wiltshire County Offices, Trowbridge 98

Winchester College 54–6, *55*, 313
Winnington-Ingram, Bishop 399
Winter, Jay 54, 63
Wodehouse, P. G. 286 and n.
Wolseley House, Piccadilly, London 117, *118*
Wood, Derwent 53n.
Wood, Edgar 132, 481–2
Woodfalls, Melchet Court 228
Woodford, James *151*
Woodland Way, Petts Wood 7
Woodside Ventilation Station *257*, 258
Wornum, George Grey 26, 129, 149–51, 167, 364–6, *365*, 455–6, *490*
Wornum, Miriam 370
Worthing Town Hall 106, 353
Worthington, Percy S. 150
Wren, Sir Christopher 9–10, 19–20, 34, 42, 90–5, 97, 116, 122, 126, 216, 249, 340, 343, 354, 378, 397–8, 440
Wren Society 90
'Wrennaissance' 90–1, 95, 114, 128
Wright, Alexander 183
Wright, Frank Lloyd 136, 138, 180, 229–30, 245, 254, 256, 267, 269
Wright, Henry 229
Wyatt, James 392–3
Wychden, Seal 287
Wylie, Edward G. 183
Yaffle Hill, Poole 228–9; Plate 20
Yerbury, F. R. 13, 30, 131, 134, 136–7, 141, 151, 152, 171, 343, 382, 422
York & Sawyer 182
York Minster 411
Yorke, F. R. S. 21, 31, 446 and n., 454, 457, 468, 475, 481, 488, 500, 504
Youth Hostel Association 285
Ypres 69–70, *71*
Zweig, Stefan 70